YOU JUST GAINED ACCESS TO

ATLAS™

YOUR ONLINE LEARNING PLATFORM!

Atlas will take you through this book and give you access to a host of additional resources, including:

• A free, full-length adaptive practice exam that simulates the real test, plus in-depth performance analytics and thorough explanations

• Additional official-format problems to hone your skills and test-wide strategies for maximizing your performance

HOW TO ACCESS ATLAS

If you purchased this guide from Manhattan Prep's online store:
Your resources are already in your account! Go to manhattanprep.com/gmat/studentcenter and log in with the same username and password you used to create your account.

If you purchased this guide at a retail location:
Go to manhattanprep.com/gmat/access and follow the instructions on the screen.

Online resource access can only be granted for a single account; the guide cannot be registered a second time for a different account.

You have one year from the date of purchase to complete your registration.

MANHATTAN
PREP

GMAT®

Advanced Quant

This supplemental guide provides in-depth and comprehensive explanations of the advanced math skills necessary for the highest-level performance on the GMAT.

Acknowledgments

A great number of people were involved in the creation of the book you are holding.

Our Manhattan Prep resources are based on the continuing experiences of our instructors and students. The overall vision for this edition was developed by Chelsey Cooley, who determined what new areas to cover and who wrote all of the problems that are new to this edition.

Chelsey served as the primary author of this edition and Emily Meredith Sledge was the primary editor; Emily also served as the primary author of the first edition of this guide. Mario Gambino managed production for the many—and quite complicated—images that appear in this guide.

Matthew Callan coordinated the production work for this guide. Once the manuscript was done, Naomi Beesen and Ben Ku edited and Cheryl Duckler and Stacey Koprince proofread the entire guide from start to finish. Carly Schnur designed the covers.

Retail ISBN: 978-1-5062-4993-3
Retail eISBN: 978-1-5062-4994-0
Course ISBN: 978-1-5062-4995-7
Course eISBN: 978-1-5062-4996-4

GMAT® Strategy Guides

GMAT All the Quant

GMAT All the Verbal

GMAT Integrated Reasoning and Essay

Strategy Guide Supplements

Math

GMAT Foundations of Math

GMAT Advanced Quant

Verbal

GMAT Foundations of Verbal

January 7, 2020

Dear Student,

Thank you for picking up a copy of *Advanced Quant*. I hope this book provides just the guidance you need to get the most out of your GMAT studies.

At Manhattan Prep, we continually aspire to provide the best instructors and resources possible. If you have any questions or feedback, please do not hesitate to contact us.

Email our Student Services team at gmat@manhattanprep.com or give us a shout at 212-721-7400 (or 800-576-4628 in the United States or Canada). We try to keep all our books free of errors, but if you think we've goofed, please visit manhattanprep.com/GMAT/errata.

Our Manhattan Prep Strategy Guides are based on the continuing experiences of both our instructors and our students. The primary author of the this edition of the Advanced Quant guide was Chelsey Cooley and the primary editor was Emily Meredith Sledge. Project management and design were led by Matthew Callan and Mario Gambino. I'd like to send particular thanks to instructors Stacey Koprince and Ben Ku for their content contributions.

Finally, we are indebted to all of the Manhattan Prep students who have given us excellent feedback over the years. This book wouldn't be half of what it is without their voice.

And now that *you* are one of our students too, please chime in! I look forward to hearing from you. Thanks again and best of luck preparing for the GMAT!

Sincerely,

Chris Ryan
Executive Director,
Product Strategy

www.manhattanprep.com/gmat   138 West 25th Street, 7th Floor, New York, NY 10001   Tel: 212-721-7400
Fax: 646-514-7425

TABLE OF CONTENTS

Introduction

In This Chapter

Introduction

A Qualified Welcome

Welcome to *GMAT Advanced Quant*! In this venue, we decided to be a little nerdy and call the introduction Chapter 0. After all, the point (0, 0) in the coordinate plane is called the *origin*, isn't it? (That's the first and last math joke in this book.)

Unfortunately, we have to qualify our welcome right away, because **this book isn't for everyone**. At least, it's not for everyone *right away*.

Who Should Use This Book

You should use this book if you meet the following conditions:

- You have achieved a scaled score of at least 47 (out of 51) on the Quant section of either the Manhattan Prep practice test or the official practice computer-adaptive test (CAT).

- You have worked through the Manhattan Prep *All the Quant* guide, which covers all of the topics and strategies you need for the Quant section, or you have worked through similar material from another company. This material should include the following:

  - Algebra
  - Fractions, Decimals, Percents, and Ratios
  - Geometry
  - Number Properties
  - Word Problems

- You are already comfortable with the core principles in these topics.

- You want to raise your performance to a scaled score of 49 or higher.

- You want to become a significantly smarter test-taker.

If you match this description, then please turn the page.

If you don't match this description, then you will probably find this book too difficult at this stage of your preparation.

For now, you are better off working on topic-focused material, as found in the *All the Quant* guide, and ensuring that you have mastered that material *before* you return to this book.

Try It Yourself

Throughout the chapters of this guide, you'll see Try-It problems—problems designed to test your skills on certain aspects of GMAT problems. Take a look at the following three Try-It problems, which are very difficult. They are at least as hard as any real GMAT problem—probably even harder.

Go ahead and give these problems a try. You should not expect to solve any of them in two minutes. In fact, you might find yourself completely stuck. If that's the case, switch gears. Do your best to eliminate some incorrect answer choices and take an educated guess.

Try-It #0-1

A jar is filled with red, white, and blue tokens that are equivalent except for their color. The chance of randomly selecting a red token, replacing it, then randomly selecting a white token is the same as the chance of randomly selecting a blue token. If the number of tokens of every color is a multiple of 3, what is the smallest possible total number of tokens in the jar?

(A) 9

(B) 12

(C) 15

(D) 18

(E) 21

Try-It #0-2

Arrow $\overrightarrow{AB}$, which is a line segment exactly 5 units long with an arrowhead at A, is constructed in the xy-plane. The x- and y-coordinates of A and B are integers that satisfy the inequalities $0 \le x \le 9$ and $0 \le y \le 9$. How many different arrows with these properties can be constructed?

(A)   50

(B) 168

(C) 200

(D) 368

(E) 536

Try-It #0-3

In the diagram to the right, the value of x is closest to which of the following?

(A) $2 + \sqrt{2}$

(B) 2

(C) $\sqrt{3}$

(D) $\sqrt{2}$

(E) 1

(Note: This problem does not require any non-GMAT math, such as trigonometry.)

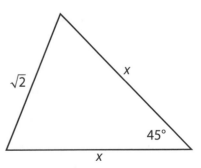

The Purpose of This Book

This book is designed to prepare you for the *most difficult* math problems on the GMAT.

So...what *is* a difficult math problem, from the point of view of the GMAT?

A difficult math problem is one that most GMAT test-takers get wrong under exam conditions. In fact, this is essentially how the GMAT measures difficulty: by the percent of test-takers who get the problem wrong.

So what kinds of math questions do most test-takers get wrong? What characterizes these problems? There are two kinds of features:

1. **Topical nuances or obscure principles**

   - Connected to a particular topic
   - Inherently hard to grasp or unfamiliar
   - Easy to mix up

   These topical nuances are largely covered in the Extra sections of the Manhattan Prep *All the Quant* guide. This book includes many problems that involve topical nuances. However, the exhaustive theory of divisibility and primes, for instance, is not repeated here.

2. **Complex structures**

   - May use simple principles in ways that aren't obvious
   - May require multiple steps
   - May make you consider many cases
   - May combine more than one topic
   - May need a flash of real insight to complete
   - May make you change direction or switch strategies along the way

   Complex structures are essentially *disguises* for simpler content. These disguises may be difficult to pierce. The path to the answer is twisted or clouded somehow.

   To solve problems that have simple content but complex structures, you need approaches that are both *more general* and *more creative*. This book focuses on these more general and more creative approaches.

   The three problems on the previous page have complex structures; the solutions are a bit later in this chapter. In the meantime, take a look at another problem.

An Illustration

Give this problem a whirl. Don't go on until you have spent a few minutes on it—or until you have figured it out.

Try-It #0-4

What should the next number in this sequence be?

1   2   9   64   —

Note: This problem is *not* exactly GMAT-like, because there is no mathematically definite rule. However, you'll know when you've solved the problem. The answer will be elegant.

This problem has very simple content but a complex structure. Researchers in cognitive science have used sequence-completion problems such as this one to develop realistic models of human thought. Here is one such model, simplified but practical.

Top-Down Brain and Bottom-Up Brain

To solve the sequence-completion problem above, you need two kinds of thinking:

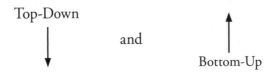

You might even say that you need two types of brain.

The top-down brain is your conscious self. If you imagine the contents of your head as a big corporation, then your top-down brain is the CEO, responding to input, making decisions, and issuing orders. In cognitive science, the top-down brain is called the *executive function*. Top-down thinking and planning is indispensable to any problem-solving process.

But the corporation in your head is a big place. For one thing, how does information get to the CEO? And how preprocessed is that information?

The bottom-up brain is your *preconscious* processor. After raw sensory input arrives, your bottom-up brain processes that input extensively *before* it reaches your top-down brain.

For instance, to your optic nerve, every word on this page is just a lot of black squiggles. Your bottom-up brain immediately turns these squiggles into letters, joins the letters into words, summons relevant images and concepts, and finally serves these images and concepts to your top-down brain. This all happens automatically and swiftly. In fact, it takes effort to *interrupt* this process. Also, unlike your top-down brain, which does things one at a time, your bottom-up brain can easily do many things at once.

How does all this relate to solving the sequence problem above?

Each of your brains needs the other one to solve difficult problems.

Your top-down brain needs your bottom-up brain to notice patterns, sniff out valuable leads, and make quick, intuitive leaps and connections.

But your bottom-up brain is inarticulate and distractible. Only your top-down brain can build plans, pose explicit questions, follow procedures, and state findings.

Imagine that you are trying to solve a tough murder case. To find all the clues in the woods, you need both a savvy detective and a sharp-nosed bloodhound.

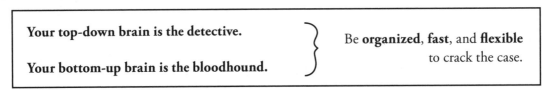

To solve difficult GMAT problems, try to harmonize the activity of your two brains by following an organized, fast, and flexible problem-solving process.

| Organized |

You need a general step-by-step approach to guide you. One such approach, inspired by expert mathematician George Pólya, is Understand, Plan, Solve (UPS):

1. **Understand** the problem first.
2. **Plan** your attack by adapting known techniques in new ways.
3. **Solve** by executing your plan.

You may never have thought explicitly about steps 1 and 2 before. It may have been easy or even automatic for you to *Understand* easier problems and to *Plan* your approach to them. As a result, you may tend to dive right into the *Solve* stage. This is a bad strategy. Mathematicians know that the real math on hard problems is not *Solve*; the real math is *Understand* and *Plan*.

| Fast |

Speed is important for its own sake on the GMAT, of course. What you may not have thought as much about is that being fast can also lower your stress level and promote good process. If you know you can *solve* quickly, then you can take more time to comprehend the question, consider the given information, and select a strategy. To this end, make sure that you can complete calculations and manipulations fairly rapidly so that you can afford to spend some time on the *Understand* and *Plan* stages of your problem-solving process. A little extra time invested up front can pay off handsomely later.

| Flexible |

To succeed against difficult problems, you sometimes have to "unstick" yourself. Expect to run into brick walls and encounter dead ends. Returning to first principles and to the general process (e.g., making sure that you fully *Understand* the problem) can help you back up out of the mud.

Let's return to the sequence problem and play out a sample interaction between the two brains. The path is not linear; there are several dead ends, as you would expect. This dialog will lead to the answer, so don't start reading until you've given the problem a final shot (if you haven't already solved it). The top-down brain is labeled TD; the bottom-up brain is labeled BU.

Sequence	Dialogue
1 2 9 64 ___	TD: "Okay, let's *Understand* this thing. At a glance, they've given me an increasing list of numbers, and they want me to find the number that "should" go in the blank, whatever "should" means. What's a good *Plan*? Hmm. No idea. Stare at the numbers given?" *BU notices that $9 = 3^2$ and $64 = 8^2$. Likes the two squares.*
1 2 3^2 8^2 ___	TD: "Write in the two squares."
1 2 3^2 8^2 ___	*BU notices that 1 is a square, too.*
sq no sq sq ___	TD: "Are they all perfect squares? No, since 2 isn't." *BU doesn't like this break in the pattern.*
1 2 3^2 2^6 ___	TD: "Wait, back up. What about primes, factoring all the way. $8 = 2^3$, and so $8^2 = (2^3)^2 = 2^6$." *BU notices $6 = 2 \times 3$, but so what?*
1 2 3^2 $(2^3)^2$ ___	TD: "Let's write 2^6 as $(2^3)^2$. Anything there?" *BU notices lots of 2's and 3's, but so what?*
	TD: "Okay, keep looking at this. Are the 2's and 3's stacked somehow?" *BU notices no real pattern. There's 2–3–2 twice as you go across, but so what? And the 1 is weird by itself.*
1 2 9 64 ___ 1 7 55	TD: "No good leads there. Hmm...time to go back to the original and try taking differences." *BU notices no pattern. The numbers look even uglier.*
1 2 9 64 ___	TD: "Hmm. No good. Go back to original numbers again. What's going on there?" *BU notices that the numbers are growing quickly, like squares or exponentials.*
1^2 2 3^2 8^2 ___	TD: "Must have something to do with those squares. I should look at those again." *BU notices a gap on the left, among the powers.*

$1^?$	2^1	3^2	8^2	——	TD: "How about looking at 2. Write it with exponents: $2 = 2^1$. Actually, 1 doesn't have to be 1^2. One can be to any power and still be 1. The power is a question mark." *BU notices 2^1 then 3^2. Likes the counting numbers.* *BU really wants 1, 2, 3, 4 somehow.*
$1^?$	2^1	3^2	$4^{??}$	——	TD: "Try 4 in that last position. Could the last term be 4 somehow?" *BU likes the look of this. 8 and 4 are related.*
$1^?$	2^1	3^2	4^3	——	TD: "64 is 4 to the what? $4^2 = 16$, times another 4 equals 64, so it's 4 to the third power. That fits." *BU is thrilled: 1, 2, 3, 4 below and 1, 2, 3 up top.*
1^0	2^1	3^2	4^3	——	TD: "Extend left. It's 1^0. Confirmed. The bases are 1, 2, 3, 4, etc., and the powers are 0, 1, 2, 3, etc." *BU is content.*
1^0	2^1	3^2	4^3	5^4	TD: "So the answer is 5^4, which is 25^2, or 625."

Your own process was almost certainly different in the details. Also, your internal dialog was very rapid—parts of it probably only took fractions of a second to transpire. After all, you think at the speed of thought.

The important thing is to recognize how the bottom-up bloodhound and the top-down detective worked together in the case above. The TD detective set the overall agenda and then pointed the BU bloodhound at the clues. The bloodhound did practically all the "noticing," which in some sense is where all the magic happened. But sometimes the bloodhound got stuck, so the detective had to intervene, consciously trying a new path. For instance, 64 reads so strongly as 8^2 that the detective had to actively give up on that reading.

There are so many possible meaningful sequences that it wouldn't have made sense to apply a strict *recipe* from the outset: "Try X first, then Y, then Z…" Such an algorithm would require hundreds of possibilities. Should you always look for 1, 2, 3, 4? Should you *never* find differences or prime factors because they weren't that useful here? Of course not! A computer can rapidly and easily apply a complicated algorithm with hundreds of steps, but humans can't. (If you are an engineer or programmer, maybe you *wish* you could program your own brain, but so far, that's not possible!)

What humans *are* good at, though, is noticing patterns. The bottom-up brain is extremely powerful—far more powerful than any computer yet built.

As you gather problem-solving tools, the task becomes **knowing when to apply which tool**. This task becomes harder as problem structures become more complex. But if you deploy your bottom-up bloodhound according to a general problem-solving process such as Understand, Plan, Solve, then you can count on the bloodhound to notice the relevant aspects of the problem—the aspects that tell you which tool to use.

 9

You can break down Understand, Plan, Solve into several discrete steps:

Understand   *Glance* at the problem briefly: does anything stand out?

                            Read the problem.

                            Jot down any obvious formulas or numbers.

Plan   *Reflect* on what you were given: what clues might help tell you how to approach this problem?

                            Organize your approach: choose a solution path.

Solve   *Work* the problem!

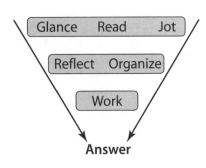

You'll get lots of practice using the UPS process throughout this guide.

Learning How to Think

This book is intended to make you smarter.

It is also intended to make you *scrappier*.

That description encompasses two main ideas: employing GMAT strategies as well as textbook solution methods and knowing when to let go.

If you have traditionally been good at paper-based standardized tests, then you may be used to solving practically every problem the "textbook" way. Problems that forced you to get down and dirty—to work backwards from the choices, to estimate and eliminate—may have annoyed you.

A major purpose of this book is to help you learn to choose the best GMAT approach. On the hardest Quant problems, the textbook approach is often *not* the best GMAT approach.

Unfortunately, advanced test-takers are sometimes very stubborn. Sometimes they feel they *should* solve a problem according to some theoretical approach. Or they fail to move to Plan B or C rapidly enough, so they don't have enough time left to execute that plan. In the end, they might wind up guessing purely at random—and that's a shame.

GMAT problems often have *back doors*—ways to solve that don't involve crazy computation or genius-level insights. Remember that in theory, GMAT problems can all be solved in two minutes. By searching for the back door, you might avoid all the bear traps that the problem writer set out by the front door!

In addition to learning alternative solution methods, you also need to learn when to *let go*. As you know, the GMAT is an adaptive test. If you keep getting questions correct, the test will keep getting harder...and harder...and harder...

At some point, there will appear a monster problem, one that announces "I must break you." In your battle with this problem, you could actually *lose* the bigger war—even if you ultimately conquer this particular problem. Maybe it takes you eight minutes, or it beats you up so badly that your head starts pounding. This will take its toll on your score.

This will happen to *everyone*, no matter how good you are at the GMAT. Why?

The GMAT is not an academic test, though it certainly appears to be. Business schools are primarily interested in whether you're going to be an effective businessperson. Good businesspeople are able to assess a situation rapidly, manage scarce resources, distinguish between good opportunities and bad ones, and make decisions accordingly.

The GMAT wants to put you in a situation where the best decision is, in fact, to guess and move on, because business schools are interested in learning whether you have the presence of mind to recognize a bad opportunity and the discipline to let it go.

Show the GMAT that you know how to manage your scarce resources (time and mental energy) and that you can recognize and cut off a bad opportunity.

Plan of This Book

The rest of this book has three parts:

Part One: Problem Solving and Data Sufficiency Strategies

> Chapter 1: Problem Solving: Advanced Principles
> Chapter 2: Problem Solving: Strategies & Tactics
> Chapter 3: Data Sufficiency: Principles
> Chapter 4: Data Sufficiency: Strategies & Tactics

Part Two: Strategies for All Problem Types

> Chapter 5: Pattern Recognition
> Chapter 6: Common Terms & Quadratic Templates
> Chapter 7: Visual Solutions
> Chapter 8: Hybrid Problems

Part Three: Practice

> Workouts 1–16: Sixteen sets of 10 problems each

The four chapters in Part I focus on principles, strategies, and tactics related to the two types of GMAT math problems: Problem Solving (PS) and Data Sufficiency (DS). The next four chapters, in Part II, focus on techniques that apply across several topics but are more specific than the approaches in Part I.

Each of the eight chapters in Part I and Part II contains the following:

- **Try-It Problems** embedded throughout the text
- **Problem Sets** at the end of the chapter

Many of these problems will be GMAT-like in format, but many will not.

Part III contains sets of GMAT-like **Workout problems**, designed to exercise your skills as if you were taking the GMAT and seeing its hardest problems. Several of these sets contain clusters of problems relating to the chapters in Parts I and II, although the problems within each set do not all resemble each other in obvious ways. Other Workout problem sets are mixed by both approach and topic.

Note that these problems are *not* arranged in order of difficulty. Also, you should know that some of these problems draw on advanced content covered in the Manhattan Prep *All the Quant* guide.

Solutions to Try-It Problems

If you haven't tried to solve the first three Try-It problems in the Try It Yourself section at the beginning of this chapter, then go back and try them now. Think about how to get your top-down brain and your bottom-up brain to work together like a detective and a bloodhound. Come back when you've tackled the problems, even if you don't get to an answer (in this case, do make a guess).

In these solutions, we'll outline sample dialogs between the top-down detective and the bottom-up bloodhound.

Try-It #0-1

A jar is filled with red, white, and blue tokens that are equivalent except for their color. The chance of randomly selecting a red token, replacing it, then randomly selecting a white token is the same as the chance of randomly selecting a blue token. If the number of tokens of every color is a multiple of 3, what is the smallest possible total number of tokens in the jar?

(A)   9

(B)   12

(C)   15

(D)   18

(E)   21

Solution to Try-It #0-1

...**jar** is filled with **red, white, and blue tokens** ...**chance** of **randomly** selecting...	TD: "I need to *Understand* this problem first. There's a jar, and it's got red, white, and blue tokens in it." *BU notices "chance" and "randomly." That's probability.* TD: "All right, this is a probability problem. Now, what's the situation?" *BU notices that there are two situations.*
...**chance of** randomly selecting **a red token**, replacing it, **then** randomly selecting **a white token** is the **same** as the **chance of** randomly selecting **a blue token**.	TD: "Let's rephrase. In simpler words, if I pick a red, then a white, that's the same chance as if I pick a blue. *Jot* that down. Okay, what else?"
...number of tokens of every color is a multiple of 3...	*BU doesn't want to deal with this "multiple of 3" thing yet.*
...**smallest possible total number** of tokens in the jar?	TD: "Okay, what are they asking me?" *BU notices "smallest possible total number." Glances at answer choices. They're small, but not tiny. Hmm.*
	TD: "Let's *Reflect* for a moment to figure out a *Plan*. How can I approach this? How about algebra—if I name the number of each color, then I can represent each fact and also what I'm looking for. Okay, I use R, W, and B. Make probability fractions. Multiply red and white fractions. Simplify algebraically."
$$\frac{R}{R+W+B} \times \frac{W}{R+W+B} = \frac{B}{R+W+B}$$ $$\frac{RW}{(R+W+B)^2} = \frac{B}{R+W+B}$$ $$RW = B(R+W+B)$$ $$RW = BR + BW + B^2$$	*BU is now unsure. No obvious path forward.*
The chance of randomly selecting a red token, replacing it, then randomly selecting a white token is the same as the chance of randomly selecting a blue token...	TD: "Let's start over conceptually. Reread the problem. Can I learn anything interesting?" *BU notices that blues are different.* TD: "How are blues different? Hmm. Picking a red, then a white is as likely as picking a blue. What does that mean?" *BU notices that it's unlikely to pick a blue. So there aren't many blues compared to reds or whites.*

Fewer blues than reds or whites

$B < R$ and $B < W$

In the very first equation above, each fraction on the left is less than 1, so their product is even smaller. The denominators of the three fractions are all the same.

So the numerator of the product (B) must be smaller than either of the other numerators (R and W).

If the number of tokens of every color is a multiple of 3, what is the smallest possible total number of tokens in the jar?

$$B = 3$$
$$RW = 3R + 3W + 9$$
$$1 = \frac{3}{W} + \frac{3}{R} + \frac{9}{RW}$$

Neither R nor W can equal 3 (since B is smaller than either).

Let $R = W = 6$.

(A) and (B) are out now. The smallest possible total is now 15.

$$\text{Is } 1 = \frac{3}{6} + \frac{3}{6} + \frac{9}{36}? \text{ No.}$$

Let $R = 6$ and $W = 9$.

$$\text{Is } 1 = \frac{3}{6} + \frac{3}{9} + \frac{9}{54}?$$
$$\text{Is } 1 = \frac{1}{2} + \frac{1}{3} + \frac{1}{6}? \text{ Yes.}$$

TD: "Are there fewer blues? Yes. Justify this. Focus on the algebraic setup."

BU notices fractions less than 1. All positive.

TD: "Two positive fractions less than 1 multiplied together give an even smaller number."

TD: "Yes, there are fewer blues."

BU is quiet.

TD: "Time to go back and reread the rest of the problem."

BU again notices "multiple of 3," also in answer choices. Small multiples.

TD: "Change of *Plan*: Algebra by itself isn't getting me there. What about plugging in a number? Try the most constrained variable: B. Since it's the smallest quantity, but still positive, pretend B is 3. Execute this algebraically. Divide by RW."

BU likes having only two variables.

TD: "Need to test other numbers. Apply constraints I know—B is the smallest number. Rule out answer choices as I go."

TD: "6 and 6 don't work, because the right side adds up to larger than 1. (C) is out too. Try the next possibility."

BU doesn't like breaking the symmetry between R and W. They seem to be alike.

TD: "Does it matter whether $R = 6$ and $W = 9$ or the other way around? No, it doesn't. One is 6, the other is 9. Plug in and go."

TD: "This works. The answer is $3 + 6 + 9 = 18$."

The correct answer is (D). Let's look at another pathway—one that moves more quickly to the back door.

Alternative Solution to Try-It #0-1

…**chance** of randomly selecting…	*BU notices "chance." BU doesn't like probability.* TD: "Oh man, probability. Okay, let's make sense of this and see whether there are any back doors. That's the *Plan*."
…the number of tokens of every color is a **multiple of 3**…	*BU notices that there are only limited possibilities for each number.* TD: "Okay, every quantity is a multiple of 3. That simplifies things. There are 3, 6, 9, etc., of each color."
A jar is filled with red, white, and blue tokens…	*BU is alert—what about 0?* TD: "What about 0? Hmm…the wording at the beginning assumes that there actually are tokens of each color. So there can't be 0 tokens of any kind."
(A) 9 (B) 12 (C) 15 (D) 18 (E) 21	TD: "Now let's look at the answer choices." *BU notices that they're small.*
(A) 9	TD: "Try plugging in the choices. Let's start at the easy end—in this case, the smallest number." *BU notices $9 = 3 + 3 + 3$.*
Select a red: $\frac{3}{9} = \frac{1}{3}$ Select a white: $\frac{3}{9} = \frac{1}{3}$ $\frac{1}{3} \times \frac{1}{3} = \frac{1}{9}$, which is not "select a blue"	TD: "The only possible way to have 9 total tokens is to have 3 reds, 3 whites, and 3 blues. So…does that work? Plug into probability formula."
~~(A) 9~~ (B) 12 (C) 15 (D) 18 (E) 21 (B) 12	TD: "No, that doesn't work. This is good. Knock out (A). Let's keep going. Try (B)." *BU notices $12 = 3 + 3 + 6$.*
	TD: "Only way to have 12 total is 3, 3, and 6. Which one's which? Picking a red and then a white is the same as picking a blue, so the blue should be one of the 3's. Let's say red is 3 and white is 6."
Select a red: $\frac{3}{12} = \frac{1}{4}$ Select a white: $\frac{6}{12} = \frac{1}{2}$ $\frac{1}{4} \times \frac{1}{2} = \frac{1}{8}$, which is not "select a blue"	
~~(A) 9~~ ~~(B) 12~~ (C) 15 (D) 18 (E) 21	TD: "That doesn't work either. Knock out (B). Keep going."

(C) 15	*BU notices 15 has a few options.*
Select a red: $\dfrac{6}{15} = \dfrac{2}{5}$	TD: "I can make 15 by 3, 6, and 6 or by 3, 3, and 9. Try 3–6–6; make blue the 3."
Select a white: $\dfrac{6}{15} = \dfrac{2}{5}$	
$\dfrac{2}{5} \times \dfrac{2}{5} = \dfrac{4}{25}$, which is not "select a blue"	TD: "Nope. What about 3–3–9."
$\dfrac{3}{15} \times \dfrac{9}{15} = \dfrac{1}{5} \times \dfrac{3}{5} = \dfrac{3}{25}$, which is not "select a blue"	TD: "Not this one either."
~~(A) 9~~ ~~(B) 12~~ ~~(C) 15~~ (D) 18 (E) 21	TD: "Knock out (C). Try (D)."
(D) 18	TD: "Maybe 3–6–9 first. Make blue the 3."
$\dfrac{6}{18} \times \dfrac{9}{18} = \dfrac{1}{3} \times \dfrac{1}{2} = \dfrac{1}{6} = \dfrac{3}{18}$, which IS "select a blue"	TD: "That's it! Answer's (D)."

Many people find this second approach less stressful and more efficient than the textbook approach. In fact, there is no way to find the correct answer by pure algebra. Ultimately, you have to test suitable numbers.

Try-It #0-2

Arrow $\overline{AB}$, which is a line segment exactly 5 units long with an arrowhead at A, is constructed in the xy-plane. The x- and y-coordinates of A and B are integers that satisfy the inequalities $0 \le x \le 9$ and $0 \le y \le 9$. How many different arrows with these properties can be constructed?

(A)   50
(B)   168
(C)   200
(D)   368
(E)   536

Solution to Try-It #0-2

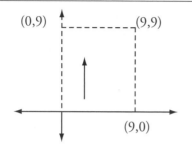

How many different arrows with these properties can be constructed?

...exactly 5 units long with an arrowhead at A... the x- and y-coordinates of A and B are to be integers that satisfy the inequalities $0 \leq x \leq 9$ and $0 \leq y \leq 9$.

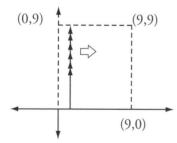

In one column, there are 5 positions for the arrowhead: $y = 5, 6, 7, 8,$ or 9. That's the same as $9 - 5 + 1$, by the way.

There are 10 identical columns: $x = 0$ through $x = 9$. $5 \times 10 = 50$ possible positions for the arrow pointing straight up.

BU notices "xy-plane."
TD: "Let's *Understand* first. This is a coordinate-plane problem. Sketch it out. Put in boundaries as necessary."

BU wonders where this is going.

TD: "What is the question asking for again? Reread the question."
BU wonders which properties.

TD: "What are the properties of the arrows supposed to be again? Each arrow is 5 units long."

BU notices "integers" and "coordinates" and pictures a pegboard.

TD: "*Reflect.* The tip and the end of the arrow have to touch holes in the pegboard exactly. Okay. The *Plan* is to start counting. How to *Organize*?"

BU imagines many possible arrows. Brute force can't be the right way forward. The arrows can point in all sorts of different ways.

TD: "Let's simplify the *Plan*. Let's *focus* on just one orientation of arrows—pointing straight up. Draw this situation. How many places can the arrow be?"

BU wants to go up & down, then right & left.

TD: "Count the positions in *one* column, then multiply by the number of columns. Be careful to count endpoints."

$50 \times 2 = 100$ possible positions for the arrow if it points straight up or to the right.

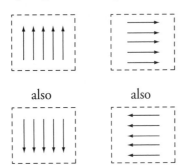

$50 \times 4 = 200$ possible positions

Answer seems to be (C).

Three up, four across:

Four up, three across:

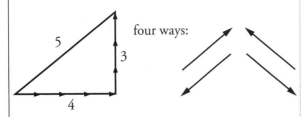

Three up, four across, pointing up to the right:

There are 7 positions vertically for the arrowhead $(9 - 3 + 1)$ and 6 positions horizontally $(9 - 4 + 1)$, for a total of $7 \times 6 = 42$ positions.

$8 \times 42 = 336$ possible positions at an angle.

In total, there are $200 + 336 = 536$ positions.

TD: "Great. I've *Solved* one part. Other possibilities?"

BU notices the square is the same vertically as horizontally. Go right.
TD: "I get the same result for arrows pointing right. 50 more positions. Is that it? Am I done?"

BU wonders about "down" and "left."
TD: "These arrows can point straight *down* or straight *left*, too. Those would have the same result. So there are 50 positions in each of the four directions. Calculate at this point and evaluate answers. Eliminate (A) and (B)."

BU is suspicious: somehow too easy.
TD: "Tentative answer is (C), but I'm not done."
BU wonders about still other ways for the arrows to point.

TD: "Could the arrows be at an angle?"
BU notices that the arrow is 5 units long, associated with 3–4–5 triangles.
TD: "3–4–5 triangles. Yes. Put the arrow as the hypotenuse of a 3–4–5 triangle. How can this be done? Try to place the arrow. Remember the reversal. Looks like there are four ways if I go 3 up and 4 across: up right, up left, down right, down left."
BU is happy. This is the trick.
TD: "Likewise, there must be four ways if I go 4 up and 3 across: again, up right, up left, down right, and down left. By the way, the answer must be (D) or (E)."

TD: "Now count just one of these ways. Same ideas as before. Be sure to include endpoints."
BU notices the symmetry. The 3 up, 4 across is the same as the 4 up, 3 across, if you turn the square.

TD: "Each of these angled ways will be the same. There are 8 ways to point the arrow at an angle. Finish the calculation and confirm the answer."

The correct answer is (E). There isn't much of an alternative to the approach above. With counting problems, it can often be very difficult to estimate the answer or work backwards from the answer choices.

Try-It #0-3

In the diagram to the right, the value of *x* is closest to which of the following?

(A) $2 + \sqrt{2}$

(B) 2

(C) $\sqrt{3}$

(D) $\sqrt{2}$

(E) 1

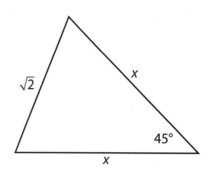

Solution to Try-It #0-3

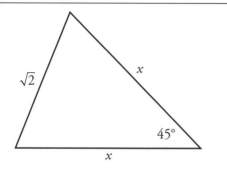

$180° - 45° = 135°$.

Divide 135° equally across the two missing angles. So each angle is 67.5°.

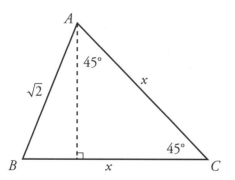

TD: "Okay, let's *Understand* this. Redraw the figure. The problem wants the value of *x*. Now…how about a *Plan*?"

BU notices this is an isosceles triangle, because there are two sides labeled x. *How about the two equal angles?*

TD: "Figure out the two missing angles. Use the 180° rule."

BU doesn't recognize this triangle.

TD: "Hmm…here's a *Plan*: add a perpendicular line to make right triangles. Drop the line from the top point. I'll label corners while I'm at it. Now fill in angles."

BU notices 45–45–90 and is happy.

Introduction

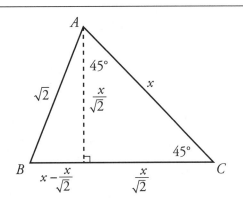

TD: "Use the 45–45–90 to write expressions for its sides. Then $\overline{BC}$ can be split up into two pieces, and I can set up the Pythagorean theorem."

BU feels that this process is kind of ugly.

$$\left(\frac{x}{\sqrt{2}}\right)^2 + \left(x - \frac{x}{\sqrt{2}}\right)^2 = \left(\sqrt{2}\right)^2$$

TD: "Let's push through. Write the Pythagorean theorem for the small triangle on the left, using the $\sqrt{2}$ as the hypotenuse."

BU thinks this equation is really ugly.

$$\frac{x^2}{2} + x^2 - \frac{2x^2}{\sqrt{2}} + \frac{x^2}{2} = 2$$

TD: "Push through. Expand the quadratic and simplify."

BU doesn't like the square root on the bottom.

$$2x^2 - \frac{2x^2}{\sqrt{2}} = 2$$

$$2x^2\sqrt{2} - 2x^2 = 2\sqrt{2}$$

$$x^2\left(2\sqrt{2} - 2\right) = 2\sqrt{2}$$

TD: "Multiply by $\sqrt{2}$ to get rid of it on the bottom of the fraction."

BU has no idea how to take the square root of this.

$$x^2 = \frac{2\sqrt{2}}{2\sqrt{2} - 2} = \frac{\sqrt{2}}{\sqrt{2} - 1}$$

$$x^2 = \frac{1.4}{1.4 - 1} = \frac{1.4}{0.4} = \frac{14}{4} = 3.5$$

TD: "Neither do I. Let's try estimating. If x^2 is about 3.5, then the square root must be a bit less than 2 (since the square root of 4 is 2). 18^2 is 324 and 19^2 is 361, so the answer is around 1.8 or 1.9."

(A) $2 + \sqrt{2}$

(B) 2

(C) $\sqrt{3}$

(D) $\sqrt{2}$

(E) 1

TD: "Answer (A) is about 3.5; that matches the squared value, not the square root. The answer needs to be less than 2, so (B) is also wrong. $\sqrt{3}$ is about 1.7. Answers (D) and (E) are too small, so the answer is (C)."

The correct answer is (C).

The method you just saw is algebraically intensive, and so your bottom-up bloodhound might have kicked up a fuss along the way. Sometimes, your top-down brain needs to ignore the bottom-up brain. Remember, when you're actually taking the GMAT, you have to solve problems quickly—and you don't need to publish your solutions in a mathematics journal. What you want is to get the correct answer as quickly and as easily as possible. In this regard, the solution above works perfectly well.

Alternatively, the question stem asks for an approximate answer, so you can also try estimating from the start. Draw the triangle *carefully* and start with the same perpendicular line as before. This line is a little shorter than the side of length $\sqrt{2}$ (which is about 1.4). Call the two shorter legs 1.2 and calculate the hypotenuse. It equals 1.2 multiplied by 1.4, or approximately 1.7. (Bonus question: How can you estimate that math quickly? Answer below.)

Now, examine the answer choices using 1.4 for $\sqrt{2}$ and 1.7 for $\sqrt{3}$:

- (A) 3.4
- (B) 2
- (C) 1.7
- (D) 1.4
- (E) 1

They're all close, but you can pretty confidently eliminate answers (A) and (E). Furthermore, the answer needs to be less than 2, so (B) can't be it. Answer (C) is closer than (D), so (C) is probably it. Unfortunately, you might guess wrong at this point. But the odds are much better than they were at the outset.

It is worthwhile to look for multiple solution paths as you practice. Your top-down brain will become faster, more organized, and more flexible, enabling your bottom-up brain to have more flashes of insight.

That was a substantial introduction. Now, on to Chapter 1!

Problem Solving and Data Sufficiency Strategies

In This Part

Problem Solving: Advanced Principles

In This Chapter

CHAPTER 1 Problem Solving: Advanced Principles

Chapters 1 and 2 of this book focus on the more fundamental of the two types of GMAT math questions: Problem Solving (PS). Some of the content applies to any kind of math problem, including Data Sufficiency (DS). However, Chapters 3 and 4 deal specifically with DS issues.

This chapter outlines broad principles for solving advanced PS problems. You've already seen very basic versions of the first three principles in the introduction, in the dialogs between the top-down and the bottom-up brain.

As mentioned earlier, these principles draw on the work of George Pólya, who was a brilliant mathematician and teacher of mathematics. Pólya was teaching future mathematicians, not GMAT test-takers, but what he said still applies. His little book *How to Solve It* has been in print since 1945—it's worth getting a copy.

In the meantime, keep reading.

Principle #1: Understand the Basics

Take time to think and plan before you start solving a difficult problem. If Quant is your strength, you may want to dive straight into every problem as soon as you see it, without pausing to consider all of the angles. There are two good reasons to slow down:

1. You need to manage your time and mental energy across the entire GMAT. If you pause briefly to find a more efficient solution, you'll save time and energy for other problems.
2. If you start doing math without thinking first, you might have to change your approach later in the problem, which takes time that you don't have. You also risk falling for traps.

To remind yourself to slow down and plan, *understand* each problem by taking three steps:

> Glance   Read   Jot

Glance at the entire problem: is it PS or DS? If it's PS, glance at the answer choices. If it's DS, glance at the statements. Knowing what type of problem you're dealing with will help you read more effectively.

Pólya recommended that you ask yourself simple questions as you *read* a problem. Here are some great Pólya-style questions that can help you *understand*:

- **What exactly is the problem asking for?**
- **What information would I need in order to find the answer?**
- **What information do I already have?**

1

- **What information *don't* I have?**
  - Sometimes you care about something you don't know. This could be an intermediate unknown quantity that you didn't think of earlier.
  - Other times, you don't know something, and you don't care. For instance, if a problem includes the quantity 11! (11 factorial), you will practically never need to know the exact value of that quantity.
- **What is this problem testing?** In other words, why is this problem on the GMAT? What aspect of math are they testing? What kind of reasoning do they want me to demonstrate?
- **Have I seen a problem like this before?** Have you already solved a similar problem? What approach worked best?

You don't need to meticulously go through every one of these questions whenever you solve a problem. (However, that's a good thing to do when you review a problem!) They're here to help you consider how you might read more productively.

As you read the problem, *jot* down any given numbers or formulas on your scrap paper. That doesn't mean you should start doing math while you're trying to read. If you start trying to solve the problem when you haven't even finished reading it, you're getting ahead of yourself.

Start the following problem by taking these three steps: Glance, Read, and Jot.

Try-It #1-1

$x = 9^{10} - 3^{17}$ and $\frac{x}{n}$ is an integer. If n is a positive integer that has exactly two factors, how many different values for n are possible?

(A) One
(B) Two
(C) Three
(D) Four
(E) Five

Glance. This is a PS problem. The answers are numbers but in written form; this format is reserved for problems that ask for the number of numbers or number of possibilities for something. The numbers are small.

Read. Dive into the text. Here are some possible answers to the Pólya questions:

What exactly is the problem asking for?	The number of possible values for n.
	This means that n might have multiple possible values. In fact, it probably can take on more than one value.
	I may not need these actual values. I just need to count them.
What are the quantities I care about?	I'm given x and n as variables. These are the quantities I care about.

What do I know?	$x = 9^{10} - 3^{17}$
	That is, $x =$ a specific large integer, expressed in terms of powers of 9 and 3.
	$\frac{x}{n}$ is an integer.
	That is, x is divisible by n, or n is a factor of x.
	Finally, n is a positive integer that has exactly two factors.
	Prime numbers have exactly two factors. So I can rephrase the information: n is prime. (Primes are always positive.)
What *don't* I know?	Here's something I don't know: I don't know the value of x as a series of digits. Using a calculator or Excel, I could find out that x equals 3,357,644,238. But I don't know this number at the outset. Moreover, because this calculation is far too cumbersome, it must be the case that I don't *need* to find this number.
What is this problem testing?	From the foregoing, I can infer that this problem is testing Divisibility & Primes. I will probably also need to manipulate exponents, since I see them in the expression for x.

You can ask these questions in whatever order is most helpful for the problem. For instance, you might not look at what the problem is asking for until you've understood the given information.

Jot. As you decide that a piece of information is important, jot it down on your scrap paper. At this point, your scrap paper might look something like this:

$$\frac{x}{n} = \text{int} \quad n = \text{prime}$$
$$x = 9^{10} - 3^{17}$$

Principle #2: Build a Plan

Next, think about *how* you will solve the problem:

Reflect   Organize

Reflect. Here are some Pólya questions that help you think about what you know and come up with a *plan*:

Is a good approach already obvious?	From your answers above, you may already see a way to reach the answer. If you can envision the rough outlines of the correct path, then go ahead and get started.
If not, what in the problem can help me figure out a good approach?	If you are stuck, look for particular *clues* to tell you what to do next. Revisit your answers to the basic questions. What do those answers mean? Can you rephrase or reword them? Can you combine two pieces of information in any way, or can you rephrase the question, given everything you know?
Can I remember a similar problem?	Try relating the problem to other problems you've faced. This can help you categorize the problem or recall a solution process.

1

Organize. For the Try-It #1-1 problem, some of the information is already rephrased (reorganized). Go further now, combining information and simplifying the question:

Given:	n is a prime number AND n is a factor of x.
Combined:	**n is a prime factor of x.**
Question:	How many different values for n are possible?
Combined:	How many different values for n, **a prime factor of x**, are possible?
Rephrased:	**How many distinct prime factors does x have?**

You need the prime factorization of x. Notice that n is not even in the question anymore. The variable n just gave you a way to ask this underlying question.

Consider the other given fact: $x = 9^{10} - 3^{17}$. It can be helpful initially to put certain complicated facts to the side. At this stage, however, you know that you need the prime factors of x. So now you have the beginning of a plan: factor this expression into its primes.

Principle #3: Solve—and Put Pen to Paper

The third step is to do the work: *solve*.

Work

You'll want to execute that solution in an error-free way—it would be terrible to get all the thinking correct, then make a careless computational mistake. That's why we say you should *put pen to paper*.

In the expression $9^{10} - 3^{17}$, the 3 is prime but the 9 is not. Since the problem is asking about prime factors, rewrite the equation in terms of prime numbers:

$$x = \left(3^2\right)^{10} - 3^{17} = 3^{20} - 3^{17}$$

Next, pull out a common factor from both terms. The largest common factor is 3^{17}:

$$x = 3^{20} - 3^{17} = 3^{17}\left(3^3 - 1\right) = 3^{17}(27 - 1) = 3^{17}(26) = 3^{17}(13)(2)$$

Now, you have what you need: the prime factorization of x. The number x has three distinct prime factors: 2, 3, and 13. The correct answer is (C).

The idea of putting pen to paper also applies when you get stuck *anywhere* along the way on a monster problem.

Think back to those killer Try-It problems in the introduction. Those are not the kinds of problems you can figure out just by looking at them.

When you get stuck on a tough problem, take action. Do not just stare, hoping that you suddenly get it.

Instead, ask yourself the Pólya questions again and write down whatever you can:

- Reinterpretations of given information or of the question
- Intermediate results, whether specific or general
- Avenues or approaches that *didn't* work

This way, your top-down brain can help your bottom-up brain find the correct leads—or help it let go. In particular, it's almost impossible to abandon an unpromising line of thinking without writing something down.

Think back to the sequence problem in the introduction. You'll keep seeing 64 as 8^2 unless you try *writing* it in another way.

Do not try to juggle everything in your head. Your working memory has limited capacity, and your bottom-up brain needs that space to work. A multistep problem cannot be solved in your brain as quickly, easily, and accurately as it can be on paper.

As you put pen to paper, there are three themes you'll want to keep in mind.

1. Look for Patterns

Every GMAT Quant problem has a two-minutes-or-faster solution path, which may depend upon a pattern that you'll need to extrapolate. You'll know a pattern is needed when a problem asks something that would be impossible to calculate (without a calculator) in two minutes. When this happens, write out the first five to eight items in the sequence or list in order to try to spot the pattern.

Try-It #1-2

$S_n = \dfrac{-1}{S_{n-1}+1}$ for all integer values of n greater than 1. If $S_1 = 1$, what is the sum of the first 61 terms in the sequence?

(A) −48

(B) −31

(C) −29

(D)   1

(E)   30

Nobody is going to write out all 61 terms and then add them up in two minutes. There must be a pattern. The recursive definition of S_n doesn't yield any secrets upon first glance. So write out the early cases in the sequence, starting at $n = 1$ and looking for a pattern:

$$S_1 = 1$$

$$S_2 = \frac{-1}{1+1} = -\frac{1}{2}$$

$$S_3 = \frac{-1}{-\frac{1}{2}+1} = \frac{-1}{\frac{1}{2}} = (-1)(2) = -2$$

$$S_4 = \frac{-1}{-2+1} = \frac{-1}{-1} = 1$$

$$S_5 = \frac{-1}{1+1} = -\frac{1}{2}$$

$$S_6 = \frac{-1}{-\frac{1}{2}+1} = -2$$

etc.

The terms of the sequence are $1, \dfrac{1}{2}, -2, 1, \dfrac{1}{2}, -2 \dots$. Three terms repeat in this cyclical pattern forever; every third term is the same. Note: If you don't spot a pattern within the first five to eight terms, stop using this approach and see whether there's another way (including guessing!).

1

The problem asks for the sum, so find the sum of each group of three consecutive terms:

$1 + \left(-\frac{1}{2}\right) + (-2) = -\frac{3}{2}$. There are 20 groups in the first 61 terms, and one additional term that hasn't been counted yet. So the sum of the first 61 terms is as follows:

$$(\text{Number of groups})(\text{Sum of one group}) + (\text{Uncounted terms}) = (20)\left(-\frac{3}{2}\right) + 1 = -29$$

The correct answer is (C).

It is almost impossible to stare at the recursive definition of this sequence and discern the resulting pattern.

The best way to identify the pattern is to calculate a few values of the sequence and look for the pattern. You will learn more about pattern recognition in Chapter 5.

2. Draw It Out

Some problems are much easier to solve if you draw out what's happening in the problem. Whenever a story problem describes something that could actually happen in the real world, you could try to draw out the solution. For instance, if a problem involves motion, you can draw snapshots representing the problem at different points in time.

Try-It #1-3

> Truck A is on a straight highway heading due south at the same time Truck B is on a different straight highway heading due east. At 1:00 p.m., Truck A is exactly 14 miles north of Truck B. If both trucks are traveling at a constant speed of 30 miles per hour, at which of the following times will they be exactly 10 miles apart?
>
> (A) 1:10 p.m.
> (B) 1:12 p.m.
> (C) 1:14 p.m.
> (D) 1:15 p.m.
> (E) 1:20 p.m.

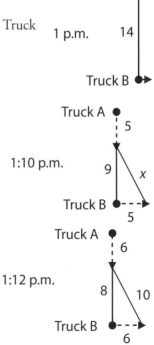

Represent Truck A and Truck B as of 1:00 p.m. How does the distance between Truck A and Truck B change as time goes by?

Try another point in time. Since the answers are all a matter of minutes after 1:00 p.m., try a convenient increment of a few minutes. After 10 minutes, each truck will have traveled 5 miles (30 miles per 60 minutes = 5 miles in 10 minutes). How far apart will the trucks be then? On the diagram to the right, the distance is represented by x.

Because Truck A is traveling due south and Truck B is traveling due east, the triangle must be a right triangle.

Therefore, $x^2 = 9^2 + 5^2$.

At this point, you could solve the problem in one of two ways. The first is to notice that once both trucks travel 6 miles, the diagram will contain a 6 : 8 : 10 triangle. Therefore, $\frac{6}{30} = \frac{1}{5}$ of an hour later, at 1:12 p.m., the trucks will be exactly 10 miles apart.

Alternatively, you could set up an algebraic equation and solve for the unknown number of miles traveled, such that the distance between the trucks is 10. Call that distance y:

$$10^2 = y^2 + (14 - y)^2$$
$$100 = 2y^2 - 28y + 196$$
$$50 = y^2 - 14y + 98$$
$$0 = y^2 - 14y + 48$$
$$0 = (y - 6)(y - 8)$$

Therefore, y could equal 6 or 8 miles. In other words, the trucks will be exactly 10 miles apart at 1:12 p.m. and at 1:16 p.m. Either way, the correct answer is (B).

Notice how instrumental these diagrams were for the solution process. You may already accept that Geometry problems require diagrams. However, many other kinds of problems can benefit from visual thinking. You will learn more about advanced visualization techniques in Chapter 7.

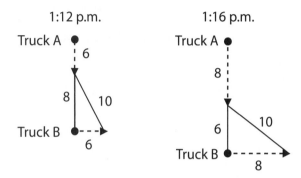

3. Solve an Easier Problem

A problem may contain large numbers or complicated expressions that actually distract you from the task at hand: finding a solution path.

When this happens, one tactic is to simplify part of the problem and solve that. Once you understand how the math works, return to the more complex problem and apply the same solution path.

Try-It #1-4

If x and y are positive integers and $\dfrac{1{,}620x}{y^2}$ is the square of an odd integer, what is the smallest possible value of xy?

(A)   1
(B)   8
(C)   10
(D)   15
(E)   28

As you read, jot down the given information.

Note that you might not immediately write down the *square of an odd integer* info if you still have to puzzle out what it means:

$$x, y = \text{int}$$
$$\frac{1{,}620x}{y^2}$$

1

What does the square of an odd integer look like? List out a few examples, on paper or in your head:

$$1^2 = 1$$
$$3^2 = 9$$
$$5^2 = 25$$
$$7^2 = 49$$

Are there any patterns or commonalities? All of the numbers are odd. All of the numbers are perfect squares. Therefore, $\frac{1,620x}{y^2}$ is an odd perfect square. Add that to your notes.

The question asks for the smallest possible value of xy. What do you need to figure out in order to find that?

If the $\frac{1,620x}{y^2}$ expression is distracting you, try figuring out what this would mean for a simpler version of the expression.

> **Simpler problem:** What if $\frac{20x}{y}$ is an odd perfect square?
>
> In order for the number to be odd, you have to get rid of the even number 20 (because an even number times any number equals an even number). The only way to get rid of the even part is to divide it out by y. If y is 4, then the expression would become $\frac{20x}{4} = 5x$. As long as x is an odd number, $5x$ will be odd, too.

Interesting. How can you apply that thinking to the real problem?

It's still true that, in order for $\frac{1,620x}{y^2}$ to be odd, you have to get rid of the even factors in the numerator.

In other words, y^2 must cancel out all the even factors in 1,620. The y^2 must contain at least two 2's, so y itself has to contain at least one 2.

Okay, that takes care of y: at minimum, y must be 2. If so, then the expression becomes $\frac{1,620x}{(2)^2} = 405x$.

Now, what about x? If you're not sure, return to your simpler problem thinking.

> **Simpler problem:** In the last step, in order to make $5x$ odd, x has to be odd. $5x$ also has to be a perfect square. If you make $x = 5$, then $5x = 25$, an odd perfect square.
>
> Why does that work? A perfect square must contain two of each factor: 5 and 5, for example. The expression $5x$, therefore, needs a second 5 to make this a perfect square.

Back to the real problem. Make sure that $405x$ has two pairs of every factor. 405 contains only one 5, so x must contain another 5. Also contained in 405 is 81, which is 9^2. That set of factors already represents a perfect square, so the minimum requirement is that x equals 5.

If y must be 2, at minimum, and x must be 5, at minimum, then the smallest possible value of xy is 10.

You can generalize this approach. If a problem has many complexities, you can attack it by ignoring some of the complexities at first. Solve a simpler problem. Then, see whether you can adjust the solution to the simpler problem in order to solve the original.

To recap, put your work on paper. Don't try to solve hard problems in your head. Instead, do the following:

- Find a pattern: Write out the first few cases.

- Visualize a scene: Draw it out!

- Solve an easier problem, then apply your method to the harder problem.

In general, jot down intermediate results as you go. You may see them in a new light and consider how they fit into the solution.

Also, try to be organized. For instance, make tables to keep track of cases. The more organized you are, the more insights you will have into difficult problems.

Principle #4: Review Your Work

When you are done with a test or practice set, you are not really done. When you first do a problem under timed conditions, your brain is too busy solving the problem to effectively learn and remember. What you *learn* from a new problem comes after you've finished it and picked your answer, when you look at it with a clear head and no timer. Give yourself twice as much time to review each problem as you spent doing the problem in the first place.

Here are some things you might consider as you review a problem. Most of these questions are useful *even if you got the problem correct*. Don't restrict yourself to reviewing problems you got wrong. Review any problem you might learn something from and ask yourself:

- What are all of the pathways to the answer? Which is the best? What is the easiest and fastest way to implement it?

- What clues in the problem told me to use a certain approach or take a certain step? If I see one of those clues in a different problem, what should I do?

- What traps or tricks are built into this problem?

- Where could I have made a mistake?

- If I did make a mistake, what went wrong in my problem-solving process? Do I need to change how I approach similar problems?

- What could I take from this problem to help me solve other problems in the future?

When you do the following problem set, apply the first three principles from this chapter to each problem: Understand, Plan, and Solve. Then, review each problem in depth. As you review, do two things:

1. Identify exactly what the problem is asking for and what that means in the simplest possible terms.

2. Note at least one general takeaway that might be useful on other problems in the future.

The solutions include our own responses to these two tasks. Yours might look different, and that's fine!

Problem Set

1. Each factor of 210 is inscribed on its own plastic ball and all of the balls are placed in a jar. If a ball is randomly selected from the jar, what is the probability that the ball is inscribed with a multiple of 42 ?

   (A) $\frac{1}{16}$

   (B) $\frac{5}{42}$

   (C) $\frac{1}{8}$

   (D) $\frac{3}{16}$

   (E) $\frac{1}{4}$

2. If x is a positive integer, what is the units digit of $(24)^{5 + 2x}(36)^6(17)^3$?

   (A) 2

   (B) 3

   (C) 4

   (D) 6

   (E) 8

3. A baker makes a combination of chocolate chip cookies and peanut butter cookies for a school bake sale. His recipes only allow him to make chocolate chip cookies in batches of 7 and peanut butter cookies in batches of 6. If he makes exactly 95 cookies for the bake sale, what is the minimum number of chocolate chip cookies that he could make?

   (A) 7

   (B) 14

   (C) 21

   (D) 28

   (E) 35

1

4. A rectangular solid is changed such that the width and length are each increased by 1 inch and the height is decreased by 9 inches. Despite these changes, the new rectangular solid has the same volume as the original rectangular solid. If the width and length of the original rectangular solid are equal and the height of the new rectangular solid is 4 times the width of the original rectangular solid, what is the volume of the rectangular solid?

    (A) 18

    (B) 50

    (C) 100

    (D) 200

    (E) 400

5. The sum of all distinct solutions for x in the equation $x^2 - 8x + 21 = |x - 4| + 5$ is equal to which of the following?

    (A) -7

    (B) 7

    (C) 10

    (D) 12

    (E) 14

1

Solutions

Each solution addresses the two steps from the instructions:

1. Identify exactly what the problem is asking for, and what that means in the simplest possible terms.

2. Note at least one general takeaway that might be useful on other problems in the future.

1. **(C)** $\frac{1}{8}$:

   1. What it's asking: The problem is asking for the probability that the selected ball is a multiple of 42.

   The quantities you care about are the factors of 210.

What you know:	There are many balls, each with a different factor of 210. Each factor of 210 is represented. One ball is selected randomly. Some balls have a multiple of 42 (e.g., 42 itself); some do not (e.g., 1).
What you don't know:	How many factors of 210 there are How many of these factors are multiples of 42
What the problem is testing:	Probability; Divisibility & Primes

   The real question:

   $$\text{Probability (multiple of 42)} = \frac{\text{\# of factors of 210 that are multiples of 42}}{\text{\# of factors of 210}} = ?$$

   Plan: 210 to primes → build full list of factors from prime components → distinguish between multiples of 42 and non-multiples → count factors → compute probability.

   Alternatively, you could list all the factors of 210 using factor pairs.

1	**210**
2	105
3	70
5	**42**
6	35
7	30
10	21
14	15

   There are 16 factors of 210, and two of them (42 and 210) are multiples of 42.

   You can also count the factors using 210's prime factorization: $(2)(3)(5)(7) = (2^1)(3^1)(5^1)(7^1)$.

Here's a shortcut to determine the number of distinct factors of 210. Add 1 to the power of each prime factor and multiply:

$$2^1 : 1 + 1 = 2$$

$$3^1 : 1 + 1 = 2$$

$$5^1 : 1 + 1 = 2$$

$$7^1 : 1 + 1 = 2$$

There are 16 different factors of 210: $2 \times 2 \times 2 \times 2 = 16$.

How many of these 16 factors are multiples of 42? 42 itself is a multiple of 42, of course. To find any others, divide 210 by 42 to get 5. This number is a prime, so the only other possible factor is 42×5, or 210. There are two multiples of 42 out of a total of 16 factors, so the probability is $\frac{2}{16} = \frac{1}{8}$.

The correct answer is **(C)**.

2. At least one takeaway: The problem is straightforward in one sense: it says the word *factor* explicitly. Listing all the factors is feasible in two minutes, but you do need to be going down that solution path fairly quickly because it will take some time. It may be slightly faster to use the factor-counting shortcut, but only if you do know how to deal with the multiples of 42.

2. **(A) 2:**

1. What it's asking: The problem asks for the units digit. Because the problem talks about a product, you care only about the units digits, not the overall values. Furthermore, the problem provides crazy numbers; you are absolutely not going to multiply these out. There must be some kind of pattern at work. Use the Last Digit Shortcut (discussed in the *All the Quant* guide).

What jumps out? If x is a positive integer, then $2x$ must be even and $5 + 2x$ must be odd.

Units digit of $(24)^{5+2x}$ = units digit of $(4)^{\text{odd}}$. The pattern for the units digit of $4^{\text{integer}} = [4, 6]$. Thus, the units digit is 4.

Units digit of $(36)^6$ must be 6, as every power of 6 ends in 6.

Units digit of $(17)^3$ = units digit of $(7)^3$. The pattern for the units digit of $7^{\text{integer}} = [7, 9, 3, 1]$. Thus, the units digit is 3.

The product of the units digits is $(4)(6)(3) = 72$, which has a units digit of 2. The correct answer is **(A)**.

2. At least one takeaway: Patterns were very important on this one! If you forget any of the units digit patterns, start listing out the early cases. At most, you'll need to list four cases to find the pattern.

3. **(E) 35:**

1. What it's asking: The problem asks for the minimum number of chocolate chip cookies.

Given: The baker only makes chocolate chip (*C*) or peanut butter (*P*) cookies. He can only make chocolate chip cookies in batches of 7 and peanut butter cookies in batches of 6. He makes exactly 95 cookies total.

What jumps out? C and P must be integers. Therefore:

$$95 = 7C + 6P$$

The answer choices are small multiples of 7, so *work backwards* from the answers on this problem. Because the problem asks you to minimize the number of chocolate chip cookies, start with the smallest answer choice.

Make a chart:

7C	6P = 95 − 7C	Is 6P a multiple of 6? (i.e., Is P an integer?)
7	88	N
14	81	N
21	74	N
28	67	N
35	60	Y

Use the answer choices to calculate the value of $6P$. Cross off an answer choice if $6P$ is not a multiple of 6. The first answer choice that works is the last one. The correct answer is **(E)**.

2. At least one takeaway: The two competing constraints made testing choices the most efficient method.

4.   **(E) 400:**

1. What it's asking: The question asks for the volume of the box. Draw out the scenarios:

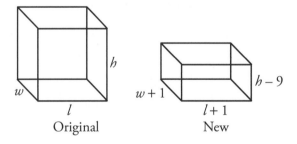

Original   New

Constraints: $w = l$

$h - 9 = 4w$

$w \times l \times h = (w + 1)(l + 1)(h - 9)$ (i.e., the volumes are equal)

There are three equations and three variables. What is the easiest way to solve for the volume?

The width, w, appears in all three constraint equations, so solve for the other variables *in terms of w* and substitute into the longest constraint:

$l = w$

$h = 4w + 9$

Substitute:

$$w \times l \times h = (w + 1)(l + 1)(h - 9)$$

Since w can't be zero, you can divide it out safely.

$$w(w)(4w + 9) = (w + 1)(w + 1)(4w)$$
$$w(4w + 9) = 4(w + 1)(w + 1)$$
$$4w^2 + 9w = 4\left(w^2 + 2w + 1\right)$$
$$4w^2 + 9w = 4w^2 + 8w + 4$$
$$w = 4$$

Solve for all variables:

$$l = w = 4$$
$$h = 4w + 9 = 4(4) + 9 = 25$$
$$Volume = w \times l \times h = (4)(4)(25) = 400$$

The correct answer is **(E)**.

2. At least one takeaway: The question is complex enough that you could check your work at the end by also calculating the volume of the new solid $(w + 1)(l + 1)(h - 9)$. As always, you have to decide whether to spend that time here versus elsewhere.

Notice that, though the initial volume formula seemed long and annoying, the calculations canceled out nicely in the end. This is common on the GMAT—common enough, in fact, to suspect that you may be doing something wrong if the algebra becomes very messy.

5. **(D) 12:**

1. What it's asking: The question asks for the sum of the distinct solutions. In other words, if the number 2 were to show up twice as a solution, you would count it only once.

The question implies that there may be multiple solutions, as does the nonlinear given equation. What is the most efficient way to find those solutions?

There are actually two good approaches; choose the one that is easier for you.

Approach #1: Do the algebra. Split it into two equations, the "positive" version and the "negative" version:

Scenario 1	Scenario 2
$x - 4 \geq 0$	$x - 4 \leq 0$
$x^2 - 8x + 21 = \lvert x - 4 \rvert + 5$	$x^2 - 8x + 21 = -(x - 4) + 5$
$x^2 - 8x + 21 = x - 4 + 5$	$x^2 - 8x + 21 = -x + 4 + 5$
$x^2 - 9x + 20 = 0$	$x^2 - 7x + 12 = 0$
$(x - 5)(x - 4) = 0$	$(x - 4)(x - 3) = 0$
$x = 5$ or 4	$x = 4$ or 3

Sum of the different solutions: $5 + 4 + 3 = 12$. The correct answer is **(D)**.

Approach #2: simplify the equation and use theory to finish it off. Isolate the absolute value:

$$x^2 - 8x + 21 = |x - 4| + 5$$
$$x^2 - 8x + 16 = |x - 4|$$
$$(x - 4)(x - 4) = |x - 4|$$
$$(x - 4)^2 = |x - 4|$$

Think it through. You square a number and get the absolute value of that same number (not squared!). Only a few numbers can make that true: 1 squared equals $|1|$, 0 squared equals $|0|$, -1 squared equals $|-1|$. That's it!

$$x - 4 = -1, 0, \text{ or } 1$$
$$x = 3, 4, \text{ or } 5$$

Sum of the different solutions: $5 + 4 + 3 = 12$.

2. At least one takeaway: When a problem asks for distinct solutions, count each unique solution; ignore multiple instances of the same value. Consider whether you prefer the pure algebraic approach or the theoretical approach. Both are valid solution methods. Which one do you think you will be able to remember and use more easily?

Problem Solving: Strategies & Tactics

In This Chapter

- Advanced Strategies

- Advanced Guessing Tactics

CHAPTER 2 Problem Solving: Strategies & Tactics

Sometimes you will encounter a Problem Solving (PS) problem that you can't answer—either because its content is difficult or obscure or because you don't have enough time to solve completely in two minutes.

This chapter describes a series of different methods you might try in these circumstances. Here, we make the distinction between **solution strategies** and **guessing tactics**.

Solution strategies are broad: they apply to a wide variety of problems, they provide a complete approach, and they can be used safely in most circumstances.

In contrast, guessing tactics can help you eliminate a few answer choices, but often leave a fair amount of uncertainty. Moreover, a particular tactic may only be useful in special situations or for parts of a problem.

The first section of this chapter outlines four Problem Solving strategies:

PS Strategy 1: **Choose Smart Numbers**

One of the most productive strategies on the GMAT is to pick good numbers and plug them into unknowns. Try this when the concepts are especially complex or when conditions are placed on key inputs that are otherwise unspecified (e.g., n is a prime number).

PS Strategy 2: **Work Backwards**

Another common approach is to work backwards from the answer choices, testing to see which one fits. Doing so can often help you avoid demanding calculations or the need to set up and solve complicated algebraic expressions.

PS Strategy 3: **Test Cases**

In certain circumstances, a problem allows multiple possible scenarios, or cases. On PS questions, the problem usually asks you to find something that *must be true* or *could be true*. On these problems, you can test different numbers to eliminate answers until only one remains.

PS Strategy 4: **Avoid Needless Computation**

The GMAT rarely requires you to carry out intensive calculations to arrive at an answer. Look for opportunities to avoid tedious computation by factoring, simplifying, or estimating.

The rest of the chapter is devoted to four specialized tactics that can knock out answer choices or provide clues about how to approach the problem more effectively:

PS Tactic 1: **Look for Answer Pairs**

Some PS questions have answer choices that pair with each other in some way. The correct answer may be part of one of these pairs.

PS Tactic 2: **Apply Cutoffs**

Sometimes a back-of-the-envelope estimation can help you eliminate any answer choice above or below a certain cutoff.

PS Tactic 3: **Look at Positive/Negative**

Some PS questions include both positive and negative answer choices. In such cases, look for clues as to the correct sign of the correct answer.

PS Tactic 4: **Draw to Scale**

Many Geometry problems allow you to eliminate some answer choices using visual estimation, as long as you draw the diagram accurately enough.

Advanced Strategies

1. Choose Smart Numbers

Some types of problems allow you to pick real numbers and solve the problem arithmetically rather than algebraically. For instance, almost any Problem Solving problem that has variables in the answer choices gives you this opportunity. Likewise, you can often pick a smart number for a fraction or percent problem without specified absolute value amounts.

Other problem types allow this strategy as well. For instance, a problem may put *specific conditions* on the inputs but not give you exact numbers. In this case, you can go ahead and just pick inputs that fit the conditions. If a problem specifies that "*x* must be a positive even integer" but does not specify the value of *x*, picking 2 for *x* will probably get you to a solution quickly and easily.

The *GMAT Official Guide* contains many problems that are difficult to solve algebraically but much easier to solve with real numbers. However, as an advanced test-taker, you might consider it a point of pride *not* to plug in a number. You might want to prove a "theoretically correct" answer. Overcome your pride! The GMAT is not a math test; the GMAT tests you on your flexibility of thinking and your ability to manage a very limited amount of time. Use the easiest and most efficient solution path, not the textbook math solution path!

Try-It #2-1

Andra, Elif, and Grady each invested in a certain stock. Andra invested q dollars, which was 40% more than Elif invested. If Elif invested 25% less than Grady invested, what was the total amount invested by all three, in terms of q ?

(A) $2q$

(B) $\dfrac{41}{20}q$

(C) $\dfrac{12}{5}q$

(D) $\dfrac{18}{7}q$

(E) $\dfrac{8}{3}q$

This problem can be solved algebraically: write a couple of equations and solve for all three variables, then add them up. A glance at the answers, though, indicates that the algebra is likely to get messy. Instead, choose a real number and solve the problem arithmetically.

If you've made it to the *GMAT Advanced Quant* book, then you have likely used this strategy before (or at least learned about it). At times, you may have been frustrated because this technique didn't actually seem easier than doing the math algebraically. If so, here's the missing piece: you need to learn how to *choose smart numbers* in the best possible way.

Most of the time, you're going to choose for the variable given (in this case, q). In some cases, though, starting with the given variable doesn't make your life any easier. The problem above actually has three unknowns: one for Andra, one for Elif, and one for Grady. Take a look at the relationship between those unknowns before you decide which one is the best starting point.

Andra invests 40% more than Elif. For just these two, it would be easier to pick a number for Elif and then calculate Andra's amount.

Elif invests 25% less than Grady. For these two, it is easier to start with Grady and then calculate Elif. As a result, start with Grady, then find Elif, then find Andra.

If Grady invests $100, then Elif invests 25% less, or $75. Andra invests 40% more than Elif, or $75 + $30 = $105. Make sure to note on your scrap paper that $q = 105$.

Collectively, the three invest $100 + $75 + $105 = $280. Find the answer choice that matches $280:

(A) $2q = 2(105) = \$210$. Eliminate.

(B) $\frac{41}{20}q = \frac{41}{20}(105)$ = not an integer. Eliminate.

(C) $\frac{12}{5}q = \frac{12}{5}(105) = 12(21)$ = a number that ends in 2. Eliminate.

(D) $\frac{18}{7}q = \frac{18}{7}(105) = (18)(15) = 270$. Eliminate.

(E) $\frac{8}{3}q = \frac{8}{3}(105) = 8(35) = 280$. Correct!

The correct answer is (E).

Note a few important aspects that will help you to choose smart numbers efficiently and effectively.

First, if there are multiple unknowns and you have to choose where to start, pause to think about how to make the math as easy as possible. In the case of the problem above, if you had picked $q = 100$ for Andra, your next step would have been to figure out Elif's amount. It is *not* the case that Elif would be $60, or 40% less than Andra.

Rather, Andra is 40% more than Elif: $1.4e = \$100$, so $e = \frac{100}{1.4}$. Elif would actually equal approximately $71.42857. Nobody's going to want to go down that path! At this stage, you have two choices: you can go back and pick for someone else or you can think about what numbers would make this particular path easier. For example, a value of $q = 140$ instead of 100 would result in an easier calculation, $\frac{140}{1.4}$, and a value of 100 for Elif. (In this case, that would still result in a messy number for the next calculation; on another problem that didn't have so many numbers, though, making a one-number adjustment can still leave you well within the two-minute time frame.)

Second, you do not need to calculate the value of every answer choice. You can stop and eliminate a choice whenever you can tell that it will not equal $280. When you plug in 105 for q, answer (B) isn't an integer and answer (C)'s units digit isn't 0, so neither can be the correct answer.

Third, practice this strategy extensively in order to expose yourself to these little variations and possible sticking points. As you become proficient with the strategy, you'll be amazed at how much time and mental effort it can save you on the GMAT.

2. Work Backwards

In a number of cases, the easiest way to solve a GMAT problem is to start from the answer choices and *work backwards*. Don't be too proud to try this technique either. The GMAT doesn't reward perfect math technique; it rewards finding the correct answer as efficiently as possible or guessing when needed.

Try-It #2-2

If $\frac{2}{z} = \frac{2}{z+1} + \frac{2}{z+9}$, which of these integers could be the value of z?

(A) 0

(B) 1

(C) 2

(D) 3

(E) 4

Look at all of those fractions! Solving for z algebraically in this problem would not be easy. Instead, notice two important clues: the problem asks for the value of a single variable and the answer choices offer nice-and-easy integers. Work backwards! People often start at the beginning, with choice (A), but actually start with (B) or (D); you'll learn why in a moment:

(B) $\quad \frac{2}{1} = \frac{2}{2} + \frac{2}{10} \qquad\qquad$ INCORRECT

The right side is smaller than the left. The numerators are always 2, so what needs to happen to bring the two halves of the equation together?

The left side needs to be made smaller, so the denominator needs to be bigger; eliminate answer choice (A) as well. This is why you start with choice (B) or (D)—you can eliminate other answer choices that are too small or too large without having to test them. Try answer (D) next:

(D) $\quad \frac{2}{3} = \frac{2}{4} + \frac{2}{12} \qquad\qquad$ CORRECT

You can stop when you find an answer that works. If you are paying attention to how the math works as you solve, you can often get away with trying just two or three answer choices on these problems.

Try-It #2-3

A certain college party is attended by both male and female students. The ratio of male-to-female students is 3 to 5. If 5 of the male students were to leave the party, the ratio would change to 1 to 2. How many total students are at the party?

(A) 24

(B) 30

(C) 48

(D) 80

(E) 90

Of course, you could set up equations for the unknowns in the problem and solve them algebraically. However, the numbers in the answers are pretty straightforward integers. Try working backwards.

Again, begin with answer (B) or answer (D), whichever number looks easier for the problem:

(B) In the original ratio, you can use an unknown multiplier to represent the total number of students: $3x + 5x = 8x$. If there are 30 students total, then the unknown multiplier is $\frac{30}{8} = 3.75$, leaving you with a non-integer number of students. This is impossible, so this answer must be incorrect.

What characteristic must be true of the correct answer? It must be a multiple of 8, so eliminate answer (E). Try the remaining answers:

(A) If there are 24 total students, then the unknown multiplier is 3: there are 9 male students and 15 female students at the party. If 5 males leave, there will be 4 left, leaving a ratio of 4 : 15. Eliminate answer (A). This ratio is also pretty far away from the correct ratio of 1 : 2, so consider trying the larger remaining answer, 80, next.

(D) If there are 80 students total, then the unknown multiplier is 10, so there are 30 males and 50 females. If 5 males leave, the new ratio is 25 : 50, or 1 : 2. This is the correct answer!

Once you have found the answer using this technique, you can stop; you don't need to test any remaining answers. Also, you don't have to translate equations or figure out how to eliminate variables and solve. You just work each number through the problem until you're done.

As you work through an answer, think about how the math is playing out. Again, you will usually be able to eliminate some answers without actually having to try them.

3. Test Cases

Some problems allow you to choose real numbers to solve, but you can't choose just one set of numbers as you do when you choose smart numbers. Rather, you have to test multiple scenarios to get yourself to the one correct answer. On Problem Solving problems, this tends to occur with *must be true* or *could be true* problems.

Try It #2-4

If n is a positive integer, what must be true of $n^3 - n$?

(A) It is divisible by 4.

(B) It is odd.

(C) It is a multiple of 6.

(D) It is a prime number.

(E) It has, at most, two distinct prime factors.

This problem is asking about a theoretical concept: what mathematical characteristic must be true of this expression? In order to solve, you can test allowable cases to narrow down the answers until only one remains.

Note that in this PS problem, one of the answers must be correct. In this case, any positive integer n will help you get to the answer, so start with the simplest possible positive integer: 1. In general, when testing cases on PS or DS, start with the simplest number that fits the problem's parameters.

Try $n = 1$:

	n	$n^3 - n$
Case 1	1	0

(A) Yes, 0 is divisible by 4. (0 is divisible by any number except 0.)

(B) No, 0 is not odd. Eliminate.

(C) Yes, 0 is a multiple of 6. (0 is a multiple of any number.)

(D) No, 0 is not a prime number. Eliminate.

(E) Yes, 0 does not have more than two prime factors.

Try your next case, ignoring answers (B) and (D) from now on:

	n	$n^3 - n$
Case 2	2	6

(A) No, 6 is not divisible by 4. Eliminate.

(C) Yes, 6 is a multiple of 6.

(E) Yes, 6 does not have more than two distinct prime factors. (The prime factors are 2 and 3.)

You're down to (C) and (E). Because one of the statements talks about having more than a certain number of prime factors, try a larger number next:

	n	$n^3 - n$
Case 3	5	120

(C) Yes, 120 is a multiple of 6.

(E) No, 120 does have more than two distinct prime factors. (The prime factors are 2, 3, and 5.) Eliminate.

The correct answer is (C). You could save yourself some time on this one by recognizing that the expression $n^3 - n$ can be rewritten as:

$$n^3 - n$$
$$n\left(n^2 - 1\right)$$
$$n\left(n - 1\right)(n + 1)$$

In other words, the expression represents three consecutive integers. Test some cases to discover what must be true about the product of three consecutive integers.

Case 1: If $n = 1$, then the three consecutive integers are 0, 1, 2. This product is even and not prime, so eliminate answers (B) and (D).

Case 2: If $n = 2$, then the three consecutive integers are 1, 2, and 3. This product does not contain two 4's, so it is not a multiple of 4. Eliminate (A).

Case 3: If $n = 3$, then the three consecutive integers are 3, 4, and 5. You could multiply out the consecutive integers, but only go down the computation path if you must. In this case, you're trying to find factors, and the three consecutive integers tell you that directly; you don't need to multiply them out. (You'll learn more about avoiding unnecessary computation in the next section.)

Instead, if possible, try to notice a pattern. In every set of three consecutive numbers, you will always have at least one even number. You will also always have a multiple of 3. (In Case 1, 0 is a multiple of 3.) As a result, the product will always be a multiple of 6.

You may also notice that the problem contains no upper limit. By choosing a large enough number, you're going to be able to create a number that contains more than two distinct prime numbers.

You can test cases directly to eliminate the four incorrect answers, or you can use a few cases to help you figure out the theory underlying the problem, which will also get you to the correct answer.

4. Avoid Needless Computation

You won't see many GMAT problems that require substantial calculation to arrive at a precise answer. Rather, correct answers on difficult problems will generally be relatively easy to compute *once the difficult concept or trick in the problem has been correctly identified and addressed.*

On several types of GMAT problems, a significant amount of computation can be avoided. A simple rule of thumb is this: *if it seems that calculating the answer is going to take a lot of work, there's a good chance that a shortcut exists.* Look for the back door!

Estimation

Intelligent estimation can save you time and effort on many problems. For example, you can round to nearby benchmarks or be ready to switch a fraction to a decimal or percent, and vice versa.

Try-It #2-5

The percent change from 29 to 43 is approximately what percent of the percent change from 43 to 57?

(A)   50%

(B)   66%

(C)   110%

(D)   133%

(E)   150%

handwritten: 14 →29 = 50%
14 →43 → 33%% · 33/50 · 50/33
(E)

In this case, the question stem straight up tells you that you can estimate. Any time you see the word *approximately* (or a synonym), definitely do not try to solve for the exact answer.

The question stem is pretty complex. Use the percent change formula:

$$\text{Percent change} = \frac{\text{new} - \text{original}}{\text{original}} \times 100\%$$

A direct translation would look like this:

$$\frac{\dfrac{43-29}{29}}{\dfrac{57-43}{43}} \times 100 = ?$$

You can simplify things by solving the question in parts. First, it talks about *the percent change from 29 to 43.*

The percent change for the top half of the fraction, is $\frac{14}{29}$, but that number is cumbersome. Estimate! This is approximately $\frac{1}{2}$.

The percent change from 43 to 57 is $\frac{14}{43}$. This is about $\frac{1}{3}$. The question is really asking:

$\frac{1}{2}$ is what percent of $\frac{1}{3}$?

$$\frac{1}{2} = (x\%)\left(\frac{1}{3}\right)$$

$$\frac{3}{2} = x\%$$

The fraction $\frac{3}{2}$ is equivalent to 150%. The correct answer is (E).

The wording of the question can sometimes provide a strong clue that estimation should be used. Look for phrases such as these:

- ...the number is approximately equal to which of the following?
- ...this result is closest to which of the following?
- Which of the following is most nearly equal to...?

The test doesn't have to tell you that you can estimate, though. You can usually estimate when the answer choices are far apart.

Heavy Long Division

Very few problems on the GMAT truly require long division, even though it might appear otherwise. You can almost always approximate the answer or reduce the division by taking out common factors.

Try-It #2-6

$\frac{3.507}{10.02}$ is equivalent to which of the following?

(A) 0.35

(B) 0.3505

(C) 0.3509

(D) 0.351

(E) 0.3527

At first glance, it appears that precise long division is necessary. The answer choices are very close together, making estimation difficult. However, with some manipulation and factoring, the solution is much more straightforward.

The key to factoring this fraction is to move the decimals of both the numerator and denominator three places to the right so that you're dealing with integers. Then you might notice that 3,507 is divisible by 7 (3,500 and 7 are both divisible by 7, providing a clue that you may be able to factor out 7). Moreover, 10,020 is divisible by 10 and by 2 (10,020 ends in a 0, and 1,002 is even):

$$\frac{3.507}{10.02} = \frac{3,507}{10,020} = \frac{7(501)}{10(1,002)} = \frac{7(501)}{(10)(2)(501)} = \frac{7}{20} = 0.35$$

The correct answer is (A).

Alternatively, you might observe that 10.02 is very slightly larger than 10. Therefore, the correct answer will be slightly smaller than $\frac{3.507}{10} = 0.3507$. Guess between choices (A) and (B).

Try-It #2-7

What is the value of $\frac{81,918}{\left(10^5 - 10^2\right)}$?

(A) 8.19

(B) 8.02

(C) 0.89

(D) 0.82

(E) 0.81

Since 10^2 is extremely small compared to 10^5, and the choices are somewhat spread out, estimate:

$$\frac{81,918}{\left(10^5 - 10^2\right)} \approx \frac{81,918}{100,000} = 0.81918$$

Notice that by ignoring the 10^2 term, you made the denominator slightly larger than it originally was. Therefore, 0.81918 is slightly *smaller* than the correct answer, 0.82. The correct answer is (D).

Quadratic Expressions in Word Problems

Some Word Problems result in a quadratic equation. You are probably pretty good at solving quadratic equations, so your natural bias would be to set up and solve the equation. However, if the coefficients are huge, the equation may be very difficult to solve. In these cases, try testing the answer choices in the original problem (*not* in the translated and manipulated quadratic), especially when the answer choices contain easier numbers.

2

Try-It #2-8

A shoe cobbler charges n dollars to repair a single pair of loafers. Tomorrow, he intends to earn $240 repairing loafers. If he were to reduce his fee per pair by $20, he would have to repair an additional pair of the loafers to earn the same amount of revenue. How many pairs of loafers does he intend to repair tomorrow?

(A) 1
(B) 2
(C) 3
(D) 4
(E) 5

The problem may not seem too bad... until you try to set it up algebraically. Assign x to represent the number of pairs of loafers the cobbler intends to repair tomorrow. Using the equation for revenue gives you the following:

$$nx = 240$$

Furthermore, reducing his fee by $20 would result in the need to repair an additional pair of shoes for the same amount of revenue:

$$(n - 20)(x + 1) = 240$$

From here, the algebra gets complicated very quickly. (The algebra is shown later, if you want to see!)

Switch to a different approach—working backwards from the answer choices. Start with (B) or (D).

The revenue in answer (B), $300, is too large. Do you need to make x larger or smaller? If you're not sure, try (D) next, and notice something very important. The revenue in (D), $200, is too small. The correct revenue, therefore, should fall between (B) and (D). The answer must be (C)!

	x	n	$x \times n$	$x + 1$	$n - 20$	$(x + 1) \times (n - 20)$
(B)	2	$120	$240	3	$100	$300
(D)	4	$60	$240	5	$40	$200

If you're not sure, try that answer:

	x	n	$x \times n$	$x + 1$	$n - 20$	$(x + 1) \times (n - 20)$
(C)	3	$80	$240	4	$60	$240

Here's the algebra in case you want to see it (but it's not recommended to do this):

$$nx = 240$$
$$(n - 20)(x + 1) = 240$$
$$x = \frac{240}{n}$$
$$(n - 20)\left(\frac{240}{n} + 1\right) = 240$$
$$240 + n - \frac{4,800}{n} - 20 = 240$$
$$n - \frac{4,800}{n} - 20 = 0$$
$$n^2 - 4,800 - 20n = 0$$
$$n^2 - 20n - 4,800 = 0$$
$$(n + 60)(n - 80) = 0$$
$$n = -60 \text{ or } 80 \ \left(\text{price cannot be negative}\right)$$
$$80x = 240$$
$$x = 3$$

Advanced Guessing Tactics

To repeat, the tactics below are less universally useful than the strategies we just covered. However, when all else fails, "break the glass" and try one or more of these tactics. They're almost always better than guessing completely randomly. If you're way behind on time and you have to sacrifice a couple of problems, though, guess immediately and move on.

The examples below will not be too difficult in order to illustrate the tactic clearly and not distract you with other issues. Of course, if you can solve the problem directly, do so. But also study the tactic, so you're ready to use it on a harder problem of the same type.

1. Look for Answer Pairs   *Certainty:* Moderate

GMAT answer choices are sometimes paired in a mathematically relevant way. Pairs of answers may:

- Add up to 1 on a probability or fraction question
- Add up to 100% on questions involving percents
- Add up to 0 (be opposites of each other)
- Multiply to 1 (be reciprocals of each other)

The correct answer is sometimes part of such a pair. Why? The GMAT likes to put in a final obstacle. Say you do everything correct, except you solve for the wrong unknown or forget to subtract from 1. Under the pressure of the exam, people make this sort of penultimate error all the time (*penultimate* means next to last).

In order to catch folks in this trap, the GMAT has to make an answer choice that's paired to the correct answer—it's correct *except* for that one last step.

This means that you can often eliminate *unpaired* answer choices. Also, the way in which the answers are paired may provide clues about the correct solution method and/or traps in the problem.

Try-It #2-9

At a certain high school, the junior class is twice the size of the senior class. If $\frac{1}{3}$ of the seniors and $\frac{1}{4}$ of the juniors study Japanese, what fraction of the students in both classes do not study Japanese?

(A) $\frac{1}{6}$

(B) $\frac{5}{18}$

(C) $\frac{5}{12}$

(D) $\frac{7}{12}$

(E) $\frac{13}{18}$

Note that two pairs of answers each add up to 1: $\frac{5}{12} + \frac{7}{12}$, and $\frac{5}{18} + \frac{13}{18}$. Answer (A) is not likely to be correct, because it is not part of an answer pair. The fact that these pairs sum to 1 also provides a clue to double-check the wording of the question: *do* vs. *do not* study Japanese (the sum of the fractions of the students that *do* study Japanese and those who *do not* will equal 1).

To solve, you could use a double-set matrix that shows juniors versus seniors and Japanese studiers versus non-Japanese studiers. However, let's go back to the first strategy in this chapter and choose smart numbers. Pick a smart number that is a multiple of the denominators in the problem: $3 \times 4 = 12$.

If the junior class has 12 people, then the senior class thus has 6. If $\frac{1}{3}$ of the seniors study Japanese, then $\frac{1}{3} \times 6 = 2$ seniors study Japanese. If $\frac{1}{4}$ of the juniors study Japanese, then $\frac{1}{4} \times 12 = 3$ juniors study Japanese. There are $12 + 6 = 18$ students total, and $2 + 3 = 5$ of them study Japanese. Thus, $\frac{5}{18}$ of the students *do* study Japanese, so the fraction of the students that *do not* study Japanese is $\frac{13}{18}$. The correct answer is (E).

2. Apply Cutoffs   *Certainty:* High

You may be able to eliminate answers above or below some easily calculated threshold value. You may have to imagine that the problem is slightly different (and easier) to come up with that threshold value, but once you do, you can often get rid of two or three answer choices.

This strategy can sometimes be used in combination with an *answer pairs* strategy, as pairs of answers are often composed of a high and a low value.

In the previous problem, for example, $\frac{1}{3}$ of the seniors and $\frac{1}{4}$ of the juniors study Japanese. Therefore, somewhere between $\frac{1}{3}$ and $\frac{1}{4}$ of the students overall, or less than half, must study Japanese. This implies that the fraction of students who *do not* study Japanese must be more than half. You could eliminate answer choices (A), (B), and (C) because each of these answer choices is smaller than $\frac{1}{2}$.

Try-It #2-10

The eSoroban device is available in two colors, orange and green. In 2013, 60% of the eSoroban devices sold were purchased by women, $\frac{5}{12}$ of whom purchased the orange device. If an equal number of orange and green eSoroban devices were sold in 2013, what fraction of men who purchased an eSoroban in 2013 purchased the green device?

(A) $\frac{3}{10}$

(B) $\frac{3}{8}$

(C) $\frac{5}{12}$

(D) $\frac{1}{2}$

(E) $\frac{5}{7}$

More than half of the people purchasing this device are women, and more than half of them buy the green version. If an equal number of green and orange devices are sold, then more than half of the men must buy the orange version. Therefore, less than half of men buy the green version: eliminate answers (D) and (E).

Furthermore, women represent 60% of purchases, while men represent just 40%. Pretend for a moment that there were equal numbers of men and women. If that were the case, then $\frac{5}{12}$ of women would buy orange and $\frac{7}{12}$ would buy green. On the flip side, $\frac{5}{12}$ of men would buy green and $\frac{7}{12}$ would buy orange.

In fact, there are more women than men, so the proportion of men buying orange devices has to be higher than $\frac{7}{12}$. Fewer than $\frac{5}{12}$ must buy the green version. Eliminate answer (C).

From here, if you have a strong number sense, you might guess that answer (B) is more likely the correct answer, because a $\frac{50}{50}$ split would have made the answer $\frac{5}{12}$. The actual split is $\frac{60}{40}$, so the correct value is not that much lower than $\frac{5}{12}$. But here's the actual solution, using a double-set matrix and a smart number of 100 total people:

	Men	Women	Total
Orange		$\frac{5}{12}(60) = 25$	50
Green	$50 - 35 = 15$	$60 - 25 = 35$	50
Total	40	60	100

Because 15 men purchased a green device out of 40 men total, the proportion is $\frac{15}{40} = \frac{3}{8}$. The correct answer is (B).

3. Look at Positive/Negative   *Certainty:* High

A special case of the *cutoff strategy* occurs when some of the answer choices are positive and others are negative. In this case, focus on figuring out the sign of the correct answer, then eliminate any answer choices of the opposite sign. (Again, this is something to do when you have run out of direct approaches or you are short on time!)

Try-It #2-11

If $x \square y$ is defined to equal $\dfrac{x^2}{y}$ for all x and y, then $(-1 \square 2) \square 3$ is equivalent to which of the following?

(A) $\dfrac{4}{3}$

(B) $\dfrac{1}{3}$

(C) $\dfrac{1}{12}$

(D) $-\dfrac{1}{12}$

(E) $-\dfrac{4}{3}$

$$\frac{-1^2}{2} = \frac{1}{2} \qquad \frac{\frac{1}{2}^2}{3} \Rightarrow \frac{1}{12}$$

The negative sign in the term -1 will be extinguished, because the term before the $\square$ symbol is squared when this function is calculated. Therefore, the correct answer will be positive. Eliminate (D) and (E). By the way, the correct answer is (C).

4. Answer Properties   *Certainty:* Moderate

You may not have time, while doing a Problem Solving problem, to figure out the correct answer. However, it might take less time to figure out something *about* the correct answer. You saw two examples of this in the previous two guessing strategies: you can sometimes figure out whether the correct answer is above or below a certain value, or whether it's positive or negative. Here are some other things you may be able to determine:

- Is the correct answer even or odd?
- Is the correct answer divisible by a certain value?
- What is the units digit of the correct answer?
- Does the correct answer include square roots?
- Does the correct answer include decimals?

5. Draw to Scale   *Certainty:* Moderate

The estimation technique can be extended to some Geometry problems.

You can approximate the length of a line segment, size of an angle, or area of an object by drawing it as accurately as possible on your scrap paper. When you take the GMAT, the laminated scratch booklet is printed with a light grid. This grid can help you draw very accurate scale pictures, and often the picture alone is enough to answer the question.

Try-It #2-12

In the diagram to the right, equilateral triangle *ADE* is drawn inside square *BCDE*. A circle is then inscribed inside triangle *ADE*. What is the ratio of the area of the circle to the area of the square?

(A) $\dfrac{\pi}{12}$

(B) $\dfrac{\pi}{8}$

(C) $\dfrac{\pi}{6}$

(D) $\dfrac{\pi}{4}$

(E) $\dfrac{\pi}{2}$

If a Problem Solving question does not say that the diagram is *not* drawn to scale, then the diagram is drawn to scale. The circle is about $\dfrac{1}{2}$ the height of the square and about $\dfrac{1}{2}$ the width. Therefore, the area of the circle should be approximately $\dfrac{1}{4}$ of the area of the square. Eliminate any answer choices that are far away from that estimate:

(A) $\dfrac{\pi}{12} \approx \dfrac{3.1}{12} \approx \dfrac{1}{4}$ Ok

(B) $\dfrac{\pi}{8} \approx \dfrac{3.1}{8} \approx \dfrac{3}{8}$ On the high side

(C) $\dfrac{\pi}{6} \approx \dfrac{3.1}{6} \approx \dfrac{1}{2}$ Too high

(D) $\dfrac{\pi}{4} \approx \dfrac{3.1}{4} \approx \dfrac{3}{4}$ Too high

(E) $\dfrac{\pi}{2} \approx \dfrac{3.1}{2} \approx \dfrac{3}{2}$ Way too high

Only answers (A) and (B) are remotely reasonable, and only (A) is really close to the estimate.

The most efficient way to solve this problem fully is to assign a radius of 1 to the circle. This way, the circle has an area of π. Now work outwards.

If the center of the circle is *O*, then *OF* = 1. Because *ADE* is an equilateral triangle, angle *ADE* = 60°. *OD* bisects angle *ADE*, so angle *ODE* = 30°. Therefore, triangle *OFD* is a 30 : 60 : 90 triangle, and $DF = \sqrt{3}$. *DE* must be twice the length of *DF*, meaning that $DE = 2\sqrt{3}$, and the area of square *BCDE* = $\left(2\sqrt{3}\right)^2 = 12$.

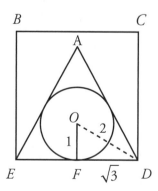

So the ratio of the area of the circle to the area of the square is $\dfrac{\pi}{12}$.

Notice how much easier the *draw to scale* tactic was! Will it work every time? No. But it works often enough that you want to think about using it.

Problem Set

Solve problems 1–12. In each case, identify whether you could use advanced strategies (Choose Smart Numbers, Work Backwards, Test Cases, or Avoid Needless Computation) and guessing tactics (Look for Answer Pairs, Apply Cutoffs, Look at Positive-Negative, or Draw to Scale) in any beneficial way. Of course, there are textbook ways to solve these problems directly; instead of trying the textbook method first, focus on applying the strategies and tactics described in this chapter.

1. A popular yoga studio that is always filled to capacity moves to a new location that is able to serve 45% more students. Unfortunately, 20% of the current students will no longer attend classes at the new location. If classes at the new location are also filled to capacity, what fraction of the students at the new location will be new students?

    (A) $\frac{25}{29}$

    (B) $\frac{20}{29}$

    (C) $\frac{16}{29}$

    (D) $\frac{13}{29}$

    (E) $\frac{9}{29}$

2. If $x < 10$, $y < 8$, and $y < x$, what must be true?

    I. $xy < 80$

    II. $\frac{x}{y} > 1$

    III. $x^2 + y^2 > 1$

    (A) None

    (B) II only

    (C) III only

    (D) I and II only

    (E) II and III only

3. If $\frac{60}{x} + \frac{288}{x^2} = 7$, which of the following could be the value of x ?

    (A) 6

    (B) 8

    (C) 9

    (D) 12

    (E) 15

4. If $\left|x^2 - 6\right| = x$, which of the following could be the value of x?

    (A) -2

    (B) 0

    (C) 1

    (D) 3

    (E) 5

5. If 154 is $\dfrac{37}{50}$ of x, approximately what is the value of $2x$?

    (A) 104

    (B) 114

    (C) 208

    (D) 228

    (E) 416

6. $\dfrac{1.206}{2.010}$ is equivalent to which of the following?

    (A) 0.6

    (B) 0.603

    (C) 0.606

    (D) 0.615

    (E) 0.66

7. In a certain clothing store, the most expensive pair of socks sells for $1 less than twice the price of the cheapest pair of socks. A customer notices that for exactly $18, she can buy three fewer pairs of the most expensive socks than the cheapest socks. What could be the number of pairs of the cheapest socks she could have purchased?

    (A) 3

    (B) 5

    (C) 6

    (D) 12

    (E) 36

8. If $\dfrac{3}{\dfrac{m+1}{m}+1} = 1$, then m must equal which of the following?

    (A) -2

    (B) -1

    (C) 0

    (D) 1

    (E) 2

9. Simplify $\dfrac{\dfrac{35^3}{72}}{\left(\dfrac{7!}{3!4!}\right)^3}$

10. If $3^x + 3^x + 3^x = 1$, what is x ?

    (A) -1

    (B) $-\dfrac{1}{3}$

    (C) 0

    (D) $\dfrac{1}{3}$

    (E) 1

11. If a and b are integers and a is a factor of b, what must be true?

    I. $a < b$

    II. The distinct prime factors of a^2 are also factors of b.

    III. $0 < \dfrac{a}{b} \le 1$

    (A) None

    (B) II only

    (C) III only

    (D) I and II only

    (E) II and III only

12. The integer k is positive but less than 400. If $21k$ is a multiple of 180, how many unique prime factors does k have?

    (A) One

    (B) Two

    (C) Three

    (D) Four

    (E) Five

Without solving problems 13–16, which answers could you confidently eliminate and why?

13. $\dfrac{69{,}300}{10^5 - 10^3} =$

    (A) 0.693

    (B) 0.7

    (C) 0.71

    (D) 6.93 –

    (E) 7.1 –

      D, E, A

14. $\dfrac{-(9.0)(0.25) - (1.5)(1.5)}{25}$ is equivalent to which of the following?

    (A) −1.8

    (B) −0.18

    (C) 0

    (D) 0.18

    (E) 1.8

    A C D E

15. In the 7-inch square to the right, another square is inscribed. What fraction of the larger square is shaded?

    (A) $\dfrac{3}{12}$

    (B) $\dfrac{24}{49}$

    (C) $\dfrac{1}{2}$

    (D) $\dfrac{25}{49}$

    (E) $\dfrac{7}{12}$

    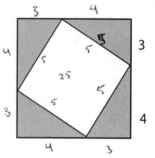

16. If Mason is now twice as old as Gunther was 10 years ago, and G is Gunther's current age in years, which of the following represents the sum of Mason's and Gunther's ages 4 years from now?

    (A) $\dfrac{3G}{2} + 3$

    (B) $3G + 28$

    (C) $3G - 12$

    (D) $8 - G$

    (E) $14 - \dfrac{3G}{2}$

Solutions

1. **(D)** $\frac{13}{29}$: (Choose Smart Numbers) Both the 45% figure and the answer choices look cumbersome, but the problem never provides a real value for the number of students, either before the move or after. Choose a smart number of 100 for this Percents problem.

    Old capacity: 100 students

    New capacity: 145 students

    Old students who will stay with the studio: 80

    If the new studio is filled to capacity, at 145 students, but only 80 old students continue to attend, then the studio will have 65 new students.

    The fraction of new students at the new location, then, is $\frac{65}{145} = \frac{13}{29}$.

    The correct answer is **(D)**.

2. **(A) None:** (Test Cases) Test real numbers to prove or disprove the statements. Make sure to choose only values that are allowed by the problem: $x < 10$, $y < 8$, and $y < x$.

    Statement I: If $x = 9$ and $y = 7$, then $xy = 63$, which is less than 80. If, on the other hand, $x = -10$ and $y = -20$, then $xy = 200$, which is greater than 80. Statement I does not have to be true. Eliminate answer (D).

    Statement II: Positive values for both x and y will make $\frac{x}{y} > 1$, but if $x = 9$ and $y = -1$, then $\frac{x}{y} = -9$, which is not greater than 1. Statement II does not have to be true. Eliminate answers (B) and (E).

    Statement III: If $x = 3$ and $y = 2$, then $x^2 + y^2$ is 13, which is greater than 1. If $x = -2$ and $y = -3$, then $x^2 + y^2$ is still 13, which is still greater than 1. Don't forget about fractions! If $x = 0.3$ and $y = 0.2$, then $x^2 + y^2 = 0.09 + 0.04$, which is *not* greater than 1. Fractions between 0 and 1 get *smaller* when squared. Eliminate answers (C) and (E).

    None of the statements must be true.

    The correct answer is **(A)**.

3. **(D) 12:** (Work Backwards) This problem can be solved algebraically, but not easily. You'd actually need to use the quadratic formula, and the equation would turn out to be really nasty. No thank you!

    Instead, notice that the problem asks for a single variable and the answer choices are decently small integers. Start with answer (B) or (D).

    $$(B)\ \frac{60}{8} + \frac{288}{8^2} = 7$$

    That math is a pain. Is answer (D) any easier? If so, start there.

    $$(D)\ \frac{60}{12} + \frac{288}{12^2} = 7$$

    Yes! Much easier: $12^2 = 144$, and that goes very nicely with 288.

    $$5 + \frac{288}{144} = 7$$

This equation simplifies to $5 + 2 = 7$, so the correct answer is **(D)**. Note that if (D) had not been the correct answer, you would have been able to tell whether to try a larger or smaller answer next based on whether (D) was too small or too large.

4. **(D) 3:** (Work Backwards) Typically, when working backwards, you start with answer (B) or (D). If you can tell that a problem isn't likely to have a consistent pattern, though, as with this absolute value equation, then just start at one end—answer (A) or answer (E)—and stop when you find the correct answer.

	x	$x^2 - 6$	$\lvert x^2 - 6 \rvert$
(A)	-2	$(-2)^2 - 6 = 4 - 6 = -2$	2
(B)	0	$(0)^2 - 6 = 0 - 6 = -6$	6
(C)	1	$(1)^2 - 6 = 1 - 6 = 5$	5
(D)	3	$(3)2 - 6 = 9 - 6 = 3$	3

The correct answer is **(D)**.

5. **(E) 416:** (Avoid Needless Computation) Not only do the numbers in the problem look ugly, but the problem asks for an approximate answer. Estimate.

It would be much easier if 154 were 150. What about that fraction? First of all, put it over 100: $\dfrac{74}{100}$. Much better! This is almost $\dfrac{3}{4}$, so use that fraction instead.

Translate the equation with the estimated values:

$$150 \approx \frac{3}{4}x$$
$$150\left(\frac{4}{3}\right) \approx x$$
$$x \approx 200$$

Finally, make sure to answer the right question that was asked! The answer is *not* (C), 208, because the question asks for the value of $2x$.

The correct answer is **(E)**.

6. **(A) 0.6:** (Avoid Needless Computation) $\dfrac{1.206}{2.010} = \dfrac{1,206}{2,010} = \dfrac{3(402)}{5(402)} = \dfrac{3}{5} = 0.6$

Alternatively, note that 2.010 is very slightly larger than 2. Therefore, the fraction is very slightly smaller than $\dfrac{1.206}{2} = 0.603$. Only (A) is smaller than 0.603. The correct answer is **(A)**.

7. **(D) 12:** (Work Backwards) This problem can be solved algebraically, but the math gets pretty challenging (see end of this explanation). It's easier to work from the answer choices. Start with (B) or (D).

Call the number of cheap pairs c and the number of expensive pairs e. Call the cost of a cheap pair $\$c$ and the cost of an expensive pair $\$e$. First, try (B).

# Cheap Pairs (c)	$\$c$ Pairs $\left(\dfrac{18}{c}\right)$	# e Pairs ($c - 3$)	$\$e$ Pairs $\left(\dfrac{18}{e}\right)$	Match? $\$e = 2(\$c) - 1?$
(B) 5	$\dfrac{\$18}{5}$	2	9	$9 = 2\left(\dfrac{18}{5}\right) - 1$ No X

Answer (B) is incorrect. Note that you don't actually have to figure out the value of the right-hand side of the equation, as long as you know that it will not equal 9. The two sides of the equation are pretty far apart, so (A) and (C) are also probably not correct answers. Try answer (D) next.

# Cheap Pairs (c)	$c Pairs $\left(\dfrac{18}{c}\right)$	# e Pairs (c − 3)	$e Pairs $\left(\dfrac{18}{e}\right)$	Match? $e = 2($c) − 1?
(D) 12	$1.50	9	$2	2 = 2(1.5) − 1 Yes ✓

Answer **(D)** makes the final equation work, so it is the correct answer.

Here's how the algebra would have to be set up. Let $c =$ the number of pairs of cheap socks, $e =$ the number of pairs of expensive socks, $x =$ the cost for one pair of cheap socks, and $y =$ the cost for one pair of expensive socks.

From sentence 1: $y = 2x - 1$

From sentence 2: $18 = cx$ and $18 = ey = (c - 3)y$

From here, you would solve the equations from sentence 2 for x and y, respectively, and plug them into the equation from sentence 1:

$$x = \frac{18}{c} \text{ and } y = \frac{18}{(c - 3)}$$

Plug in to equation 1: $\dfrac{18}{(c - 3)} = 2\left(\dfrac{18}{c}\right) - 1$

With the correct manipulation (over multiple, complicated steps!), that equation would eventually become $c^2 - 21 + 108 = 0$ and you could solve for the two solutions, $c = 9$ and $c = 12$. Only 12 is in the answer choices, so choice **(D)** is the correct answer.

8. **(D) 1:** (Work Backwards) In order for the left-hand side to equal 1, m has to be positive. Try only the three positive answer choices. In this circumstance, start with the middle number of the remaining choices. If $m = 1$, then the left-hand side simplifies to $\dfrac{3}{3} = 1$.

   The correct answer is **(D)**.

9. $\dfrac{1}{72}$: (Avoid Needless Computation)

$$\frac{\dfrac{35^3}{72}}{\left(\dfrac{7!}{3!4!}\right)^3} = \frac{\dfrac{5^3 7^3}{2^3 3^2}}{\left(\dfrac{(7)(6)(5)}{(3)(2)}\right)^3} = \frac{\dfrac{5^3 7^3}{2^3 3^2}}{7^3 5^3} = \frac{1}{2^3 3^2} = \frac{1}{72}$$

10. **(A) −1:** (Work Backwards) You might solve this one by inspection: three identical "somethings" sum to 1, so one of those "somethings" equals $\frac{1}{3}$, or $3^x = \frac{1}{3} = 3^{-1}$. Therefore, $x = -1$.

   Testing choices is fast, too. In this case, (B) and (D) are both fractions, but the other answers are integers, so try testing (A), (C), and (E) instead. Stop when you find the correct answer.

Many people would try (C) first because 0 is an easy number. Notice that it's too big. Which number should you try next, -1 or 1? Since 0 leads to a number that's too big, try -1 next.

	x	$3^x + 3^x + 3^x$
(C)	0	$1 + 1 + 1 = 3$
(A)	-1	$\frac{1}{3} + \frac{1}{3} + \frac{1}{3} = 1$

The correct answer is **(A)**.

11.   **(B) II Only:** (Test Cases) First, consider what the given information *a is a factor of b* tells you:

2 is a factor of 6

6 is not a factor of 2

1, 2, 3, and 6 are all factors of 6

Next, test the statements.

Statement I: $a < b$. A factor can be smaller than the main number, but a factor can also equal the main number: 6 is a factor of 6. Statement I does not have to be true. Eliminate answer (D).

Statement II: The distinct prime factors of a^2 are also factors of b. If $a = 2$, then $a^2 = 4$. There is just one distinct prime factor of a^2: 2. In this case, a is a factor of b, yes. If $a = 6$, then $a^2 = 36$. There are two distinct prime factors of a^2: 2 and 3. In this case, a is still a factor of b.

Notice any patterns? The distinct prime factors of a^2 are the same as the distinct prime factors of a, since a^2 is made up of a multiplied by itself. So, first, this statement is really saying that the distinct prime factors of a are also factors of b.

If a is a factor of b, then by definition all of a's prime factors also have to be factors of b. No matter what numbers you try for statement II, a will be a factor of b. Statement II must be true, so eliminate answers (A) and (C).

Statement III: $0 < \frac{a}{b} \leq 1$. If b is 6, then a could be 6, in which case $\frac{a}{b} = 1$. Alternatively, if b is 6, then a could be 2, in which case $\frac{a}{b} = \frac{1}{3}$. So far, this statement looks good.

Don't forget about negative numbers! The problem doesn't specify positive integers. What if b is -6? In this case, a could still be 2, so $\frac{a}{b} = -\frac{1}{3}$. Statement III does not have to be true. Eliminate answer (E) and choose correct answer **(B)**.

Note: The GMAT doesn't often test the factors of negative numbers, but the definitions provided in the math review of the *Official Guide* do allow for the possibility.

12.   **(C) Three:** (Choose Smart Numbers) A laborious way to solve this problem would be to determine *all* the possible values for k and take a prime factorization of each value, counting the number of different prime factors that each value has. Ugh!

An easier technique is to pick a smart number: *one* value of k that satisfies the constraints. Any value of k that fits the constraints must have the same number of different prime factors as any other legal value of k. Otherwise, the problem could not exist as written. There would be more than one correct answer.

The problem states that $21k$ is a multiple of 180, so $\frac{21k}{180} = \frac{7k}{60}$ must be an integer. In other words, k must be divisible by 60. The easiest number to choose is $k = 60$.

The prime factorization of 60 is $2 \times 2 \times 3 \times 5$, so 60 has the unique prime factors 2, 3, and 5. Thus, k has three unique prime factors. The correct answer is **(C)**.

13. **(A), (D), and (E) can be eliminated:** If you ignore the 10^3 in the denominator, the division is $\frac{69,300}{10^5} = 0.693$. This is an approximation of the answer, not an exact computation of it, so eliminate (A). You have slightly overstated the denominator, thus slightly understated the result. Answers (B) and (C) are possibilities, but (D) and (E) are both too large. The correct answer turns out to be **(B)**.

14. **(A), (C), (D), and (E) can be eliminated:** The numerator is negative, so eliminate (C), (D), and (E). The numbers in the numerator will add to more than -25 (i.e., closer to 0), so eliminate (A).

    The correct answer must be **(B)**.

15. **(A), (C), (D), and (E) can be eliminated:** Ignoring the dimensions 3 and 4 for a moment, think about the types of squares that might be inscribed in the larger square:

The shaded area can be at most $\frac{1}{2}$ of the larger square, which occurs when the smallest possible square is inscribed in the larger square. This gives you a great *cutoff*.

The larger the inscribed square, the smaller the shaded area and the more the inscribed square must be rotated from the vertical orientation of the minimum inscribed square.

Eliminate (D) and (E), since they are larger than $\frac{1}{2}$. Eliminate (C), since the labeled lengths of 3 and 4 are not equal, indicating that the inscribed square is rotated from the minimum square position.

Answer (B) is paired with (D) to sum to 1. Answer (A) is unpaired, so between (A) and (B), the more likely answer is (B). Choice **(B)** is in fact the correct answer.

There is a way to arrive at the exact answer: compute the relevant areas and take the ratio. The point of this exercise, though, is to practice guessing tactics.

16. **(D) and (E) can be eliminated:** Gunther must be at least 10 years old for him to have had a non-negative age "10 years ago" and for Mason to have a non-negative age now. Therefore, eliminate (D) and (E), as both choices will give a negative result when $G > 10$. The correct answer is in fact **(C)**.

Data Sufficiency: Principles

In This Chapter

CHAPTER 3 Data Sufficiency: Principles

The goal of every Data Sufficiency (DS) problem is the same: determine what information will let you answer the given question. This gives you a significant advantage. Once you know whether a piece of information lets you answer the given question, *you can stop calculating*. You do not have to waste time finishing that calculation.

However, this type of problem presents its own challenges. DS answer choices are never numbers, so you can't plug them back into the question to check your work. Also, answer choice (E)—that the two statements combined are NOT sufficient—leaves open the possibility that the embedded math question is not solvable even with *all* the information given. That is, unlike Problem Solving (PS), DS may contain math problems that *cannot* be solved! This aspect of DS is unsettling. (Note: If you don't already have the five DS answer choices memorized, then you are not yet ready for this chapter. Practice with other material and then return here when you feel fully comfortable with how DS works.)

On DS problems, the issue being tested is "answer-ability" *itself*—can the given question be answered, and if so, with what information? So the GMAT disguises "answer-ability" as best it can. The given facts and the question itself are generally presented in ways that make this determination difficult.

For instance, information that *seems* to be sufficient may actually be insufficient if it permits an alternative scenario that leads to a different answer. Likewise, information that seems to be *insufficient* may actually be sufficient if all the possible scenarios lead to the same answer for the question.

Advanced DS problems require you to step up your game. You will have to get really good at Testing Cases, which is even more important for advanced DS than for advanced PS problems.

You will also have to get really good at simplifying the given facts and the given question. The GMAT increases the trickiness of the *phrasing* of the question and/or statements even more than the complexity of the *underlying concepts*.

So how do you approach advanced DS problems? Unfortunately, there is no "one-size-fits-all" approach:

- The best approach may involve precise application of theory, *or* it may involve a "quick and dirty" approach.
- The statements may be easy *or* difficult to interpret.
- The question may require no rephrasing *or* elaborate rephrasing. In fact, the crux of the problem may rest entirely on a careful rephrasing of the question.

All that said, there are a few guiding principles you can follow.

Principle #1: Follow a Consistent Process

This is the most important principle. A consistent process will prevent the most common errors. It will focus your efforts at any stage of the problem. Perhaps most importantly, it will reduce your stress level, because you will have confidence in the approach that you've practiced.

Follow these rules of the road:

- **Do your work on paper, not in your head.** This fits with the *put pen to paper* concept discussed in Chapter 1. Writing down each thought as it occurs helps you keep track of the work you've done. Your mind is also freed up to think ahead. Many DS questions are *explicitly designed* to confuse you if you do all the work in your head.

- **Label everything and separate everything physically on your paper.** If you mix up the elements of the problem, you will often mess up the problem itself. Keep these four elements straight:

  - **Facts given in the question stem.** You can leave them unlabeled or you can put them with each statement.

  - **Question.** Label the question with a question mark. Obvious, right? Amazingly, many people fail to take this simple step. Without a question mark, you might think the question is a fact—and you *will* get the problem wrong. Keep the question mark as you rephrase. It's also helpful to keep the helping verb in a Yes/No question:

    - Original question: Is $x = 2$?
    - You write down: Is $x = 2$?
    - You could just write down: $x = 2$?
    - Do NOT just write down: $x = 2$ ✗

  - **Statement (1).** Label this with a (1).
  - **Statement (2).** Label this with a (2).

  It may be worth rewriting the facts from the question stem alongside each statement. Although this may seem redundant, the time is well spent if it prevents you from forgetting to use those facts.

- **Rephrase the question and statements whenever possible.** Question stems and statements are often more complex than they need to be; if you can simplify the information up front, you will save yourself time and effort later in the problem. In particular, try to rephrase the question *before* you dive into the statements.

- **Evaluate the easier statement first.** If the second statement looks much easier to you than the first, then start with the second statement.

- **Physically separate the work that you do on the individual statements.** Doing so can help reduce the risk of *statement carryover*—unintentionally letting one statement influence you as you evaluate the other.

Here is one sample schema for setting up your work on a Data Sufficiency question:

Scrapwork for Rephrasing: ~~~~		
Constraints: ~~~~		
	(1)	(2)
AD BCE	FACT from question stem: ~~~~ FACT from (1): ~~~~ ...*and any work you do to combine these facts*	FACT from question stem: ~~~~ FACT from (2): ~~~~ ...*and any work you do to combine these facts*
QUESTION: ...?	ANSWER	ANSWER

Notice the *physical separation* between statement (1) and statement (2). You might even consider going so far as to cover up the statement (1) work when evaluating statement (2). Also observe that this schema explicitly parses out the facts given in the question stem and evaluates those facts *alongside* each statement.

Try this example problem, and then take a look at what the scrap paper would look like according to this schema.

Try-It #3-1

If x and y are integers and $4xy = x^2y + 4y$, what is the value of xy ?

(1) $y - x = 0$

(2) $x^3 < 0$

Because the question stem contains an equation, simplify it before considering the statements:

$$x^2y - 4xy + 4y = 0$$

$$y\left(x^2 - 4x + 4\right) = 0$$

$$y\left(x - 2\right)^2 = 0$$

Therefore, either $x = 2$ or $y = 0$, or both. One of the following scenarios must be true:

x	y	xy = ?
2	Not 0	2y
Not 2	0	0
2	0	0

Interesting. It turns out that you only need to know the value of y. If $y = 0$, then $xy = 0$. Otherwise, x must equal 2, in which case the value of xy is still determined by the value of y.

(1) INSUFFICIENT: Rather than trying to combine this algebraically with the equation in the question stem, try a couple of the possible scenarios that fit the statement $y - x = 2$. Construct scenarios using the earlier table as inspiration:

- If $x = 2$, then $y = 2 + x = 4$, so $xy = (2)(4) = 8$.
- If $y = 0$, then $x = y - 2 = -2$, so $xy = (-2)(0) = 0$.

Since there are two possible answers, this statement is not sufficient.

(2) SUFFICIENT: If $x^3 < 0$, then $x < 0$. If x does not equal 2, then y must equal 0, according to the fact from the question stem. Therefore, $xy = 0$.

Notice how valuable it was to evaluate the fact in the question stem first and to use it to rephrase the question. Then, when you reach the statements, your work is made much easier. Here is approximately how your paper could look:

Scrapwork for Rephrasing:	$4xy = x^2y + 4y$	Does $x = 2$ or does $y = 0$?
	$x^2y - 4xy + 4y = 0$	$x = 2$, $y = 0$ or both
	$y(x^2 - 4x + 4) = 0$	If $y = 0$, value of $xy = 0$.
	$y(x - 2)^2 = 0$	If $x = 2$, value of xy depends on y
Constraints:	x and y <u>integers</u>	
	(1)	(2)
~~AD~~ (B)CE	$x = 2$ or $y = 0$ or BOTH $y - x = 2$ $y = 2 + x$ Case 1: If $x = 2$, $y = 4$, so $xy = 8$. Case 2: If $y = 0$, $x = -2$, so $xy = 0$.	$x = 2$ or $y = 0$ or BOTH $x^3 < 0$ $x < 0$ If x is negative, y must equal 0.
QUESTION: Does $y = 0$? What is y ?	INSUFFICIENT	$y = 0$ SUFFICIENT

The correct answer is (B).

If you don't rephrase the question, it is easy to fall into the trap of thinking that statement (2) alone is not sufficient.

You can lay out your paper in many other ways. For instance, you might go with this version:

Stem:	Q:…?
1)	
2)	

In this second layout, facts go on the left, while the question and any rephrasing go on the right. Then the process is always to see whether you can bridge the gap, going from left to right.

The important thing is that you develop a consistent layout that you always use. Don't give away points on Data Sufficiency because your work is sloppy or you mix up the logic.

Principle #2: Never Rephrase Yes/No as Value

All DS questions can be divided into two types: **Value** questions (such as "What is a?") and **Yes/No** questions (such as "Is x an integer?"). Value questions and Yes/No questions are fundamentally different: they require different levels of information to answer the question. Therefore, *never* rephrase a Yes/No question as a Value question. Value questions usually require more information than Yes/No questions.

Try-It #3-2

Is the integer n odd?

(1) $n^2 - 2n$ is not a multiple of 4.

(2) n is a multiple of 3.

You don't need to know *which* value n might be, just *whether n is odd*. Therefore, do not rephrase this question to "What is integer n?" Doing so unnecessarily increases the amount of information you need to answer the question. Of course, if you happen to know what n is, then great, you can answer any Yes/No question about n. But you generally don't *need* to know the value of n to answer Yes/No questions about n, and the GMAT loves to exploit that truth at your expense.

(1) SUFFICIENT: $n^2 - 2n = n(n - 2)$. If n is even, both terms in this product will be even and the product will be divisible by 4. Since $n^2 - 2n$ is not a multiple of 4, integer n cannot be even—it must be odd.

(2) INSUFFICIENT: Multiples of 3 can be either odd or even.

The correct answer is (A).

Rephrasing a Yes/No question into a Value question makes the question *unnecessarily picky*. Yes/No questions can often be sufficiently answered despite having multiple possible values for the answer. In the last question, for example, *n* could be any odd integer. If you rephrased this question to "What is *n*?" you would *incorrectly* conclude that the answer is (E).

Note that the converse of this principle is *not* always true. Occasionally, it's okay to rephrase a Value question as a Yes/No question—specifically, when it turns out that there are only two possible values.

Try-It #3-3

If x is a positive integer, what is the remainder of $\dfrac{x^2-1}{4}$?

Some quick analysis will show that $x^2 - 1$ can be factored into $(x + 1)(x - 1)$. If x is odd, then both of these terms will be even and the product will be divisible by 4, yielding a remainder of 0 when divided by 4. If x is even, then x^2 will be divisible by 4, so the remainder of $x^2 - 1$ will be 3.

There are only two possible values of the remainder: 0 and 3. So this Value question can be rephrased as the Yes/No question, "Is x odd?" or similarly, "Is x even?" Although this Value question seemed at first to have several different potential outcomes, only two are possible, so you are able to *change* the question to a Yes/No format by suitable rephrasing.

Principle #3: Work from Facts to Question

Especially for simple Yes/No questions, people often assume the answer to the question is Yes before looking at the statements. They only test cases for which the answer is Yes, rather than testing all of the possible cases allowed by the statements.

This line of thinking is backwards—and tempting, because of the order in which things are presented.

Instead ask, "If I start with the applicable facts and consider *all* possibilities, do I get a *definitive* answer to the question?"

Always work from the given facts to the question—never the reverse! This is why you have to keep the facts separated from the question and why you should always clearly mark the question on your paper.

Try-It #3-4

If $x \neq 0$, is $x = 1$?

(1) $\quad x^2 = \dfrac{1}{x^2}$

(2) $\quad x^2 = \dfrac{1}{x}$

If you work from the question to the facts, you would assume a Yes for the question, then plug this information into the statements. For instance, you would plug $x = 1$ into each statement. You would see that the value fits the equations in both statements, and you would pick (D) *incorrectly*. That's especially easy to do in this case because this particular question is much simpler to think about than the statements (which are nasty little equations).

Don't start from the question! No matter what, when you are judging sufficiency, always proceed from the *facts* to the *question*. It doesn't matter how easy or hard the question is at that point. After you've rephrased, put the question on hold and work *from* the statements and any other given facts *to* the question:

	(1)	(2)
AD BCE	$x^2 = \dfrac{1}{x^2}$ $x^4 = 1$ $x = 1$ or -1	$x^2 = \dfrac{1}{x}$ $x^3 = 1$ $x = 1$
Question: Is $x = 1$?	Maybe	Yes

The correct answer is (B).

> In a Yes/No question, when evaluating the statements, always try to determine whether the question can be answered the same way under *any possibility* that is consistent with those facts. A Yes answer means Always Yes, for all allowed scenarios. Likewise, a No answer means Always No.

Principle #4: Be a Contrarian

To avoid statement carryover and to gain insight into the nature of a problem, *deliberately* try to violate one statement as you evaluate the other statement. This will make it much harder for you to make a faulty assumption that leads to an incorrect answer. Think outside the first statement's box.

Try-It #3-5

> If $x \neq 0$, is $xy > 0$?
>
> (1) $x > 0$
>
> (2) $\dfrac{1}{x} < y$

The question is actually asking whether x and y have the same sign.

(1) INSUFFICIENT: This indicates nothing about the sign of y.

In evaluating statement (2), you might be tempted to assume that x must be positive. After all, you just read information in statement (1) that indicates that x is positive. Besides, it is natural to assume that a given variable will have a positive value, because positive numbers are much more intuitive than negative numbers.

Instead, follow Principle #4: *actively* try to violate statement (1), helping you to expose the trick in this question.

(2) INSUFFICIENT: Consider the possibility that x is negative. In this case, it is necessary to flip the sign of the inequality when you cross-multiply. That is, if $x < 0$, then $\dfrac{1}{x} < y$ means that $1 > xy$, and the answer to the question is MAYBE.

(1) & (2) SUFFICIENT: If x is positive, then statement (2) says that $1 < xy$ (do not flip the sign when cross-multiplying). Thus, $xy > 0$.

The correct answer is (C).

> When evaluating individual statements, *deliberately* trying to violate the other statement can help you see the full pattern or trick in the problem. You will be less likely to fall victim to *statement carryover*.

Principle #5: Assume Nothing

This principle is a corollary of the previous principle: avoid assuming constraints that aren't actually given in the problem—particularly assumptions that seem natural to make.

Try-It #3-6

Is z an even integer?

(1) $\frac{z}{2}$ is an even integer.

(2) $3z$ is an even integer.

The wording of this question has a tendency to bias people toward integers. After all, the "opposite" of even is odd, and odd numbers are integers, too. However, the question does not state that z must be an integer in the first place, so *do not assume* that it is.

(1) SUFFICIENT: The fact that $\frac{z}{2}$ is an even integer implies that $z = 2 \times$ (an even integer), so z must be an even integer. (In fact, according to statement (1), z must be divisible by 4.)

(2) INSUFFICIENT: The fact that $3z$ is an even integer implies that $z = \dfrac{(\text{an even integer})}{3}$, so z might not be an integer at all. For example, z could equal $\frac{2}{3}$.

One way to avoid assuming is to invoke Principle #3: *work from facts to question*. Statement (2) indicates that $3z =$ even integer $= -2, 0, 2, 4, 6, 8, 10$, etc. No even integers have been skipped over, nor have you allowed the question to suggest z values. That is how assumptions sneak in.

Next, divide the numbers in your list by 3: $z = -\frac{2}{3}, 0, \frac{2}{3}, \frac{4}{3}, 2, \frac{8}{3}, \frac{10}{3}$, etc. Is z an even integer? Maybe. Note that you could have stopped computing after the second value, since you already achieved a Yes and a No.

The correct answer is (A).

> If you had assumed that z must be an integer, you might have evaluated statement (2) with two cases:
>
> - $3 \times$ even $=$ even, so z could be even.
> - $3 \times$ odd $=$ odd, so z is definitely not odd.
>
> You would have *incorrectly* concluded that statement (2) was sufficient and therefore *incorrectly* selected answer (D).

Another common assumption is that a variable must be positive. Do not assume that any unknown is positive *unless it is stated as such* in the information given (or if the unknown counts physical things or measures some other positive-only quantity).

Problem Set

For problems 1–3, apply Principle #1 (*follow a consistent process*) from this chapter to arrive at a solution to each problem. Note that the solutions presented for problems 1–3 are specific examples. Your process may be different. Also note that the Data Sufficiency answer choices are not listed but all DS problems throughout this guide use the standard DS answers in the standard order.

1. There are 19 batters on a baseball team. Every batter bats either right-handed only, left-handed only, or both right-handed and left-handed. How many of the 19 batters bat left-handed?

    (1) Seven of the batters bat right-handed but do not bat left-handed.

    (2) Four of the batters bat both right-handed and left-handed.

2. If a is a positive integer and 81 divided by a results in a remainder of 1, what is the value of a ?

    (1) The remainder when a is divided by 40 is 0.

    (2) The remainder when 40 is divided by a is 40.

3. If a, b, c, d, and e are positive integers such that $\frac{a \times 10^d}{b \times 10^e} = c \times 10^4$, is $\frac{bc}{a}$ an integer?

    (1) $d - e \geq 4$

    (2) $d - e > 4$

Solve problems 4 and 5. Apply Principle #2 (*Never Rephrase Yes/No as Value*); describe why these Yes/No questions cannot be rephrased as Value questions.

4. If a, b, and c are each integers greater than 1, is the product abc divisible by 6 ?

    (1) The product ab is even.

    (2) The product bc is divisible by 3.

5. If n is a positive integer, is $n - 1$ divisible by 3 ?

    (1) $n^2 + n$ is not divisible by 6.

    (2) $3n = k + 3$, where k is a positive multiple of 3

6. Revisit problems 4 and 5 above, this time deliberately violating Principle #3 (*Work from Facts to Question*). Determine the incorrect answer you might have selected if you had reversed the process and worked from the *question* to the *facts*.

First, attempt to solve problem 7 by evaluating statement (1), and then evaluating statement (2) *without violating the information* in statement (1). Then, re-solve the problem by applying Principle #4 (*be a contrarian*). Do you get the same answer? Verify that applying Principle #4 leads to the correct answer, whereas not following the principle could lead to an incorrect answer.

7. Is $m \neq 0$, is $m^3 > m^2$?

    (1) $m > 0$

    (2) $m^2 > m$

For problems 8 and 9, apply Principle #5 (*assume nothing*) by identifying the explicit constraints given in the problem. What values are still permissible? Next, solve using these constraints. Verify that different (incorrect) answers are attainable if incorrect assumptions about the variables in the problem are made, and identify examples of such incorrect assumptions.

8. If $yz \neq 0$, is $0 < y < 1$?

    (1) $y = z^2$

    (2) $y < \dfrac{1}{y}$

9. Is $x > y$?

    (1) $|x - y| < |x|$

    (2) $|x| > |y|$

Solutions

(Note that the solutions presented for problems 1–3 are specific examples. Your notes may be different.)

1. **(A):**

<table>
<tr><td colspan="2">Rephrasing:</td><td></td><td>L</td><td>Not L</td><td>Total</td></tr>
<tr><td colspan="2">19 batters total → integers only!</td><td>R</td><td></td><td></td><td></td></tr>
<tr><td colspan="2">Some R only</td><td>Not R</td><td></td><td>0</td><td></td></tr>
<tr><td colspan="2">Some L only</td><td>Total</td><td>x</td><td></td><td>19</td></tr>
<tr><td colspan="2">Some R & L</td><td colspan="4"></td></tr>
<tr><td colspan="2">0 "neither"</td><td colspan="4"></td></tr>
<tr><td colspan="2">**How many left-handed batters?**</td><td colspan="4">**What is the integer x ?**</td></tr>
</table>

	(1)	(2)
Ⓐ D ~~BCE~~	<table><tr><td></td><td>L</td><td>Not L</td><td>Total</td></tr><tr><td>R</td><td></td><td>7</td><td></td></tr><tr><td>Not R</td><td></td><td>0</td><td></td></tr><tr><td>Total</td><td>x</td><td>7</td><td>19</td></tr></table>	<table><tr><td></td><td>L</td><td>Not L</td><td>Total</td></tr><tr><td>R</td><td>4</td><td></td><td></td></tr><tr><td>Not R</td><td></td><td>0</td><td></td></tr><tr><td>Total</td><td>x</td><td></td><td>19</td></tr></table>
Question: **Integer x = ?**	Can find x. (SUFFICIENT)	Can't find x. (INSUFFICIENT)

2. **(B):**

Rephrasing:	81 divided by a → remainder of 1.
	a goes evenly into 80, and $a \neq 1$.
	a is one of the factors of 80 other than 1.
	$a = 2, 4, 5, 8, 10, 16, 20, 40,$ or 80.

Which of the numbers listed above is the value of a ?

	(1)	(2)
~~AD~~ Ⓑ CE	$\dfrac{a}{40}$ → remainder of 0. 40 goes evenly into a. a is a multiple of 40.	$\dfrac{40}{a}$ → remainder of 40. a must be greater than 40.
Question: **Which of the listed numbers is a ?**	a could be 40 or 80. (INSUFFICIENT)	a must be 80. (SUFFICIENT)

3. **(D):**

Rephrasing:		
$\dfrac{a \times 10^d}{b \times 10^e} = c \times 10^4$	Is $\dfrac{bc}{a}$ an integer?	
$\dfrac{a}{b} \times 10^{d-e} = c \times 10^4$	Is 10^{d-e-4} an integer?	
$10^{d-e-4} = \dfrac{bc}{a}$	Is $d - e - 4 \geq 0$?	
	Is $d - e \geq 4$?	

A Ⓓ ~~BCE~~	(1) $d - e \geq 4$	(2) $d - e > 4$
Question: **Is $d - e \geq 4$?**	Yes (SUFFICIENT)	Yes (SUFFICIENT)

4. **(C):**

Each of the below is an accurate Yes/No rephrase:

- Is $\dfrac{abc}{6} =$ integer?
- Is $abc = 6, 12, 18, 24, 30, 36, 42, 48$, etc.?
- Is abc divisible by 2 *and* by 3 ?

Alternatively, you could ask "Is there an even integer and a multiple of 3 among a, b, and c?"

(1) INSUFFICIENT: ab is divisible by 2, but it's unclear whether it is divisible by 3 (or whether c is divisible by 3).

(2) INSUFFICIENT: bc is divisible by 3, but it's unclear whether it is divisible by 2 (or whether a is divisible by 2).

(1) AND (2) SUFFICIENT: Statement (1) indicates that a or b is even, and statement (2) indicates that b or c is divisible by 3. Therefore abc is divisible by both 2 and 3.

The correct answer is **(C)**.

3

5. **(A):**

An accurate Yes/No rephrase is the following:

$$\text{Is } \frac{n-1}{3} = \text{integer?}$$

Is $n - 1 = 3 \times$ integer?

Is $n = 3 \times$ integer $+ 1$?

Is the positive integer n one greater than a multiple of 3 ?

This narrows down the values of interest to a certain type of number, which follows a pattern: 1, 4, 7, 10, etc.

(1) SUFFICIENT: If $n^2 + n = n(n+1)$ is not divisible by 6, you can rule out certain values for n.

n	$n+1$	$n(n+1)$ **not divisible by 6**
1	2	✓
2	3	✗
3	4	✗
4	5	✓
5	6	✗
6	7	✗
7	8	✓

The pattern from the rephrasing is apparent here: n can only be 1, 4, 7, 10, etc., all integers that are one greater than a multiple of 3.

Alternatively, use theory. The integers $n - 1$, n, and $n + 1$ must be consecutive. If $n(n + 1)$ is not divisible by 3, then $n - 1$ must be divisible by 3, since in any set of three consecutive integers, one of the integers must be divisible by 3.

(2) INSUFFICIENT: If $3n = 3 \times pos\ integer + 3$, then $n = pos\ integer + 1$. Therefore, n is an integer such that $n \geq 2$. This does not resolve whether n is definitely one greater than a multiple of 3.

The correct answer is **(A)**.

6. **Revisiting #4, working incorrectly from the *Question* to the *Facts*:**

Manipulating the question to $abc = 6 \times integer$ (and losing track of the question mark), someone might be tempted to check whether it is *possible* for abc to be a multiple of 6, instead of whether abc is *definitely* a multiple of 6:

(1) $abc = 6 \times integer$, so ab is even. ✓

(2) $abc = 6 \times integer$, so bc is divisible by 3. ✓

The *incorrect* thinking would lead someone to wrong answer (D). Be sure to revisit how to do this problem correctly!

Revisiting #5, working incorrectly from the Question to the Facts:

Someone working incorrectly might try multiples of 3 for $n - 1$ to see whether they "work" with the statements:

(1) SUFFICIENT:

$n - 1$	n	$n + 1$	$n^2 + n = n(n + 1)$	not divis by 6
3	4	5	20	✓
6	7	8	56	✓
9	10	11	110	✓

(2) SEEMS SUFFICIENT (*incorrectly*): If $3n = k + 3$, then $k = 3n - 3 = 3(n - 1)$.

$n - 1$	$k = 3n - 3 = 3(n - 1)$	pos mult of 3
3	9	✓
6	18	✓
9	27	✓

This *incorrect* work would lead you to wrong answer (D). Be sure to revisit how to do this problem correctly, so you are certain how to do so for the future!

7. **(C):**

Non-Contrarian Approach	Contrarian Approach
(1) INSUFFICIENT: $m > 0$ or $m = $ pos, so "Is pos^3 > pos^2?" • Yes, if $m > 1$. • No, if m is a proper fraction or 1. (That is, $0 < m \leq 1$.)	(1) INSUFFICIENT: $m > 0$ or $m = $ pos, so "Is pos^3 > pos^2?" • Yes, if $m > 1$. • No, if m is a proper fraction or 1. (That is, $0 < m \leq 1$.)
(2) SEEMS SUFFICIENT: $m^2 > m$ implies that m is *not* a fraction or 1, therefore $m^3 > m^2$. Or, if you *assume* that $m > 0$, carrying over from (1), you might do the following: $m^2 > m$ $m > 1$ (dividing by m) Therefore, $m^3 > m^2$.	(2) INSUFFICIENT: $m^2 > m$ implies that m is *not* a fraction or 1, so if $m > 1$ then the answer is Yes. BUT, contradicting (1), **what if m is negative?** That is possible according to (2), since neg^2 > neg. Is $m^3 > m^2$? → Is neg^3 > neg^2? No!
	(1) AND (2) SUFFICIENT: Combined, the statements eliminate negative, zero, positive proper fractions, and 1 for the value of m. If $m > 1$, then $m^3 > m^2$. Definite Yes answer.
The (incorrect) answer is (B).	The correct answer is **(C)**.

Note that both solutions were hampered by inadequate rephrasing. Ideally, you would first rephrase as follows:

- Is $m^3 > m^2$?
- Is $m > 1$? (It's okay to divide by m^2, which must be positive: a square is never negative and m is also not 0, according to the question stem.)

Takeaway: With proper rephrasing, other errors are less likely. But even with inadequate rephrasing, taking a contrarian approach can save you from a wrong answer.

8. **(C):** The explicit constraint is $yz \neq 0$, which indicates that $y \neq 0$ and $z \neq 0$. Both y and z could be any nonzero value, including positive integers, negative integers, positive fractions, negative fractions, etc.

Making faulty assumptions:

For (1), a faulty assumption could be made by those who plug in values for z.

For example, if you plug in $z = -2, -1, 1, 2, 3, 4$, etc., you would get $y = 1, 4, 9, 16$, etc. That would yield a definite No answer to the question, as all the y values are at least as great as 1. The (unverbalized) assumption is that z is an integer, but that's not necessarily so.

For (2), most people would want to cross-multiply, so a potential *false* assumption is that y is positive (and this is reinforced by the fact that, in statement (1), y is in fact positive):

$$y < \frac{1}{y}$$
$$y^2 < 1$$
$$0 < y^2 < 1$$
$$\sqrt{0} < \sqrt{y^2} < \sqrt{1}$$
$$0 < y < 1$$

Conclusion: SEEMS SUFFICIENT (incorrect)

These faulty assumptions would lead to the *incorrect* answers (A) or (D).

Correct solution:

(1) INSUFFICIENT: y must be positive, but is it a fraction or an integer?

If $z = 2$, then $y = 4$, and the answer is No.
If $z = \frac{1}{2}$, then $y = \frac{1}{4}$, and the answer is Yes.

(2) INSUFFICIENT:

	If $y > 0$:	If $y < 0$:
	$y < \dfrac{1}{y}$	$y < \dfrac{1}{y}$
	$y^2 < 1$	$y^2 > 1$
	$0 < y^2 < 1$	$\sqrt{y^2} > \sqrt{1}$
	$\sqrt{0} < \sqrt{y^2} < \sqrt{1}$	$|y| > 1$
	$0 < y < 1$	$y > 1 \text{ or } y < -1$
		$y < -1$
		Since you're assuming $y < 0$, the rephrasing is $y < -1$.
Is $0 < y < 1$?	YES	NO

(1) AND (2) SUFFICIENT: Since y is positive, statement (1) indicates that $0 < y < 1$.

The correct answer is (C).

9. **(E):**

(1) INSUFFICIENT: Test cases for x and y. Avoid limiting yourself to cases in which x is greater than y. Since "Is $x > y$?" is a question and not a statement, x might be greater than or less than y. Actively seek cases that give a No answer.

x	y	$\|x - y\| < \|x\|$	Is $x > y$?
3	4	$\|-1\| < \|3\|$ (valid)	No
4	3	$\|1\| < \|3\|$ (valid)	Yes

Since x could be greater than y or less than y, given the information in the statement, this statement is insufficient.

(2) INSUFFICIENT: The second case tested above also fits this statement and yields an answer of Yes. Find another case in which $|x| > |y|$, but x is not greater than y.

x	y	$\|x\| > \|y\|$	Is $x > y$?
4	3	$\|4\| > \|3\|$ (valid)	Yes
-4	3	$\|-4\| > \|3\|$ (valid)	No

(1) AND (2) INSUFFICIENT: A case that fits both statements and gives an answer of Yes has already been found. Try to find another case for which both statements are true, but which gives an answer of No. As you test different values for x and y, you may find certain cases for which one or both statements are not true. Cross these off on your paper, and do not take them into consideration when choosing your answer.

x	y	(1) $\|x - y\| < \|x\|$	(2) $\|x\| > \|y\|$	Is $x > y$?
4	3	$\|1\| < \|3\|$ (valid)	$\|4\| > \|3\|$ (valid)	Yes
~~−4~~	~~3~~	~~$\|-7\| < \|-4\|$: (not valid)~~	~~n/a~~	~~n/a~~
−4	−3	$\|-1\| < \|-4\|$	$\|-4\| > \|-3\|$	No

The answer to the question can be either Yes (if $x = 4$ and $y = 3$) or No (if $x = -4$ and $y = -3$), so the statements together are insufficient.

The correct answer is **(E)**.

Data Sufficiency: Strategies & Tactics

In This Chapter

- Advanced Strategies

- Advanced Guessing Tactics

- Summary

- Common Wrong Answers

CHAPTER 4 Data Sufficiency: Strategies & Tactics

Sometimes you will encounter a Data Sufficiency (DS) problem that you can't answer—either because its content is difficult or obscure, or because you don't have enough time to solve completely in two minutes.

Like Chapter 2, this chapter describes a series of different methods you might try in these circumstances. Again, this chapter distinguishes between **solution strategies** and **guessing tactics**.

Strategies are broad: they apply to a wide variety of problems, they provide a complete approach, and they can be used safely in most circumstances.

In contrast, *tactics* can help you eliminate a few answer choices, but often leave a fair amount of uncertainty. Moreover, a particular tactic may only be useful in special situations or for parts of a problem.

The first section of this chapter outlines six DS strategies:

DS Strategy 1: **Compute to Completion**
For some problems, you won't necessarily be able to tell whether the answer can be calculated until you follow through on the calculations *all the way*.

DS Strategy 2: **Extract the Equation**
For many Word Problems, you need to represent the problem with algebraic equations to avoid embedded tricks that can be difficult to spot otherwise.

DS Strategy 3: **Know the Code**
The most challenging part of some DS problems is figuring out what the question and statements are actually saying. If the problem is written in "GMAT code," translate it into simple language before you do anything else.

DS Strategy 4: **Use the Constraints**
Many DS problems provide explicit constraints on the variables. In other problems, these constraints will be implicit (e.g., a variable that refers to a number of people, houses, or airplanes must be both positive and an integer). In either case, these constraints frequently determine the correct answer, so you *must* identify and use them.

DS Strategy 5: **Beware of Inequalities**
Whenever a DS problem involves inequality symbols, be especially careful—the GMAT loves to trick people with inequalities.

DS Strategy 6: **Test Cases**
One of the best ways to show that a statement is insufficient is to test different scenarios, or *cases*, in which that statement is true.

The remainder of the chapter is devoted to tactics that can knock out answer choices or provide clues as to how to approach the problem more effectively. These tactics are listed later in the chapter. As with Problem Solving (PS) tactics, some of these DS tactics work wonders when used correctly. Others only slightly improve your guessing odds.

Advanced Strategies

1. Compute to Completion

A general principle of Data Sufficiency is that once you have determined whether you can answer the question with a given set of information, you can stop calculating. For some problems, however, you cannot determine whether a single answer can be obtained until you've calculated the problem *all the way through*. This is particularly common in the following situations:

- Multiple equations are involved—particularly if they are non-linear.
- A complicated inequality expression is present.
- Variables hidden within a Geometry problem are related.

Try-It #4-1

What is the value of ab ?

(1) $a = b + 1$
(2) $a^2 = b + 1$

(1) INSUFFICIENT: Statement (1) does not answer the question. For example, if $a = 2$ and $b = 1$, then $ab = 2$, and if $a = 3$ and $b = 2$, then $ab = 6$.

(2) INSUFFICIENT: Statement (2) does not answer the question. For example, if $a = 1$ and $b = 0$, then $ab = 0$, and if $a = 2$ and $b = 3$, then $ab = 6$.

(1) AND (2) SUFFICIENT: Evaluating both statements together is trickier, however:

$$b = a - 1$$
$$a^2 = (a - 1) + 1$$
$$a^2 - a = 0$$
$$a(a - 1) = 0$$
$$a = 0 \text{ or } 1$$

Based on this work, either $a = 0$ or $a = 1$. It would be tempting at this stage to decide that since a can have two different values, statements (1) and (2) together are insufficient. However, this is *incorrect*.

Look at the values b can hold in these two scenarios:

a	b	ab
1	$a - 1 = 0$	0
0	$a - 1 = -1$	0

While it is true that *a* can take on different values, *ab* is equal to zero in *either case*. When $a = 1$, $b = 0$, and $ab = 0$. When $a = 0$, $b = -1$, and $ab = 0$. Therefore, (1) and (2) combined are SUFFICIENT to answer this *specific* question: What is the value of *ab* ?

The correct answer is (C).

>
>
> In a multiple-scenario problem, be sure to compute for the specific question asked (in this case, *ab*) in order to determine whether the end result for each scenario is *actually different*.

2. Extract the Equation

For Word Problems, setting up an algebraic representation of the question is *essential*. It is very easy to get intellectually lazy and miss an embedded trick in the problem. These tricks are usually much easier to spot if you are looking at the underlying algebra behind the problem.

Try-It #4-2

A store sells two types of bird feeders: Alphas and Bravos. Alphas feed 1 bird at a time, whereas Bravos feed 2 birds at a time. The total number of birds that can be fed at one time by bird feeders sold last month is 50. What is the total revenue generated by bird feeders sold last month?

(1) Last month, the price of each Alpha was $15 and the price of each Bravo was $30.

(2) 40 Alphas were sold last month.

From the words in the question stem, Extract the Equation. The problem indicates that Alphas can feed 1 bird at a time and Bravos 2 birds at a time. The problem also indicates that last month 50 birds could be fed at a time, so you have this:

> Total number of birds fed $= A + 2B = 50$, where *A* and *B* represent the number of bird feeders of each type that have been sold.

To calculate the revenue, it seems you will need the prices of the bird feeders and the number of bird feeders, *A* and *B*.

(1) SUFFICIENT: Again extract the equation from the wording of the question:

> Total revenue $= \$15A + \$30B = \$15(A + 2B)$

It turns out that you don't need to know *A* and *B* individually, since the question stem equation indicated that $A + 2B = 50$. Therefore, total revenue equals $\$15(A + 2B) = \$15(50) = \$750$.

It's true that there are many possible values of *A* and *B* that satisfy the condition that $A + 2B = 50$. However, mathematically *every possible combination* that satisfies this equation would lead to the same revenue of $750. The number of each type of bird feeder sold is irrelevant. In this sense, Extract the Equation can be similar to the Compute to Completion strategy because once the equation has been extracted, you may find that the multiple possibilities for the variables might converge to a single answer to the specific question that's been asked.

(2) INSUFFICIENT: If there were 40 Alphas sold, there were 5 Bravos sold. But you still don't know the prices, so you can't compute revenue.

The correct answer is (A).

> **!** Relying on intuition, which indicates a need for the prices and number of the two bird feeder types, someone might ultimately choose (C) *incorrectly*. Be sure to translate all Word Problems into math so they can be properly evaluated. These issues are sensitive to the exact numbers given.

3. Know the Code

Many DS questions and statements are intentionally written in a complicated way. Take a look at the two statements below:

1. a and b are integers such that 2 is not a factor of $7a^2b^3$.

2. a and b are both odd integers.

These statements look very different, but from the perspective of someone who's solving a DS problem, *they say exactly the same thing*. In other words, the first statement is just saying that a and b are both odd—but it's saying it in code to keep you from noticing.

There are two clues that the statement is really about odd and even numbers. First, it specifies that a and b are integers. Second, if 2 is not a factor of a certain integer, that's just another way of saying that the integer is odd. You can write that out as follows:

-   a and b are integers, and $7a^2b^3$ is odd.

The next thing to notice is that multiplying a number by 7 has no effect on whether it's odd or even. Multiplying an even number by 7 gives you an even number, and multiplying an odd number by 7 gives you an odd number. So the 7 can be removed entirely:

-   a and b are integers, and a^2b^3 is odd.

The exponents also don't matter. Squaring or cubing an odd integer gives you an odd integer, and squaring or cubing an even integer gives you an even integer. So saying that a^2b^3 is odd is no different from saying that ab is odd.

Finally, if the product of two integers is odd, both of those integers have to be odd. Multiplying an even integer by another integer always results in an even value. Here's what the statement really says:

-   a and b are odd integers.

The two statements were really the same all along. If you see something in a DS problem that looks like it could be GMAT code, try to crack the code before you go further. You may find that a complicated statement is disguising something much easier to work with.

4. Use the Constraints

Often, a DS question will provide relevant constraints on the variables in the problem—for example, that the variables must be integers or must be positive, or must be between 0 and 1. When this information is given, it is usually *essential* to the problem. If you don't *use the constraints*, you could easily end up choosing the wrong answer choice.

Try-It #4-3

If $8x > 3x + 4x$, what is the value of the integer x?

(1) $6 - 4x > -2$

(2) $3 - 2x \leq 4 - x \leq 5 - 2x$

Simplify the question stem:

$$8x > 3x + 4x$$

$$8x > 7x$$

$$x > 0 \qquad\qquad 8x \text{ can only be greater than } 7x \text{ when } x \text{ is positive.}$$

On top of that, there is also another constraint given: x must be an integer. This limits the scope of the potential values of x even further. *Make note of this type of constraint in your work on paper.* Write "$x = $ int" or something similar. You could also incorporate this information by rephrasing the question to include the constraint: "If the integer x is positive, what is the value of x?"

(1) SUFFICIENT: Solve this inequality for x:

$$6 - 4x > -2$$

$$-4x > -8$$

$$x < 2$$

Since you know from the question stem that $x > 0$, you can conclude that $0 < x < 2$. The *only integer* between 0 and 2 is 1. Therefore, $x = 1$.

(2) SUFFICIENT: Manipulate this compound inequality as follows:

$$
\begin{array}{ccccc}
3 - 2x & \leq & 4 - x & \leq & 5 - 2x \\
+2x & & +2x & & +2x \\
\hline
3 & & \leq 4 + x & \leq 5 \\
-4 & & -4 & -4 \\
\hline
-1 & \leq & x \leq 1 &
\end{array}
$$

Note that it's fine to manipulate all the parts of the compound inequality at the same time as long as you perform each manipulation to *all three* parts of the inequality.

Since the question stem indicates that $x > 0$, it must be the case that $0 < x \leq 1$. The only integer that fits this criteria is 1. Therefore, $x = 1$.

If you had overlooked the fact that x is an integer, you would have determined that there are many values between 0 and 1 or between 0 and 2. You might have chosen answer (E), incorrectly.

The correct answer is (D).

> **!** Make a note of any additional information given to you in the question stem (e.g., "*x* is positive" or "*x* is an integer"). You often will have to use this information properly to get the correct answer.
>
> Integer constraints in particular are very potent: they often limit the possible solutions for a problem to a small set. Sometimes this set is so small that it contains *only one item*.

Constraints will not always be explicitly given. The ones the GMAT doesn't explicitly give you can be called **hidden constraints**. Hidden constraints are most prevalent in Word Problems and Geometry questions. Here are some examples of hidden constraints that you should train yourself to take note of:

- The number of *countable* items must be a *non-negative integer*. Note that zero is only a possibility if it is possible for the items not to exist at all—if the problem clearly assumes that the items exist, then the number of items must be *positive*. Examples:
  - Number of people
  - Number of yachts
  - Number of books

- Many *non-countable* quantities must be *non-negative numbers*, though not necessarily integers. Again, zero is only an option if the underlying object might not exist. If the problem clearly assumes the existence and typical definition of an object, then these quantities must be *positive*. Examples:
  - The side of a triangle must have a positive length. (All geometric quantities shown in a diagram, such as lengths, areas, volumes, and angles, must be positive. The only exception is negative coordinates in a coordinate plane problem.)
  - The weight of a shipment of products must be positive in any unit.
  - The height of a person must be positive in any unit.

- Many other *non-countable* quantities are theoretically allowed to take on *negative* values. Examples:
  - The profit of a company (However, if a company *made a profit*, then that profit is positive!)
  - The growth rate of a population
  - The change in the value of essentially any variable

These sorts of constraints exist in Problem Solving, but they are even more important and dangerous on Data Sufficiency. If these constraints are important in a PS problem, then failing to take a constraint into account may make you unable to solve the problem. That will alert you to the existence of the constraints, since every PS problem must be solvable. In contrast, you will get no such signal on a DS problem. After all, solvability is the very issue that DS tests!

5. Beware of Inequalities

Whenever a DS question involves inequality symbols, be especially careful. The GMAT can employ a variety of different inequality-specific tricks. Here are six examples:

1. One inequality can imply another seemingly unrelated inequality, depending on the situation. For example, if you need to know whether $x > 0$, then knowing that $x > 5$ is sufficient. If x is greater than 5, then it must be positive, thus $x > 0$. However, the opposite is *not* the case. If you knew that $x < 5$, then you would *not* be able to determine whether $x > 0$. After all, x could be positive but less than 5, or x could be negative.

2. Inequalities can combine with integer constraints to produce a single value. For example, if $0 < x < 2$ and x is an integer, then x *must* equal 1.

3. Some Word Problems can create a hidden constraint involving inequalities. These inequalities may come into play in determining the correct answer. For example, a problem might read: "The oldest student in the class…the next oldest student in the class…the youngest student in the class…." This can be translated to the following inequality: youngest < middle < oldest.

4. Inequalities involving a variable in a denominator often involve two possibilities: a positive and a negative one. For example, if you know that $\frac{1}{y} < x$, you might be tempted to multiply by y and arrive at $1 < xy$. However, this may not be correct. It depends on whether y is a positive or negative number. If $y > 0$, then it is correct to infer that $1 < xy$. However, if $y < 0$, then $1 > xy$. Therefore, you'll need to test two cases (positive and negative) in this situation.

5. At the same time, hidden constraints may allow you to manipulate inequalities more easily. For instance, if a quantity must be positive, then you can multiply both sides of an inequality by that quantity without having to set up two cases.

6. Many questions involving inequalities are actually disguised positive/negative questions. For example, if you know that $xy > 0$, the fact that xy is greater than 0 is not in and of itself very interesting. What is interesting is that the product is positive, meaning both x and y are positive or both x and y are negative. Thus, x and y have the *same sign*. Here, the inequality symbol is used to disguise the fact that x and y have the same sign.

Take a look at some examples that illustrate these concepts.

Try-It #4-4

If $\sqrt{x}$ is a prime number, what is the value of x ?

(1) $-16 < -3x + 5 < 22$

(2) x^2 is a two-digit number

If $\sqrt{x}$ is a prime number, then possible values are 2, 3, 5, and so on. Therefore, x must be a perfect square of a prime; possible values include 4, 9, 25, and so on.

(1) SUFFICIENT: Manipulate the inequality to isolate x:

$$-16 < -3x + 5 < 22$$
$$-21 < -3x < 17$$
$$7 > x > -\frac{17}{3}$$

Since x is the square of a prime, it can't be negative or zero; it has to be positive. The smallest possible square of a prime is 4 and the next smallest possible square of a prime is 9. This inequality allows just one possible value: $x = 4$.

(2) INSUFFICIENT: According to this statement, $10 \leq x^2 \leq 99$. In addition, from the question stem, $\sqrt{x}$ is a prime number. Determine the possible value(s) for x:

If $x = 4$, then $\sqrt{x}$ is a prime number, 2, and x^2 is a two-digit number, 16.

If $x = 9$, then $\sqrt{x}$ is a prime number, 3, and x^2 is a two-digit number, 81.

Because there are two possible values for x, this statement is not sufficient.

The constraints were so specific that statement (1), which looks at a glance as though it will allow more than one possible answer, turns out to be sufficient.

The correct answer is (A).

Try-It #4-5

If $mn \neq 0$, is $m > n$?

(1) $\dfrac{1}{m} < \dfrac{1}{n}$

(2) $m^2 > n^2$

The constraint in the question stem indicates that neither m nor n equals zero.

(1) INSUFFICIENT: You can solve algebraically/theoretically or you can test cases. If you solve algebraically, be careful: you have to account for multiplying the inequality by a negative:

If m and n are both positive, then $m > n$.

If m and n are both negative, the sign flips twice, so $m > n$ again.

If only one is negative, then the sign flips once and $m < n$. In this case, m must be the negative number, since any positive is greater than any negative.

Alternatively, test cases:

If $m = 3$ and $n = 2$, then statement (1) is true and the answer to the question is Yes, $m > n$.

If $m = -3$ and $n = 2$, then statement (1) is true and the answer to the question is No, m is not greater than n.

(2) INSUFFICIENT: This statement indicates nothing about the signs of the two variables. Either one could be positive or negative.

(1) AND (2) INSUFFICIENT. If you are solving algebraically, test the scenarios that you devised for statement (1):

If m and n are both positive, then $m > n$ and $m^2 > n^2$. Both statements allow this scenario.

If m and n are both negative, then $m > n$ but m^2 is *not* greater than n^2. Discard this scenario, since it makes statement (2) false.

If m is negative and n is positive, then $m < n$. It could also be true that $m^2 > n^2$, as long as m's magnitude is larger than n's. If you're not sure, test cases (see below).

Alternatively, start by testing whether the cases you already tried for statement (1) also apply to statement (2):

If $m = 3$ and $n = 2$, then $m > n$ and $m^2 > n^2$. Both statements allow this scenario.

If $m = -3$ and $n = 2$, then $m < n$ and $m^2 > n^2$. Both statements allow this scenario.

Because there are scenarios in which $m > n$ and $m < n$, both statements together are still insufficient to answer the question. If you forgot to account for the positive and negative cases, you may end up with (A) or (D) as your (*incorrect*) answer.

The correct answer is (E).

6. Test Cases

In a Data Sufficiency problem, a statement is insufficient if, given the information in the statement, the question still has more than one possible answer. One way to show that this is true is by testing cases. Write down several scenarios, or *cases*, in which the statement is true. For instance, you might think of different possible values for the variables in the statement. For each of these cases, determine the answer to the question. If the question has different answers depending on which case you're testing, the statement is insufficient. If the question always has the same answer in every case you try, the statement is likely sufficient.

As an advanced test-taker, you might be biased against case testing or "plugging in numbers": it might somehow seem less advanced than theoretical approaches. However, the theory required to answer a question may be cumbersome to figure out in two minutes. If implemented correctly, testing cases can be fast, easy, and accurate, so it should be part of your toolbox. Particularly, testing cases is often the simplest way to show that a statement is not sufficient.

Plugging in random numbers as they come to mind is the most common approach to testing cases, and while this strategy can be successful, it is inherently ad hoc and therefore not the most reliable process. It's easy to overlook a salient scenario. The key is to have a *systematic approach* to testing cases. This relies on three approaches: the *standard number set for testing*, *discrete number listing*, and *case testing with concepts*. Sometimes testing enough cases will also allow you to notice a pattern to help you deduce whether the statement is sufficient.

Standard Number Set for Testing

The GMAT often tests odd/even rules, positive/negative rules, fraction/integer rules, proper vs. improper fractions, etc. On any given problem, you may have trouble identifying which rule is relevant, and in fact the GMAT may test more than one rule within a given question. Therefore, if you must pick and test numbers, consider a set of numbers that covers every possible combination of properties:

	Odd	Even	Proper Fraction	Improper Fraction
Negative	−1	−2	$-\dfrac{1}{2}$	$-\dfrac{3}{2}$
Zero		0		
Positive	1	2	$\dfrac{1}{2}$	$\dfrac{3}{2}$

This set includes integers, non-integers, positive and negative numbers, and numbers greater than and less than 1. Thus, a comprehensive set of test numbers (to memorize and apply) would be as follows:

$$\left\{-2, -\frac{3}{2}, -1, -\frac{1}{2}, 0, \frac{1}{2}, 1, \frac{3}{2}, 2\right\}$$

Remember this list as "every integer and half-integer between −2 and 2."

Not all of these numbers will be relevant or possible on every problem. For example, if the variable has to be positive, five of the nine values presented above can be ignored. The question itself may suggest certain values to test, but always keep in mind the *potential* need to test a value of each relevant type—and if a problem really might entail testing nine different cases, consider whether that problem is really worth your time. Using the Standard Set ensures that you don't get tripped up by forgetting to try a particular type of value that will give you a different answer, thereby allowing you to prove definitively that the statement is not sufficient.

Try-It #4-6

Is $a < 0$?

(1) $a^3 < a^2 + 2a$

(2) $a^2 > a^3$

This problem presents inequalities, and the question asks whether a is negative. Therefore, test different values of a to see which values fit the statements.

The question stem doesn't provide any constraints, so begin by testing some easier integers and then move to fractions if needed:

(1) $a^3 - a^2 - 2a < 0$

(2) $a^2 - a^3 > 0$

(1) INSUFFICIENT: Test the possible integers from the *standard number set*:

a	$a^3 - a^2 - 2a < 0$	$a < 0$?
−2	$(-2)^3 - (-2)^2 - 2(-2) = -8$ (valid)	Yes
−1	$(-1)^3 - (-1)^2 - 2(-1) = 0$ (invalid)	
0	$(0)^3 - (0)^2 - 2(0) = 0$ (invalid)	
1	$(1)^3 - (1)^2 - 2(1) = -2$ (valid)	No

Stop when you find two valid cases that return different answers to the question.

(2) INSUFFICIENT: Try integers first:

a	$a^2 - a^3 > 0$	$a < 0$?
−2	$(-2)^2 - (-2)^3 = 12$ (valid)	Yes
−1	$(-1)^2 - (-1)^3 = 2$ (valid)	Yes
0	$(0)^2 - (0)^3 = 0$ (invalid)	
1	$(1)^2 - (1)^3 = 0$ (invalid)	
2	$(2)^2 - (2)^3 = -4$ (invalid)	

Be careful: You're not done. Try a fraction. Because a positive and a negative number figured into the mix for statement (1), try one positive and one negative fraction:

a	$a^2 - a^3 > 0$	$a < 0?$
-2	$(-2)^2 - (-2)^3 = 12$ (valid)	Yes
-1	$(-1)^2 - (-1)^3 = 2$ (valid)	Yes
0	$(0)^2 - (0)^3 = 0$ (invalid)	
1	$(1)^2 - (1)^3 = 0$ (invalid)	
2	$(2)^2 - (2)^3 = -4$ (invalid)	
$-\dfrac{1}{2}$	$\left(-\dfrac{1}{2}\right)^2 - \left(-\dfrac{1}{2}\right)^3 = \dfrac{3}{8}$ (valid)	Yes
$\dfrac{1}{2}$	$\left(\dfrac{1}{2}\right)^2 - \left(\dfrac{1}{2}\right)^3 = \dfrac{1}{8}$ (valid)	No

Statement (2) is *insufficient*. When $a = \dfrac{1}{2}$, the constraint is fulfilled, but a is positive.

Combining statements (1) and (2) shows that whenever $a = -2$, $-\dfrac{3}{2}$, or $\dfrac{1}{2}$, both conditions are fulfilled. The variable a could thus be positive or negative. The correct answer is (E).

Notice that you did not need to test every possible value for a. For example, when $a = -2$, both conditions are easily satisfied. That means that testing $-\dfrac{3}{2}$ was unlikely to be necessary, since that value is not much different from -2. Furthermore, when you do find a contradictory answer, you can stop testing. For a Yes/No question, all you need to do is find *one* valid Yes and *one* valid No to prove insufficiency.

This problem can also be solved algebraically, but it takes more conceptual work. First solve the inequality as though it were an equation, then map the solutions on a number line and test to see in which regions the inequality is true.

(1) INSUFFICIENT:

$$a^3 - a^2 - 2a = 0$$
$$a(a^2 - a - 2) = 0$$
$$a(a - 2)(a + 1) = 0$$
$$a = 2, 0, \text{ or } -1$$

This number line demonstrates that either $a < -1$ *or* $0 < a < 2$.

(2) INSUFFICIENT:

$$a^2 - a^3 > 0$$
$$a^2(1 - a) > 0 \qquad \text{Since } a \text{ can't be zero, and } a^2 \text{ must be positive, you can divide by } a^2.$$
$$1 - a > 0$$
$$a < 1$$

(1) AND (2) INSUFFICIENT: Overlapping the possible ranges, either $a < -1$ *or* $0 < a < 1$. This is still not enough information to tell whether a is negative. The correct answer is (E).

In some cases, the *standard number testing* list may not quite suffice; try the partial DS example below.

Try-It #4-7

> If *x* is positive, is $x \leq 1$?
>
> (1) $x^2 \leq 1.3$

If you used the standard number testing list of $\left\{\frac{1}{2}, 1, \frac{3}{2}, 2\right\}$ (ignoring the non-positive values in the set), all of the values for *x* above 1 would *fail* to fit statement (1) and all of the values for *x* equal to or below 1 would *fit* statement (1). Therefore, the standard number testing list would indicate that statement (1) is sufficient. However, *x* could be 1.1, in which case $x^2 = 1.21$, which is less than 1.3. So statement (1) is actually insufficient.

You could figure out that *x could* be greater than 1 upon a quick inspection of this problem. You might think to try a number slightly larger than 1. However, if the problem were more complicated, it might not be so obvious. In cases like these, use the **boundary principle**: test values that are *close to boundaries* given in the problem. In this case, the boundary value is 1, so add 0.9 and 1.1 to your list of numbers to test. You might even try 0.99 or 1.01. You should know that −1, 0, and 1 are natural boundaries, because numbers behave differently on either side of them (that's why the standard list contains numbers in the ranges defined by −1, 0, and 1).

Discrete Number Listing

In the previous problems, the variables *a* and *x* were not constrained, so you had to test a series of different numbers to solve the problem. By contrast, many questions suggest specific constraints: *x* must be odd, for example, or *x* must be a positive integer. In these cases, just *list* a series of consecutive numbers that fit these criteria and test them all. For example, if *x* must be positive and even, test *x* = 2, 4, 6, 8, 10.

Discrete number listing can be used whenever a problem specifies a sequence of discrete (separate) values that a variable or an expression can take on:

- Integers (the classic case): ... −3, −2, −1, 0, 1, 2, 3...
- Odd/even integers:... −3, −1, 1, 3...or...−4, −2, 0, 2, 4...
- Positive perfect squares: 1, 4, 9, 16, 25...
- Positive multiples of 5: 5, 10, 15, 20...
- Any set that is "integer-like," with well-defined, separated values

By contrast, some problems describe a *smooth range* of potential values for a variable or expression (e.g., $0 < x < 1$ or *x* must be negative). In these cases, don't list consecutive values to test because the set of possible values is *not* discrete. If the variable can take on any real number in a range, then rely on the standard number testing list, potentially with some modifications, as described in the previous section.

A key to the *discrete number listing* process is to **test consecutive values** that fit the criteria—it would be too easy to leave out the one exception that proves insufficiency. Never skip numbers that fit the constraint. This is especially important if you are listing discrete numbers to equal an expression, not just a variable. By the way, remember to work from the facts to the question, not the other way around! Don't assume that the question should be answered Yes and only test values that make it so.

Try-It #4-8

Is x a multiple of 12 ?

(1) $\sqrt{x-3}$ is odd.

(2) x is a multiple of 3.

Since statement (1) indicates that $\sqrt{x-3}$ is odd and the square root sign implies a positive answer, list 1, 3, 5, 7, 9, etc.

Notice that you're picking values for $\sqrt{x-3}$, *not x*. It would be far too much work to test different values for x to determine which make $\sqrt{x-3}$ odd, and you could potentially miss some values that fit the statement. Do not plug in numbers for x here! Instead, list consecutive odd values for $\sqrt{x-3}$, a quick and easy process. Then, solve for x in each case.

For this problem, your work on paper may look something like this:

(1) INSUFFICIENT: $\sqrt{x-3} = $ odds $= 1, 3, 5, 7, 9$, etc.

   $x - 3 = 1, 9, 25, 49, 81$, etc.

   $x = 4, 12, 28, 52, 84$, etc.

   Is x divisible by 12? Maybe. For example, 12 is, while 28 is not.

(2) INSUFFICIENT: $x = $ multiples of $3 = 3, 6, 9, 12, 15$, etc.

   Is x divisible by 12? Maybe. For example, 12 is, while 15 is not.

(1) AND (2) SUFFICIENT: Combine these statements by selecting only the values for x that are in both lists. On your paper, circle the following values: $x = 12$ and $x = 84$. These are the values calculated in statement (1) that fit the criteria in statement (2). This seems to be SUFFICIENT—the values for x that fit both statements are multiples of 12. At this point, if you wanted to check another value, you could, or you could go with the trend, which is likely going to be correct after testing this many cases.

The correct answer is (C).

> In retrospect, it may seem obvious that statement (1) indicates that x is a multiple of 4. But if you tried to evaluate statement (1) with algebra, you might reason that $\sqrt{x-3}$ is odd, so $(x-3)$ is odd^2, or an odd perfect square. Thus, x is an odd perfect square plus 3. One might conclude that x is even, which is a true but incomplete description! Listing numbers is an easy way to see that these numbers are all multiples of 4.

As in the previous example, trying to solve statement (1) algebraically is tricky. Yes, it's worth knowing how to do this algebra. The point is that a discrete number testing process is quick and simple, so it's also worth knowing how to do.

(1) INSUFFICIENT: $\sqrt{x-3} = 2k+1$ where k is an integer.

$$x - 3 = (2k+1)^2 = 4k^2 + 4k + 1$$
$$x = 4k^2 + 4k + 4 = 4\left(k^2 + k + 1\right)$$

x must be divisible by 4.

(2) INSUFFICIENT: x is a multiple of 3, so x must be divisible by 3.

(1) AND (2) SUFFICIENT: x is divisible by 3 and by 4, so x is divisible by 12.

Case Testing with Concepts

You don't need to use actual numbers to do case testing. In fact, it's sometimes more efficient to case test using *concepts*, rather than numbers.

Try-It #4-9

> If *a*, *b*, and *c* are integers, is $abc > 0$?
>
> (1) $ab > 0$
> (2) $bc > 0$

You could test cases in the traditional way: find specific values for *a*, *b*, and/or *c* that fit one statement or the other, then multiply those three values together and check whether their product was greater than zero. However, doing that much actual multiplication would be overkill. Instead of case testing by checking specific numbers, try case testing with *concepts*.

(1) INSUFFICIENT: Instead of choosing appropriate values for *a*, *b*, and *c*, think about whether they could be positive or negative. For instance, one scenario that fits the statement is that *a*, *b*, and *c* are all positive. Another scenario is that *a* and *b* are positive, but *c* is negative. You can put this information in a chart, just as you would with ordinary case testing:

a	b	c	ab > 0	abc > 0?
+	+	+	(+)(+) = + (valid)	Yes
+	+	−	(+)(+) = + (valid)	No

(2) INSUFFICIENT:

a	b	c	bc > 0	abc > 0?
+	+	+	(+)(+) = + (valid)	Yes
−	+	+	(+)(+) = + (valid)	No

Neither statement is sufficient on its own, so try them together. (1) AND (2) INSUFFICIENT:

a	b	c	(1): ab > 0	(2): bc > 0	abc > 0?
+	+	+	(+)(+) = + (valid)	(+)(+) = + (valid)	Yes
−	−	−	(−)(−) = + (valid)	(−)(−) = + (valid)	No

The answer to this problem is (E). It was never necessary to work with specific numbers to solve this problem.

This strategy doesn't only work on positive/negative or odd/even problems. You can use it for other types of Data Sufficiency problems as well. Before reading the explanation, try to figure out how to solve the following problem using concepts (not specific numbers) to test cases.

Try-It #4-10

At a certain company, the bonus pool is divided among a group of employees consisting entirely of engineers and managers so that each engineer receives a bonus of e dollars and each manager receives a bonus of m dollars. Is m at least 20% greater than e ?

(1) At least 20% of the employees in the group are managers.

(2) The total amount awarded to managers is at least 20% greater than the total amount awarded to engineers.

Here's how you might case test while solving this Data Sufficiency problem:

(1) INSUFFICIENT: At least 20% of the employees in the group are managers, but the amount earned by each employee is unknown. There could be a lot of managers who each earn a large bonus or there could be a lot of managers who each earn a small bonus. Think about scenarios on the extreme end of the range, ones that could result in a different answer to the question.

# of Engineers	# of Managers	e	m	At least 20% managers?	$m > 1.2e$?
Few	Many	Small	Large	Lots of managers, and each manager earns a large bonus: (valid)	Yes
Few	Many	Large	Small	Lots of managers, but each manager earns almost no bonus: (valid)	No

(2) INSUFFICIENT: This statement tells you about the total amount awarded to the managers. However, this total amount could be received by only a single manager or split across a huge number of managers.

# of Engineers	# of Managers	e	m	m total 20% + greater than e total?	$m > 1.2e$?
Many	One	Very small	Very large	Only one manager, but that manager gets most of the bonus pool: (valid)	Yes
Few	Many	Equal	Equal	Everybody gets the same bonus, but there are significantly more managers, so most of the pool goes to managers: (valid)	No

(1) AND (2) INSUFFICIENT: Even considering both statements, there are multiple possible situations. For instance, the group could be composed mostly of managers. This matches statement (1). Everyone in the group could earn the same bonus, fitting statement (2), since the number of managers is much greater than the number of engineers. In this case, since $e = m$, the answer to the question is No.

Another possibility is that the group contains an equal number of managers and engineers. This fits statement (1). If the managers earn very large bonuses, and the engineers earn very small bonuses, then statement (2) is also true, since most of the bonus pool will go to managers. Finally, since m is much greater than e, the answer to the question is Yes.

# of Engineers	# of Managers	e	m	(1) 20% + man?	(2) m total 20% + greater than e total?	$m > 1.2e$?
Few	Many	Equal	Equal	✓ (valid)	✓ (valid)	No
Equal	Equal	Very small	Very large	✓ (valid)	✓ (valid)	Yes

Without doing any mathematical calculation, or using any specific numbers, you can prove that the answer to this problem is (E).

Try one more problem, this time testing cases based on odd and even numbers.

Try-It #4-11

If a, b, and c are integers, is abc divisible by 4 ?

(1) $a + b + 2c$ is even.

(2) $a + 2b + c$ is odd.

Evaluate the possible odd/even combinations of a, b, and c without testing specific numbers.

(1) INSUFFICIENT: $2c$ must be even because c is an integer. This statement implies that $a + b$ is even, which occurs when a and b have the same odd/even parity. (There is no constraint on c.)

a	b	c	$a + b + 2c =$ **Even**	Is abc divisible by 4?
Even	Even	Even	✓ (valid)	Yes
Even	Even	Odd	✓ (valid)	Yes
Odd	Odd	Even	✓ (valid)	Maybe (only if c is divisible by 4)

Stop here! MAYBE indicates insufficient.

(2) INSUFFICIENT: $2b$ must be even because b is an integer. Thus, this statement implies that $a + c$ is odd, which occurs when a and c have opposite odd/even parity. (There is no constraint on b.)

a	b	c	$a + b + 2c =$ **Odd**	Is abc divisible by 4?
Even	Even	Odd	✓ (valid)	Yes
Even	Odd	Odd	✓ (valid)	Maybe

Stop here! MAYBE indicates insufficient.

(1) AND (2) INSUFFICIENT: From (1) you know that a and b have the same odd/even parity, while from (2) you know that a and c have opposite odd/even parity.

a	b	c	(1) $a + b + 2c =$ **Even**	(2) $a + 2b + c =$ **Odd**	Is abc divisible by 4?
Even	Even	Odd	✓ (valid)	✓	Yes
Odd	Odd	Even	✓ (valid)	✓ (valid)	Maybe

Even with these constraints, you do not have a definitive answer to the question. The correct answer is (E).

Notice that in evaluating statements (1) and (2) together, you would not need to test completely new cases. You can reuse the work from statement (1) and statement (2) to determine the answer (e.g., by circling the cases in one chart that also appear in the other chart). Be careful as you do this! Know what case you're considering.

Advanced Guessing Tactics

The rest of this chapter is devoted to scrappy tactics that can raise your odds of success. There will be fewer opportunities to apply these tactics than the strategies mentioned previously. However, when all else fails, these tactics may be your only friend. The tactics are listed according to their reliability: the earlier tactics nearly always work, while the later tactics provide only a modest improvement over random guessing.

1. Spot Identical Statements   *Certainty:* Very High

(...)

(1) $3y - 6 = 2x$

(2) $y = \frac{2}{3}x + 2$

By adding 6 to both sides of statement (1) and multiplying statement (2) by 3, you can see that both statements indicate that $3y = 2x + 6$. Depending on the question, either each statement will be sufficient or each will not—because they are identical, there cannot be any benefit from looking at the statements together. The answer must be (D) or (E).

2. Spot Clear Sufficiency   *Certainty:* Very High

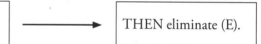

Try-It #4-12

If $Z = \dfrac{m + \dfrac{m}{3}}{n + \dfrac{2}{n^{-1}}}$ and $mn \neq 0$, what is the value of Z?

(1) $m = \dfrac{15}{n^{-1}}$

(2) $m = 5$

It is obvious that you could plug $m = 5$ into statement (1) to get a value for n, then plug values for m and n into the expression for Z. So you can knock out (E) for sure.

Note that this tactic does *not* imply that you should assume, or even *lean toward*, choosing answer choice (C). Many of these types of problems are trying to trap you into choosing (C) because it's so obvious that the two combined statements are sufficient. Quite often, some algebraic work will reveal that one or both of the statements will be sufficient on their own. Indeed, in the example problem given above, statement (1) alone is sufficient to answer the question, so the correct answer is (A).

3. Spot One Statement Inside the Other   *Certainty:* Very High

IF one statement is "contained within" (i.e., is a subset of) the other... → THEN *eliminate* (C) and "broader statement only."

(Some question involving x)

(1) $x > 50!$

(2) $x > 10!$

This trick only shows up occasionally, but when it does, it's useful. Notice that narrow statement (1) is completely contained within broad statement (2). In other words, any value that satisfies statement (1) *also* satisfies statement (2). Therefore, if statement (2) is sufficient, statement (1) *must* be sufficient also. However, the reverse is not true. If (2) is insufficient, (1) could still possibly be sufficient on its own.

Either way, it is impossible for both of the statements to be required together to answer the question. It is also impossible for statement (2) to be sufficient without statement (1) being sufficient also. So you can definitively eliminate (B), as it corresponds to the broader statement, as well as (C) (the together option).

This situation can occur with inequalities. Whenever one statement defines a range that is completely encompassed by the other statement's range, you can eliminate (C), as well as the broader statement alone.

Be careful with this tactic, though. It can be easy to think—incorrectly—that one statement is a subset of the other.

(Some question involving x)

(1) x is an odd number.

(2) x is a prime number.

At first, it might seem that statement (2) is a subset of statement (1), but 2 is a prime number that is not odd. *Almost* every prime number is odd, but *not all*. Therefore, statement (2) is *not* a subset of statement (1). Even if just one value escapes, you cannot use this tactic.

4. Spot One Statement Adding Nothing   *Certainty:* High

| IF one statement adds no information to the other… | $\longrightarrow$ | THEN eliminate (C). |

(Some question involving x, y, and z)

(1) $y^x + (-y)^x = z$

(2) $y < 0$

This tactic may seem identical to the previous one, but it is not. Notice in this example that statement (1) does not determine whether y is positive or negative, and statement (2) does not even include z. Therefore, neither statement is a subset of the other.

That said, the fact that y is negative *does not change anything* in statement (1), because regardless of the value of y, z will remain the same if you swap y and $-y$. If $y = 4$, then you'd get $4^x + (-4)^x = z$. If $y = -4$, then you'd get $(-4)x + 4x = z$. Those equations are the same! The sign of y doesn't matter because y and $-y$ are symmetric. So knowing the sign of y adds no information to statement (1).

Note that in this example, (A), (B), (D), and (E) are all still possible answers, depending upon the question. Only (C) can be eliminated.

5. Spot a (C) Trap   *Certainty:* Moderate

IF it is *very obvious* that the combined statements would be sufficient, but you can't eliminate the possibility that one statement alone is sufficient…	→	THEN eliminate (C) and (E).

A *(C) Trap* is a DS problem that tries to trick you into incorrectly choosing answer (C). It does this by giving you two statements that are obviously sufficient when you put them together. The test writers hope that you'll jump to putting the two statements together, without testing each statement individually first. The trap is that one or both statements are actually sufficient alone, so the correct answer is really (A), (B), or (D).

(C) Traps frequently appear in Combo problems, which require you to solve for a complicated value, rather than a single variable. The following problem is one example.

Try-It #4-13

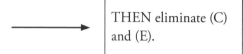

If $K = \dfrac{\frac{1}{3a} + \frac{1}{b}}{\frac{5}{ab}}$ and $ab \neq 0$, what is the value of K?

$\dfrac{9b}{5}K = \dfrac{1}{9} + \dfrac{1}{b}$ $\dfrac{9+b}{9b} = \dfrac{9bK}{5}$ $\dfrac{(9b)^2}{5}K$

(1) $a = 3$ ✗

(2) $b - 3(5 - a) = 0$

You can prove that the two statements combined are sufficient without actually doing any math. If you wanted to, you could plug the value of *a* from statement (1) into statement (2) to solve for the value of *b*. Then, you could plug those values into the question to solve for *K*.

Immediately be skeptical. Answer (C) should seem too easy. After all, you didn't do anything to the question stem. Your next thought should be that one of the statements *alone* may be sufficient. Make an informed guess among (A), (B), and (D). In some problems, the individual statements may appear equally informative; you would favor choice (D) in such a situation. In this problem, statement (2) gives more information than statement (1) does (two variables vs. just one), so you should favor choice (B) as a preliminary guess.

Start by rephrasing the question:

$$K = \frac{\frac{1}{3a} + \frac{1}{b}}{\frac{5}{ab}}$$

$$= \frac{\frac{b}{3ab} + \frac{3a}{3ab}}{\frac{5}{ab}}$$

$$= \frac{b + 3a}{3ab} \times \frac{ab}{5}$$

$$= \frac{b + 3a}{15}$$

"What is the value of K?" rephrases to "What is the value of $b + 3a$?" Statement (2) provides the answer:

$$b - 3(5 - a) = 0$$
$$b - 15 + 3a = 0$$
$$b + 3a = 15$$

The correct answer is (B). In these cases, the more complicated statement may be enough.

This is not a tactic to use at lower levels of the test. If you're doing easier Quant problems, something that looks like a (C) Trap might just be a straightforward problem with a correct answer of (C). This is one of many reasons why the material in this book is only appropriate if you have achieved a certain level of proficiency on the math side of the GMAT.

6. Use Basic Algebraic Reasoning   *Certainty:* Moderate

Quite often, basic intuition about algebra can lead you to the correct answer. For example, you might have the intuition on a problem that "I have two unknowns and only one equation, so I can't solve" or "This statement doesn't even mention the variable(s) that I care about." Often, you will discover that your intuition is correct.

Try-It #4-14

A sales manager at an industrial company has an opportunity to switch to a new, higher-paying job in another state. If his current annual salary is $50,000 and his current state tax rate is 5%, how much income after state tax would he make at the new job?

(1)   His new salary will be 10% higher than his old salary.

(2)   His annual state taxes will total $2,200 in the new state at his new job.

You may reason that in order to answer this question, you need to know how much his new salary will be and how much his taxes will increase by. This reasoning will lead you to conclude that the correct answer is (C). And you'll be right.

Of course, you need to be *very careful* about using this tactic. Many problems on the GMAT are designed to hoodwink your algebraic reasoning—usually to make you think that you need to know every value precisely to answer the question.

For example, suppose the question in the previous problem were changed to "Will the manager make more money at the new job, after state taxes?" The correct answer in this case is (B). The problem explicitly states that the new job is higher-paying, so you only need to check whether the change in state tax might lead to a lower after-tax compensation. Statement (2) indicates that his new state taxes ($2,200) will be lower than his current state taxes (5% of $50,000 = $2,500), so his after-state-tax compensation will definitely be higher in the new job. You do *not* need to find out how much higher his pre-tax salary would be to answer this question.

Because the GMAT frequently uses traps involving basic algebraic reasoning, you should only resort to using it if you are *truly stuck*.

7. Spot Cross-Multiplied Inequalities   *Certainty:* Low

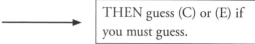

IF a Y/N question involves inequalities with variables to cross-multiply…   →   THEN guess (C) or (E) if you must guess.

When you are presented with an inequality problem in Data Sufficiency in which one or more variables appears in a denominator, you may need to know the sign of the variable or variables to answer the question. This might be the hidden trick.

Try-It #4-15

Is $xy < 1$?

(1) $\dfrac{2}{x} > 3y$

(2) $x > 0$

Statement (1) might imply that $xy < \dfrac{2}{3}$, but *only* if x is positive. If it is negative, you would need to flip the sign: $xy > \dfrac{2}{3}$. You need to know the sign of x—information that is provided in statement (2). The correct answer is (C).

These types of problems may have an (A) or (B) trap, in that you might fail to realize that you have to set up negative and positive cases when you multiply or divide an inequality by a variable.

Watch out! On some GMAT problems, you *can* assume the sign of the variables because the variables represent countable quantities of physical things. In those cases, you can assume that the variables are positive, and you can cross-multiply inequalities involving those variables at will.

8. Judge by Appearance   *Certainty:* Low

IF a statement is tricky and you don't know what to do with it…   →   THEN take a guess by "judging by appearance."

Sometimes a statement will leave you completely bewildered. In that case, the best (and only!) tactic is to guess whether it will be sufficient judging by how it looks:

- Does it look like it might be sufficient, even if you can't see how?
- Does it use the variables you are looking for?
- Could it likely be manipulated into a form *similar* to that of the question?

The general rule is this: if the information in a statement has a *structure* and *complexity* similar to the question, and has the right ingredients (variables, coefficients, etc.), it's more likely to be sufficient than otherwise. This won't crack every case by any means, but you'd be surprised at how much mileage you can get from this tactic.

Try-It #4-16

Does $4^a = 4^{-a} + b$?

(1) $16^a = 1 + \dfrac{2^{2a}}{b^{-1}}$

(2) $a = 2$

Depending on your level of comfort with exponent manipulations, you may be able to prove that statement (1) alone is sufficient:

$$16^a = 1 + \frac{2^{2a}}{b^{-1}}$$

$$16^a = 1 + \left(2^{2a}\right)b$$

$$4^{2a} = 1 + \left(4^a\right)b$$

$$\frac{4^{2a}}{4^a} = \frac{1 + \left(4^a\right)b}{4^a}$$

$$4^a = \frac{1}{4^a} + b$$

$$4^a = 4^{-a} + b$$

However, what if you find yourself at a temporary loss on the test? Your exponent engine may shut down for a problem or two. Then what do you do?

One line of reasoning might be as follows: "Statement (2) is clearly not sufficient, since it tells me nothing about b. Now, let's look at statement (1). It's a very complicated expression, but it seems to have the right ingredients. It contains a and b and uses a as an exponent. Also, the exponential terms in statement (1) are powers of 2 (2, 4, 16), just like the exponential terms in a. I'll bet if I manipulate this equation right, it will answer the question. I'll guess (A)." And you'd be correct. The GMAT never needs to know that you guessed.

Summary

That was a lot of information! To summarize, the following advanced strategies and guessing tactics can be used to solve Data Sufficiency problems effectively or to increase your chances of success:

Advanced Data Sufficiency Strategies

1. **Compute to Completion:** If you can't tell for certain whether the answer can be calculated in theory, keep going on the calculations *all the way*.

2. **Extract the Equation:** Represent Word Problems with algebraic equations to avoid embedded tricks that can be difficult to find otherwise.

3. **Know the Code:** Translate complicated questions and statements into simpler language.

4. **Use the Constraints:** Bring explicit and implicit constraints to the surface. These constraints will often be necessary to determine the correct answer.

5. **Beware of Inequalities:** Whenever a problem involves inequality symbols, *be careful*—there are many ways in which inequalities can be used to trick you.

6. **Test Cases:** There may be many possible scenarios in which a particular statement is true. Methodically write down these cases and check to see whether they result in different answers to the question.

Data Sufficiency Guessing Tactics

1. **Spot Identical Statements (High):** If the two statements say the same thing (after rephrasing), then the answer must be (D) or (E).

2. **Spot Clear Sufficiency (High):** If the two statements together are clearly sufficient, then eliminate (E).

3. **Spot One Statement Inside the Other (High):** If a narrow statement is completely contained within a broader statement, then eliminate (C) and "broader statement only" (either (A) or (B)).

4. **Spot One Statement Adding Nothing (High):** If one statement adds no value to the information given in the other statement, then eliminate (C).

5. **Spot a (C) Trap (Moderate):** If the two statements together are *very* clearly sufficient and at least one of the statements is complex enough that it could be sufficient, then (C) could be a trap answer, so eliminate (C).

6. **Use Basic Algebraic Reasoning (Moderate):** Apply basic knowledge of algebra, such as considering the number of unknowns relative to the number of known equations, to guide your thought process.

7. **Spot Cross-Multiplied Inequalities (Low):** If a Yes/No question involves inequalities with variables in a denominator, then guess (C) or (E) if you must guess.

8. **Judge by Appearance (Low):** If you're completely unsure what to do, then make your best guess as to whether it *appears* to be sufficient.

Common Wrong Answers

There are two ways to get a Data Sufficiency problem wrong:

1. You thought that a statement or both statements together were **sufficient**, but they were actually **insufficient**.

2. You thought that a statement or both statements together were **insufficient**, but they were actually **sufficient**.

Let's call the first type of error a *Type 1 error*: you thought that a statement was sufficient, but it wasn't. In other words, you thought that it gave you an exact answer to the question, but it was actually possible to get at least two different answers to the question. Here's why that might happen:

- If you tested cases, you might have missed a critical case. For instance, maybe the question has a different answer when you plug in a fraction or a negative value.

- You might have used information from the other statement without meaning to. This can make it seem as though you have enough information to answer the question, when you actually don't. Keep the two statements completely separate on your paper and test them individually before you put them together.

The second type of DS error is a *Type 2 error*. If you made this type of error, you thought that a statement *wasn't* sufficient, but it actually was. It looked like you didn't have enough information to answer the question, but you actually had more information than you thought:

- You may have assumed that you needed a specific value to answer a Yes/No question. The question might have asked something like "is x even?" If you treat this question as though you need to know the exact value of x, you'll make Type 2 errors.

- You may have fallen for a (C) Trap. If you assume that you need both statements in order to answer the question, it's easy to miss the fact that one statement is actually sufficient on its own as well.

- Not testing cases often leads to this type of error. Many statements *look* insufficient, because they don't appear to include a lot of information. However, testing cases sometimes reveals that the question only has one answer.

The common thread in many of these errors is that they stem from assumptions. The easiest way to miss a DS problem is to assume that a statement is or isn't sufficient, rather than proving it. You won't always have time on test day to meticulously prove whether a statement is sufficient. But neither should you decide whether a statement is sufficient just by glancing at it. At the very least, briefly think about how the statement bears on the specific question you're being asked. And if you have time, *prove* your suspicions about each statement before moving on.

4

Problem Set

For problems 1–3, list five values that satisfy each of the following constraints.

1. n is a prime number.   *[handwritten: $n = 2, 3, 5, 7, 11, 13, 17, 19, 23, 29, 31, 37, 41, 43, 47, 51, 53, 57, 61$]*

2. $x^2 > 0$ *[handwritten: $-2, -1, 0, 1, 2$]*

3. $\frac{M}{7} = N + \frac{3}{7}$, where M and N are positive integers.   *[handwritten: $M = 7N + 3$; $M = 0, 1, 2, 3, -1, -2, 10$; $N = -\frac{3}{7}, -\frac{2}{7}, -\frac{1}{7}, 0, \frac{4}{7}, -\frac{4}{7}, -\frac{5}{7}, 1$]*

For problems 4–6, solve the problem by Testing Cases. Note which method is appropriate for each problem: testing the standard number set, listing discrete numbers, or case testing with concepts rather than numbers.

4. If $a \neq 0$, is $a + a^{-1} > 2$?

    (1) $a > 0$ *[handwritten: (A)]*

    (2) $a < 1$

    [margin: 4]

5. At a certain florist shop, roses can be purchased either individually or as a bouquet of 12 at a discount of p percent. What is the greatest number of roses that can be purchased with \$45 ?

    (1) The greatest number of roses that can be purchased with \$30 is 24.

    (2) $p = 20$

6. Is $y^3 \leq |y|$?

    (1) $y < 1$

    (2) $y < 0$

For problems 7–9, Test cases to show that one or both statements are insufficient.

7. If a, b, and c are positive integers, is abc an even integer?

    (1) $a + b$ is even.

    (2) $b + c$ is odd.

8. Twenty-eight students were each assigned to one of five classes: Anthropology, Biology, Geology, Musicology, and Sociology. Was at least one of the classes assigned fewer than 5 students?

    (1) At least 6 students were assigned to each of Biology, Geology, and Sociology.

    (2) Geology and Sociology were not assigned the same number of students.

9. Set A consists of the four integers x, x^2, x^3, and x^4, and set B consists of the four integers x, $2x$, $3x$, and $4x$. What is the probability that a randomly selected integer from 1 to 100, inclusive, is a member of neither set A nor set B ?

    (1) $x > 5$

    (2) $x < 10$

For problems 10–15, solve the problem. Note the **strategies** used to solve the problem, and also note any **guessing tactics** that could be employed to help eliminate answer choices. Even if you weren't certain as to the correct answer, which answer choices could you eliminate and why? Also, which guessing tactics would *not* work, and why?

The following advanced strategies and guessing tactics were discussed in this chapter:

Advanced Strategies	Guessing Tactics
(1) Compute to Completion	(1) Spot Identical Statements
(2) Extract the Equation	(2) Spot Clear Sufficiency
(3) Know the Code	(3) Spot One Statement Inside the Other
(4) Use the Constraints	(4) Spot One Statement Adding Nothing
(5) Beware of Inequalities	(5) Spot a (C) Trap
(6) Test Cases	(6) Use Basic Algebraic Reasoning
	(7) Spot Cross-Multiplied Inequalities
	(8) Judge by Appearance

4

10. The average (arithmetic mean) of the original six prices for six coats at a clothing store was $85. After two of the six coats were each discounted by 20%, the average price of the six coats was $76. Was the coat with the lowest original price one of the two coats that were discounted?

     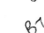

    (1) One of the discounted coats was the one with the highest original price.

     (2) Before the discount, none of the coats had a price greater than $180.

11. Amanda and Todd purchase candy, popcorn, and pretzels at the stadium. If a package of candy costs half as much as a bag of popcorn, how much more money did Amanda and Todd spend on the candy than on the popcorn and pretzels combined?

    (1) The cost of a bag of popcorn is equal to the cost of a pretzel.

     (2) Amanda and Todd purchased 24 packages of candy, 6 pretzels, and 6 bags of popcorn.

12. What is the value of $|x + 4|$?

    (1) $x^2 + 8x + 12 = 0$

    (2) $x^2 + 6x = 0$

13. If $abcd \neq 0$, is $abcd < 0$?

    (1) $\dfrac{a}{b} > \dfrac{c}{d}$

     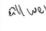

    (2) $\dfrac{b}{a} > \dfrac{d}{c}$

14. If m and n are positive integers, is n a multiple of 24 ?

    (1) $n = \dfrac{(m+7)!}{(m+3)!}$

    (2) n is a multiple of $(m + 4)$.

15. What is the value of $x(1 - y)(1 + y)$?

    (1) $x^2 = x$

    (2) $y^2 = x$

Solutions

1. $n = 2, 3, 5, 7, 11, 13, 17, 19, 23$, etc.

2. $x = 0.5, 2, 3, 6.7, 0, -1$, etc. (Note that the list should include integers and non-integers, positive and negative values—although the items you choose do not need to match these exact values. Anything other than 0 will work!)

3. $M = 10, 17, 24, 31, 38$, etc., and $N = 1, 2, 3, 4, 5$, etc.:

   M must have a remainder of 3 when divided by 7:

   $$M = 7 + 3, 14 + 3, 21 + 3, 28 + 3, 35 + 3, \text{ etc.}$$
   $$M = 10, 17, 24, 31, 38, \text{ etc.}$$
   $$N = 1, 2, 3, 4, 5, \text{ etc.}$$

   Note that successive values of M differ by 7 and the corresponding values of N are consecutive integers.

   One way to generate this list is to pick consecutive numbers for N and then calculate values for M:

   $$\frac{M}{7} = N + \frac{3}{7}$$
   $$M = 7N + 3$$
   $$N = 1, 2, 3, 4, 5, \text{ etc.}$$
   $$M = 7(1) + 3 = 10, 7(2) + 3 = 17, 7(3) + 3 = 24, 7(4) + 3 = 31, 7(5) + 3 = 38, \text{ etc.}$$

4. **(C):** Because there are no constraints on a, use the *standard number set*. The inequality can be rephrased as follows:

   $$\text{Is } a + a^{-1} > 2 ? \quad \rightarrow \quad \text{Is } a + \frac{1}{a} > 2 ?$$

   (1) INSUFFICIENT:

a	$a + \dfrac{1}{a}$	$> 2?$
$\dfrac{1}{2}$	$\dfrac{1}{2} + \dfrac{1}{\frac{1}{2}} = \dfrac{5}{2}$	Yes
1	$1 + 1 = 2$	No

   (2) INSUFFICIENT:

a	$a + \dfrac{1}{a}$	$> 2?$
-1	$-1 + (-1) = -2$	No
$-\dfrac{1}{2}$	$-\dfrac{1}{2} + \dfrac{1}{-\frac{1}{2}} = -\dfrac{5}{2}$	No
$\dfrac{1}{2}$	$\dfrac{1}{2} + \dfrac{1}{\frac{1}{2}} = \dfrac{5}{2}$	Yes

(1) AND (2) SUFFICIENT: Combining the two constraints, $0 < a < 1$. Within the standard number set, only $\frac{1}{2}$ is within this range. In addition, test numbers close to the boundaries of the range.

a	$a + \dfrac{1}{a}$	$> 2?$
$\dfrac{1}{10}$	$\dfrac{1}{10} + \dfrac{1}{\frac{1}{10}} = \dfrac{101}{10}$	Yes
$\dfrac{1}{2}$	$\dfrac{1}{2} + \dfrac{1}{\frac{1}{2}} = \dfrac{5}{2}$	Yes
$\dfrac{9}{10}$	$\dfrac{9}{10} + \dfrac{10}{9} = \dfrac{181}{90}$	Yes

It seems that at the extreme edges, the values are greater than 2, so statements (1) and (2) appear to be SUFFICIENT.

The correct answer is **(C)**.

5. **(E):** The question asks you to maximize the number of roses that can be purchased for $45. To do so, first purchase as many 12-rose bouquets as possible, then purchase as many individual roses as possible with the remaining money.

    (1) INSUFFICIENT: The greatest number of roses that can be purchased with $30 is 24. In other words, two bouquets can be purchased for $30, and any leftover money is not enough to purchase one individual rose. Test cases to determine how many roses could be purchased with $45.

    Case 1: If a bouquet of 12 roses costs exactly $15, then exactly 24 roses can be purchased with $30, and exactly 36 roses can be purchased with $45.

    Case 2: Try to find a case in which only 24 roses can be purchased with $30, but more than 36 roses can be purchased with $45. This will happen if two bouquets cost less than $30 and the leftover money isn't enough to purchase any more individual roses. But the leftover money from $45 when three bouquets are purchased is just enough to purchase an additional rose.

    For instance, suppose that a bouquet costs $14 and an individual rose costs $2.50 before the discount. (Since this is a Data Sufficiency problem, it isn't necessary to find the exact value of p for which this will occur, as long as you're confident that such a value exists.) In this case, only 24 roses could be purchased with $30, since the $2 change wouldn't be enough to purchase any individual roses. However, 37 roses could be purchased with $45: three bouquets for $42 and one additional $2.50 rose with the remaining $3.

    Since either 36 or 37 roses could be purchased for $45, this statement is insufficient.

    (2) INSUFFICIENT: The price of an individual rose is unknown. Therefore, any number of roses might be purchased for $45.

    (1) AND (2) INSUFFICIENT: First, use the case in which exactly 36 roses can be purchased for $45. Then, look for a case in which more than 36 roses can be purchased for $45.

Case 1: If a bouquet of roses costs exactly $15, then exactly 36 roses can be purchased for $45. (For reference, this implies each rose in a bouquet cost $\frac{\$15}{12} = \$1.25$, so the individual [not discounted] rose price is $\frac{\$1.25}{0.8} = \$1.5625$.)

Case 2: Determine whether more than 36 roses could be purchased for $45. If roses cost only slightly less than they did in Case 1, it might still only be possible to purchase 24 roses for $30, but it might also be possible to purchase one extra individual rose with the leftover money. Try a cost of $1.50 per rose.

If a rose costs $1.50 individually, then a bouquet costs $12(\$1.50)(0.80) = \$14.40$.

Since two bouquets cost $2(\$14.40) = \$28.80$, there isn't enough money left over to purchase another single rose. Therefore, this case fits statement (1).

Now three bouquets cost $3(\$14.40) = \$43.20$, and one more rose can be purchased for $1.50, bringing the total purchase to $44.70. In this case, 37 roses can be purchased with $45.

Since either 36 or 37 roses could be purchased for $45, the two statements are insufficient together.

The correct answer is (**E**).

6. (**D**): Because there are no constraints on y, use the *standard number set*, displayed here in number line graphic form:

	-2	$-\frac{3}{2}$	-1	$-\frac{1}{2}$	0	$\frac{1}{2}$	1	$\frac{3}{2}$	2
y^3	-8	$-\frac{27}{8}$	-1	$-\frac{1}{8}$	0	$\frac{1}{8}$	1	$\frac{27}{8}$	8
$\lvert y \rvert$	2	$\frac{3}{2}$	1	$\frac{1}{2}$	0	$\frac{1}{2}$	1	$\frac{3}{2}$	2
$y^3 \le \lvert y \rvert$?	Y	Y	Y	Y	Y	Y	Y	N	N

Statement (1): $y < 1$. If y is less than 1, all tested values show $y^3 \le \lvert y \rvert$. SUFFICIENT.

Statement (2): $y < 0$. If y is less than 0, all tested values show $y^3 \le \lvert y \rvert$. SUFFICIENT.

Notice that you could use Guessing Tactic 3: *spot one statement inside the other.* $y < 0$ is more limiting than $y < 1$, so if statement (1) is sufficient, statement (2) must be sufficient.

The correct answer is (**D**).

7. (**B**): In order for abc to be even, what must be true? If just one of the numbers is even, then the product will be even. The only case that will produce an odd is when all three numbers are odd. Keep this in mind when testing the statements.

(1) INSUFFICIENT: If $a + b$ is even, then the two variables are either both even or both odd:

a	b	c	abc even?
Even	Even	Even	Yes
Odd	Odd	Odd	No

(2) SUFFICIENT: $b + c$ is odd, so one of b and c is odd and the other is even. In other words, it is impossible for all three variables to be odd. Therefore, the product abc must be even.

The correct answer is (**B**).

8. **(C):** Set up a table and try to find contradictory scenarios.

    (1) INSUFFICIENT:

A	B	G	M	S	$<$ 5 in one class?
5	6	6	5	6	No
4	6	6	6	6	Yes

    (2) INSUFFICIENT:

A	B	G	M	S	$<$ 5 in one class?
6	6	4	6	6	Yes
6	5	5	6	6	No

    (1) AND (2) SUFFICIENT:

A	B	G	M	S	$<$ 5 in one class?
4	6	6	5	7	Yes

    Since Geology and Sociology each have to have a minimum of 6 students, and they can't have the same number of students, one of the two classes has to have at least 7 students. Between Biology, Geology, and Sociology, then, the minimum number of students is $6 + 6 + 7 = 19$, leaving 9 students to be split among the other two classes. In this case, it's impossible to have 5 or more students in both of those two remaining classes.

    The correct answer is **(C)**.

9. **(C):** The question asks for the probability that a randomly selected integer, from 1 to 100, will be in neither one of the two sets. To calculate this probability, you need to know the total number of integers that are in one or both of the two sets, as well as within the 1 to 100 range.

    Jot down the definitions of the two sets. Integer x is contained in both sets, so, at most, the two sets will contain seven distinct integers between them. However, some of these integers might be less than 1 or greater than 100, and there might be more integers that overlap between the two sets, decreasing the number of possible values that overlap with the selected integer to less than 7. A statement is sufficient if every possible value of x yields the same number of distinct values between 1 and 100, inclusive.

    (1) INSUFFICIENT: Test a straightforward case first, then test a case that might yield a different value.

    Case 1: The smallest possible value for x that fits the statement is 6. If $x = 6$, then set A consists of four integers: 6, 6^2, 6^3, and 6^4. Two of those integers, 6 and $6^2 = 36$, are smaller than 100. As long as you know that 6^3 and 6^4 are greater than 100, there is no need to calculate their exact values. Set B also consists of four integers: 6, 12, 18, and 24.

    Therefore, the sets contain a total of five distinct integers between 1 and 100, inclusive.

    Case 2: Try an extreme case, such as $x = 1,000$. In this case, all of the integers in both set A and set B are much greater than 100. Therefore, the sets contain no integers between 1 and 100.

    (2) INSUFFICIENT: The first case tested above, with $x = 6$, also fits this statement. In this case, there are five distinct integers within the range, as described above.

Try another extreme case, such as $x = -2$. In this case, the only positive integers in either set will be $(-2)^2 = 4$ and $(-2)^4 = 16$, which are both between 1 and 100. Therefore, there are exactly two distinct integers within the range. Since the set could contain five integers or two integers within the given range, this statement is also insufficient.

(1) AND (2) SUFFICIENT: $x = 6$ yields five distinct integers that are within the range 1 to 100. Check to see whether this is also true for $x = 7$, 8, and 9.

For $x = 7$, 8, or 9, set A contains two integers that are within the range 1 to 100: x and x^2. In all three cases, x^3 and x^4 are outside of the range. Also, set B contains four integers that are within the range, but one of them, x itself, is also contained in set A. So in every case in which x is between 5 and 10, there are exactly five distinct integers in the range that are contained in one or both sets.

The correct answer is **(C)**.

10. **(B):** The average price of six coats was originally \$85. So the sum of the six prices was originally $6(\$85) = \$510$.

Two of the prices were discounted by 20%, resulting in a \$9 reduction in the average price, or a $6(\$9) = \$54$ reduction in the overall price. Since 20% (or $\frac{1}{5}$) of the cost of these two coats came to \$54, the original price of these two coats must have been five times this, or $5(\$54) = \$270$.

Given that the sum of the original prices of the two discounted coats was \$270, did one of these two coats have the lowest original price?

(1) INSUFFICIENT: From the question stem, the two discounted coats had a total price of \$270, and according to this statement, one of those two coats was the most expensive. Test cases to see whether the other coat could have been the least expensive. Note that the four non-discounted coats had a total price of $\$510 - \$270 = \$240$.

Case 1: If the discounted coats originally cost \$1 and \$269 and the other four coats each cost $\frac{\$240}{4} = \$60$, then the least expensive coat was one of the two that was discounted, and the answer is Yes.

Case 2: If the discounted coats originally cost \$130 and \$140 and the other four coats each cost $\frac{\$240}{4} = \$60$, then the least expensive coat was not one of the two that was discounted, and the answer is No.

(2) SUFFICIENT: This statement limits the possible original costs of the two discounted coats. Since none of the coats originally cost more than \$180, the two discounted coats could not have cost, for example, \$50 and \$220, or \$70 and \$200. Since neither of the coats could have cost more than \$180, the less expensive of the two discounted coats must have cost at least $\$270 - \$180 = \$90$.

However, this coat could not have been the one with the lowest original price, as \$90 is greater than the original average price. The least number in any set cannot be greater than the average of that set. Therefore, neither of the two discounted coats could have been the one with the lowest price. The answer to the question is definitely No, and this statement is sufficient.

The correct answer is **(B)**.

11. **(C):** Assign variables to the unknowns in the problem.

C = packages of candy P_c = price of a package of candy

P = bags of popcorn P_p = price of a bag of popcorn

R = number of pretzels P_r = price of a pretzel

Algebraically, the question asks: What is $P_c \times C - (P_p \times P + P_r \times R)$?

The question stem indicates that $P_c = \frac{1}{2} \times P_p$.

(1) INSUFFICIENT: $P_r = P_p$. Substitute and rephrase the question:

What is $P_c \times C - (P_p \times P + P_r \times R)$?

What is $\left(\frac{1}{2} \times P_p\right) \times C - \left(P_p \times P + \left(P_p\right) \times R\right)$?

What is $P_p \times \left(\frac{1}{2} \times C - P - R\right)$?

There are four unknown variables, so statement (1) is not sufficient.

(2) INSUFFICIENT: $C = 24$, $P = 6$, and $R = 6$:

What is $P_c \times C - (P_p \times P + P_r \times R)$?

What is $\left(\frac{1}{2} \times P_p\right) \times 24 - \left(P_p \times 6 + P_r \times 6\right)$?

What is $12P_p - 6P_p - 6P_r$?

What is $6P_p - 6P_r$?

There are two unknown variables, so statement (2) is not sufficient.

(1) AND (2) SUFFICIENT:

From statement (2): What is $6P_p - 6P_r$?

From statement (1): What is $6P_p - 6(P_p)$?

Rephrased question: What is 0 ?

Given the relative prices of the candy, popcorn, and pretzels, and the quantity of each purchased, the cost of the candy will always equal the combined cost of the popcorn and pretzels, even though it's impossible to calculate the exact prices. Statements (1) and (2) combined are SUFFICIENT to answer the question.

The correct answer is **(C)**.

12. **(A):** It's tempting to rephrase the question as "What is x?" but that is dangerous when the question contains absolute value symbols. It's possible that two different values of x would resolve to the same value of $|x + 4|$. Leave the question as it is.

(1) SUFFICIENT: $x^2 + 8x + 12 = 0$. Factor the equation:

$(x + 2)(x + 6) = 0$

$x = -2 \text{ or} - 6$

Plug these answers into the question stem:

$$|(-2) + 4| = |2| = 2 \qquad |(-6) + 4| = |-2| = 2$$

The two different values resolve to the same final value for $|x + 4|$, so statement (1) is sufficient.

(2) INSUFFICIENT: $x^2 + 6x = 0$. Factor the equation:

$$x(x + 6) = 0$$
$$x = 0 \text{ or } -6$$

Plug both values into the question stem:

$$|(0) + 4| = 4 \qquad |(-6) + 4| = |-2| = 2$$

There are two different values for the expression $|x + 4|$, so statement (2) is not sufficient.

The correct answer is **(A)**.

13. **(C):** If $abcd \neq 0$, then none of the variables equals 0. In order for the product $abcd$ to be negative, you would need to have an odd number of negatives in the mix:

Scenario	Product *abcd*
All 4 positive or all 4 negative	+
3 positive, 1 negative	−
2 positive, 2 negative	+
1 positive, 3 negative	−

(1) INSUFFICIENT: Beware of inequalities.

  If b and d are both positive or both negative, then $ad > bc$.

  If one is positive and one is negative, then $ad < bc$.

  This statement indicates nothing about a and c, though.

(2) INSUFFICIENT:

  If a and c are both positive or both negative, then $bc > ad$.

  If one is positive and one is negative, then $bc < ad$.

  This statement indicates nothing about b and d, though.

(1) AND (2) SUFFICIENT: Here's where the trick comes in. The two statements allow two possible scenarios:

If $ad > bc$, then b and d have the same sign but a and c have opposite signs. In this case, three signs are the same and one is not, so there are an odd number of negatives in the mix, and the product of all four variables must be negative.

If $ad < bc$, b and d have opposite signs, but a and c have the same signs. In this case, three signs are the same and one is not; as before, the product of all four variables must be negative.

Either way, the two statements together are sufficient to answer the question.

The correct answer is **(C)**.

14. **(A):** The question stem asks whether $n = 24, 48, 72, \ldots$

    (1) SUFFICIENT: Rewrite and simplify:

    $$n = \frac{(m+7)(m+6)(m+5)(m+4)(m+3)!}{(m+3)!}$$
    $$n = (m+7)(m+6)(m+5)(m+4)$$

    In other words, n is the product of four consecutive integers. In any four consecutive integers, one number must be divisible by 3 and two numbers must be even. Furthermore, of the two even numbers, one must be divisible by 4. As a result, the product of any four consecutive integers is divisible by $(3)(2)(4) = 24$.

    Alternatively, you could figure this out by testing a few cases:

    $m = 1$: $(8)(7)(6)(5)$, which is divisible by $(8)(3) = 24$
    $m = 2$: $(9)(8)(7)(6)$, which is divisible by $(8)(3) = 24$
    $m = 3$: $(10)(9)(8)(7)$, which is divisible by $(8)(3) = 24$

    (2) INSUFFICIENT: If $m = 1$, then n could equal 5, which is not a multiple of 24. If $m = 20$, then n could equal 24, which is a multiple of 24.

    The correct answer is **(A)**.

15. **(C):** This algebra problem includes a special quadratic: $(1 - y)(1 + y) = 1 - y^2$. Rephrase the question as "What is the value of $x(1 - y^2)$?"

    (1) INSUFFICIENT: This statement appears to provide little information. However, it significantly limits the possible values of x.

    $$x^2 = x$$
    $$x^2 - x = 0$$
    $$x(x - 1) = 0$$
    $$x = 1 \; or \; 0$$

    If $x = 1$, the answer to the question is the value of $1 - y^2$, which is unknown. If $x = 0$, the answer to the question is 0.

    (2) INSUFFICIENT: If $y^2 = x$, then the question simplifies to "What is the value of $x(1 - x)$?" Different values of x produce different answers, so this statement is insufficient.

    (1) AND (2) SUFFICIENT: According to statement (1), the value of x is either 0 or 1.

    If the value of x is 0, then, according to statement (2), $y^2 = x = 0$. In this case, the answer is $x(1 - y^2) = 0(1 - 0) = 0$.

    If the value of x is 1, then, according to statement (2), $y^2 = x = 1$. In this case, the answer is $x(1 - y^2) = 1(1 - 1) = 0$.

    Since the answer to the question is always 0, the two statements together are sufficient.

    The correct answer is **(C)**.

Strategies for All Problem Types

CHAPTER 5

Pattern Recognition

In This Chapter

- Pattern Recognition Problems

- Sequence Problems

- Units (Ones) Digit Problems

- Remainder Problems

- Other Pattern Problems

CHAPTER 5 Pattern Recognition

Pattern Recognition Problems

In the context of the GMAT, pattern recognition involves spotting a repeating cycle or other simple relationship underlying a series of numbers. If you can grasp the rule, you can predict numbers that appear later in the series. The series may be part of a defined sequence or it may arise from a general list of possibilities. Either way, if you can spot the pattern, you can eliminate a lot of unnecessary calculation. In fact, often the only feasible way to get the answer in two minutes (e.g., finding the 100th number in some series) is to recognize the underlying pattern. Here's an example.

Try-It #5-1

> Each number in a sequence is 3 more than the previous number. If the first number is 4, what is the value of the 1,000th term in the sequence?

Obviously, finding the 1,000th number the long way (by computing every intervening number) is impossible in the time allotted on the GMAT. You can solve this problem in several ways, but one powerful way is to compute the first several terms, spot the underlying *pattern*, figure out *the rule*, and then apply it.

The first five terms of the sequence are 4, 7, 10, 13, 16. Notice that you repeatedly add 3 to get the next value. Repeated addition is just multiplication, so match these numbers to the multiples of 3. The first five multiples of 3 are 3, 6, 9, 12, 15—all 1 less than the numbers in the sequence. Thus, the rule for generating the sequence is "take the corresponding multiple of 3, and add 1." Therefore, the 1,000th term of the sequence is 1 more than the 1,000th multiple of 3, which is $3,000 + 1 = 3,001$. Once you spot the pattern, you can skip over vast amounts of unnecessary work.

The two most basic patterns are these:

1. The *counting numbers* (1, 2, 3, 4...), also known as the *positive integers*. As simple as this pattern may seem, it is the basis for many other patterns. For instance, the sequence of the multiples of 7 (7, 14, 21, 28...) can be derived from 1, 2, 3, 4... by multiplying by 7. You can write this sequence as $S_n = 7n$, where *n* is the basic sequence of positive integers.

2. A *repeating cycle* of numbers. For instance, the sequence 4, 2, 6, 4, 2, 6, 4, 2, 6... has a repeating cycle of three terms: 4, 2, 6. Repeating cycles can be derived in various ways from the counting numbers (e.g., when you raise an integer to increasing powers, the units digits of the results repeat themselves). However, it is often easier to think of repeating cycles *on their own terms*, separately from the counting numbers and related patterns.

When you are examining a string of numbers for a pattern, follow these steps:

1. Compute the first five to eight terms and try to match them to a pattern that you already know. The most basic pattern is the counting numbers, but you should also have these related patterns up your sleeve:

    a. Multiples (e.g., $7 \times 1 = \mathbf{7}, 7 \times 2 = \mathbf{14}, 7 \times 3 = \mathbf{21}, 7 \times 4 = \mathbf{28}, 7 \times 5 = \mathbf{35} \dots 7n \dots$)

    b. Squares ($1^2 = \mathbf{1}, 2^2 = \mathbf{4}, 3^2 = \mathbf{9}, 4^2 = \mathbf{16}, 5^2 = \mathbf{25} \dots n^2 \dots$)

    c. Powers ($2^1 = \mathbf{2}, 2^2 = \mathbf{4}, 2^3 = \mathbf{8}, 2^4 = \mathbf{16}, 2^5 = \mathbf{32} \dots 2^n \dots$)

    For each of these sequences, notice exactly where the counting numbers come into play. For instance, in the squares series, the counting numbers are the *bases*, but in the powers series, the counting numbers are the *exponents*.

2. Look for repeating cycles. As soon as you generate a repeated term, see whether the sequence will repeat itself from that point onward. Repeating cycles on the GMAT typically begin repeating every four terms (or fewer), so five to eight terms should be sufficient to identify the pattern. Of course, some cycles repeat every single term—that is, it's the same number over and over again!

3. If you are stuck, look for patterns within *differences between terms* or *sums across terms*:

    a. Look at the difference between consecutive terms. For instance, this process can help you spot linear sequences (sequences of multiples plus a constant):

Sequence:	10		17		24		31		$\dots$	$7n + 3 \dots$
Differences:		7		7		7		7	(constant difference)	

    b. Also look at the *cumulative sum* of all the terms up to that point. This is helpful if the terms get closer to zero or alternate in sign:

Sequence:	$\frac{1}{2}$	$\frac{1}{4}$	$\frac{1}{8}$	$\frac{1}{16}$	$\dots$	$\frac{1}{2^n}$	$\dots$
Cumulative Sum:	$\frac{1}{2}$	$\frac{3}{4}$	$\frac{7}{8}$	$\frac{15}{16}$	$\dots$	$\dfrac{\left(2^n - 1\right)}{2^n}$	$\dots$

    Notice that the cumulative sum for this sequence approaches 1.

    c. Some sums involve *matching pairs* that sum to the same number (or even cancel each other out). Be on the lookout for such matching pairs.

    What is the sum of 1, 5, 8, 10, 11, 11, 12, 14, 17, and 21 ?

    You can, of course, sum these numbers in order, but look to make natural intermediate sums (subtotals) with matching pairs. In this example, spot the repeated 11's in the middle and sum them to 22. Working outward, 10 and 12 sum to 22 as well. So do 8 and 14, 5 and 17, and 1 and 21. In all, there are five subtotals of 22, for a grand total of 110.

4. Look at characteristics of the numbers: positive/negative, odd/even, integer/non-integer, etc. Once you have extended the pattern for several terms, these characteristics will generally repeat or alternate in some predictable way.

Perhaps the most important principle to apply on Pattern Recognition problems is to *put pen to paper,* as discussed in Chapter 1. Often, the pattern will be completely hidden until you actually compute the first several values of the sequence or other initial results.

Several types of problems frequently involve underlying patterns. When you see these types of problems on the GMAT, be ready to analyze the pattern so you can find the rule:

1. **Sequence Problems:** Nearly all sequence problems involve a pattern in the elements (or terms) of the sequence. Sequences can be defined either directly (i.e., each value in the series is a function of its *location* in the order of the sequence) or recursively (i.e., each value is a function of the *previous items* in the sequence).

2. **Units (Ones) Digit Problems:** Questions involving the last digit (sometimes called the *units* or *ones* digit) of an integer almost always involve some sort of repeating cycle pattern that can be exploited.

3. **Remainder Problems:** Remainders from the division of one integer into another will result in a pattern. For example, when divided by 5, the counting numbers will exhibit the following repeating remainder pattern: 1, 2, 3, 4, 0, 1, 2, 3, 4, 0... The units digit of an integer is a special case of a remainder: it's the remainder after division by 10.

4. **Other Pattern Problems:** Some pattern problems do not involve deciphering a string of numbers and discovering the rule. For instance, you may have to count a set of numbers that all fit some constraint. The point is to discover a simple rule or group of rules that let you account for all the numbers—and therefore count them—without having to generate each one. Here are some ideas:

   - Break the problem into sub-problems. For instance, a sum may be split into several smaller sums. Or you might count a larger total, then subtract items that do not fit the constraint. You even might multiply a larger total by the proportion of suitable items, if that fraction is easy to calculate.

   - Recall counting and summing methods from Manhattan Prep's *All the Quant* guide:

     a. Number of Choices: When you have a series of successive decisions, you multiply the number of choices you have at each stage to find the number of total choices you have. For instance, if you can choose 1 appetizer out of 6 possible appetizers and 1 main course out of 7 possible main courses, then you could have $6 \times 7 = 42$ possible meals.

     b. Number of Items in a Consecutive Set of Integers: The number of integers in a consecutive set of integers equals the largest minus the smallest, plus 1.

     c. Sum of a Consecutive Set of Integers: The sum of a consecutive set of integers equals the number of integers (computed above) multiplied by the average, which is the average of the largest integer and the smallest integer. This is also equal to the median, or "middle," number in the set.

   - As you go, always check that the extreme cases are still valid. Two or three constraints can interact in surprising ways, eliminating some of the values that would seem to work otherwise.

Sequence Problems

Any question that involves the definition of a sequence (usually involving subscripted variables, such as A_n and S_n) is very likely to involve patterns. These patterns can range from relatively straightforward linear patterns to much more complicated ones.

When you are given a sequence definition, list a few terms of the sequence, starting with any particular terms you are given, and look for a pattern.

Do not be intimidated by a *recursive* definition for a sequence, in which each term is defined using *earlier* terms. (By contrast, a direct definition defines each term using the *position* or *index* of the term.) To illustrate the difference, here are two ways to define the series of positive odd integers {1, 3, 5, 7, 9, etc.}:

Recursive Definition	Direct Definition
$A_n = A_{n-1} + 2$ where $n > 1$ and $A_1 = 1$	$A_n = 2n - 1$, where $n \geq 1$
Translation:	Translation:
"This term = the *previous term* + 2, and the first term is 1."	"This term = the *index number* $\times$ 2, minus 1. Thus, the first term is $(2)(1) - 1 = 1$."

Try-It #5-2

The sequence X_n is defined as follows: $X_n = 2X_{n-1} - 1$ whenever n is an integer greater than 1. If $X_1 = 3$, what is the value of $X_{20} - X_{19}$?

The pattern underlying this sequence is not obvious, so begin computing a few of the terms in the set:

n	X_n
1	3
2	$2(3) - 1 = 5$
3	$2(5) - 1 = 9$
4	$2(9) - 1 = 17$
5	$2(17) - 1 = 33$
6	$2(33) - 1 = 65$
7	$2(65) - 1 = 129$

You might notice that there appears to be a repeating pattern among the units digits of the elements of X_n (3, 5, 9, 7, 3, 5, 9...). However, this does not help to answer the question, which asks about the *difference* between two consecutive elements later in the set. Instead, look at the differences between consecutive elements:

n	X_n	$X_n - X_{n-1}$
1	3	—
2	$2(3) - 1 = 5$	$5 - 3 = 2$
3	$2(5) - 1 = 9$	$9 - 5 = 4$
4	$2(9) - 1 = 17$	$17 - 9 = 8$
5	$2(17) - 1 = 33$	$33 - 17 = 16$
6	$2(33) - 1 = 65$	$65 - 33 = 32$
7	$2(65) - 1 = 129$	$129 - 65 = 64$

The pattern quickly emerges: the difference between consecutive terms in the sequence appears to always be a power of 2. Specifically, $X_2 - X_1 = 2 = 2^1$, $X_3 - X_2 = 4 = 2^2$, $X_4 - X_3 = 8 = 2^3$, etc.

You can determine the pattern for the sequence: $X_n - X_{n-1}$ equals 2^{n-1}. Therefore, $X_{20} - X_{19} = 2^{19}$. This is a *difference pattern*—a pattern or rule that exists among the differences between consecutive terms in the sequence. Be careful at this last step! When you extrapolate the pattern, you might accidentally think that the number you want is 2^{20}. Always explicitly match to the index, and realize that you might be slightly shifted. In this case, the difference you want is *not* 2^n. The difference is 2^{n-1}.

Try-It #5-3

If $A_n = \dfrac{1}{n(n+1)}$ for all positive integers n, what is the sum of the first 100 elements of A_n?

Once again, compute the first few elements of A_n. Because you need to know the sum of the first 100 elements, also track the cumulative sum:

n	A_n	Sum through A_n
1	$\dfrac{1}{1 \times 2} = \dfrac{1}{2}$	$\dfrac{1}{2}$
2	$\dfrac{1}{2 \times 3} = \dfrac{1}{6}$	$\dfrac{1}{2} + \dfrac{1}{6} = \dfrac{3+1}{6} = \dfrac{2}{3}$
3	$\dfrac{1}{3 \times 4} = \dfrac{1}{12}$	$\dfrac{2}{3} + \dfrac{1}{12} = \dfrac{8+1}{12} = \dfrac{3}{4}$
4	$\dfrac{1}{4 \times 5} = \dfrac{1}{20}$	$\dfrac{3}{4} + \dfrac{1}{20} = \dfrac{15+1}{20} = \dfrac{4}{5}$
5	$\dfrac{1}{5 \times 6} = \dfrac{1}{30}$	$\dfrac{4}{5} + \dfrac{1}{30} = \dfrac{24+1}{30} = \dfrac{5}{6}$

The sum of the first n terms of A_n equals $\dfrac{n}{n+1}$. Therefore, the sum of the first 100 terms is $\dfrac{100}{101}$. This is a *summing pattern*—a pattern or rule that exists among the cumulative sum of the terms in the sequence.

Units (Ones) Digit Problems

When you raise an integer to a power, the units digit always displays some kind of pattern as you increase the power.

Try-It #5-4

What is the units digit of 4^{674} ?

Observe what happens to the units digit of the consecutive powers of 4, starting with 4^1:

$$4^1 = 4 \quad\quad \rightarrow \quad \text{last digit of } 4 = 4$$
$$4^2 = 4(4^1) \quad \rightarrow \quad \text{last digit of } 4(4) = \text{last digit of } 16 = 6$$
$$4^3 = 4(4^2) \quad \rightarrow \quad \text{last digit of } 4(6) = \text{last digit of } 24 = 4$$
$$4^4 = 4(4^3) \quad \rightarrow \quad \text{last digit of } 4(4) = \text{last digit of } 16 = 6$$

Because the computations $(4 \times 4 = 16)$ and $(4 \times 6 = 24)$ keep repeating, the units digit will continue to alternate $[4, 6]$.

Thus, 4^x will have a units digit of 4 whenever x is odd and a units digit of 6 whenever x is even (assuming, of course, that x is positive). The units digit of 4^{674} is therefore 6.

Also notice that in determining the value of the units digit of a product, *all of the other digits* besides the units digit are irrelevant. Therefore, 14^{674} and $3,184^{674}$ will both also have units digits of 6. This is also true for multiplication of *any* two integers, as well as the *addition* of any integers:

$$
\begin{array}{r}
5,879 \\
\times\ 1,642 \\
\hline
11,758 \\
235,160 \\
3,527,400 \\
+\ 5,879,000 \\
\hline
9,653,318
\end{array}
$$

Only the units digits $(2 \times 9 = 18)$ contribute to the units digit of the result, since the other units digits in the multiplication are zeros.

$$
\begin{array}{r}
3\,4\,5 \\
2\,6\,2 \\
+\ 1\,4\,9 \\
\hline
7\,5\,6
\end{array}
$$

Only the sum of $5 + 2 + 9 = 16$ affects the units digit of the sum.

As mentioned earlier, every integer raised to different positive exponents has a units digit pattern. As an exercise, derive several of the patterns yourself for the units digits 2, 3, 5, 7, and 8; you can check your work using the table below:

Series	Consecutive Powers	Units Digit Pattern
1^x	**1**; **1**; **1**; **1**; **1**; **1**; etc.	[1]
2^x	**2**; **4**; **8**; **16**; **32**; **64**; etc.	[2, 4, 8, 6]
3^x	**3**; **9**; **27**; **81**; **243**; **729**; etc.	[3, 9, 7, 1]
4^x	**4**; **16**; **64**; **256**; **1,024**; **4,096**; etc.	[4, 6]
5^x	**5**; **25**; **125**; **625**; **3,125**; **15,625**; etc.	[5]
6^x	**6**; **36**; **216**; **1,296**; **7,776**; **46,656**; etc.	[6]
7^x	**7**; **49**; **343**; **2,401**; **16,807**; **117,649**; etc.	[7, 9, 3, 1]
8^x	**8**; **64**; **512**; **4,096**; **32,768**; **262,144**; etc.	[8, 4, 2, 6]
9^x	**9**; **81**; **729**; **6,561**; **59,049**; **531,441**; etc.	[9, 1]
10^x	**10**; **100**; **1,000**; **10,000**; **100,000**; **1,000,000**; etc.	[0]

You can either memorize this chart or know how to regenerate these patterns quickly. The units digits 1, 5, 6, and 0 just repeat the same digit forever; there's no real pattern to memorize. That leaves you with six possibilities to memorize (or to re-create when you need them). Note that no pattern goes beyond four numbers before repeating, so you don't have to check beyond the first four terms of any pattern.

Try-It #5-5

What is the units digit of 19^{40} ?

As shown in the table above, $9^1 = 9$, $9^2 = 81$, $9^3 = 729$, etc., and 19 will have the same units digit pattern as 9. Therefore, the pattern is a two-term repeating pattern: 9, 1, 9, 1.... This pattern alternates every two items, just like odd and even integers. Since 40 is an even number, the units digit of 19^{40} will equal 1. Try another example:

What is the remainder when 19^{40} is divided by 10 ?

This alternative question is asking the exact same thing as the original question. The remainder whenever an integer is divided by 10 will always be the same as the units digit of the original number:

$$\frac{84}{10} = 8\frac{4}{10} \rightarrow 8 \text{ remainder } 4 \qquad\qquad \frac{361}{10} = 36\frac{1}{10} \rightarrow 36 \text{ remainder } 1$$

$$\frac{7,819}{10} = 781\frac{9}{10} \rightarrow 781 \text{ remainder } 9$$

Remainder Problems

In general, remainders provide a means by which the GMAT can disguise an underlying pattern. For example, notice that when the positive integer n is divided by 4, the remainders follow a pattern as n increases consecutively:

$$\left. \begin{array}{l} 1 \div 4 \rightarrow \text{remainder } 1 \\ 2 \div 4 \rightarrow \text{remainder } 2 \\ 3 \div 4 \rightarrow \text{remainder } 3 \\ 4 \div 4 \rightarrow \text{remainder } 0 \\ 5 \div 4 \rightarrow \text{remainder } 1 \end{array} \right\}$$
A *repeating cycle* of [1, 2, 3, 0] emerges for the remainders when dividing the counting numbers by 4. The number of terms in the repeat equals the divisor in this case.

Conversely, you can calculate all of the numbers that have a certain remainder when divided by a certain value, because they appear at regular intervals as well. For instance, the numbers that have a remainder of 3 when divided by 4 are 3, 7, 11, 15, 19, 23, etc. Notice that those numbers are evenly spaced exactly 4 apart.

When a problem discusses remainders, look for patterns and take advantage of them.

Try-It #5-6

If x and y are positive integers, what is the remainder when 5^x is divided by y ?

(1) $x = 3$
(2) $y = 4$

$\dfrac{5^x}{y}$ $x = 3 \rightarrow \dfrac{125}{4}$ AB   C

(1) INSUFFICIENT: $5^3 = 125$. The problem provides no information about the value of y, however. For example, if $y = 5$, then the remainder equals 0. If $y = 6$, then the remainder is 5.

(2) SUFFICIENT: This statement may not initially appear to be sufficient, but test some different values for x:

x	5^x	Remainder of $\frac{5^x}{4}$
1	5	1
2	25	1
3	125	1
4	625	1

The pattern is clear: no matter what exponent 5 is raised to, the remainder when divided by 4 will always equal 1—a fact that you probably did not expect before testing the rule for this problem.

The correct answer is (B).

This problem is an example of a (C) Trap. If you used both statements, you could calculate the exact remainder. However, that would be too easy for a tough GMAT Quant problem. You don't actually *need* both statements to determine that the answer to the question is 1. Thanks to the remainder pattern, statement (2) is sufficient on its own.

Other Pattern Problems

Many questions will not at first glance demonstrate an obvious pattern. For example, a Word Problem involving counting a collection of objects or maximizing some number may hide some sort of regularity. The point is to discover a simple rule or group of rules that let you account for all the possibilities—and therefore count or maximize them—without having to generate each possibility separately.

Try-It #5-7

How many of the integers between 1 and 400, inclusive, are not divisible by 4 and do not contain any 4's as a digit?

This problem involves a *counting pattern*. It's clear that there are 400 integers between 1 and 400, inclusive. You'll need to subtract the integers that are divisible by 4 or contain a 4 as a digit. The tricky part is the overlap: some numbers, such as 64 and 124, violate both constraints.

It is easier to determine the number of multiples of 4. Since there are 400 integers in the set, and those 400 integers are consecutive, there must be $\frac{400}{4} = 100$ integers that are divisible by 4. There are $400 - 100 = 300$ integers remaining.

Next, consider the remaining numbers that have a 4 among their digits. These numbers have a 4 among their digits but *are not* themselves multiples of 4.

Only one of the integers between 1 and 400, inclusive, has a 4 in the hundreds place: 400. You have already eliminated that one from the count because it is a multiple of 4.

To eliminate integers with a 4 in the tens place, of the form $x4y$, count only those that are not multiples of 4. These are the numbers whose last two digits are 41, 42, 43, 45, 46, 47, or 49. There are seven such numbers in each set of "hundreds," that is, the 300's, the 200's, the 100's, and the no hundreds. That is a total of $7 \times 4 = 28$ terms. There are $300 - 28 = 272$ integers remaining.

Last, count and eliminate the integers with 4 in the units digit, of the form $xy4$, that have not already been subtracted. These are the numbers whose last two digits are 14, 34, 54, 74, or 94 (numbers with an even integer in the tens place and 4 in the units are all divisible by 4, so they have been eliminated already). There are 5 such numbers in each set of "hundreds," so that is a total of $5 \times 4 = 20$ terms. There are $272 - 20 = 252$ integers remaining.

The correct answer is $400 - 100 - 28 - 20 = 252$.

Try-It #5-8

$x = 10^{10} - z$, where z is a two-digit integer. If the sum of the digits of x equals 84, how many values for z are possible?

The first thing to do in solving this problem is to subtract any two-digit number from 10^{10} and look for a pattern. Try subtracting 24:

$$10^{10} = 10,000,000,000$$

$$
\begin{array}{r}
10,000,000,000 \\
-24 \\
\hline
9,999,999,976
\end{array}
$$

Notice the pattern: the first eight digits of x are all 9's, so those digits sum to 72. This will be true no matter which two-digit integer you try for z. Therefore, the final two digits of x must sum to $84 - 72 = 12$.

What possibilities would work for these final two digits of x? 39, 48, 57, 66, 75, 84, and 93 all add to 12. When subtracted from 100, these numbers will have to produce a two-digit integer. Try subtracting from 100 to find the pattern:

$$100 - 39 = 61 \qquad 100 - 48 = 52$$

Hmm. Each successive number is larger, so it will result in a smaller two-digit integer. Do the numbers actually drop to one digit at some point? Jump to the other end of the scale and try 93:

$$100 - 93 = 7$$

In order for x to end in 93, z would have to be 7, which is not a two-digit integer. According to the GMAT, a two-digit integer must have a nonzero tens digit and zeros for all higher places. What about the next number up? If x ends in 84, then it would result in the two-digit integer $100 - 84 = 16$. All of the other numbers are two-digit integers; only 93 doesn't work.

Therefore, the final two digits of x can only be 39, 48, 57, 66, 75, and 84, resulting in six possible values for z.

As the two previous problems demonstrate, unusual patterns can appear in problems on the GMAT. Sometimes you must "think outside the box" to identify the wanted pattern.

Look for the examples in the following chart:

Pattern Type	Example	Comments
Repeats	1, 3, −2, 1, 3, −2, 1, etc.	Often, these repeating patterns can only be identified by listing out a few values in the pattern. On the GMAT, the cycle is usually 4 numbers or fewer (the cycle in the example shown is 3).
Consecutive Integers	10, 11, 12, 13, 14, etc.	Can be defined as follows: $A_n = n + k$, where n and k are integers. In this example, $A_n = n + 9$, so that the first term is $1 + 9 = 10$. Note that the average term = the median term = $\frac{1}{2} \times$ (First + Last).
Consecutive Multiples	7, 14, 21, 28, etc.	Consecutive multiples of 7, for example, can be defined as follows: $A_n = 7n$, where n is a set of consecutive integers. The evens are just a special case (multiples of 2, or $2n$). Note that the average term = the median term = $\frac{1}{2} \times$ (First + Last).
Evenly Spaced Sets	9, 16, 23, 30, etc. (Constant difference of 7 between consecutive terms)	When dividing this series by 7, each of the terms leaves a remainder of 2. Can be defined as a multiple plus/minus a constant: $A_n = 7n + k$, where n is a set of consecutive integers, in this example. The odds are a special case (multiples of 2, plus 1, or $2n + 1$). Note that the average term = the median term = $\frac{1}{2} \times$ (First + Last), as for consecutive multiples.
Non-Uniform Spacing that Itself Follows a Pattern	0, 1, 3, 6, 10, 15, etc. (Spacing between terms follows 1, 2, 3, 4, 5, etc. pattern.)	Another example of this type is the perfect squares: 0, 1, 4, 9, 16, 25, etc. (Spacing between squares = 1, 3, 5, 7, 9, etc. = the odd integers!)
Alternating Sign	−1, 1, −2, 2, −3, 3, etc.	Can result from a $(-1)^n$ term in a direct sequence definition, or a $(-(A_{n-1}))$ term in a recursive sequence definition.

In general, listing five to eight examples or terms will usually be sufficient to identify a pattern on the GMAT—you can stop with fewer examples if you've identified the pattern by that point.

Problem Set

For the following problems, use the Pattern Recognition techniques discussed in this chapter to solve.

1. In the sequence 4, 9, 14, 19 ..., each term is 5 greater than the previous term. What is the remainder when the 75th term is divided by 9 ?

2. If x and y are integers between 0 and 9, inclusive, and the units digit of x^y is 5, what are the possible values of x and y ?

3. What is the remainder when $13^{17} + 17^{13}$ is divided by 10 ?

4. If y is a positive integer, what is the units digit of y ?

    (1) The units digit of y^2 equals 6.

    (2) The units digit of $(y + 1)^2$ equals 5.

5. If y is a positive integer, what is the units digit of y ?

    (1) The units digit of $y^2 = 1$.

    (2) The units digit of y does not equal 1.

6. In sequence A, $A_1 = 1$, $A_2 = 100$, and the value of A_n is strictly between the values of A_{n-1} and A_{n-2} for all $n \geq 3$. Which of the following must be true?

    (A) $A_{100} < A_{200} < A_{300} < A_{400}$

    (B) $A_{100} < A_{300} < A_{400} < A_{200}$

    (C) $A_{200} < A_{400} < A_{300} < A_{100}$

    (D) $A_{400} < A_{200} < A_{300} < A_{100}$

    (E) $A_{400} < A_{300} < A_{200} < A_{100}$

7. If x is an integer, what is the remainder when x is divided by 5 ?

    (1) x^2 has a remainder of 4 when divided by 5.

    (2) x^3 has a remainder of 2 when divided by 5.

8. If x and y are positive integers, what is the remainder when 5^x is divided by y ?

    (1) x is an even integer.

    (2) $y = 3$

9. a, b, c, and d are positive integers. If $\frac{a}{b}$ has a remainder of 9 and $\frac{c}{d}$ has a remainder of 10, what is the minimum possible value for bd ?

10. What is the sum of the numbers in the grid below?

1	−2	−1	2	3
3	−4	−2	3	6
5	−6	−3	4	9
7	−8	−4	5	12
9	−10	−5	6	15
11	−12	−6	7	18

(handwritten: 90, +15, 105, 42, 63)

(handwritten below table: 36, −42, −21, 27, 63, 90)

11. The sequence $a_1, a_2, a_3 \ldots a_n$ is defined such that $a_n = a_{n-1} + 9 + n$ for all $n > 1$. If $a_1 = 10$, what is the value of a_{11}?

12. The sequence S is defined as follows for all $n \geq 1$:

$$S_n = (-1)^n \frac{1}{n(n+1)}$$

The sum of the first 10 terms of S is

(A) Between -1 and $-\frac{1}{2}$

(B) Between $-\frac{1}{2}$ and 0

(C) Between 0 and $\frac{1}{2}$

(D) Between $\frac{1}{2}$ and 1

(E) Greater than 1

13. In sequence Q, the first number is 3, and each subsequent number in the sequence is determined by doubling the previous number and then adding 2. How many times does the digit 8 appear in the units digit of the first 10 terms of the sequence?

14. $\blacklozenge P \blacklozenge$ is defined as the product of all even integers r such that $0 < r \leq P$. For example, $\blacklozenge 14 \blacklozenge = 2 \times 4 \times 6 \times 8 \times 10 \times 12 \times 14$. If $\blacklozenge K \blacklozenge$ is divisible by 4^{11}, what is the smallest possible value for K?

(A) 22

(B) 24

(C) 28

(D) 32

(E) 44

15. Mitchell plans to work at a day camp over the summer. Each week, he will be paid according to the following schedule: At the end of the first week, he will receive $1. At the end of each subsequent week, he will receive $1, plus an additional amount equal to the sum of all payments he's received in previous weeks. How much money will Mitchell be paid in total during the summer, if he works for the entire duration of the 8-week-long camp?

Solutions

1. **5:** The sequence starts with the number 4, then adds 5 to each subsequent term. The math plays out in this way:

   1st term: 4

   2nd term: $4 + 5$

   3rd term: $4 + 5 + 5 = 4 + 5(2)$

   4th term: $4 + 5(3)$

   The sequence pattern is $4 + 5(n - 1)$, where n is the number of the term. The 75th term in the sequence is therefore $4 + 5(75 - 1) = 4 + 5(74) = 374$.

   In order to find the remainder, first find the multiple of 9 closest to 374 but smaller than that number. 360 is a multiple of 9, and so is 369. Therefore, $\frac{369}{9}$ has a remainder of 0, so $\frac{374}{9}$ has a remainder of 5.

2. $x = 5; 1 \leq y \leq 9$: Only the integer 5 can be raised to a power to result in a units digit of 5. Any power of 5 will have a units digit of 5, other than zero, because $5^0 = 1$. The integer y, on the other hand, can have any value except for 0.

3. **0:** The remainder when dividing an integer by 10 always equals the units digit. Ignore all but the units digits and rephrase the question: "What is the units digit of $3^{17} + 7^{13}$?"

   The pattern for the units digits of 3 is [3, 9, 7, 1]. Every fourth term is the same. The 17th power is 1 past the end of the repeat. Since 3^{16} ends in 1, 3^{17} must end in 3.

   The pattern for the units digits of 7 is [7, 9, 3, 1]. Every fourth term is the same. The 13th power is 1 past the end of the repeat. Since 7^{12} ends in 1, 7^{13} must end in 7.

   The sum of these units digits is $3 + 7 = 10$. Thus, the units digit is 0.

For problems #4 and #5, reference the following chart:

For integers ending in a certain digit, the table shows the units digit pattern. For example, integers ending in 2 have a units digit pattern of 2, 4, 8, 6. Integers ending in 9 have a units digit pattern of 9, 1.

	1	2	3	4	5	6	7	8	9	0
y^1	1	2	3	4	5	6	7	8	9	0
y^2	1	4	9	6	5	6	9	4	1	0
y^3	1	8	7	4	5	6	3	2	9	0
y^4	1	6	1	6	5	6	1	6	1	0

4. **(B):**

   (1) INSUFFICIENT: According to the Units Digit Patterns chart above, both 4 and 6 yield a units digit of 6 when raised to the second power. (Notice that you would only need to check even numbers for this statement, as odd numbers to any power cannot end in a 6, an even number.)

(2) SUFFICIENT: Only 5 yields a units digit of 5 when raised to *any* power. Since the units digit of $y + 1$ is 5, the units digit of y must be 4.

The correct answer is **(B)**.

5. **(C):** Begin with statement (2).

    (2) INSUFFICIENT: The statement indicates only that the units digit does not equal 1, but it could still be any other digit.

    (1) INSUFFICIENT: Because both 1 and 9 yield a units digit of 1 when raised to the second power, there are two possible values for the units digit.

    (1) AND (2) SUFFICIENT: The two statements together indicate that the units digit of y must be 9.

    The correct answer is **(C)**.

6. **(E)** $A_{400} < A_{300} < A_{200} < A_{100}$: The answer choices refer to terms that are very late and very far apart in the sequence. Since there isn't time to calculate that many terms, there must be a pattern. Write down what you know about the first few terms in order to identify that pattern.

    Each term in the sequence is *strictly between* the two terms that come immediately before it. To keep track of this, draw a number line on your paper. Put the third term of the sequence somewhere between the first two terms:

    Continue to add terms to the number line, making sure to put each term between the two that came before it. The first eight terms have been plotted on the number line shown below:

    The odd-numbered terms of the sequence appear in increasing order, so that $A_1 < A_3 < A_5 < A_7$ and so on. The even-numbered terms are in decreasing order so that $A_2 > A_4 > A_6 > A_8$, etc.

    The answer choices only refer to even-numbered terms, so the terms should be in decreasing order, with A_{100} being the greatest and A_{400} being the least.

    The correct answer is **(E)**.

7. **(B):** Because the question is asking about the remainder when *x* is divided by 5, you only need to check the units digits 0 through 4. The pattern will recycle for the next set of 5 (5 through 9) and for every set of 5 after that.

(1) INSUFFICIENT:

x	x^2	$\frac{x^2}{5}$ = remainder of 4	$\frac{x}{5}$ = remainder of ?
0	0	No (invalid)	
1	1	No (invalid)	
2	4	Yes	$\frac{2}{5}$ = 0 remainder 2
3	9	Yes	$\frac{3}{5}$ = 0 remainder 3

There are at least two possible values for the remainder.

(2) SUFFICIENT:

x	x^3	$\frac{x^3}{5}$ = remainder of 2	$\frac{x}{5}$ = remainder of ?
0	0	No (invalid)	
1	1	No (invalid)	
2	8	No (invalid)	
3	27	Yes	$\frac{3}{5}$ = 0 remainder 3
4	64	No (invalid)	

There is only one possible remainder: 3.

If you aren't sure that you only need to test these five cases, try the next five values for *x*. Note the repeat of the remainder pattern. Only every third term (3, 8, 13, and so on) will be valid based on the information from statement (2) and will always have a remainder of 3.

The correct answer is **(B)**.

8. **(C):** 5^x will always end in 5.

(1) INSUFFICIENT: If *x* is even, then $5^x = 25, 625$, and so on. This statement provides no information about *y*, though. For example if *y* = 5, then $\frac{25}{5}$ = 5 remainder 0. If *y* = 4, then $\frac{25}{4}$ = 6 remainder 1.

(2) INSUFFICIENT: Test some different values for *x*.

x	5^x	Remainder of $\frac{5^x}{3}$
1	5	2
2	25	1
3	125	2
4	625	1

After testing the first two numbers, it's clear that statement (2) is not sufficient. Because you will have to test the two statements together, continue testing another couple of numbers to see whether there is a pattern. When 5 is raised to an odd power, the remainder is 2, but when 5 is raised to an even power, the remainder is 1.

(1) AND (2) SUFFICIENT: When $5^{\text{even integer}}$ is divided by 3, the remainder is always 1.

The correct answer is **(C)**.

9. **110:** The remainder must always be smaller than the divisor. Thus, *b* must be at least 10, and *d* must be at least 11. Therefore, *bd* must be at least 110. The purpose of this problem is to remind you of these constraints on remainders.

10. **63:** Each column contains a series of evenly spaced integers. To avoid calculation, cancel out as many values as possible before summing the remaining values.

In each row, the sum of the integers in the first two columns is −1, and the sum of the integers in the third and fourth columns is 1. Therefore, the sum of the integers in the first four columns in each row is −1 + 1 = 0. Only the integers in the fifth column need to be considered.

The integers in the fifth column can be rewritten as follows:

$$3(1) + 3(2) + 3(3) + 3(4) + 3(5) + 3(6)$$
$$3(1 + 2 + 3 + 4 + 5 + 6)$$

The sum of the integers is therefore 3(21) = 63.

11. **165:** Write out the first few terms of the sequence to find the pattern.

$$a_1 = 10$$
$$a_2 = a_1 + 9 + 2$$
$$a_3 = a_2 + 9 + 3$$
$$a_4 = a_3 + 9 + 4$$
$$\dots$$

5

To simplify the calculation, these terms can be rewritten as follows:

$$a_1 = 10$$
$$a_2 = a_1 + 10 + 1$$
$$a_3 = a_2 + 10 + 2$$
$$a_4 = a_3 + 10 + 3$$
$$\ldots$$
$$a_{11} = a_{10} + 10 + 10$$

Therefore, the nth term in the sequence can be found by adding 10 a total of n times, then adding the sum of the integers from 1 to $n - 1$, inclusive. For $n = 11$, this value is equal to $10(11) + (1 + 2 + 3 + \ldots + 10)$, which equals $10(11) + 55 = 165$.

12. **(B) Between $-\dfrac{1}{2}$ and 0:** Compute the first few elements of S_n.

n	S_n
1	$(-1)^1 \dfrac{1}{1 \times 2} = -\dfrac{1}{2}$
2	$(-1)^2 \dfrac{1}{2 \times 3} = \dfrac{1}{6}$
3	$(-1)^3 \dfrac{1}{3 \times 4} = -\dfrac{1}{12}$
4	$(-1)^4 \dfrac{1}{4 \times 5} = \dfrac{1}{20}$
5	$(-1)^5 \dfrac{1}{5 \times 6} = -\dfrac{1}{30}$

Use a number line to track the sum:

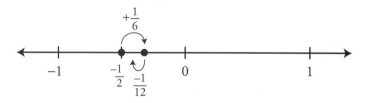

Place the first term, $-\dfrac{1}{2}$, on the number line. The second term is $+\dfrac{1}{6}$, so the sum will move to the right (closer to 0) on the number line. The third term is $-\dfrac{1}{12}$, so the sum will move to the left, but it can't go as far as $-\dfrac{1}{2}$ again, because you're only subtracting $\dfrac{1}{12}$ this time—the distance is smaller than the first $\dfrac{1}{6}$ hop that you made.

Each subsequent hop flips back and forth between positive and negative but also keeps getting smaller and smaller, so you'll never "break out" of the range $-\dfrac{1}{2}$ to 0.

The correct answer is **(B)**.

13.   **9:** Calculate the first several terms of the sequence to find the pattern:

$$Q_1 = 3$$
$$Q_2 = 2(3) + 2 = 8$$
$$Q_3 = 2(8) + 2 = 18$$
$$Q_4 = 2(18) + 2 = 38$$
$$Q_5 = 2(38) + 2 = 78$$
$$\dots$$

The pattern should continue, so 8 will be the units digit 9 out of the first 10 times.

14.   **(B) 24:** This is a counting pattern problem. In order for ◆K◆ to be divisible by 4^{11}, it must be divisible by $(2^2)^{11} = 2^{22}$. Thus, ◆K◆ must contain 22 twos in its prime factorization.

If $K = 10$, for example, then ◆K◆ equals $2 \times 4 \times 6 \times 8 \times 10$. The number 2 has one 2 in its prime factorization; 4 has two 2's; 6 has one 2 (and a 3); 8 has three 2's; 10 has one 2 (and a 5). This amounts to a total of only eight 2's:

Number	2	4	6	8	10
Prime Factor(s)	2	2, 2	2, 3	2, 2, 2	2, 5
Total 2's in PF	1	2	1	3	1
Cumulative 2's	1	3	4	7	8

Keep adding even numbers to the result until you get to 22 twos in total:

Number	2	4	6	8	10	12	14	16	18	20	22	24
Prime Factor(s)	2	2, 2	2, 3	2, 2, 2	2, 5	2, 2, 3	2, 7	2, 2, 2, 2	2, 3, 3	2, 2, 5	2, 11	2, 2, 2, 3
Total 2's in PF	1	2	1	3	1	2	1	4	1	2	1	3
Cumulative 2's	1	3	4	7	8	10	11	15	16	18	19	22

Thus, the smallest possible value for K is 24. Notice the pattern in the number of 2's in each even number: 1, 2, 1, 3, 1, 2, 1, 4, 1, 2, 1 ...

The correct answer is **(B)**.

15. **$255 (or $2^8 - 1$):** At the end of the first week, Mitchell receives $1. At the end of the second week, he gets $1, plus $1 for the total he had been paid up to that point, for a total of $2. At the end of the third week, he gets $1, plus ($1 + $2), or $3, for the total he had been paid up to that point, so this third week's total is $4. Put this in a table:

Week #	Paid This Week ($)	Cumulative Pay Including This Week ($)
1	1	1
2	$1 + 1 = 2$	$1 + 2 = 3$
3	$1 + 3 = 4$	$3 + 4 = 7$
4	$1 + 7 = 8$	$7 + 8 = 15$
5	$1 + 15 = 16$	$15 + 16 = 31$
6	$1 + 31 = 32$	$31 + 32 = 63$
7	$1 + 63 = 64$	$63 + 64 = 127$
8	$1 + 127 = 128$	$127 + 128 = 255$

This calculation is not so bad, but you may notice that this payment schedule is a geometric sequence, 2^{n-1}, where n is the number of the week in which Mitchell is being paid. Summing that sequence is equivalent to $2^t - 1$, where t is the total number of weeks. In other words, the cumulative pay is one less than the next power of 2.

The correct answer is $2^8 - 1 = \$255$.

5

Common Terms & Quadratic Templates

In This Chapter

- Common Terms
- Quadratic Templates
- Quadratic Templates in Disguise

CHAPTER 6 Common Terms & Quadratic Templates

You are probably already familiar with the *mechanics* of algebraic manipulations—what is allowed and what is not:

- You can substitute one expression for another if they are equal.
- You can add some number to one side of an equation as long as you do the same on the other side of the equation.
- You can cross-multiply to simplify equations with fractions on each side of the equals sign. And so on.

But of all the steps you *could* take, how do you decide which steps you *should* take?

Two indicators can often help you on the GMAT:

1. Common Terms
2. Quadratic Templates

Common Terms

If you spot common terms, you can often spot the path all the way to the solution. Common terms appear on the GMAT in three typical ways.

1. Algebra

Look for terms that appear in the same form more than once. Those recurring expressions might also appear in slightly modified form such as reciprocal, negative, or raised to a power:

If $\dfrac{a}{b} = \dfrac{3}{5}$, then $\dfrac{b+a}{a} = ?$	$\dfrac{b}{a}$ is the reciprocal of $\dfrac{a}{b}$.	$\dfrac{b+a}{a} = \dfrac{b}{a} + \dfrac{a}{a} = \dfrac{5}{3} + 1 = \dfrac{8}{3}$
Is $\dfrac{1}{a^2 - b^2} < b^2 - a^2$?	$b^2 - a^2$ is negative $a^2 - b^2$.	Is $\dfrac{1}{x} < -x$? where $a^2 - b^2 = x$
$\left(\dfrac{x}{3y}\right)^2 + 2\left(\dfrac{x}{3y}\right)(3y) + (3y)^2$ $\underbrace{\quad}_{a} \qquad \underbrace{\quad}_{b}$	$\dfrac{x}{3y}$ and $3y$ appear both squared and multiplied together.	This expression is of the form: $a^2 + 2ab + b^2 = (a+b)^2$ (More on Quadratic Templates later in this chapter)

Try-It #6-1

If $y \neq 3$, simplify as much as possible: $\dfrac{2y^2(3-y)-3+y}{3-y}$

Spot the common term $(3-y)$. Note that $(-3+y)$ is $-(3-y)$, or $-1 \times (3-y)$.

Factor out the common term $(3-y)$ and cancel: $\dfrac{\cancel{(3-y)}\left(2y^2-1\right)}{\cancel{3-y}} = 2y^2 - 1.$

By the way, the condition that y could not equal 3 just prevented you from dividing by 0 and ending up with an undefined number.

2. Exponents

Exponents can be manipulated when either bases or exponents are common. Also look for bases that have common factors, such as 3 and 12 (common factor of 3). You can often create a common base. For example:

$$(16^x)(4^2) = 256$$

4 is a factor of 4, 16, and 256.

Similarly, 4, 16, and 256 are all powers of 4.

$$\left(16^x\right)\left(4^2\right) = 256$$
$$\left(4^2\right)^x\left(4^2\right) = 4^4$$
$$4^{2x+2} = 4^4$$
$$2x + 2 = 4$$
$$x = 1$$

Try-It #6-2

If $3^x + 243 = 2(3^x)$, what is the value of x?

Note the common term 3^x, and note the fact that $243 = 3^5$:

$$\boxed{3^x} + \boxed{243} = 2\left(3^x\right)$$
$$3^x + 243 = 3^x + 3^x$$
$$243 = 3^x$$
$$3^5 = 3^x$$
$$5 = x$$

3. Factors and Multiples

When many terms share a factor, pull that shared factor *out to the side*. These can appear in algebraic or numerical expressions:

$$x^{18} + 2x^{16} + x^{14} \quad \rightarrow \quad x^{14} \text{ is a factor of each term} \quad \rightarrow \quad x^{14}(x^4 + 2x^2 + 1) = x^{14}(x^2+1)^2$$

$$\dfrac{\frac{8}{15} - \frac{2}{5}}{\frac{1}{3} + \frac{2}{15}} \quad \rightarrow \quad \text{get common denominators, then cross them all off} \quad \rightarrow \quad \dfrac{\frac{8}{15} - \frac{6}{15}}{\frac{5}{15} + \frac{2}{15}} = \dfrac{(8-6)}{(5+2)} = \dfrac{2}{7}$$

Factorials are particularly noteworthy, as they often have an abundance of shared factors. For any integer n, the factorial $n!$ is calculated as follows: $n! = n(n - 1)(n - 2)(n - 3)\ldots 1$. Thus, all the terms in $4! = (4)(3)(2)(1)$ are also common factors of $6! = (6)(5)(4)(3)(2)(1) = (6)(5)(4!)$.

More generally, factorials are "super multiples." Without ever computing their precise value, you can tell that they're divisible by all sorts of numbers. For example:

| If x is an integer between $7! + 2$ and $7! + 4$, inclusive, is x prime? | x is one of the following integers:

$7! + 2 = (7)(6)(5)(4)(3)(\mathbf{2})(1) + \mathbf{2}$
$7! + 3 = (7)(6)(5)(4)(\mathbf{3})(2)(1) + \mathbf{3}$
$7! + 4 = (7)(6)(5)(\mathbf{4})(3)(2)(1) + \mathbf{4}$ | x has one of the following factors, if x is:

$7! + 2 = \mathbf{2} \times$ Integer
$7! + 3 = \mathbf{3} \times$ Integer
$7! + 4 = \mathbf{4} \times$ Integer $\ldots$ so x is not prime! |

Sometimes a common factor is just a random number buried inside a couple of larger numbers. Find it and pull it out:

| $\dfrac{10.1010}{5.0505} =$ | 10's in the numerator line up with 5's in the corresponding digit place of the denominator:

$\dfrac{10\,10\,10}{5\,05\,05}$ | $\dfrac{10.1010}{5.0505} = \dfrac{10(1.0101)}{5(1.0101)}$

$= \dfrac{10}{5}$

$= 2$ |

Try-It #6-3

If n is a positive integer and $\sqrt{(45)(14)(7^n) - (15)(7^{n-1})(54)}$ is a positive integer, what is the value of n?

(1) n is prime.

(2) $n < 3$

What would need to be true in order for the square root to be a positive integer? The number under the square root symbol would have to be a perfect square. Rearrange the expression to determine whether there are any restrictions that could help narrow down the possibilities before going to the statements. Try to break the numbers down into primes to locate and pull out any existing perfect squares:

$$\sqrt{(45)(14)(7^n) - (15)(7^{n-1})(54)}$$

$$\sqrt{(3^2)(5)(2)(7)(7^n) - (3)(5)(7^{n-1})(3^3)(2)}$$

Pull out common terms:

$$\sqrt{(3^2)(5)(2)\left[(7^{n+1}) - (7^{n-1})(3^2)\right]}$$

It turns out that you can also pull out the term 7^{n-1}. The term $7^{n+1} = (7^{n-1})(7^2)$:

$$\sqrt{(3^2)(5)(2)(7^{n-1})[7^2 - 3^2]}$$
$$\sqrt{(3^2)(5)(2)(7^{n-1})[49 - 9]}$$
$$\sqrt{(3^2)(5)(2)(7^{n-1})(40)}$$
$$\sqrt{(3^2)(400)(7^{n-1})}$$

The first two terms are both perfect squares and can be pulled out of the square root sign:

$$(3)(20)\sqrt{7^{n-1}}$$

What would need to be true in order for 7^{n-1} to be pulled out of the square root sign? It would also have to be a perfect square, so $n - 1$ must be even and n itself must be odd.

The question is: "If n is odd, what is the value of n?"

(1) INSUFFICIENT: This statement allows multiple possible odd values of n.

(2) SUFFICIENT: The question stem indicates that n is a positive integer, and this statement specifies that $n < 3$. The only odd, positive integer less than 3 is the number 1.

The correct answer is (B).

6

Quadratic Templates

On the GMAT, quadratic expressions take three common forms called the Quadratic Templates. Memorize these templates, and get comfortable transforming back and forth between factored and distributed form:

	Factored	$\leftrightarrow$	Distributed
Square of a Sum	$(a + b)^2$	$=$	$a^2 + 2ab + b^2$
Square of a Difference	$(a - b)^2$	$=$	$a^2 - 2ab + b^2$
Difference of Two Squares	$(a + b)(a - b)$	$=$	$a^2 - b^2$

Quick Manipulation

Expressions with both squared and non-squared common terms should make you suspect that you are looking at a Quadratic Template.

Try-It #6-4

Factor $\left(\dfrac{x}{3}\right)^2 + 2\left(\dfrac{x}{3}\right)(5y) + (5y)^2$.

This problem requires you to manipulate a rather complicated expression. However, by using the common terms, you can put the problem in the more basic template form to solve:

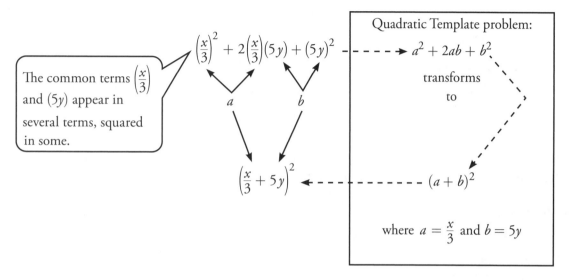

Once you are comfortable with Quadratic Templates, you can manipulate even complicated expressions quickly, as in the middle box above. Until then, write down the templates and the substitution of the common terms, as in the box on the right.

The very same problem could have been presented in disguise:

Factor $\dfrac{x^2}{9} + \dfrac{10xy}{3} + 25y^2$.

The common terms are slightly harder to spot in this form. In such a case, start with the squared terms, $\dfrac{x^2}{9}$ and $25y^2$. Then, try to untangle their square roots, $\dfrac{x}{3}$ and $5y$, from the remaining term. The factored form is:

$$\left(\dfrac{x}{3} + 5y\right)^2$$

Consider all three of the common Quadratic Templates before deciding which one or ones are most convenient to use.

The Middle Term: 2ab

The *square of a sum* and *square of a difference* templates have something in common: the middle term is $\pm 2ab$. The only difference is the sign of that middle term.

When you *add* these two templates, the middle terms cancel, leaving the *end* terms:

	Factored	⟷	Distributed
Square of a Sum	$(a+b)^2$	$=$	$a^2 + 2ab + b^2$
+ Square of a Difference	$(a-b)^2$	$=$	$a^2 - 2ab + b^2$
Addition:	$(a+b)^2 + (a-b)^2$	$=$	$2a^2 + 0 + 2b^2$ $2(a^2 + b^2)$

In contrast, when you *subtract* these two templates, the end terms cancel, leaving the *middle* term:

	Factored	⟷	Distributed
Square of a Sum	$(a+b)^2$	$=$	$a^2 + 2ab + b^2$
+ Square of a Difference	$(a-b)^2$	$=$	$a^2 - 2ab + b^2$
Subtraction:	$(a+b)^2 - (a-b)^2$	$=$	$0 + 4ab + 0$

This is handy for simplification. Also, whenever you see the *sum of two squares* $(a^2 + b^2)$, which is not itself a Quadratic Template, remember that it can be derived from this sum of two templates.

Try It #6-5

What is the sum of $9{,}999^2$ and $10{,}001^2$?

(A) 99,980,001

(B) 199,999,998

(C) 200,000,002

(D) 399,999,996

(E) 400,000,004

These numbers all look seriously cumbersome. If only they had given the easier number of 10,000 instead…

When wishful thinking pops up, try to use it to make the problem easier. If you changed both of these numbers to the form 10,000 plus or minus a number, what would that be?

$$(10{,}000 - 1)^2 + (10{,}000 + 1)^2 = ?$$

These are the Quadratic Templates! In this case, $a = 10{,}000$ and $b = 1$. If you've memorized the *sum* term, plug these in:

$$\text{Sum} = 2\left(a^2 + b^2\right)$$
$$\text{Sum} = 2\left(10{,}000^2 + 1^2\right)$$

Now, notice something: the part in the parentheses is going to have a units digit of 1. Multiply the number by 2, and the end result will have a units digit of 2. Only answer choice (C) fits.

Not sure about that? Go ahead and do the math:

$$2(100{,}000{,}000 + 1) =$$
$$200{,}000{,}002$$

The correct answer is (C).

Even if you don't memorize the sum term of the Quadratic Templates, the math is still far easier to do in this rewritten form:

$$(10,000 - 1)^2 + (10,000 + 1)^2 =$$
$$(100,000,000 - 20,000 + 1) + (100,000,000 + 20,000 + 1)$$
$$200,000,000 + 2$$
$$200,000,002$$

Quadratic Templates in Disguise

Quadratic Templates can be disguised in arithmetic computations.

Try-It #6-6

What is 198×202 ?

You can round each number and quickly estimate the result to be about 200^2. Or, you could laboriously multiply two 3-digit numbers by hand to get an exact result. But if you need an exact result quickly, you can use a Quadratic Template, as shown in the previous section. You just need to turn 198 into $(200 - 2)$ and 202 into $(200 + 2)$ as shown here:

$$198 \times 202 = (200 - 2)(200 + 2)$$
$$= 200^2 - 2^2$$
$$= 40,000 - 4$$
$$= 39,996$$

Another place to hide a Quadratic Template is in an advanced right-triangle problem:

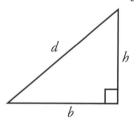

You know that Area $= \frac{1}{2}bh$ and $d^2 = b^2 + h^2$ (by the Pythagorean theorem). Do the common terms b^2, h^2, and bh look familiar? Use the Square of a Sum template:

$$(b + h)^2 = b^2 + 2bh + h^2 = (b^2 + h^2) + 4\left(\frac{bh}{2}\right)$$
$$(b + h)^2 = d^2 + 4(\text{Area})$$

Likewise, there is a similar relationship based on the Square of a Difference template:

$$(b - h)^2 = b^2 - 2bh + h^2 = \left(b^2 + h^2\right) - 4\left(\frac{bh}{2}\right)$$
$$(b - h)^2 = d^2 - 4(\text{Area})$$

An advanced GMAT problem can draw on these complicated relationships. For instance, you can compute the area of a right triangle directly from the sum of the shorter sides and the hypotenuse:

$$(b + h)^2 = d^2 + 4(\text{Area})$$

$$\frac{(b + h)^2 - d^2}{4} = (\text{Area})$$

You should absolutely *not* memorize these particular formulas. Rather, be able to recognize when the GMAT is indirectly testing these generic Quadratic Templates.

6

Problem Set

For the following problems, use the Pattern Recognition techniques discussed in this chapter to solve.

1. If $xy > 0$, is $\left(5^x\right)^{\frac{1}{y}} > 25$?

   (1) $\quad 2\left(\dfrac{xy^4}{x^2}\right)^2 = \dfrac{16y^5}{x^2}$

   (2) $\quad x > 2y$

   For problems 2–4, if $x < -1$, which of the following inequalities must be true?

2. Is $x^4 > x^2$?

3. Is $x^3 + x^4 > x^3 + x^2$?

4. Is $x^6 - x^7 > x^5 - x^6$?

5. If, $\dfrac{(x+y)^2}{xy+y^2} = 3$ and $|x| \neq |y|$, what is the ratio of x to y ?

   (A) $4:1$

   (B) $3:1$

   (C) $2:1$

   (D) $3:2$

   (E) $1:3$

6. If $\dfrac{a}{b} = \dfrac{1}{8}$, what is the value of $\dfrac{a^2+b^2}{ab}$?

7. If n is an integer and $(-3)^{4n} = 3^{7n-3}$, then $n = ?$

8. If $(ax+by)^2 = (bx+ay)^2$, what is the value of $a - b$?

   (1) $\quad x^2 > y^2$

   (2) $\quad a$ and b are positive integers.

9. If x and k are both integers, $x > k$, and $x^{-k} = 625$, what is x ?

   (1) $\quad |k|$ is a prime number.

   (2) $\quad x + k > 20$

   Distribute the expression in problems 10–14 without FOILing (doing the math the long way). Use the Quadratic Templates.

10. $\left(x + \dfrac{1}{x}\right)^2$

11. $\left(x^2 - y\right)^2$

12. $\left(z^2 + \dfrac{1}{z}\right)\left(z^2 - \dfrac{1}{z}\right)$

13. $\left(5 - \sqrt{21}\right)\left(5 + \sqrt{21}\right)$

14. $\left(a - \dfrac{b}{2}\right)^2$

Factor problems 15–19 according to the Quadratic Templates.

15. $y^4 - 2 + \dfrac{1}{y^4}$

16. $4 + 4a + a^2$

17. $81 - x^4$

18. $x + 2\sqrt{xyz} + yz$

19. $4x^2 - 12xy + 9y^2$

For problems 20–23, simplify the expressions completely.

20. $\left(\sqrt{x} + \sqrt{y}\right)^2 + \left(\sqrt{x} - \sqrt{y}\right)^2$

21. $\left(\sqrt{x} + \sqrt{\dfrac{1}{x}}\right)^2 - \left(\sqrt{x} - \sqrt{\dfrac{1}{x}}\right)^2$

22. $(111)(89)$

23. $350^2 - 320^2$

24.

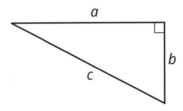

In the right triangle below, side a is 7 inches longer than side b. If the area of the triangle is 30 inches^2, what is the length of hypotenuse c ?

Solutions

1. **(C):** From $xy > 0$, you know that neither x nor y equals 0, and they must have the same sign $(++ \text{ or } --)$.

   Combine the exponent in the question to get $5^{\frac{x}{y}} > 25$.

   What is the significance of the inequality in the question stem? If the exponent equals 2, then $5^2 = 25$. In order to be greater than 25, the exponent has to be greater than 2. The question can be rephrased as "Is $\frac{x}{y} > 2$?"

   You may want to start with statement (2).

   (2) INSUFFICIENT: If y is positive, then $\frac{x}{y} > 2$. If, on the other hand, y is negative, then $\frac{x}{y} < 2$.

   (1) INSUFFICIENT: Simplify the equation:

   $$2\left(\frac{xy^4}{x^2}\right)^2 = \frac{16y^5}{x^2}$$

   $$2\left(\frac{y^8}{x^2}\right) = \frac{16y^5}{x^2}$$

   $$2y^8 = 16y^5$$

   $$y^8 = 8y^5$$

   Therefore, y^3 must equal 8, so $y = 2$. This provides no information about x, however.

   (1) AND (2) SUFFICIENT: If $y = 2$, then you can plug into statement (2) to find the range of values for x. Since $x > 2y$ and y is positive, you can divide the expression by y, giving $\frac{x}{y} > 2$.

   The correct answer is **(C)**.

For questions 2–4: since $x \neq 0$, divide by the common terms, making sure to flip the inequality sign if the common term is negative.

2. **TRUE:**

$x^4 > \boxed{x^2}$	Note: x^2 is positive.
$x^2 > 1?$	Divide both sides by x^2, leaving the sign as it is.
True	The square of a number smaller than -1 will be greater than positive 1.

3. **TRUE:**

$x^3 + x^4 > x^3 + \boxed{x^2}$	Note: x^2 is positive.
$x + x^2 > x + 1$	Divide both sides by x^2, leaving the sign as it is.
$x^2 > 1$	Subtract x from both sides.
True	(Or, you might have subtracted x^3 immediately.)

4. **TRUE:**

$$x^6 - x^7 > \boxed{x^5} - x^6 \qquad \text{Note: } x^5 \text{ is negative.}$$

$$x - x^2 < 1 - x \qquad \text{Divide both sides by } x^5, \text{ flipping the inequality sign.}$$

$$2x - 1 < x^2 \qquad \text{Group like terms.}$$

$$\text{neg} < \text{pos?}$$

True

5. **(C) 2 : 1:** Try to find like terms in order to simplify the left-hand side of the equation:

$$\frac{(x+y)^2}{xy + y^2} = 3$$

$$\frac{(x+y)^2}{y(x+y)} = 3$$

$$\frac{x+y}{y} = 3$$

$$\frac{x}{y} + \frac{y}{y} = 3$$

$$\frac{x}{y} + 1 = 3$$

$$\frac{x}{y} = 2$$

The ratio of x to y is 2 : 1.

The correct answer is **(C)**.

6. $\dfrac{\mathbf{65}}{\mathbf{8}}$: Since $\dfrac{a}{b} = \dfrac{1}{8}$, $\dfrac{a^2 + b^2}{ab} = \dfrac{a^2}{ab} + \dfrac{b^2}{ab} = \dfrac{a}{b} + \dfrac{b}{a} = \dfrac{1}{8} + 8 = \dfrac{65}{8}$

7. $\mathbf{\mathit{n} = 1:}$ Since n is an integer, $4n$ is even. An even exponent "hides the sign" of the base, so you can treat the (-3) base as a (3):

$$(-3)^{4n} = (3)^{7n-3}$$

$$(3)^{4n} = (3)^{7n-3}$$

$$4n = 7n - 3$$

$$3 = 3n$$

$$1 = n$$

8. **(C):** Begin by simplifying the equation in the question stem, making it look as similar as possible to the question itself:

$$\left(ax + by\right)^2 = \left(bx + ay\right)^2$$
$$a^2x^2 + 2abxy + b^2y^2 = b^2x^2 + 2abxy + a^2y^2$$
$$a^2x^2 + b^2y^2 = b^2x^2 + a^2y^2$$
$$a^2x^2 - a^2y^2 = b^2x^2 - b^2y^2$$
$$a^2\left(x^2 - y^2\right) = b^2\left(x^2 - y^2\right)$$

Do not divide by $x^2 - y^2$, since it may equal 0. Instead, subtract $b^2(x^2 - y^2)$ from both sides of the equation, then factor:

$$a^2\left(x^2 - y^2\right) - b^2\left(x^2 - y^2\right) = 0$$
$$\left(a^2 - b^2\right)\left(x^2 - y^2\right) = 0$$

So either $a^2 - b^2 = 0$ (in which case $a^2 = b^2$), or $x^2 - y^2 = 0$ (in which case $x^2 = y^2$). One or both of these must be true.

(1) INSUFFICIENT: If $x^2 > y^2$, then x^2 cannot equal y^2. Therefore, $a^2 = b^2$.

Case 1: It is possible that a and b are equal, in which case $a - b = 0$, so the answer is 0.

Case 2: It is also possible that a and b are equal in absolute value but have opposite signs. For example, $a = -2$ and $b = 2$. In this case, the answer is $a - b = -4$.

More than one answer is possible, so this statement is not sufficient.

(2) INSUFFICIENT: This statement only says that a and b are positive integers, but does not give further indication of what they could be. There are many possible answers for the value of $a - b$, so this statement is insufficient.

(1) AND (2) SUFFICIENT: According to statement (1), $a^2 = b^2$. Thus, either $a = b$ or $a = -b$. According to statement (2), a and b are both positive, so it is not possible that $a = -b$. Therefore, $a = b$, and the answer to the question is $a - b = 0$. The statements together are sufficient.

The correct answer is **(C)**.

9. **(A):** The fact that x and k are both integers (and that $x > k$) significantly limits the possible values for x and k. The possible pairings are as follows:

x	k
5	−4
25	−2
625	−1

(1) SUFFICIENT: If the absolute value of k is prime, then only the second possibility works: $x = 25$ and $k = -2$.

(2) INSUFFICIENT: The second and third possibilities both make this statement true, so it isn't possible to determine a single value for x.

10. $x^2 + 2 + \dfrac{1}{x^2}$

11. $x^4 - 2x^2 y + y^2$

12. $z^4 - \dfrac{1}{z^2}$

13. **4:**

$$5^2 - \left(\sqrt{21}\right)^2 = 25 - 21 = 4$$

14. $a^2 - ab + \dfrac{b^2}{4}$

15. $\left(y^2 - \dfrac{1}{y^2}\right)^2$

16. $(2 + a)^2$

17. $\left(9 + x^2\right)(3 + x)(3 - x)$:

$$\left(9 + x^2\right)\left(9 - x^2\right) = \left(9 + x^2\right)(3 + x)(3 - x)$$

18. $\left(\sqrt{x} + \sqrt{yz}\right)^2$

19. $(2x - 3y)^2$

20. $2(x + y)$

21. **4:**

$$4\sqrt{x}\sqrt{\dfrac{1}{x}} = 4\sqrt{\dfrac{x}{x}} = 4$$

22. **9,879:**

$$(100 + 11)(100 - 11) = \left(100^2 - 11^2\right) = 10{,}000 - 121 = 9{,}879$$

23. **20,100:**

$$(350 + 320)(350 - 320) = (670)(30) = 20{,}100$$

24. $(a - b) = 7$ and $\frac{1}{2}ab = 30$: From the Pythagorean theorem, $a^2 + b^2 = c^2$.

Use the Square of a Difference template:

$$(a - b)^2 = a^2 - 2ab + b^2$$
$$= \left(a^2 + b^2\right) - 2ab$$
$$= \left(c^2\right) - 4\left(\frac{1}{2}ab\right)$$

Plug in the values:

$$7^2 = \left(c^2\right) - 4(30)$$
$$49 + 120 = c^2$$
$$169 = c^2$$
$$13 = c$$

Visual Solutions

In This Chapter

- Representing Objects with Pictures

- Rubber Band Geometry

- Baseline Calculations for Averages

- Number Line Techniques for Statistics Problems

CHAPTER 7 Visual Solutions

Visual interpretations—good pictures, essentially—can help you solve certain types of GMAT problems. This chapter highlights some of these types of problems and demonstrates how you can use visual techniques to solve these problems more confidently, accurately, and quickly.

Many problems discussed in this chapter can be solved with other techniques. Still, visual thinking is a powerful tool. It can expand your comprehension of a topic. It may enable you to solve particular problem types more easily or "break through" on a difficult problem. In fact, visualization is the only realistic way to approach certain problems. So it's worth trying your hand with visual approaches.

In this chapter, we will discuss the following Visual Solution techniques:

- **Representing Objects with Pictures:** Many Word Problems and Geometry problems do not provide a diagram alongside the problem. Drawing a good picture will make the problem-solving process easier and less error-prone.

- **Rubber Band Geometry:** For Geometry questions involving both constraints and flexibility (especially in Data Sufficiency), drawing different "rubber band" scenarios according to those constraints and freedoms can often help you solve the problem without doing *any* computation.

- **Baseline Calculations for Averages:** Visual techniques can help you compute averages (both basic and weighted) and can also foster a better understanding of those calculations.

- **Number Line Techniques for Statistics Problems:** You can solve a variety of common problems involving statistics by using a number line to visualize and manipulate the problem.

Representing Objects with Pictures

For Word Problems that describe a physical object, or for Geometry problems that do not give a diagram alongside the problem, drawing a picture is often the best approach. Sometimes it's the *only* viable approach! Even if you are good at visualizing objects in your head, draw the picture anyway. It's just too easy to make a mistake on many of these questions.

Try-It #7-1

A rectangular wooden dowel measures 4 inches by 1 inch by 1 inch. If the dowel is painted on all surfaces and then cut into $\frac{1}{2}$-inch cubes, what fraction of the resulting cube faces are painted?

(A) $\frac{1}{3}$

(B) $\frac{3}{8}$

(C) $\frac{7}{16}$

(D) $\frac{1}{2}$

(E) $\frac{9}{16}$

If you draw a picture, this problem becomes a matter of counting:

$$\text{Total cubes} = (4 \text{ inches} \times 2 \text{ cubes per inch}) \times (1 \times 2) \times (1 \times 2) = 32 \text{ cubes}$$

$$\text{Total cube faces} = 32 \text{ cubes} \times 6 \text{ faces per cube} = 192 \text{ faces total}$$

Now, consider the faces that were painted on the front and back of the dowel, the top and bottom of the dowel, and the ends of the dowel. In the diagram above, you can see 16 faces on the front, 16 faces on the top, and 4 faces on the end shown. Of course, there are other sides: the back, the bottom, and the other end. Now you can find the number of painted cubes:

$$\text{Painted cube faces} = (16 \text{ faces} \times 2) + (16 \text{ faces} \times 2) + (4 \text{ faces} \times 2) = 32 + 32 + 8 = 72$$

Front & Back   Top & Bottom   Ends

Therefore, the fraction of faces that are painted is $\dfrac{72}{192} = \dfrac{24(3)}{24(8)} = \dfrac{3}{8}$. The correct answer is (B).

Notice that there is no shortcut to solving this kind of problem, so don't waste time looking for one—just draw the diagram and count.

!	Even if you can easily picture 3-D shapes and objects in your head, it is still better to draw a picture on your scrap paper.
	The test will usually include among the incorrect answers numbers that you might get by losing track of your progress as you process the object in your mind.

This kind of process can also help you with questions that deal with the relative size of different objects.

Try-It #7-2

Bucket A has twice the capacity of Bucket B, and Bucket A has $\frac{1}{3}$ the capacity of Bucket C. Bucket B is full of water and Bucket C is half full of water. When the water from Bucket B is poured into Bucket C, Bucket C will be filled to what fraction of its capacity?

You could attempt to solve this problem algebraically, but the equations get messy very quickly. Instead, try drawing buckets A, B, and C in correct proportion to one another. Then think through the problem:

$$A_{capacity} = 2B_{capacity}$$

$$A_{capacity} = \frac{1}{3}C_{capacity}$$

$$B_{water} = B_{capacity}$$

$$C_{water} = \frac{1}{2}C_{capacity}$$

$$\frac{B_{water} + C_{water}}{C_{capacity}} = ?$$

Alternatively:

$$A = 2B$$

$$A = \frac{1}{3}C$$

$$\frac{B + \frac{1}{2}C}{C} = ?$$

Algebra   **Picture**

The algebra and the picture say the same thing, but the picture has several advantages:

- It's much easier to comprehend at a glance.
- It's harder to mistake relative sizes (e.g., accidentally thinking A is smallest).
- You can easily represent both total capacity and amount of water visually.
- It prompts you to pursue the smartest, easiest solution: picking numbers for the capacities of the buckets.

Based on this picture, you might pick a capacity of 1 for Bucket B, yielding a capacity of 2 for Bucket A and 6 for Bucket C. Bucket B would contain 1 unit of water and Bucket C, 3 units. When the contents of B are poured into C, Bucket C would then be $\frac{4}{6} = \frac{2}{3}$ full.

Notice that the buckets are not labeled in alphabetical order, even though that would be easy to incorrectly assume. The GMAT frequently adds little layers of disguise and complexity such as this to induce you to make a mistake. By drawing the buckets carefully, you minimize the chance that you will fall into a trap on a problem such as this one.

Rubber Band Geometry

Many Geometry problems—particularly of the Data Sufficiency (DS) variety—describe objects for which only partial information is known. We call these questions *Rubber Band Geometry* problems, because they simultaneously involve constraints and flexibility. Some parts of the diagram can stretch like a rubber band as you open or close angles.

Your job is to figure out what specifics in the problem are constrained and what specifics are flexible.

For example, if a problem specifies that a line has a slope of 2, it will be steep and upward-sloping. In fact, it will always "rise" 2 units for every unit of "run." However, you don't know where the line will appear.

The line is *constrained* in its slope, but it is *flexible* in that it can be moved up or down, right or left. You can draw many different lines with a slope of 2 (these lines will all be parallel, of course).

If, however, the problem only specifies that a line must go through the point (4, 0) in the coordinate plane, then the line is "fixed" at that point. However, the slope of the line would now be flexible. You could draw many different lines with different slopes that run through that point.

If you knew both of these specifications—that the line must have a slope of 2 and must run through the point (4, 0)—then you would be able to calculate the exact line that is being described. The slope of the line and a point that the line goes through specify the line precisely—there is no remaining flexibility for either the slope or the location of the line. (Note that in this example, the line is described by the equation $y = 2x - 8$.)

Given these specifications, every other feature of this line is also known: its *x*-intercept, its *y*-intercept, whether it goes through some fixed point, which quadrants it crosses, etc. In a DS problem, you could answer any such questions about this line without actually calculating the answer.

Therefore, for these types of problems, your goal is to figure out what combination of information "cements" the problem in place—in other words, what combination of information removes all of the remaining flexibility. No flexibility means sufficiency. And by using rubber band geometry thinking, you can often do this without using any calculation or algebra at all.

For each piece of information that you're given in this type of problem, think about what is *fixed* and what is *flexible*. Try to draw multiple versions of each object (if possible), testing the boundaries of this flexibility. The following everyday objects may be useful as analogies in your thinking:

- Rubber band: Determines a straight line segment. Can stretch between any two points.
- Drinking straw: Determines a straight line segment, but with fixed length.
- Thumbtack: Fixes a point, but can allow rotations through that point in many cases.
- Wedge: Fixes an angle.

Here are some common examples of how these objects can be used to help you think through these problems:

Constrained	Flexible	Analogous Object(s)	Mental Picture/ Simplified Sketch
A line passes through a specified point.	Slope of the line	Drinking straw = line Thumbtack = point	 Line free to spin about a point.
Two lines intersect at a specified point.	Slope of the lines	Drinking straw = line Thumbtack = point	 Both lines free to spin about a point. The angle is free to change.

7

Constrained	Flexible	Analogous Object(s)	Mental Picture/ Simplified Sketch
A line passes through two points.	Nothing flexible	Drinking straw = Line Thumbtacks = Points	Two points pin down a line—no flexibility.
Specified distance between two points	Absolute or relative location of the points	Thumbtacks = Points Drinking straw = distance between points	Fix one point temporarily. Line (straw) free to spin about one point, tracing the circle of possible locations of the other point.
Slope of a line	Location of the line, or points the line may pass through	Drinking straw = line	Line is free to "float around" but not rotate.
Points are on a line (either in the coordinate plane or on a basic number line).	Distance between the points	Rubber band = stretched between points	"Stretchy" distance between points
Points on a line are a specified distance apart.	Order of the points (left-to-middle-to-right) Manipulation will be determined by other stated constraints, but thinking of the points as the endpoints of rigid straws will ensure that you do not forget the distance constraint.	Drinking straws = fixed lengths between points	A (or) B B A Lines could be laid end-to-end, overlapping, separated, and flipped right-to-left.
Triangle with a fixed area and a fixed base (and therefore a fixed height)	Position of the third vertex along a line parallel to the base	Straw = fixed base Rubber bands = other sides of the triangle Thumbtacks = endpoints of the base	B A

This is not intended to be an exhaustive list. The idea is to show you a new way of thinking through some difficult Geometry problems.

Try-It #7-3

A circle in a coordinate plane has a center at point A and a diameter of 6. If points B and C also lie in the same coordinate plane, is point B inside the circle?

(1) The distance between point A and point C equals 2.

(2) The distance between point B and point C equals 2.

The exact locations of points A, B, and C do not matter—only the relative locations of the points matter. Therefore, you can arbitrarily assign point A to a specific location (when possible, choose the origin of the coordinate plane) and draw a circle with a radius of 3 units around it.

Is B inside the circle?

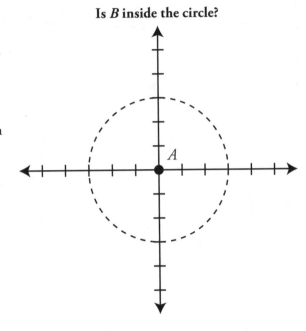

(1) INSUFFICIENT: Statement (1) does not indicate anything about point B, so it is not sufficient. However, it does indicate that A and C are 2 units apart, so statement (1) enables you to place point C anywhere along the gray circle.

(1) The distance between A and C is 2.

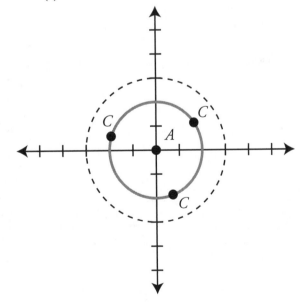

(2) The distance between _B_ and _C_ is 2.

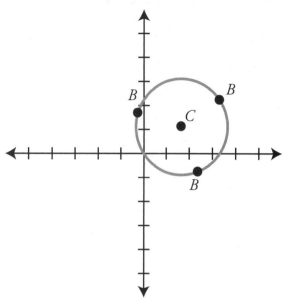

(2) INSUFFICIENT: Statement (2) does not indicate anything about point _B relative_ to point _A_, so it is not sufficient. However, it does constrain point _B_ to be exactly 2 units away from wherever point _C_ is. You could imagine point _C_ at the center of a circle of size 2, with point _B_ somewhere on the circle around it (and this circle could pick up and move anywhere on the coordinate plane).

(1) and (2) combined

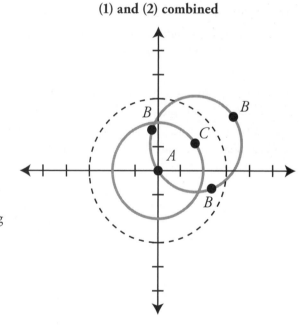

(1) AND (2) INSUFFICIENT: Finally, combine these two statements to see that depending on where point _C_ is drawn, point _B_ may be inside the dotted circle, and it may not be.

The correct answer is (E).

As long as you can achieve a visual proof of the answer, you don't need to prove it algebraically.

That's what rubber band geometry is all about: testing scenarios for Geometry problems _without_ the need to plug in numbers or use algebra. All you need is a visual environment that can be manipulated—one that preserves all key constraints and freedoms in the problem and allows you to see and test them.

7

Baseline Calculations for Averages

Basic Averages

Try-It #7-4

What is the average (arithmetic mean) of 387, 388, and 389 ?

Without even calculating, you may be able to see that the average is 388. How did you arrive at that answer?

It's very unlikely that you calculated the average the classical way:

$$\text{Average} = \frac{\text{Sum}}{\text{Number of terms}} = \frac{387 + 388 + 389}{3} = \frac{1{,}164}{3} = 388$$

You probably noticed that the numbers are very close together and evenly spaced: 387 is 1 less than 388, and 389 is 1 greater than 388. Thus, the average must be 388—right in the middle.

Whether you realize it or not, you're using a relatively advanced technique to solve this problem: a *baseline calculation*. The baseline in this case is 388—the middle number. This concept can be applied to more difficult calculations of averages, making the calculation process much easier.

Try-It #7-5

A consumer finds that five bags of popcorn contain 257, 261, 273, 280, and 259 corn kernels per bag, respectively. What is the average (arithmetic mean) number of corn kernels per bag of popcorn?

First, note that all of the bags have at least 257 kernels, so the average must be greater than 257. How much greater than 257? First, consider how much each term differs from 257. Represent every number with a column rising above the baseline value (in this example, 257). The biggest numbers rise the highest; a number equal to the baseline has no height. The height of the column thus represents the difference between the number and the baseline value:

Calculate the sum of the differences: $0 + 4 + 16 + 23 + 2 = 45$.

Divide by the number of terms: the average difference is $45 \div 5 = 9$.

Therefore, the average number of kernels per bag equals baseline + average difference: $257 + 9 = 266$.

Simply put, a baseline picture is a column chart. The columns don't show the actual value of any number—rather, they show the difference between the baseline and the number.

> The baseline can be *any* convenient number. Consider the following when choosing a baseline:
>
> - The smallest term in the set
> - The largest term in the set
> - The median term in the set
> - A round number near the range of values

For sets with apparent symmetry, choosing a baseline in the *middle* is a good way not only to confirm the symmetry, but also to compute the average. In this scenario, represent numbers lower than the baseline with columns that drop *below* the baseline. As before, the size of the column represents the difference between the number and the baseline.

Use trial and error to pick a possible average baseline, then adjust the drawing and calculations if necessary.

Try-It #7-6

If a small business paid quarterly taxes last year of $10,079, $10,121, $10,112, and $10,088, what was the average (arithmetic mean) quarterly tax payment last year?

In this case, some of the numbers are below $10,100 and others are above $10,100, so $10,100 is a natural first guess:

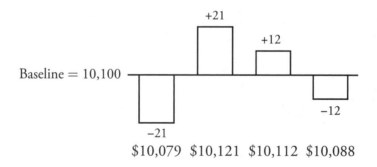

If the baseline is the average, then the sum of the differences from the baseline will be zero. Since the differences from the baseline do in fact sum to zero, $10,100 is indeed the average of this set.

Weighted Averages

Some sets may have many terms, but each of those terms has one of only two possible values. Rather than add each individual term together, simplify the calculations by using a *weighted average* calculation.

For weighted averages, use visualization to advance your understanding of the math. Two real-life analogies can make it easier to remember how the *relative weights* of high and low values determine where the weighted average falls.

| Teeter-Totter | Hanging Scale |

These pictures represent the values in a set as horizontal positions—left-to-right, as on a number line, not as vertical columns. (It may help to imagine the balance beam or lever marked off in equal units like a number line.) Each pin or weight corresponds to the presence of a value in a set. The X in each picture marks the *equilibrium point*—in other words, the weighted average.

Both visual interpretations regard weighted averages as a kind of balancing act: *the weighted average will be closer to the end of the range that has more weight.* In the pictures, there are more instances of the left-hand side number in the set, so the X is relatively closer to the left-hand side. You can think of this point as the point where the weight would be "balanced" between the two sets.

Try-It #7-7

A convenience store stocks soda in 12-ounce and 24-ounce bottles. If the average capacity of all the bottles in the store is 22 ounces, then what fraction of the bottles in the store are 12 ounces?

Note that 22 is much closer to 24 than to 12. This implies that there will be many more 24-ounce bottles than 12-ounce bottles. Because the question asks about 12-ounce bottles, you could strategically eliminate any answer greater than or equal to $\frac{1}{2}$.

Use your understanding of weighted averages as a balancing act to work backwards from the weighted average to the ratio of high-to-low terms:

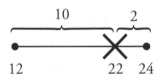

The total range between the high and low values (24 and 12) is 12 units. Mark off the distance from each end to the average of 22. Because the weighted average is closer to 24, that side of the teeter-totter is assigned the greater weight of 10 out of 12. The other side, 12, is assigned the smaller weight of 2 out of 12. Therefore, the 24-ounce bottles constitute $\frac{10}{12} = \frac{5}{6}$ of the total number of bottles. The 12-ounce bottles constitute $\frac{2}{12} = \frac{1}{6}$ of the total number of bottles.

When using this technique, it is important to remember that the weighted average is *closer* to (i.e., *fewer* units away from) the side that has greater weight, so that side should always be assigned the higher fraction. It is easy to reverse this logic accidentally when solving a weighted average problem with this technique, so be very careful! Just remember: *the weighted average point will be closer to the side with **more** weight.*

Try-It #7-8

Darla decides to mix lemonade with limeade to make a new drink called citrusade. The lemonade is 50% water, 30% lemon juice, and 20% sugar. The limeade is 40% water, 28% lime juice, and 32% sugar. If the citrusade is more than 45% water and more than 24% sugar, which of the following could be the ratio of lemonade to limeade?

(A) 3 : 1

(B) 7 : 3

(C) 3 : 2

(D) 4 : 5

(E) 3 : 4

The citrusade is more than 45% water. The lemonade is 50% water and the limeade is 40% water, so the lemonade must be more heavily weighted:

Therefore, the lemonade must make up more than 50% of the mixture. Eliminate answers (D) and (E).

Next, the citrusade is more than 24% sugar. The lemonade is 20% sugar and the limeade is 32% sugar, so what else can you figure out about the relative weighting?

Since lemonade is more heavily weighted (the mixture is to the right of 50/50), the weighting of the mixture is somewhere between 24% and the 50/50 weighting of the sugar, 26%. What weighting does the 24% figure represent?

The weighting is at most $\frac{8}{12}$ lemonade, or $\frac{2}{3}$. The weighting, then, must be between $\frac{1}{2}$ and $\frac{2}{3}$ lemonade and the rest limeade.

Answer (A) represents a weighting of $\frac{3}{4}$ lemonade. Answer (B) represents a weighting of $\frac{7}{10}$ lemonade. Only answer (C) offers a weighting in the correct range: $\frac{3}{5}$ or 3 : 5 lemonade.

The correct answer is (C).

Number Line Techniques for Statistics Problems

Several other common types of questions involving statistics can be solved with visualization. Specifically, using a number line can help simplify the work for many of these problems.

Median Relative to Mean

Most questions involving the term *median* are really asking about the order of terms in a set: you line up the terms in a set in order of size, then select the middle term. By contrast, the *average*, or arithmetic mean, is the sum of all of the terms divided by the number of terms. It can be visualized as the balancing point of all the terms laid out on the number line, as in the discussion of the balancing point for weighted averages in the previous section. For Data Sufficiency questions involving median, you generally need to picture the placement of the unknown terms *relative to* the given terms in the problem.

This technique is similar to rubber band geometry discussed earlier in this chapter, except this technique applies to problems involving sets rather than problems involving the coordinate plane. In this technique, you must place *fixed* terms in order from least to greatest (as you would on a number line), then move *variable* terms around according to the constraints. By doing so, you can visualize what impact these changes have on the answer.

Try-It #7-9

> If set S consists of the numbers n, -2, and 4, is the mean of set S greater than the median of set S?
>
> (1) $n > 2$
> (2) $n < 3$

The mean of set S is $\dfrac{n + (-2) + 4}{3} = \dfrac{n + 2}{3}$. The median depends on where n falls relative to -2 and 4: below -2, between -2 and 4, or above 4. One approach to this question is to think through the potential answers for all possible n values in the likely range (you can glance at the statements and other values in the list to get a sense of the relevant range) and draw out the scenarios on a number line. Try numbers around the relevant numbers, including a smaller and larger one at the far ends of the range; note that, by definition, all numbers in a set are different, so n cannot be -2 or 4:

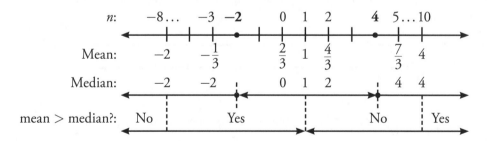

This requires a fair amount of up-front work, but evaluating the statements is fast as a result. Statement (1) indicates that $n > 2$, which is not sufficient. If $n = 5$, for example, the mean would equal $\dfrac{7}{3}$ and the median would equal 4. By contrast, if $n = 10$, the mean would equal 4 and the median would still equal 4.

Similarly, statement (2) indicates that $n < 3$, which is not sufficient. If $n = -3$, for example, the mean would equal $-\frac{1}{3}$ and the median would equal -2. By contrast, if $n = -8$, the mean would equal -2 and the median would still equal -2.

Taken together, however, any number in the range of $2 < n < 3$ would feature a median greater than the mean.

The correct answer is (C).

Notice from this problem that as you move the variable terms, the mean *always* changes when the value of the variable terms change, but the median typically changes in *jumps*. The median can get stuck while the number you're changing doesn't affect *which* number is in the middle.

Changes in Standard Deviation

The GMAT will rarely (if ever) ask you to calculate the *standard deviation* of a list of numbers. However, the exam will expect you to have some intuition about standard deviations.

One way in which the GMAT might test your intuitive knowledge of standard deviations is by *changing numbers within a list* and asking you what the impact on standard deviation would be. The relationship is relatively straightforward:

- Moving terms away from the mean increases the standard deviation of the list.
- Moving terms toward the mean decreases the standard deviation of the list.

You might also see the term *variance*, which is also a measure of the spread of numbers in a set or list. Variance and standard deviation indicate the same information. A variance of 0 indicates that all of the numbers are identical, as does a standard deviation of 0. The larger the variance, or standard deviation, the more the numbers are spread out. (Variance and standard deviation are never negative.)

Try-It #7-10

Last Year	9	9.5	10	10	11	11	11	11	11	12.5	13	13
This Year	9	x	10	10	11	11	11	11	11	y	13	13

The monthly sales (in thousands of $) at a certain restaurant for the past two years are given in the chart above. If the standard deviation of the monthly sales is greater this year than last year, which of the following are possible values for x and y ?

(A) 9 and 12.5

(B) 10 and 11

(C) 10 and 12.5

(D) 11 and 11

(E) 11 and 12.5

Except for x and y, the two lists of monthly sales numbers are identical, so focus exclusively on those terms that changed: 9.5 and 12.5 from last year were replaced by x and y this year. If this year's standard deviation is greater, then this year's numbers must be more spread out from the mean than last year's. The numbers are close enough together to indicate that the average should be somewhere around 11.

Visually, here are the interesting terms from last year:

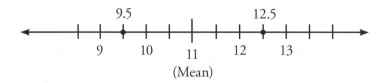

This problem does not require actual computation of the standard deviation using the new *x* and *y* values. The math would be too complex to complete in two minutes. Instead, determine visually which *x* and *y* values increase the standard deviation: the pair of *x* and *y* values *that are farther from the mean* than are 9.5 and 12.5 will increase the standard deviation.

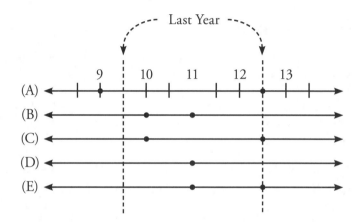

All of the sets have either one point or both points shifted in toward the mean EXCEPT (A), which has one of the points shifted away from the mean while the other is unchanged. Only in this case is the deviation greater.

The correct answer is (A).

The GMAT may also test you on standard deviations by adding numbers to a list. When new terms are added, the GMAT will often ask you to compare the old list to the new list, or to compare various options for the new list, or to do both. You must have a technique to evaluate the standard deviation of different lists *relative to one another*. Again, pictures make for great comparison tools!

Try-It #7-11

A list of 12 test scores has an average (arithmetic mean) of 500 and a standard deviation of 50. Which of the following lists of additional test scores, when combined with the original list of 12 test scores, must result in a combined list with a standard deviation less than 50 ?

(A)   6 test scores with average of 450 and standard deviation of 50

(B)   6 test scores with average of 500 and standard deviation of 25

(C)   6 test scores with average of 550 and standard deviation of 25

(D)   12 test scores with average of 450 and standard deviation of 25

(E)   2 test scores with average of 550 and standard deviation of 50

It is not generally true that all of the terms in a list are within 1 standard deviation of the mean. However, standard deviation *is* a measure of the spread of the terms of a list, so you could represent the original list of scores this way:

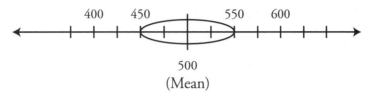

The oval spans ±1 standard deviation from the mean, where many of the scores will likely be. This simplification is acceptable as long as you represent all of the other lists the same way so that you can compare the *relative* effects of the new test scores systematically.

For each of the answer choices, overlay the representative ovals for the new data on top of the oval for the original data:

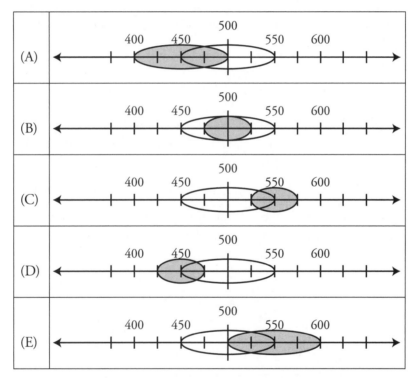

Only answer (B) concentrates the list of scores closer to the original average of 500. Thus, adding the data in answer (B) will result in a smaller standard deviation than that found in the original data. The correct answer is (B).

In general, these are the rules for adding a single term to a list:

- Adding a new term *more than* 1 standard deviation from the mean generally *increases* the standard deviation.

- Adding a new term *less than* 1 standard deviation from the mean generally *decreases* the standard deviation.

Note that mathematically this is a slight oversimplification, but for the purpose of adding terms to a list of numbers on the GMAT, you can accept this simplification as true.

Floating Terms in a Set

On GMAT Statistics problems involving elements (i.e., terms) in a list, you can usually focus your attention on a single term or two. These terms could be considered the *floating terms*—the terms that are unknown or not completely defined among a list of more clearly defined terms.

As you approach a question of this type, try to rephrase the question quickly so that you focus on the unknown, or *floating*, terms rather than on the known terms.

Try-It #7-12

List *A* contains 5 positive integers, and the average (arithmetic mean) of the integers in the list is 7. If the integers 6, 7, and 8 are in List *A*, what is the range of List *A* ?

(1) The integer 3 is in List A.

(2) The largest term in List A is greater than 3 times and less than 4 times the size of the smallest term.

The average of all five integers in the list is 7. Three of the integers in the list are given (6, 7, and 8), and they all have an average of 7. Therefore, the floating terms in this problem must also have an average of 7. Assign *x* and *y* to represent these terms:

$$\frac{x + y}{2} = 7$$
$$x + y = 14$$

The rephrased question is thus, "Given that $x + y = 14$, what is either *x* or *y*?" Once you know one of the values, you can solve for the other and thereby determine the range of the list.

(1) SUFFICIENT: If 3 is one of the unknown integers, the other must be 11. The range is thus $11 - 3 = 8$.

(2) SUFFICIENT: This statement might seem a little too vague to be sufficient, but by visually listing the possible pairs that add up to 14, you can rule out pairs that don't fit the constraint from this statement:

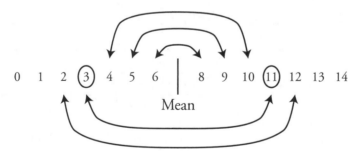

Notice that the pairings represent the constraint $x + y = 14$. Visually, this means that *x* and *y* are balanced around 7.

Among these pairs:

- 8 is 1.33 times the size of 6 (the ratio is too low).

- 9 is 1.8 times the size of 5 (the ratio is too low).

- 10 is 2.5 times the size of 4 (the ratio is too low).

- 11 is 3.66 times the size of 3 (an acceptable ratio).

- 12 is 6 times the size of 2 (the ratio is too high).

Only one pair of integers results in a ratio strictly between 3 and 4. The unknown terms must therefore be 3 and 11, and the range is $11 - 3 = 8$.

The correct answer is (D).

In this problem, the constraint $x + y = 14$ is a *fixed sum*. Another common constraint is a *fixed difference*, such as $a - b = 2$. A fixed difference can be represented visually as a fixed distance between a and b on the number line, with a to the right because it is larger. That distance could move left or right:

Maximizing (or Minimizing) One Term

Another visual technique for statistics involves maximizing (or minimizing) the value of a term in a set or list of numbers, subject to some constraints. Such problems will usually employ the word *maximum* or *minimum*. For these problems, you often should maximize (or minimize) the term by minimizing (or maximizing) the *other* terms, because the constraints usually involve mathematical trade-offs.

Try-It #7-13

In a certain lottery drawing, five balls are selected from a tumbler in which each ball is printed with a different two-digit positive integer. If the average (arithmetic mean) of the five numbers drawn is 56 and the median is 60, what is the greatest value that the lowest number selected could be?

(A) 43
(B) 48
(C) 51
(D) 53
(E) 56

The goal is to maximize the value of the lowest-numbered ball. All balls contain a two-digit positive integer, and none of the balls have the same number. The problem provides enough information to calculate the sum and to lay out a visual listing of the numbers:

$$56 = \frac{\text{Sum}}{5}$$

$$\underline{\quad}\underset{\text{Max}}{\quad} \underline{\quad} \underset{60}{\underline{\quad}} \underline{\quad} \underline{\quad}$$

$$280 = \text{Sum}$$

In order to maximize the value of the first (lowest) number in the set, what do you need to do to the other numbers?

You'd want to minimize them. Select the smallest numbers that you can for the remaining slots:

$$\underline{\quad x \quad}\ \underline{\ x+1\ }\ \underline{\ 60\ }\ \underline{\ 61\ }\ \underline{\ 62\ }$$

In some problems, you might actually make different slots equal to each other (e.g., the three largest numbers could be 60, 60, and 60). This problem, though, specifies that the integers are all different.

The five numbers must sum to 280, so you can set up an algebraic equation and solve. Can you think of a way to minimize the arithmetic needed to solve in that way?

The three numerical values, 60, 61, and 62, are all larger than the average of 56. Specifically, they are +4, +5, and +6 away from that average.

The other two numbers, then, need to make up for that overage of $4 + 5 + 6 = 15$:

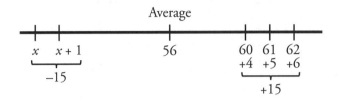

The numbers x and $x + 1$ are also consecutive, so they need to be −8 and −7 away from the average of 56. The two remaining numbers are 48 and 49. (We call this the *over/under approach*, by the way.)

The correct answer is (B).

Try-It #7-14

The average (arithmetic mean) of six numbers is 18 and the median of the six numbers is 16. What is the minimum possible value for the greatest number in the list?

(A) 19

(B) 20

(C) 21

(D) 22

(E) 23

This time, the goal is to minimize the largest number:

$$18 = \frac{\text{Sum}}{6}$$

$$108 = \text{Sum} \qquad \underline{} \; \underline{} \; \overbrace{\underline{} \; \underline{}}^{\substack{\text{Median} \\ 16}} \; \underline{} \; \underset{\text{Min}}{\underline{}}$$

In order to minimize the final term, you'd want to maximize all of the other terms. This time, though, the list contains an even number of terms, so you can't just set the median to the middle number. The two middle numbers average to 16.

The pair (16, 16) averages to 16, as does the pair (15, 17). The first pair, though, is better when the goal is to minimize the final term, since the terms to the right have to be equal to or greater than the terms to the left.

In other words, when trying to minimize the final term, it's true that you want to maximize the earlier terms, but you also have to think about how to do so in a way that doesn't make the final term too large (since it has to be larger than the earlier terms). In this case, the first four terms are all 16:

$$\underline{16} \quad \underline{16} \quad \underline{16} \quad \underline{16} \quad \underline{} \quad \underset{\text{Min}}{\underline{}}$$

In order to minimize the final term, set the last two terms equal to each other and solve algebraically:

$$108 - (16)(4) = 44 \text{ and } \frac{44}{2} = 22$$

Or you can use the over/under approach:

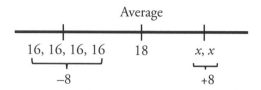

Those last two terms have to make up for the -8 on the other side, so each x must be 4 over the average, or 22.

Taking and Giving

Another common scenario involves taking value from one term in a list and giving it to another term. The relative value of the terms in the list will change, leading to some interesting results.

Try-It #7-15

Jake	51
Keri	63
Luke	15
Mia	38
Nora	22

The table above shows the number of points held by five players of a certain game. If an integer number of Keri's points were taken from her and given to Luke, and the median score of the five players increased, how many points were transferred from Keri to Luke?

(A) 23

(B) 24

(C) 25

(D) 26

(E) 27

The key to this problem is that by taking enough points from Keri and giving them to Luke, *the median of the list can change*.

Set it up visually. Order the scores from low to high on a number line, and represent the change in Luke's score with x:

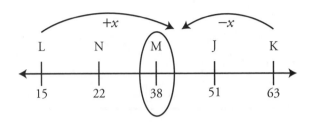

The current median is Mia's 38, circled in the diagram. In order for the median to change, Luke's score must leap-frog those of Nora and Mia, pushing Mia into the bottom two scores and making Luke's score the median. But be careful! You don't want to decrease Keri's score *so much* that Luke and Mia surpass her, leaving Mia once again in the median score position.

If $15 + x = 38$, Luke would *match* the current median score. That is $x = 23$, and Keri's new score would be $63 - 23 = 40$. However, the median score would remain 38, with both Luke and Mia having that score. Therefore, x must be greater than 23.

Try $x = 24$. Luke's new point value is $15 + 24 = 39$. Keri's new point value is $63 - 24 = 39$. Both Nora and Mia are below Luke (and Keri), so the new median is 39:

The correct answer is (B).

7

Problem Set

Use the Visual Solutions techniques discussed in this chapter to solve the following problems.

1. Does a rectangular mirror have an area greater than 10 square centimeters?

    (1) The perimeter of the mirror is 24 cm.

    (2) The diagonal of the mirror is less than 11 cm.

2. A number line is numbered with the integers from 0 to 50 inclusive. An ant walks along the number line as follows: First, it walks in the positive direction until it reaches a multiple of 5 that it hasn't previously reached. Then, it walks in the negative direction for at least 1 unit, stopping when it reaches any multiple of 2. The ant starts at 0 on the number line and repeats this process until it first reaches the point marked 50. How many units does it travel in total?

    (A) 60

    (B) 65

    (C) 76

    (D) 80

    (E) 90

3. If a, b, and c are positive, is $a > \dfrac{b+c}{2}$?

    (1) On the number line, a is closer to b than it is to c.

    (2) $b > c$

4. The length of one edge of a cube equals 4. What is the distance between the center of the cube and one of its vertices?

5. A test is taken by 100 people and possible scores are the integers between 0 and 50, inclusive. For each of the following scenarios, determine whether the average (arithmetic mean) score would be greater than 30 (answer Yes, No, or Uncertain).

    (A) More than 70 people scored 40 or higher.

    (B) 75 people scored 40 or higher.

    (C) Fewer than 10 people scored 50.

    (D) No more than 2 test-takers scored any given score.

7

6.

As part of an experiment, a student repeatedly tests the temperature of a light bulb. The bar graph above displays the number of readings the student recorded at various temperatures, measured in degrees Fahrenheit. What was the average (arithmetic mean) temperature reading of the light bulb?

7. In a certain dance troupe, there are 55 women and 33 men. If all of the women are 62 inches tall and all of the men are 70 inches tall, what is the average height of the dancers in the troupe?

8.

Note: Not drawn to scale.

Anton and Lena start at the same point on a circular track, measuring 10 meters in diameter, and begin walking counterclockwise at the same time, with Anton walking more quickly than Lena. When Anton has traveled exactly halfway around the track, they both stop walking. They then observe that the distance between them along a straight line measures exactly $5\sqrt{3}$ meters, as shown above. What fraction of the track has Lena covered?

(A) $\frac{1}{8}$

(B) $\frac{1}{6}$

(C) $\frac{1}{5}$

(D) $\frac{1}{4}$

(E) $\frac{1}{3}$

9.   Eddy, Mario, and Peter have $32, $72, and $98, respectively. They pool their money and redistribute the entire amount among themselves. If Eddy now has the median amount of money in the group, what is the greatest amount of money that Eddy could now have?

   (A) $72

   (B) $85

   (C) $98

   (D) $101

   (E) $202

10.

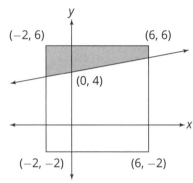

A square is drawn in the coordinate plane with its vertices at the points $(-2, -2)$, $(-2, 6)$, $(6, 6)$, and $(6, -2)$, and a non-vertical line is drawn that passes through the point $(0, 4)$. The portion of the coordinate plane that lies within the square, but above the line, is then shaded as shown above. If A is the area of the shaded region in square units, which of the following specifies all the possible values of A ?

   (A) $8 \leq A \leq 16$

   (B) $8 \leq A < 48$

   (C) $16 \leq A < 48$

   (D) $8 < A \leq 32$

   (E) $16 < A \leq 32$

Solutions

1. **(C):** Because the formula for the area of a rectangle is $A = lw$, rephrase the question. Is $lw > 10$?

    (1) INSUFFICIENT: The perimeter is 24 cm. The area of a quadrilateral is maximized when the quadrilateral is a square, so first try $l = w = 6$. In this case, the area is 36 cm^2 and the answer to the question is Yes.

    If, on the other hand, $l = 11.5$ and $w = 0.5$, the perimeter is still 24, but the area is $(11.5)(0.5) = 5.75$ cm^2. In this case, the answer to the question is No.

    (2) INSUFFICIENT: The diagonal of the rectangle is less than 11. If the diagonal is less than 11, then the sides must also be less than 11. If $l = w = 6$, then the diagonal is shorter than 11 and, as last time, the area is 36. In this case, the answer to the question is Yes.

    If, on the other hand, $l = 3$ and $w = 1$, the diagonal is less than 11, but the area is $(3)(1) = 3$ cm^2. In this case, the answer to the question is No.

    (1) AND (2) SUFFICIENT: The sides must be less than 11 and the perimeter must be 24. The case of the square still maximizes the area: $l = w = 6$ and the area is 36.

    The largest possible length is just under 11, making the width just over 1. $(<11)(>1) =$ something larger than 10. The area must be greater than 10.

    The correct answer is **(C)**.

2. **(C) 76:** The problem describes an ant walking along a number line in a complex way. It starts at 0, then walks to the right until it reaches a multiple of 5:

    Then, it walks to the left until it reaches a multiple of 2. The problem specifies that the ant must walk to the left at least one unit. Therefore, even if it is already standing on a multiple of 2, it must walk to the next one. In this case, it walks left until it reaches 4:

    Then it walks to the right again until it reaches a new multiple of 5:

    The question asks how far the ant walks, in total, to reach the number 50 for the first time. Since this is too many units to realistically count by hand, there must be an underlying pattern.

    Write down the first few distances that the ant walks, using your number line:

    5, 1, 6, 2, 7, 1, 6, 2, 7, 1 . . .

There is a repeating cycle of four numbers. Starting at 5 on the number line, the ant moves left 1, then right 6, then left 2, then right 7, which takes it to 15 on the number line. That is, the ant walks a total of $1 + 6 + 2 + 7 = 16$ units to move from 5 to 15. Then it walks another 16 units to move from 15 to 25, from 25 to 35, and from 35 to 45. In total, the ant walks $4(16) = 64$ units to move from 5 to 45.

To get from 45 to 50, the ant first walks one unit left to 44, then six units right to 50. In total, the ant walks $64 + 1 + 6 = 71$ units to move from 5 to 50.

Finally, add the five units it walks from the beginning: $71 + 5 = 76$.

It is also possible to estimate the answer. As established above, traveling 10 points on the number line (from 15 to 25, from 25 to 35, and so on) requires the ant to travel 16 units. To begin at 0 and end at 50, the ant would travel approximately $5(16) = 80$ units. This is enough to let you eliminate answers (A), (B), and (E). By estimation alone, the answer must be either (C) or (D).

The correct answer is **(C)**.

3. **(C):** The problem indicates that a, b, and c are positive and asks whether a is greater than $\dfrac{b + c}{2}$, which is the *average* (or arithmetic mean) of b and c.

Draw a picture and rephrase the question: "On the number line, is a positioned to the right of the midpoint between b and c?"

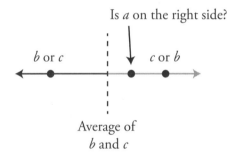

(1) INSUFFICIENT: It isn't clear whether b or c is the larger value—the point on the right—so a could be closer to the smaller number (making a less than the average) or the larger number (making a greater than the average).

(2) INSUFFICIENT: This statement indicates nothing about a, so it can't be sufficient.

(1) AND (2) SUFFICIENT: Together, the two statements indicate that b is the point on the right, so a must be on the right side of the midpoint.

The correct answer is **(C)**.

4. $2\sqrt{3}$: Draw it out!

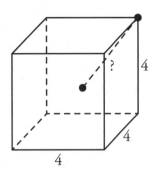

The length of any side of the cube is 4, and the problem asks for the distance between the center of the cube and any of its vertices (corners). Chop up the cube into eight smaller cubes to see that the distance from the center of the $4 \times 4 \times 4$ cube to any corner is the diagonal of a $2 \times 2 \times 2$ cube.

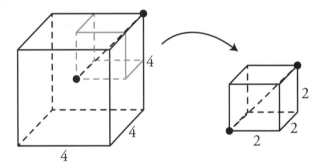

You can find the diagonal of a cube in a variety of ways. Probably the fastest (besides applying a memorized formula) is to use the "Super Pythagorean" theorem, which extends to three dimensions:

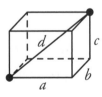

$$a^2 + b^2 + c^2 = d^2$$

In the special case when the three sides of the box are equal, as they are in a cube, use this equation:

$$s^2 + s^2 + s^2 = d^2$$
$$3s^2 = d^2$$
$$s\sqrt{3} = d$$

Since $s = 2$, $d = 2\sqrt{3}$.

5. To visualize this set of *weighted averages* problems, imagine a teeter-totter that is 50 meters long, marked off from 0 to 50 to represent scores. One hundred people of equal weight sit on the teeter-totter at their respective scores. The weighted average is the position where the teeter-totter would balance. Thus, to answer whether the average score is greater than 30, take extremes according to the given conditions and see whether you can swing the balance to either side of 30 (or whether you are forced to balance on one side of 30 only).

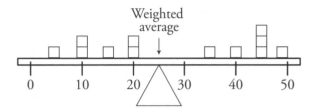

(A) **Uncertain:** More than 70 people scored 40 or higher. If all 100 scored 40 (or higher), then the average is above 30.

If, on the other hand, 71 people scored 40 and the other 29 scored 0, does the average drop to 30 or lower?

Match up the 29 people who scored 0 with 29 of the people who scored 40. These 58 people together have an average score of 20. The other 42 people have a score of 40. If you average these two groups, the average must be below 30, since 58 is larger than 42.

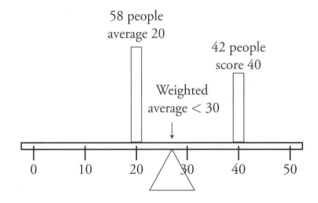

(B) **Uncertain:** Seventy-five people scored 40 or higher. If all 100 scored 40, then the average is higher than 30. If 75 scored 40 and the other 25 scored 0, then what?

Match the 25 people who scored 0 with 25 people who scored 40. These 50 people have an average score of 20. The remaining 50 people have an average score of 40, so the overall average is exactly 30. It is possible, therefore, to have an average that is higher than 30 or an average that is not higher than 30:

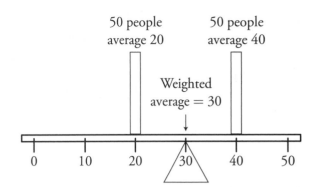

(C) **Uncertain:** Fewer than 10 people scored 50. Say that 1 person scored 50 and the other 99 scored 0. The average is definitely below 30. If on the other hand, 1 person scored 50 and the other 99 scored 40, then the average is definitely above 30.

(D) **No:** Each score was achieved by no more than 2 people. There are 51 integers between 0 and 50, inclusive. In other words, there are 102 possible scores to spread among the test-takers. Since there are 100 test-takers, almost every score is taken.

The highest possible average will occur when nobody scores 0 points. If 2 test-takers score 1, 2 test-takers score 2, and so on up to 50, then the average score will be approximately 25. As this is the highest allowable average for this scenario, it's impossible for the average to be greater than 30.

6. **112°:** Eyeball the graph. The average looks like it's in the 112° range. Calculate the *over/under* with 112° as the assumed baseline.

   The four 110° readings are each 2° below the baseline, and the three 111° readings are each 1° below the baseline, for a total of 11° below baseline.

   On the other side, the 113°, 114°, and 115° readings are a total of 11° above the baseline. They balance perfectly! The average is exactly 112°.

7. **65 inches:** Algebraic solution:

$$\text{Average} = \frac{55(62 \text{ inches}) + 33(70 \text{ inches})}{(55 + 33)}$$

$$= \frac{3,410 + 2,310}{88} \text{ inches}$$

$$= \frac{5,720}{88} \text{ inches}$$

$$= 65 \text{ inches}$$

Visual solution:

"Pull" the average $\frac{55}{88} = \frac{5}{8}$ toward the women's end of the teeter-totter.

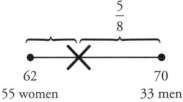

62
55 women

70
33 men

The weighted average is

$$70 - \left(\frac{5}{8}\right)(8) = 70 - 5 = 65.$$

8. **(B)** $\frac{1}{6}$: Draw a diagram showing the track, and label all of the given information. Because Anton has walked exactly halfway around the track, the distance between Anton and the starting point is the diameter.

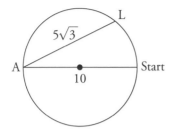

The answer choices are fractions that are fairly far apart from each other, suggesting that visual estimation could be effective. If you use this approach, carefully draw your diagram to scale. Since $5\sqrt{3}$ is approximately $5(1.7) = 8.5$, the line between Anton and Lena is only slightly shorter than the diameter of the circle. Therefore, Lena is closer to the starting point than she is to Anton, so Lena has traveled less than one-quarter of the circle: eliminate answers (D) and (E).

At the other extreme, choice (A) is quite small, suggesting that the distance between Anton and Lena would be closer to 10 than it actually is. The only reasonable answer choices are (B) and (C).

To calculate the exact answer, observe that Anton, Lena, and the starting line form the three vertices of a triangle. Because one side of the triangle is the diameter of the circle, the triangle is a right triangle with hypotenuse 10. The known leg is equal to $5\sqrt{3}$.

You can either use the Pythagorean theorem to calculate the missing leg (the straight line between Lena and the starting point) or you can note that the known leg and the hypotenuse have a ratio of $x\sqrt{3}:2x$, so the triangle must be a 30–60–90 triangle and the remaining side must equal 5.

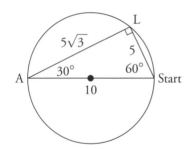

The arc of the circle that Lena traveled has a corresponding inscribed angle of 30 degrees (the vertex at point A). The corresponding central angle is twice the inscribed angle, or 60 degrees.

Alternatively, the distance between Lena and the starting line is equal to the radius of the circle. Therefore, the triangle with vertices at Lena, the starting line, and the center of the circle is an equilateral triangle, and all of its angles equal 60 degrees. So Lena has covered 60 degrees out of the 360 degrees in a full circle, or a fraction of $\frac{60}{360} = \frac{1}{6}$.

The correct answer is **(B)**.

9. **(D) $101:** The pool of money is $32 + $72 + $98 = $202. After the redistribution, each person will have an amount between $0 and $202, inclusive. Call the amounts L, M, and H (low, median, high). To maximize M (Eddy's share), minimize L and H.

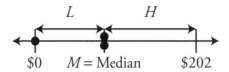

$$L \qquad\qquad H$$

$$\$0 \qquad M = \text{Median} \qquad \$202$$

Minimum $L = \$0$

Minimum $H = M$

Maximum $M = $ Total pool of money $-$ Minimum $L -$ Minimum H

$M = \$202 - \$0 - M$

$2M = \$202$

$M = \$101$

The correct answer is **(D)**.

10. **(B) $8 \leq A < 48$:** On your paper, draw the square in the coordinate plane. The line passes through the point $(0, 4)$, so label that point as well. Since the slope of the line could vary, sketch several possible lines that pass through the point, being certain to test extreme cases.

If the slope is very positive, then the line is nearly vertical, and the area above the line will be very close to $2(8) = 16$:

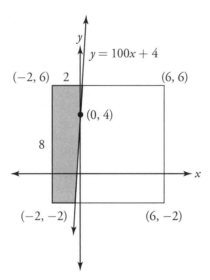

As the slope decreases, the area above the line will decrease. If the slope is 1, the area above the line is the area of a triangle with base 4 and height 4, which is equal to $\frac{1}{2}(4)(4) = 8$.

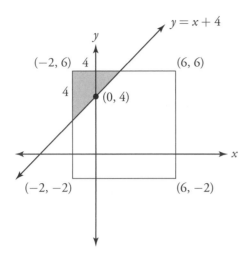

Then, as the slope continues to decrease, the area above the line will once again increase steadily. The greatest area is found when the slope is very negative, since the area will be slightly less than $(6)(8) = 48$.

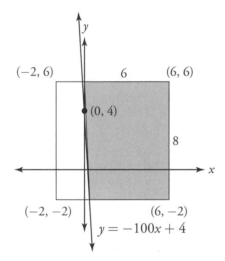

The area of the shaded region can be a minimum of exactly 8 and can be a maximum of almost, but not equal to, 48 (since the line cannot be vertical).

The correct answer is **(B)**.

Hybrid Problems

In This Chapter

CHAPTER 8 Hybrid Problems

Pop Quiz!

Try these four hybrid problems.

Try-It #8-1

Set *A* consists of four consecutive positive integers. Set *B* is constructed as follows: each integer in set *A* is randomly either increased by 10% or decreased by 10%, and the four resulting values compose set *B*. What is the range of set *B* ?

(1)   The smallest integer in set *A* was increased by 10% when set *B* was constructed.

(2)   The greatest integer in set *A* was increased by 10% when set *B* was constructed.

Try-It #8-2

Set *S* contains 100 consecutive integers. If the range of the negative elements of set *S* equals 80, what is the average (arithmetic mean) of the positive numbers in the set?

Try-It #8-3

If *a* and *b* are consecutive positive integers, is *ab* divisible by 30 ?

(1) a^2 is divisible by 25.

(2)   63 is a factor of b^2.

Try-It #8-4

A carnival card game gives the contestant a one in three probability of successfully choosing the correct card and thereby winning the game. If a contestant plays the game repeatedly, what is the minimum number of times that he must play the game so that the probability that he never loses is less than 1% ?

Hybrid Problems

Hybrid problems blend topics together. They contain two or more qualitatively different kinds of obstacles that you must surmount on the way to the answer.

Some hybrid problems feature content areas that are fairly closely related. Other hybrid problems feature content areas that share little in common; these problems must be solved in separate steps.

The difficulty of a hybrid problem is related to the following questions:

- **How closely related are the subjects being tested?** Are the content areas covered in the same section of the Manhattan Prep *All the Quant* guide? The more closely related the subjects, the easier it will be to navigate the problem.

- **How important is each of the subject areas?** Are each of the subject areas fundamental to the problem or is one of them just a low-level disguise that can be quickly disposed of? The more important each topic is in solving the problem, the more difficult the problem will usually be.

Problems with minor additional content areas are generally easier to solve than hybrids that blend topics together in an unusual, fundamental, and clever way. The best hybrids are one of a kind. You will have to bring your A game to solve them.

But solve them you can. That's why you're reading this chapter!

Identify and Sequence the Parts

When you encounter a hybrid problem, first pick out all of the topics tested. Take a look at the first problem from the pop quiz:

> **Try-It #8-1**
>
> Set *A* consists of four consecutive positive integers. Set *B* is constructed as follows: each integer in set *A* is randomly either increased by 10% or decreased by 10%, and the four resulting values compose set *B*. What is the range of set *B* ?
>
> (1)   The greatest integer in set *A* was increased by 10% when set *B* was constructed.
> (2)   The smallest integer in set *A* was increased by 10% when set *B* was constructed.

This problem refers to consecutive integers, but it involves percents and also asks for the range of a set of numbers, which is a statistics concept. Which aspect of the problem should you tackle first?

In this problem, a set begins as four consecutive integers and is then changed. So you might start your approach by jotting down some sets of consecutive integers—either as numbers or in terms of a variable. Then, apply the percent change described in the problem and, finally, check the range of the resulting set.

In general, start with wherever you feel the logical beginning is or whichever part you feel is an easier, cleaner starting point.

Where to Start

Starting at the Beginning

As you contemplate the logical order of steps, you might feel less confident with the second stage than with the first. If so, go ahead and start at the beginning. Just articulate very clearly, "What *intermediate result* will I get once I'm finished with the first part of the problem?"

Begin by defining set *A*. Set *A* consists of four consecutive integers, such as 1, 2, 3, 4, or 10, 11, 12, 13.

Next, choose a statement to work with first. Statement (1) says that the smallest integer in set *A* is increased by 10%. The other integers might have been either increased or decreased. Using one of your cases, calculate what might happen to the set:

Set *A*	Scenarios	Set *B*
1, 2, 3, 4	All values increased by 10%	1.1, 2.2, 3.3, 4.4
1, 2, 3, 4	Smallest value increased by 10%, other values decreased by 10%	1.1, 1.8, 2.7, 3.6

Finally, calculate the range of the resulting set. The *range* of a set is the difference between the greatest number and the smallest number in the set.

Set *A*	Scenarios	Set *B*	Range
1, 2, 3, 4	All values increased by 10%	1.1, 2.2, 3.3, 4.4	4.4−1.1 = 3.3
1, 2, 3, 4	Smallest value increased by 10%, other values decreased by 10%	1.1, 1.8, 2.7, 3.6	3.6−1.1 = 2.7

Since different ranges are possible, the statement is insufficient. Eliminate answers (A) and (D).

Starting at the End

You might decide that it is easier to start at the end and work backwards. That's fine. Just ask yourself, "What information do I need to have as a *last step* before arriving at a solution to the question?"

In this problem, you might first consider what would cause set *B* to have a different range. The range of a set is the difference between the greatest and smallest numbers in the set. If the difference between these two numbers can vary, the range can vary as well.

According to statement (2), the greatest integer in set *A* was increased by 10%. However, the smallest integer might have increased by 10%, bringing it closer to the greatest integer, or it might have decreased by 10%, bringing it farther from the greatest integer. Therefore, the range of the set can vary, so statement (2) is insufficient. Eliminate answer (B).

Now, put the two statements together. One option is to try a few different cases, making sure to increase the smallest integer in set *A* and decrease the greatest integer in set *A*. One of the two cases used for statement (1) works here as well:

Set *A*	Scenario	Set *B*	Range
1, 2, 3, 4	All values increased by 10%	1.1, 2.2, 3.3, 4.4	4.4−1.1 = 3.3

Try another case, using different numbers:

Set *A*	Scenario	Set *B*	Range
10, 11, 12, 13	All values increased by 10%	11, 12.1, 13.2, 14.3	14.3−11 = 3.3

The range is the same, but this doesn't mean that the statements are sufficient together. To see why, use a different approach. Set *A* always contains the numbers x, $x + 1$, $x + 2$, and $x + 3$. When the smallest value in set *A* is increased by 10%, it goes from x to $1.1x$. When the greatest value is increased by 10%, it goes from $x + 3$ to $1.1x + 3.3$. So these two values differ by 3.3.

However, you can't assume that the smallest and greatest values in set *A* always become the smallest and greatest values in set *B*. If two of the values switch places, the range might change. Here's an example:

Set *A*	Scenarios	Set *B*	Range
10, 11, 12, 13	Smallest and largest values increased by 10%, other values decreased by 10%	11, 9.9, 10.8, 14.3	14.3−9.9 = 4.4

The range of the set might vary, even when both statements are used. The correct answer is (E).

Let's look at another example:

Try-It #8-2

Set *S* contains 100 consecutive integers. If the range of the negative elements of set *S* equals 80, what is the average (arithmetic mean) of the positive numbers in the set?

In this problem, information is given about the *range* of numbers in a set. Thus, knowing how to work with statistics techniques will be important in solving the problem.

Solving this problem also requires using consecutive integers techniques—namely, counting consecutive integers and computing their average. These two topics are closely related but still cover different ideas.

If you start with the statistics piece of the problem, then you'll be able to find the highest and lowest negative numbers in the set of consecutive integers. This will act as an input to the formulas for computing the largest and smallest positive integers in the set, and subsequently the average of the positive integers in the set.

First, determine what set of consecutive negative integers will result in a range of 80. Range is defined as the difference between the highest and lowest numbers in a set:

$$\text{High} - \text{Low} = \text{Range}$$

The high number among the negative terms is the largest negative integer, -1:

$$-1 - \text{Low} = 80$$
$$-\text{Low} = 80 + 1$$
$$\text{Low} = -81$$

Therefore, the lowest number in set *S* is -81. Use this result to jump to the consecutive integers portion of the solution. In this case, -81 is the smallest or "first" element in the set:

$$\text{Last} - \text{First} + 1 = \text{Count}$$
$$\text{Last} - (-81) + 1 = 100$$
$$\text{Last} + 82 = 100$$
$$\text{Last} = 18$$

Therefore, the highest or "last" number in set *S* is 18.

Finally, calculate the average of the *positive* terms in the set using 1 as the smallest positive integer ("first pos") and 18 as the largest positive integer ("last pos"):

$$\text{Average of Pos} = \frac{\text{Last Pos} + \text{First Pos}}{2} = \frac{18 + 1}{2} = \frac{19}{2} = 9.5$$

The average of the positive numbers in the set is 9.5.

If instead you decided to start with the second step, you would write the formula for the average of consecutive integers first, focusing on the positive integers:

$$\text{Average of Pos} = \frac{\text{Last Pos} + \text{First Pos}}{2}$$

The two unknowns you need to solve for are the greatest positive integer and the least positive integer because the question asks only about the *positive* integers in the set.

Some of the integers in set S are negative and some are positive, so clearly the least positive integer will be 1. Therefore, you only need to figure out what the greatest integer in the set will be. This is the information needed in the *last step* of solving the problem.

In order to calculate this number, you would now need to apply the definition of range:

$$\text{High} - \text{Low} = \text{Range}$$

The greatest negative integer (the "high" number) is −1:

$$-1 - \text{Low} = 80$$
$$-\text{Low} = 80 + 1$$
$$\text{Low} = -81$$

Therefore, the least number in the set is −81; plug this into the formula for counting consecutive integers:

$$\text{Last} - \text{First} + 1 = \text{Count}$$
$$\text{Last} - (-81) + 1 = 100$$
$$\text{Last} + 82 = 100$$
$$\text{Last} = 18$$

Therefore, the highest number in the set is 18.

Finally, plug 18 into the average formula:

$$\text{Average of Pos} = \frac{\text{Last Pos} + \text{First Pos}}{2} = \frac{18 + 1}{2} = \frac{19}{2} = 9.5$$

Whether you start solving this problem from the beginning or from the end, study how the steps hook together: the output of one step becomes the input to another. These are the "turns" you have to make in solving any hybrid problem. Often, a number that plays one role in a particular formula or calculation plays a completely different role in the next step.

Minor Hybrids

In minor hybrid problems, one of the following conditions applies:

1. The content areas in the problem are closely related. For instance, they are covered in the same section of the Manhattan Prep *All the Quant* guide.

2. One of the content areas is a low-level disguise or some other minor feature.

These problems can be easier to solve than major hybrids. However, you will still benefit greatly from paying close attention to the turns as you move through the stages of the solution.

Try-It #8-3

If a and b are consecutive positive integers, is ab divisible by 30 ?

(1) a^2 is divisible by 25.

(2) 63 is a factor of b^2.

This problem tests your skill with both Divisibility & Primes and Consecutive Integers. Consecutive integer concepts often lend themselves well to questions about divisibility.

To be divisible by 30, a number must have 2, 3, and 5 as prime factors. Thus, the question becomes: "Does ab have 2, 3, and 5 as prime factors?"

Next, use a concept from consecutive integers: a and b are consecutive positive integers. Thus, either a or b is an even number, which means that the product ab is automatically divisible by 2. The question can be further simplified: "Does the product ab have 3 and 5 as prime factors?"

(1) INSUFFICIENT: Statement (1) indicates that 25 is a factor of a^2, meaning that 5 and 5 are prime factors of a^2. Knowing that 5 is a prime factor of a indicates that 5 is a factor of ab, but does not indicate whether 3 is a factor.

(2) INSUFFICIENT: Statement (2) indicates that 63 is a factor of b^2, which means that 3, 3, and 7 are prime factors of b^2 ($3 \times 3 \times 7 = 63$). Knowing that 3 is a prime factor of b indicates that 3 is a factor of ab, but does not indicate whether 5 is a factor.

(1) AND (2) SUFFICIENT: According to the combined statements, a is divisible by 5 and b is divisible by 3. This is sufficient information to answer the rephrased question.

The correct answer is (C).

Notice that the solution never indicated exactly what consecutive integers a and b are—this isn't necessary. Also notice a potential trap in this problem—assuming that $a < b$ because of the way the question is phrased. This assumption would not be fatal in this case, but if you realize that a and b can come in *either* order, then it's easier to create an accurate list of different scenarios for a and b.

Try-It #8-4

> A carnival card game gives the contestant a one in three probability of successfully choosing the correct card and thereby winning the game. If a contestant plays the game repeatedly, what is the minimum number of times that he must play the game so that the probability that he never loses is less than 1% ?

This problem primarily tests Probability theory. In addition, Exponents are needed to represent the impact of playing multiple games on the probability of the outcomes. The probabilities are given in fractions, yet the question is asked in terms of percents, so Fraction, Decimal, and Percent (FDP) connections are relevant. Finally, the question is phrased in terms of an inequality, so Inequalities come into play.

"The probability that he never loses" can be rephrased as "the probability that he always wins." This probability can be expressed as $\left(\frac{1}{3}\right)^n$, where $\frac{1}{3}$ is the chance of winning on a single play and n is the number of times the contestant plays.

Track scenarios in a chart:

Number of Plays	P(All Wins)	Approx. Equivalent
1	$\frac{1}{3}$	$0.33 = 33\%$
2	$\frac{1}{9}$	$0.11 = 11\%$
3	$\frac{1}{27}$	$\frac{4}{100} = 0.04 = 4\%$
4	$\frac{1}{81}$	$\frac{1}{80} = \frac{1.25}{100} = 1.25\%$
5	$\frac{1}{243}$	$\frac{1}{250} = \frac{0.4}{100} = 0.4\% < 1\%$

You might also have noticed that only the denominator in the probabilities mattered, as the numerator was always 1. To have a probability of less than 1%, the fractional probability must be "1 over something greater than 100." In order for $3^n > 100$, n must be at least 5.

The correct answer is 5.

Problem Set

Solve the following problems and identify the topics being tested.

1. The average (arithmetic mean) of a list of six numbers is equal to 0. What is the positive difference between the number of positive numbers in the list and the number of negative numbers in the list?

   (1) Each of the positive numbers in the list equals 10.

   (2) Each of the negative numbers in the list equals −5.

2. Simplify: $\dfrac{2^2 + 2^3 + 2^4 + 2^5}{\left(\sqrt{5} + \sqrt{3}\right)\left(\sqrt{5} - \sqrt{3}\right)}$.

3. If a, b, and c are positive, is $a > b$?

   (1) $\dfrac{a}{b+c} > \dfrac{b}{a+c}$

   (2) $b + c < a$

4. If c is randomly chosen from the integers 20 to 99, inclusive, what is the probability that $c^3 - c$ is divisible by 12 ?

5. If x and y are positive integers greater than 1 such that $x - y$ and $\dfrac{x}{y}$ are both even integers, which of the following numbers must be non-prime integers?

   I. x

   II. $x + y$

   III. $\dfrac{y}{x}$

   (A) I only

   (B) II only

   (C) III only

   (D) I and II only

   (E) I, II, and III

8

6. A number cube with faces numbered 1 through 6 has an equal chance of landing on any face when rolled. If the number cube is rolled twice, what is the probability that the sum of the two rolls is a prime number?

7. The function $\{x\}$ is defined as the area of a square with diagonal of length x. If $x > 0$ and $\{x^2\} = x^2$, what is the value of x ?

   (A) 1

   (B) $\sqrt{2}$

   (C) $\sqrt{3}$

   (D) 2

   (E) 4

8. A circular microchip with a radius of 2.5 centimeters is manufactured by following a circular diagram. The scale of the diagram is such that a measurement of 1 centimeter on the diagram corresponds to a measurement of 0.5 millimeters on the microchip. What is the area of the diagram, in square centimeters? (1 centimeter = 10 millimeters)

9. Three consecutive integers are selected from the integers 1 to 50, inclusive. What is the sum of the remainders that result when each of the three integers is divided by x ?

   (1) When the greatest of the consecutive integers is divided by x, the remainder is 0.

   (2) When the least of the consecutive integers is divided by x, the remainder is 1.

10. If x, y, and z are all distinct positive integers, and the percent increase from x to y is equal to the percent increase from y to z, what is x ?

   (1) y is prime.

   (2) $z = 9$

Solutions

1. **(E):** Since the average of the six numbers in the list is 0, the sum of the six numbers is 0. There could be positive numbers and negative numbers in the set. Zero is not mentioned, but this does not rule it out. In order for the sum of the numbers in the set to be 0, either all the terms are 0 or there are some positives and some negatives.

   (1) INSUFFICIENT: Statement (1) indicates that the list contains at least one positive number and that each positive term is 10. The list could be $\{-2, -2, -2, -2, -2, 10\}$, and the positive difference between the number of positive terms and the number of negative terms would be 4. Alternatively, the list could be $\{-20, -20, 10, 10, 10, 10\}$, and the positive difference would be 2.

   (2) INSUFFICIENT: Statement (2) indicates that the list contains at least one negative number and that each negative term is -5. The set could be $\{-5, 1, 1, 1, 1, 1\}$, and the positive difference between the number of positive terms and the number of negative terms would be 4. The set could be $\{-5, -5, -5, 5, 5, 5\}$, and the positive difference would be 0.

   (1) AND (2) INSUFFICIENT: The statements together suggest that the set has twice as many -5 terms as 10 terms, in order to maintain a sum of 0. If every term is negative or positive, then the set would have to be $\{-5, -5, -5, -5, 10, 10\}$, and the positive difference would be 2. However, zero terms are possible, so the set could be $\{-5, -5, 0, 0, 0, 10\}$, and the positive difference would be 1.

   The correct answer is **(E)**.

2. **30:** You could simplify the numerator arithmetically (multiply out the terms and then add). Alternatively, factor a 2^2 out of the numerator. Then, distribute the denominator (which becomes the difference of squares).

$$\frac{2^2\left(1 + 2 + 2^2 + 2^3\right)}{\left[\left(\sqrt{5}\right)^2 - \left(\sqrt{3}\right)^2\right]} = \frac{2^2(1 + 2 + 4 + 8)}{5 - 3}$$

$$= \frac{4(15)}{2}$$

$$= 30$$

3. **(D):** Statement (2) appears to be a bit easier to work with so begin there.

   (2) SUFFICIENT: If a, b, and c are all positive, then $a > b + \text{positive}$. Therefore, a must be *greater* than b. You could also prove this fact by testing cases.

Case	$b + c < a$	Is this case possible according to (2)?
$a > b$	$b + \text{positive} < \text{number greater than } b$	Possible
$a = b$	$b + c < b$	Impossible, since c is positive
$a < b$	$b + c < \text{number less than } b$	Impossible, since c is positive

Only the $a > b$ case is possible, so the answer is a definite Yes.

8

(1) SUFFICIENT: Statement (1) can be cross-multiplied without flipping the inequality sign, since the denominators are positive.

$$a(a + c) > b(b + c)$$
$$a^2 + ac > b^2 + bc$$
$$a^2 + ac - b^2 - bc > 0$$

$$a^2 - b^2 + ac - bc > 0 \qquad \text{Group similar terms to simplify.}$$
$$[a^2 - b^2] + [ac - bc] > 0 \qquad \text{Note the Quadratic Template.}$$
$$(a - b)(a + b) + c(a - b) > 0$$
$$(a - b)[(a + b) + c] > 0 \qquad \text{Factor out } a - b.$$

Therefore, $a + b + c$ is positive, because all three additive terms are positive. So $(a - b)(\text{positive}) > 0$. By Number Properties sign rules, $(a - b)$ must also be positive in order for the product to be greater than 0. Thus, $a > b$.

This algebra is very tough; it is hard to see where to begin or what series of manipulations will be productive. If you did not see this, you could try testing cases to see which are allowed by statement (1). Note: LT = less than and GT = greater than. GTb means "a number greater than b."

Case	$\dfrac{a}{(b + c)} > \dfrac{b}{(a + c)}$	Is this case possible according to (1)?
$a > b$	$\dfrac{\text{GT}b}{(b + c)} > \dfrac{b}{\text{GT}(b + c)}$	Possible. The left is greater than the right.
$a = b$	$\dfrac{b}{(b + c)} > \dfrac{b}{(b + c)}$	Impossible; the two expressions are equal.
$a < b$	$\dfrac{\text{LT}b}{(b + c)} > \dfrac{b}{\text{LT}(b + c)}$	Impossible; the left side is actually less than the right side, not greater than as (1) requires.

The correct answer is **(D)**.

4. $\dfrac{3}{4}$: The words *divisible* and *probability* are used, so this question is about Divisibility & Primes and Probability.

Probability is $\dfrac{(\text{Favorable outcomes})}{(\text{Total \# of possibilities})}$. There are $99 - 20 + 1 = 80$ possible values for c, so the unknown is how many of these c values yield a $c^3 - c$ that is divisible by 12.

The prime factorization of 12 is $2 \times 2 \times 3$. There are at least two ways to think about this: numbers are divisible by 12 if they are divisible by 3 and by 2 twice, or if they are multiples of both 4 and 3.

The expression involving c can be factored.

$$c^3 - c = c\left(c^2 - 1\right)$$
$$= c(c - 1)(c + 1)$$

These are consecutive integers. It may help to put them in increasing order: $(c-1)c(c+1)$. Thus, this question has a lot to do with Consecutive Integers, and not only because the integers 20 to 99 themselves are consecutive.

In any set of three consecutive integers, a multiple of 3 will be included. Thus, $(c-1)c(c+1)$ is always divisible by 3 for any integer c. This takes care of part of the 12. So the question becomes: "How many of the possible $(c-1)c(c+1)$ values are divisible by 4?" Since the prime factors of 4 are 2's, it makes sense to think in terms of Odds and Evens.

For example, $(c-1)c(c+1)$ could be (E)(O)(E), which is definitely divisible by 4, because the two evens would each provide at least one separate factor of 2. Thus, $c^3 - c$ is divisible by 12 whenever c is odd, which are the cases $c = 21, 23, 25 \ldots 95, 97, 99$. That's $\left(\dfrac{99-21}{2}\right) + 1 = \left(\dfrac{78}{2}\right) + 1 = 40$ possibilities.

Alternatively, $(c-1)c(c+1)$ could be (O)(E)(O), which will only be divisible by 4 when the even term itself is a multiple of 4. Thus, $c^3 - c$ is also divisible by 12 whenever c is a multiple of 4, which are the cases $c = 20, 24, 28, \ldots, 92, 96$. That's $\left(\dfrac{96-20}{4}\right) + 1 = \left(\dfrac{76}{4}\right) + 1 = 20$ possibilities.

The probability is thus $\left(\dfrac{40+20}{80}\right) = \dfrac{60}{80} = \dfrac{3}{4}$.

5. **(D) I and II only:** x cannot equal y, as that would make $\dfrac{x}{y} = 1 \neq$ even. So either $x > y$ or $y > x$. x and y are both positive and $\dfrac{x}{y}$ is an integer, so $x > y$.

Since $x - y$ is even, either x and y are both even or they are both odd.

Since $\dfrac{x}{y} = $ an even integer, $x = y \times$ (even integer).

Therefore, x is an even integer, as is y.

I.   TRUE. x and y are both positive even integers, and $x > y$. No even number greater than 2 is prime, so x can't be prime.

II.   TRUE. x and y are each positive even integers and $x > y$. Thus, $x + y$ is even and the least possible value of $x + y = 4 + 2 = 6$. All even numbers greater than or equal to 6 are non-prime.

III. FALSE. It could be that $x = 4$ and $y = 2$, so $\dfrac{y}{x} = \dfrac{1}{2}$, which is not prime, but is also not an integer. In fact, if $\dfrac{x}{y} = $ an even integer, then $\dfrac{y}{x} = \dfrac{1}{\text{an even integer}} = $ positive fraction.

The correct answer is **(D)**.

8

6. $\frac{5}{12}$: First, think about the prime numbers less than 12, the maximum sum of the numbers. These primes are 2, 3, 5, 7, 11.

   The probability of rolling 2, 3, 5, 7, or 11 is equal to the number of ways to roll any of these sums divided by the total number of possible outcomes. The total number of possible outcomes is $6 \times 6 = 36$.

   Sum of 2 can happen 1 way: $1 + 1$

   Sum of 3 can happen 2 ways: $1 + 2, 2 + 1$

   Sum of 5 can happen 4 ways: $1 + 4, 2 + 3, 3 + 2, 4 + 1$

   Sum of 7 can happen 6 ways: $1 + 6, 2 + 5, 3 + 4, 4 + 3, 5 + 2, 6 + 1$

   Sum of 11 can happen 2 ways: $5 + 6, 6 + 5$

   That's a total of $1 + 2 + 4 + 6 + 2 = 15$ ways to roll a prime sum.

   Thus, the probability is $\frac{15}{36}$, or $\frac{5}{12}$.

7. **(B)** $\sqrt{2}$: The problem defines the function in words; you'll need to translate into math.

   "The function $\{x\}$ is defined as the area of a square with diagonal of length x."

   $\{x\} = s^2$, where s is the side of the square.

   If the diagonal equals x, then the side of the square equals $\frac{x}{\sqrt{2}}$.

   Therefore:

   $$\{x\} = \left(\frac{x}{\sqrt{2}}\right)^2$$

   $$\{x\} = \frac{x^2}{2}$$

   The question stem also indicates that $\{x^2\} = x^2$. In other words, applying the defined function to x^2 will result in an answer of x^2. First, find $\{x^2\}$.

   $$\{x^2\} = \frac{\left(x^2\right)^2}{2} = \frac{x^4}{2}$$

   Now, set that equal to x^2 and solve.

   $$\frac{x^4}{2} = x^2$$

   $$x^4 = 2x^2$$

   $$x^2 = 2$$

   (Note: It is acceptable to divide by x^2 because the question stem indicates that $x \neq 0$.) Therefore, x is equal to $-\sqrt{2}$ or $\sqrt{2}$. Since the question stem indicates that $x > 0$, only $x = \sqrt{2}$ is a valid solution.

   Alternatively, you could work backwards from the answers. Start with (B) or (D).

8

(B) If $x = \sqrt{2}$, then $x^2 = 2$. Next, the question specifies that that $\{x^2\} = x^2 \cdot \left\{\left(\sqrt{2}\right)^2\right\}$ becomes $\{2\}$, so what does this function return?

"The function $\{x\}$ is defined as the area of a square with diagonal of length x."

The function $\{2\}$ is defined as the area of a square with diagonal length 2. The side length of this square is $\dfrac{2}{\sqrt{2}}$, so the area of this square is $\left(\dfrac{2}{\sqrt{2}}\right)^2 = \dfrac{4}{2} = 2$. Therefore, $\{2\} = 2$, which matches the question stem specification that $\{x^2\} = x^2$.

The correct answer is **(B)**.

8. **2,500π:** Microchip radius $= (2.5 \text{ cm})(10 \text{ mm/cm}) = 25 \text{ mm}$

$$\text{Diagram radius} = 1 \text{ cm per every } 0.5 \text{ mm on the microchip}$$
$$= 10 \text{ mm per every } 0.5 \text{ mm on the microchip}$$
$$= \left(\frac{10 \text{ mm}}{0.5 \text{ mm on microchip}}\right)(25 \text{ mm on microchip})$$
$$= \left(\frac{10 \text{ mm}}{0.5}\right)(25)$$
$$= \left(\frac{100 \text{ mm}}{5}\right)(25)$$
$$= (100 \text{ mm})(5)$$
$$= 500 \text{ mm}$$
$$= (500 \text{ mm})\left(\frac{1 \text{ cm}}{10 \text{ mm}}\right)$$
$$= 50 \text{ cm}$$

$$\text{Diagram area} = \pi \times r^2$$
$$= \pi \times (50 \text{ cm})^2$$
$$= 2,500\pi \text{ cm}^2$$

9. **(C):** When consecutive integers are divided by the same number, the remainders follow a repeating pattern. For instance, when consecutive integers are divided by 4, the remainders form a repeating pattern of [1, 2, 3, 0], with every fourth integer being divisible by 4.

(1) INSUFFICIENT: This statement indicates that the greatest of the three integers is divisible by x. However, the sum of the remainders depends on the value of x. For instance, if $x = 10$, the three remainders would be 8, 9, and 0, respectively, and their sum would be 17. If $x = 5$, the three remainders would be 3, 4, and 0, with a sum of 7.

(2) INSUFFICIENT: Statement (2) indicates that the least of the three integers is one greater than a multiple of x. However, the sum of the remainders again depends on the value of x. If $x = 10$, the three remainders would be 1, 2, and 3, with a sum of 6. If $x = 2$, the three remainders would be 1, 0, and 1, with a sum of 2.

(1) AND (2) SUFFICIENT: Call the three consecutive integers y, $y + 1$, and $y + 2$. The remainder when y is divided by x is 1 and the remainder when $y + 2$ is divided by x is 0. Write out the known remainders and write out enough other terms to see where the pattern repeats. In this case, the term $y - 1$ also has a remainder of 0, so the pattern repeats every three terms.

$y - 1$	y	$y + 1$	$y + 2$
0	1	?	0

The only way for the remainders to have a consistent repeating pattern is for the missing remainder to equal 2 (in which case x must equal 3). Therefore, the sum of the three remainders is $1 + 2 + 0 = 3$.

10. **(A):** The question asks for the value of x. Translate the equation given in the question stem.

$$\frac{y - x}{x} = \frac{z - y}{y}$$

$$y^2 - xy = zx - xy$$

$$y^2 = zx$$

$$x = \frac{y^2}{z}$$

The problem stem specifies that x is an integer, so the right-hand side of the equation must also be an integer. Therefore, z must be a factor of y^2.

The question asks for the value of x.

(1) SUFFICIENT: If y is prime, then there are two possible scenarios.

Case 1: $y = z$. This isn't allowed, though, because the question stem indicates that the variables represent three different positive integers.

Case 2: $y^2 = z$, in which case x must equal 1. This is the only possible case, so statement (1) is sufficient.

(2) INSUFFICIENT: If $z = 9$, then y^2 is a multiple of 9, so z must be a multiple of 3. It's possible that $z = 9$, $y = 3$, and $x = 1$. It's also possible that $z = 9$, $y = 36$, and $x = 4$.

The correct answer is **(A)**.

Practice

CHAPTER 9
Workout Sets

In This Chapter

CHAPTER 9 Workout Sets

Workout Set 1

1.

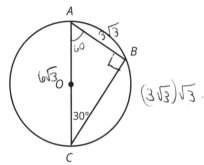

Figure not drawn to scale.

The circle with center O has a circumference of $6\pi\sqrt{3}$. If AC is a diameter of the circle, what is the length of BC ?

(A) $\dfrac{3}{\sqrt{2}}$

(B) 3

(C) $3\sqrt{3}$

(D) 9

(E) $9\sqrt{3}$

$C = 2\pi r$

$r = 3\sqrt{3}$

2. A batch of widgets costs $p + 15$ dollars for a company to produce and each batch sells for $p(9 - p)$ dollars. For which of the following values of p, does the company make a profit?

(A) 3

(B) 4

(C) 5

(D) 6

(E) 7

$P = R - C$

$\text{Profit} = P(9-p) - (P+15)$

$9p - p^2 - p - 15$

$= -p^2 + 8p - 15$

$3 \quad -9 \quad 24 \quad -15 = \emptyset$

$4 = \quad -16 \quad 32 \quad -15 = 1 \checkmark$

$5 \quad \quad -25 \quad +40 \quad -15 = \emptyset \times$

3. If K is the sum of the reciprocals of the consecutive integers from 41 to 60 inclusive, which of the following is less than K?

   I. $\dfrac{1}{4}$

   II. $\dfrac{1}{3}$

   III. $\dfrac{1}{2}$

   (A) None

   (B) I only

   (C) II only

   (D) I and II only

   (E) I, II, and III

   [handwritten: $\frac{1}{41} + \frac{1}{42} \cdots \frac{1}{60}$]
   [handwritten: $\frac{1}{50} = 2\% \times 10$]
   [handwritten: $1/2 = 50\%$]
   [handwritten: $1/3 = 33.3\%$]
   [handwritten: $1/4 = 25\%$]

4. Triplets Adam, Bruce, and Charlie enter a triathlon. There are nine competitors in the triathlon. If every competitor has an equal chance of winning, and three medals will be awarded, what is the probability that at least two of the triplets will win a medal?

   (A) $\dfrac{3}{14}$

   (B) $\dfrac{19}{84}$

   (C) $\dfrac{11}{42}$

   (D) $\dfrac{15}{28}$

   (E) $\dfrac{3}{4}$

   [handwritten: $\dfrac{9!}{6!}$]
   [handwritten: $1-p$]

5. Floyd started at one end of a trail at 8:07 a.m. and hiked the entire 5 miles to the other end of the trail at an average rate of 3 miles per hour. Connie started at the same end of the trail at 8:30 a.m. and hiked the entire length of the trail at an average rate of 2.5 miles per hour. Finally, Karen started her hike in the same place at 10:00 a.m. and hiked the entire length of the trail at an average rate of 4 miles per hour. During approximately what percent of the 4-hour period from 8:00 a.m. to noon were at least two of the three hikers on the trail?

   (A) 34%

   (B) 45%

   (C) 55%

   (D) 59%

   (E) 68%

   [handwritten: Fl 8:07 $\xrightarrow[1:40]{3mph \times 5mi}$ 9:47   8:30 ~ 9:47]
   [handwritten: C 8:30 $\xrightarrow{2.5mph \times 5mi}$ 10:30   9:47 - 10:30]
   [handwritten: K 10:00 $\xrightarrow[1:15]{4mph \times 5mi}$ 11:15]
   [handwritten: 2 hrs → 60   120 min]
   [handwritten: 3:08 → 188]
   [handwritten: $\frac{30}{47} \leftarrow \frac{60}{94} \leftarrow \frac{120}{188}$]

6. Half an hour after Car A started traveling from Newtown to Oldtown, a distance of 62 miles, Car B started traveling along the same road from Oldtown to Newtown. The cars met each other on the road 15 minutes after Car B started its trip. If Car A traveled at a constant rate that was 8 miles per hour greater than Car B's constant rate, how many miles had Car B driven when they met?

   (A) 14
   (B) 12
   (C) 10
   (D) 9
   (E) 8

7. If $x = 2^b - (8^8 + 8^6)$, for which of the following b values is x closest to zero?

   (A) 20
   (B) 24
   (C) 25
   (D) 30
   (E) 42

8. If $k > 1$, which of the following must be equal to $\dfrac{2}{\sqrt{k+1} + \sqrt{k-1}}$?

   (A) 2
   (B) $2\sqrt{2k}$
   (C) $2\sqrt{k+1} + \sqrt{k-1}$
   (D) $\dfrac{\sqrt{k+1}}{\sqrt{k-1}}$
   (E) $\sqrt{k+1} - \sqrt{k-1}$

9. If y is 20% less than 90% of x and z is 25% more than 130% of y, then z is what percent of x ?

   (A) 72%
   (B) 92.5%
   (C) 108.5%
   (D) 117%
   (E) 135%

10. Set A consists of three consecutive positive multiples of 3, and set B consists of five consecutive positive multiples of 5. If the sum of the integers in set A is equal to the sum of the integers in set B, what is the least number that could be a member of set A ?

   (A) 69
   (B) 72
   (C) 75
   (D) 78
   (E) 81

Workout Set 1 Answer Key

1. **D**
2. **B**
3. **D**
4. **B**
5. **B**
6. **A**
7. **B**
8. **E**
9. **D**
10. **B**

Workout Set 1 Solutions

1. **(D) 9:** If AC is a diameter of the circle, then triangle ABC is a right triangle, with angle $ABC = 90$ degrees. The shortest side of a triangle is across from its least angle and the longest side of a triangle is across from its greatest angle. Therefore, $AC > BC > AB$.

    The circumference of the circle $= \pi d = 6\pi\sqrt{3}$, so $d = 6\sqrt{3} \approx 6(1.7) = 10.2$. Thus, $AC \approx 10.2$ and $BC < 10.2$. Answer (E) is too great and answer (D), while less than 10.2, is questionable, because side BC is opposite a 60-degree angle. The value should be less than 9.

    Since angle ACB is 30 degrees, angle CAB is 60 degrees.

    The sides in a 30–60–90 triangle have the ratio $x : x\sqrt{3} : 2x$, so use the ratio to compute the desired side, BC.

    $$2x = 6\sqrt{3}$$
    $$x = \frac{6\sqrt{3}}{2}$$
    $$x = 3\sqrt{3}$$

    Find the length of BC.

    $$BC = x\sqrt{3} = \left(3\sqrt{3}\right)\left(\sqrt{3}\right)$$
    $$BC = 9$$

    Therefore, BC has length 9.

    The correct answer is **(D)**.

2. **(B) 4:** You can *work backwards* from the answers. Start with (B) or (D).

    > (D) $p = 6$
    > Cost: $6 + 15 = 21$
    > Revenue: $6(9 - 6) = 18$
    > Profit: $18 - 21 = -3$ Loss, not profit!

    Eliminate (D) and try (B) next.

    > (B) $p = 4$
    > Cost: $4 + 15 = 19$
    > Revenue: $4(9 - 4) = 20$
    > Profit: $20 - 19 = 1$

    The company makes a profit when $p = 4$.

9

Alternatively, profit equals revenue minus cost. The company's profit is:

$$p(9-p)-(p+15)=9p-p^2-p-15$$
$$=-p^2+8p-15$$
$$=-\left(p^2-8p+15\right)$$
$$=-(p-5)(p-3)$$

Profit will be zero if $p=5$ or $p=3$, which eliminates answers (A) and (C). For $p>5$, both $(p-5)$ and $(p-3)$ are positive. In that case, the profit is negative (i.e., the company loses money). The profit is only positive if $(p-5)$ and $(p-3)$ have opposite signs, which occurs when $3<p<5$.

The correct answer is **(B)**.

3. **(D) I and II only:** The sum $\frac{1}{41}+\frac{1}{42}+\frac{1}{43}+\cdots+\frac{1}{60}$ has 20 fractional terms. It is impossible to compute this by hand in two minutes. Instead, look at the maximum and minimum possible values for the sum.

Maximum: The greatest fraction in the sum is $\frac{1}{41}$. K is definitely less than $20\times\frac{1}{41}$, or $\frac{20}{41}$, which is less than $\frac{20}{40}=\frac{1}{2}$.

Minimum: The least fraction in the sum is $\frac{1}{60}$. K is definitely greater than $20\times\frac{1}{60}=\frac{1}{3}$.

Therefore, $\frac{1}{3}<K<\frac{1}{2}$.

   I. $\frac{1}{4}<\frac{1}{3}<K$ Yes

   II. $\frac{1}{3}<K$ Yes

   III. $\frac{1}{2}>K$ No

The correct answer is **(D)**.

4. **(B)** $\frac{19}{84}$: With nine competitors and only three medals awarded, only $\frac{1}{3}$ of the competitors will win overall. Although a simplification, it is reasonable for each competitor to see his or her chance of winning a medal as $\frac{1}{3}$, or to expect to win $\frac{1}{3}$ of a medal (pretending for a moment that medals can be shared).

The question asks for the probability that *at least* two of the triplets will win a medal. In other words, you want $\frac{2}{3}$ to $\frac{3}{3}$ of the triplets to win medals or for each triplet to win $\frac{2}{3}$ to $\frac{3}{3}$ of a medal. Since $\frac{2}{3}$ and $\frac{3}{3}$ are both greater than $\frac{1}{3}$, you are looking for the probability that the triplets will win medals at a rate greater than that expected for competitors overall. In other words, this would be an unusual outcome. Thus, the probability should be less than $\frac{1}{2}$. Eliminate (D) and (E). You could then guess from among the remaining answers with a 1 in 3 chance of guessing correctly.

To solve, use the probability formula and combinatorics.

$$\text{Probability} = \frac{\text{Specified outcome}}{\text{All possible outcomes}} = \frac{\text{\# of ways at least 2 triplets win medal}}{\text{\# of ways 3 medals can be awarded}}$$

First, find the total number of outcomes for the triathlon. There are nine competitors; three will win medals and six will not. Set up an anagram grid where Y represents a medal, N no medal.

Competitor	C_1	C_2	C_3	C_4	C_5	C_6	C_7	C_8	C_9
Medal	Y	Y	Y	N	N	N	N	N	N

Therefore, the number of ways three medals can be awarded is $\frac{9!}{3!6!} = \frac{(9)(8)(7)}{(3)(2)(1)} = (3)(4)(7) = 84$.

Now, determine the number of instances when *at least two* brothers win a medal. Practically speaking, this could happen when 1) exactly three brothers win or 2) exactly two brothers win.

Start with *all three* triplets winning medals, where Y represents a medal.

Triplet	A	B	C	Non-triplet	C_1	C_2	C_3	C_4	C_5	C_6
Medal	Y	Y	Y	Medal	N	N	N	N	N	N

The number of ways this could happen is $\frac{3!}{3!} \times \frac{6!}{6!} = 1$. This makes sense, as there is only one instance in which all three triplets would win medals and all of the other competitors would not. (If you recognize this immediately, no need to write out the math.)

Next, calculate the instances when *exactly two* of the triplets win medals.

Triplet	A	B	C	Non-triplet	C_1	C_2	C_3	C_4	C_5	C_6
Medal	Y	Y	N	Medal	Y	N	N	N	N	N

Since both triplets and non-triplets win medals in this scenario, consider the possibilities for both sides of the grid. For the triplets, the number of ways that two could win medals is $\frac{3!}{2!1!} = 3$.

For the non-triplet competitors, the number of ways that one could win the remaining medal is $\frac{6!}{1!5!} = 6$.

Multiply these two numbers to get the total number of instances: $3 \times 6 = 18$.

The brothers win *at least two* medals in $18 + 1 = 19$ cases. The total number of cases is 84, so the probability is $\frac{19}{84}$.

The correct answer is (**B**).

5. **(B) 45%:** To answer the question, you'll need to identify the periods of time during which different numbers of hikers are on the trail. To organize your work, start by drawing out a diagram showing the four hours between 8:00 a.m. and noon.

Next, identify the time period during which each hiker was on the trail. Floyd traveled the 5 miles at a rate of 3 miles per hour (mph), so he spent $\frac{5 \text{ miles}}{3 \text{ mph}} = 1$ hour and 40 minutes on the trail. Therefore, Floyd was on the trail from 8:07 to 9:47.

Connie traveled the 5 miles at a rate of 2.5 mph, so she spent $\frac{5 \text{ miles}}{2.5 \text{ mph}} = 2$ hours on the trail. Connie was on the trail from 8:30 to 10:30.

Finally, Karen traveled the 5 miles at a rate of 4 mph, so she spent $\frac{5 \text{ miles}}{4 \text{ mph}} = 1$ hour 15 minutes on the trail. Karen was on the trail from 10:00 to 11:15.

Plot each of these time periods on your drawing.

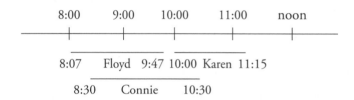

There were no periods of time during which all three hikers were on the trail. However, there were two periods during which exactly two of the three hikers were on the trail. Floyd and Connie were both on the trail from 8:30 to 9:47, and Connie and Karen were both on the trail from 10:00 to 10:30. This represents a total of 1 hour and 47 minutes, or approximately 1.75 hours.

1.75 hours is more than a third of 4 hours, but less than half of 4 hours. Therefore, the only reasonable answer is (B). It is also possible to simplify the fraction more precisely.

$$\frac{1.75}{4} = \frac{1.75 \times 25}{4 \times 25} = \frac{43.75}{100} \approx 45\%$$

The correct answer is **(B)**.

6. **(A) 14:** Draw a diagram to illustrate the moment at which Car A and Car B pass each other moving in opposite directions.

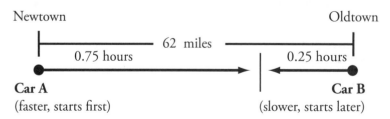

Try working backwards from the answers, starting with (B) or (D).

	B's Distance (miles)	B's Rate (mph) $= \dfrac{D}{T} = \dfrac{D}{0.25}$	A's Rate (mph) = B's Rate + 8	A's Distance (miles) $= R \times T$ $= R \times 0.75$	Total Distance = 62?
(B)	12	48	56	42	54

The total distance is not 62, so answer (B) is incorrect. Furthermore, a distance of 54 is too short, so the answer must be (A). If you aren't sure, confirm by checking answer (A).

	B's Distance (miles)	B's Rate (mph) $= \dfrac{D}{T} = \dfrac{D}{0.25}$	A's Rate (mph) = B's Rate + 8	A's Distance (miles) $= R \times T$ $= R \times 0.75$	Total Distance = 62?
(A)	14	56	64	48	62

Alternatively, you could solve algebraically, using a rate–time–distance (RTD) chart. Note that you must convert 15 minutes to 0.25 hours.

	Rate	Time	Distance
Car A	$(r + 8)$ mph	0.75 hours	$(0.75)(r + 8)$ miles
Car B	r mph	0.25 hours	$0.25r$ miles
Total			62 miles

Set up and solve an equation for the total distance.

$$(0.75)(r + 8) + (0.25r) = 62$$
$$0.75r + 6 + 0.25r = 62$$
$$r = 56$$

Therefore, in 15 minutes, Car B traveled a distance of $0.25r = (0.25)(56) = 14$ miles.

The correct answer is **(A)**.

7. **(B) 24:** Testing the choices would be a natural way to solve this problem, since the question doesn't ask you to solve for b in general, but rather "for which of the following is x closest to zero?" However, numbers between 2^{20} and 2^{42} are too great to plug and compute. Instead, manipulate the terms with base 8 to see how they might balance with 2^b.

$$x = 2^b - \left(8^8 + 8^6\right)$$

$$0 \approx 2^b - \left(8^8 + 8^6\right)$$

$$2^b \approx \left(8^8 + 8^6\right)$$

$$2^b \approx \left(8^6\right)\left(8^2 + 1\right) \text{ Since 1 is very small in comparison to the other numbers,}$$
$$\text{assume that}\left(8^2 + 1\right) \approx 8^2.$$

$$2^b \approx \left(8^6\right)\left(8^2\right)$$

$$2^b \approx 8^8$$

$$2^b \approx \left(\left(2^3\right)^8\right)$$

$$2^b \approx 2^{24}$$

$$b \approx 24$$

The correct answer is **(B)**.

8. **(E)** $\sqrt{(k+1)} - \sqrt{(k-1)}$: Since there are variables in the answer choices, *choose a smart number to solve*. If $k = 2$, then $\dfrac{2}{\sqrt{k+1} + \sqrt{k-1}} = \dfrac{2}{\sqrt{3} + \sqrt{1}} \approx \dfrac{2}{1.7 + 1} = \dfrac{2}{2.7}$, which is less than 1. Now, test the answer choices and try to match the target; stop if you can tell that an answer won't equal the target.

(A)   2 Too high. Eliminate.

(B) $2\sqrt{2k} = 2\sqrt{4}$ Too high. Eliminate.

(C) $2\sqrt{k+1} + \sqrt{k-1} = 2\sqrt{3} + \sqrt{1} \approx 2(1.7) + 1$ Too high. Eliminate.

(D) $\dfrac{\sqrt{k+1}}{\sqrt{k-1}} = \dfrac{\sqrt{3}}{\sqrt{1}} \approx 1.7$ Too high. Eliminate.

(E) $\sqrt{k+1} - \sqrt{k-1} = \sqrt{3} - \sqrt{1} \approx 1.7 - 1 = 0.7$ Correct!

Alternatively, solve the problem algebraically. The expression given is of the form $\dfrac{2}{a+b}$, where $a = \sqrt{k+1}$ and $b = \sqrt{k-1}$.

9

You need to either simplify or cancel the denominator, as none of the answer choices have the starting denominator and most of the choices have no denominator at all. First, try to eliminate the radical signs entirely, leaving only a^2 and b^2 in the denominator. To do so, multiply by a fraction that is a convenient form of 1.

$$\frac{2}{(a+b)} = \frac{2}{(a+b)} \times \frac{(a-b)}{(a-b)}$$

$$= \frac{2(a-b)}{a^2 - b^2}$$

Notice the "difference of two squares" special product created in the denominator.

Substituting for a and b:

$$\frac{2}{\left(\sqrt{k+1} + \sqrt{k-1}\right)} \times \frac{\left(\sqrt{k+1} - \sqrt{k-1}\right)}{\left(\sqrt{k+1} - \sqrt{k-1}\right)} = \frac{2\left(\sqrt{k+1} - \sqrt{k-1}\right)}{(k+1) - (k-1)}$$

$$= \frac{2\left(\sqrt{k+1} - \sqrt{k-1}\right)}{2} = \sqrt{k+1} - \sqrt{k-1}$$

The correct answer is **(E)**.

9. **(D) 117%:** An algebraic setup would be fairly ugly on this problem, but a combination of two other techniques work quite nicely: choose smart numbers and *estimate*.

There are no real values for the variables, so choosing smart numbers is a valid approach. Furthermore, the answer choices are far enough apart that you can estimate if the smart numbers get a little messy.

Of the three variables, it is easiest to pick for x. If you were to pick for y or z, you would have to do "reverse" calculations to find the other variables. Since this is a percent problem, try 100 first.

$x = 100$
90% of $x = 90$
$y = 20\%$ less than $90 = 90 - 18 = 72$

This number is a little ugly, so round down to 70. Therefore, $y = 70$, so 130% of y is equal to $70 + 21 = 91$.

The next step requires you to take 25% of that number, so 91 is going to get messy. Estimate again, but this time round up a little bit (to offset the error you introduced when you rounded down earlier). Round to the nearest number that is divisible by 4, which is 92. Next, find 25% more than 92.

$z = 92 + 23 = 115$

If $x = 100$ and $z \approx 115$, then the final calculation is $\frac{115}{100} \approx 115\%$, which is closest to 117%.

The correct answer is **(D)**.

10. **(B) 72:** The values in set A and set B are unknown. Jot them down in terms of variables. If x is a positive integer, then x, $x + 1$, and $x + 2$ are consecutive integers, and $3x$, $3(x + 1)$, and $3(x + 2)$ are three consecutive multiples of 3. Similarly, set B contains $5y$, $5(y + 1)$, $5(y + 2)$, $5(y + 3)$, and $5(y + 4)$, where y is a positive integer. Do not use the same variable for both sets, since it is unclear whether or how they are related.

Sum the numbers in each set.

$$\text{Set } A\text{: } 3x + 3(x + 1) + 3(x + 2) = 3(3x + 3)$$

$$\text{Set } B\text{: } 5y + 5(y + 1) + 5(y + 2) + 5(y + 3) + 5(y + 4) = 5(5y + 10)$$

The sums of the sets are equal. Set them equal to each other and simplify as much as possible.

$$3(3x + 3) = 5(5y + 10)$$

$$9(x + 1) = 25(y + 2)$$

Because x and y are positive integers, the right side of the equation is a multiple of 25 and the left side is a multiple of 9. In other words, each side of the equation must be a multiple of both 9 and 25. Because 9 and 25 have no common factors, $x + 1$ must be a multiple of 25 and $y + 2$ must be a multiple of 9. The least possible value for x is $x = 24$, and the least number that could be a member of set A is $3x = 3(24) = 72$.

Alternatively, the sum of the integers in set A can be calculated by working backwards from the choices. Manually add them up or note that for an evenly spaced set the sum is (# of terms) $\times$ (the median term).

The integers in set B are multiples of 5, so the sum of set B is a multiple of 5. By extension, the (equivalent) sum of set A must be a multiple of 5. Try the answer choices; since the problem asks for the least value, start with answer (A).

(A) $\{69, 72, 75\}$ sums to $3(72) = $ not a multiple of 5. Eliminate.

(B) $\{72, 75, 78\}$ sums to $3(75) = $ a multiple of 5.

The problem asks for the least value that could be a member of set A, so the correct answer is **(B)**.

Workout Set 2

11. If $a \neq b$, is $\dfrac{1}{a-b} > ab$?

    (1) $|a| > |b|$

    (2) $a < b$

12. If $m = 4n + 9$, where n is a positive integer, what is the greatest common factor of m and n ?

    (1) $m = 9s$, where s is a positive integer

    (2) $n = 4t$, where t is a positive integer

13. A museum sold 30 tickets on Saturday. Some of the tickets sold were $10 general exhibit tickets and the rest were $70 special exhibit tickets. How many general exhibit tickets did the museum sell on Saturday?

    (1) The museum's total revenue from ticket sales on Saturday was greater than $1,570 and less than $1,670.

    (2) The museum sold more than 20, but fewer than 25, special exhibit tickets on Saturday.

14. If x and y are integers, is $x^y = y^x$?

    (1) $x - y = 2$

    (2) $xy = 8$

15. If $ab^3c^4 > 0$, is $a^3bc^5 > 0$?

    (1) $b > 0$

    (2) $c > 0$

16. What is the perimeter of isosceles triangle ABC ?

    (1) The length of side AB is 9.

    (2) The length of side BC is 4.

17. If x, y, and z are integers and $2^x \, 5^y \, z = 6.4 \times 10^6$, what is the value of xy ?

    (1) $z = 20$

    (2) $x = 9$

18. Is $x > y$?

    (1) $y^2 < z^2 < x^2$

    (2) $z < x$

19. A school has *a* students and *b* teachers. If $a < 150$, $b < 25$, and classes have a maximum of 15 students, can the *a* students be distributed among the *b* teachers so that each class has the same number of students? (Assume that any student can be taught by any teacher.)

    (1) It is possible to divide the students evenly into groups of 2, 3, 5, 6, 9, 10, or 15.

    (2) The greatest common factor of *a* and *b* is 10.

20. A set of five distinct positive integers has a median of 3 and a range of 12. What is the mean of the set of integers?

    (1) The product of the integers in the set is a multiple of 14.

    (2) The sum of the integers in the set is a multiple of 13.

Answers and explanations follow on the next page. ▶ ▶ ▶

Workout Set 2 Answer Key

11. **E**
12. **A**
13. **A**
14. **C**
15. **B**
16. **C**
17. **A**
18. **C**
19. **E**
20. **D**

Workout Set 2 Solutions

11. **(E):** You can cross-multiply the inequality, as long as you consider both cases.

> If $a - b$ is negative, the question becomes "Is $1 < ab(a - b)$?" (FLIPPED inequality sign)

> If $a - b$ is positive, the question becomes "Is $1 > ab(a - b)$?" (ORIGINAL inequality sign)

This is a conditional rephrased question—importantly, one with completely opposite questions as possibilities. *Any statement that doesn't at least answer the question of whether* $a - b$ *is positive or negative is unlikely to be sufficient.* You would also have to carry each statement through both questions, so this path is not very efficient. It's better to use the original inequality to *test cases* in order to eliminate the incorrect answers.

(1) INSUFFICIENT: *Test cases* to determine whether this statement is sufficient.

	a	b	$\lvert a \rvert > \lvert b \rvert$	Is $\dfrac{1}{a-b} > ab$?
Case 1	2	1	✓	$\dfrac{1}{1} > 2$? No
Case 2	2	−1	✓	$\dfrac{1}{3} > -2$? Yes

(2) INSUFFICIENT: Test cases again.

	a	b	$a < b$	Is $\dfrac{1}{a-b} > ab$?
Case 1	−2	1	✓	$\dfrac{1}{-3} > -2$? Yes
Case 2	−2	−1	✓	$\dfrac{1}{-1} > 2$? No

(1) AND (2) INSUFFICIENT: Whenever possible, reuse cases you've already tested (you can only do this when the case makes both statements true). The pairs tested for statement (2) are also valid for statement (1).

	a	b	Valid?	Is $\dfrac{1}{a-b} > ab$?
Case 1	−2	1	✓	$\dfrac{1}{-3} > -2$? Yes
Case 2	−2	−1	✓	$\dfrac{1}{-1} > 2$? No

Once again, two valid sets of numbers return two different answers, so even together, the statements are insufficient. The correct answer is **(E)**.

12. **(A):** The greatest common factor (GCF) of any two numbers is given by the product of the shared or overlapping primes in the two numbers. Any such question can be rephrased accordingly: "What exactly are the overlapping factors of m and n?"

(1) SUFFICIENT: This statement indicates that m must be a multiple of 9. If m is a multiple of 9 and $m = 4n + 9$, then this equation is really saying:

> multiple of $9 = 4n + 9$

In order for this to be true, $4n$ must also be a multiple of 9. The number 4 does not contain any factors of 9, so n itself must be a multiple of 9.

If both m and n are multiples of 9, and m is exactly 9 units away from $4n$, then the greatest possible common factor is 9, so this statement is sufficient.

(If you're not sure about the logic of that last part, test out a couple of real numbers. Remember that n must be a multiple of 9. If $n = 9$, then $m = 4(9) + 9 = 45$. The GCF of the numbers 9 and 45 is 9. If $n = 18$, then $m = 4(18) + 9 = 81$. The GCF of the numbers 18 and 81 is still 9.)

Alternatively, methodically list possible values of s, m, and n. Ignore any case for which the statement is not true; for the remaining cases, determine the answer to the question.

s = pos int	$m = 9s$	$n = \dfrac{m-9}{4}$	n = pos int	GCF of m and n?
1	9	$\dfrac{0}{4}$	Zero X	
2	18	$\dfrac{9}{4}$	Fraction X	
3	27	$\dfrac{18}{4}$	Fraction X	
4	36	$\dfrac{27}{4}$	Fraction X	
5	**45**	$\dfrac{\mathbf{36}}{\mathbf{4}} = \mathbf{9}$	✓	9
6	54	$\dfrac{45}{4}$	Fraction X	
7	63	$\dfrac{54}{4}$	Fraction X	
8	72	$\dfrac{63}{4}$	Fraction X	
9	**81**	$\dfrac{\mathbf{72}}{\mathbf{4}} = \mathbf{18}$	✓	9
10	90	$\dfrac{81}{4}$	Fraction X	

In this case, n is only a positive integer when $(s - 1)$ is a multiple of 4. Also, m and n are both multiples of 9. Here's the proof:

$$n = \frac{m-9}{4} = \frac{9s-9}{4} = 9\frac{(s-1)}{4} = 9(\text{int})$$

Try the next number in the pattern, $9 + 4 = 13$, to be confident that the apparent GCF pattern will continue.

$s =$ pos int	$m = 9s$	$n = \dfrac{m-9}{4}$	$n =$ pos int	GCF of m and n?
5	$(9)(5) = 45$	$\dfrac{36}{4} = 9 = (9)(1)$	✓	9
9	$(9)(9) = 81$	$\dfrac{72}{4} = 18 = (9)(2)$	✓	9
13	$(9)(13) = 117$	$\dfrac{108}{4} = 27 = (9)(3)$	✓	9

The variables m and n always share an overlapping factor of 9, but there is never any overlap between their remaining factors. The GCF is always 9.

(2) INSUFFICIENT: $n = 4t$, where t is a positive integer. In this case, n must be a multiple of 4. This does not allow you to deduce anything consistent about m, as statement (1) did.

$t =$ pos int	$n = 4t$	$m = 4n + 9$	GCF of m and n?
1	4	$16 + 9 = 25$	1
2	8	$32 + 9 = 41$	1
3	12	$48 + 9 = 57$	3

There is more than one possible GCF, so the statement is not sufficient.

The correct answer is **(A)**.

13. **(A):**

(1) SUFFICIENT: Use the integer constraint to test possible cases. Let g equal the number of general exhibit tickets sold. Because the special tickets are so much more expensive, begin by choosing numbers for which $(70)(\text{# of special tickets})$ is approximately $1,600.

      If $g = 7$, total revenue $= 10(7) + 70(23) = 70 + 1,610 = 1,680$. Too high.

      If $g = 8$, total revenue $= 10(8) + 70(22) = 80 + 1,540 = 1,620$. Ok.

      If $g = 9$, total revenue $= 10(9) + 70(21) = 90 + 1,470 = 1,560$. Too low.

Only $g = 8$ gives a total revenue in the given range.

Don't assume that having a *range* of values automatically means a statement is insufficient to answer a Value question. At times, a constraint (such as an integer constraint) may limit the number of cases to just one possibility.

Alternatively, you can use algebra, though that path is a bit long on this problem. Let g equal the number of general exhibit tickets sold. Then $(30 - g)$ represents the number of special exhibit tickets sold. Set up and solve the following inequality:

$$1{,}570 < 10g + 70(30 - g) < 1{,}670$$
$$1{,}570 < 10g + 2{,}100 - 70g < 1{,}670$$
$$1{,}570 < -60g + 2{,}100 < 1{,}670$$
$$-530 < -60g < -430$$
$$\frac{-530}{-60} > \frac{-60g}{-60} > \frac{-430}{-60} \quad \text{Flip the direction of the inequality when dividing by a negative.}$$
$$8.8 > g > 7.2$$

The only integer between 7.2 and 8.8 is 8, so g must be 8. The museum sold 8 general exhibit tickets.

(2) INSUFFICIENT: This statement indicates that the museum sold 21, 22, 23, or 24 special exhibit tickets. Since the museum sold a total of 30 tickets, this means that it sold 9, 8, 7, or 6 general exhibit tickets.

The correct answer is **(A)**.

14. **(C):**

(1) INSUFFICIENT: *Test cases* on this theory problem. If you can generate both Yes and No cases, you will prove insufficiency.

	x	y	x^y	y^x	Does $x^y = y^x$?
Case 1	2	0	$2^0 = 1$	$0^2 = 0$	No
Case 2	3	1	$3^1 = 3$	$1^3 = 1$	No
Case 3	4	2	$4^2 = 16$	$2^4 = 16$	Yes

(2) INSUFFICIENT: Continue to test cases.

	x	y	x^y	y^x	Does $x^y = y^x$?
Case 1	8	1	$8^1 = 8$	$1^8 = 1$	No
Case 2	4	2	$4^2 = 16$	$2^4 = 16$	Yes

(1) AND (2) SUFFICIENT: Test whether any cases work for both statements. The case $x = 4$ and $y = 2$ was already used for both statements and returned a Yes answer. Can any of the No cases work for both statements?

They don't. Now you have a choice. If you are good with numbers, you can try to find another pair of integers that will work with both equations. Since x and y have to be integers, there are only a limited number of possibilities. The two numbers need to multiply to 4 and have a difference of 2. In addition to 4 and 2, the pair -4 and -2 fit the bill, as long as $x = -2$ and $y = -4$.

Alternatively, solve algebraically to determine the possible values for x and y.

$$xy = 8$$
$$(2 + y)y = 8$$
$$2y + y^2 = 8$$
$$y^2 + 2y - 8 = 0$$
$$(y + 4)(y - 2) = 0$$

$$y = -4 \text{ or } y = 2$$

Therefore, $x = -2$ or $x = 4$.

You have already tested the case where $x = 4$ (and $y = 2$), so test the other case.

x	y	x^y	y^x	Does $x^y = y^x$?
-2	-4	$(-2)^{-4} = \dfrac{1}{16}$	$(-4)^{-2} = \dfrac{1}{16}$	Yes

In either case, $x^y = y^x$. The correct answer is **(C)**.

15. **(B):** Odd exponents do not "hide the sign" of the base. If $ab^3c^4 > 0$, then a and b must have the same sign so that their product is positive. In that case, a^3b must also be positive. As a result, in order for the inequality a^3bc^5 to be positive, c^5 must be positive. The rephrased question is, "Is $c > 0$?"

(1) INSUFFICIENT: No information about the sign of c.

(2) SUFFICIENT: Answers the rephrased question directly.

The correct answer is **(B)**.

16. **(C):** The perimeter of a triangle is equal to the sum of the three sides.

(1) INSUFFICIENT: Knowing the length of one side of the triangle is not enough to find the sum of all three sides.

(2) INSUFFICIENT: Knowing the length of one side of the triangle is not enough to find the sum of all three sides.

(1) AND (2) SUFFICIENT: Triangle ABC is an isosceles triangle, which means that two of the sides are equal in length. The statements provide two of the side lengths, so the third side, AC, must equal one of the given sides.

There is a *hidden constraint* in this problem: the triangle must be valid. Recall that the sum of the lengths of any two sides of a triangle must be greater than the length of the third side.

AB	BC	AC	Perimeter	Valid triangle?
9	4	4	$9 + 4 + 4 = 17$	$4 + 4 < 9$ No
9	4	9	$9 + 4 + 9 = 22$	$4 + 9 > 9$ Yes

9

A "triangle" with three sides of 4, 4, and 9 is not really a triangle, as it cannot be drawn with those dimensions.

Therefore, the actual sides of the triangle must be $AB = 9$, $BC = 4$, and $AC = 9$. The perimeter is 22.

The correct answer is **(C)**.

17.   **(A):** Express both sides of the equation in terms of prime numbers.

$$2^x 5^y z = 6.4 \times 10^6$$
$$= (64)\left(10^5\right)$$
$$= \left(2^6\right)\left(2^5 5^5\right)$$
$$= 2^{11} 5^5$$

The right side of the equation is composed of only 2's and 5's. The left side of the equation has x number of 2's and y number of 5's along with some factor z. This unknown factor z must be composed of only 2's and/or 5's, or it must be 1 (i.e., with no prime factors).

If $z = 1$, then $x = 11$ and $y = 5$.

If $z = 2^? 5^?$, where the exponents are not 0, then x and y will depend on the value of those exponents.

The rephrased question is thus, "How many factors of 2 and 5 are in z?"

(1) SUFFICIENT: If $z = 20 = 2^2 5^1$, then this answers the rephrased question. Incidentally, this implies that $2^x 5^y (2^2 5^1) = 2^{11} 5^5$, so $x = 9$ and $y = 4$, making $xy = 36$ (though you do not have to solve for x and y).

(2) INSUFFICIENT: $x = 9$, but the statement doesn't indicate anything about the value of y.

The correct answer is **(A)**.

18.   **(C):** This problem deals with both squares and inequalities. Remember that negative numbers become positive when squared and that squaring a number less than 1 results in a value that is even closer to 0.

(1) INSUFFICIENT: Without any more information about z, this statement only tells you that x^2 is greater than y^2. However, x could be either greater than y or less than y, depending on whether x is positive or negative.

Case 1: $x = -100$, $y = 1$. Since all squares are positive, x^2 is much greater than y^2. However, x is less than y.

Case 2: $x = 100$, $y = 1$. In this case, x^2 is greater than y^2 and x is greater than y.

(2) INSUFFICIENT: This statement does not provide any information about y, so y could be greater than, less than, or equal to x.

(1) AND (2) SUFFICIENT: According to statement (2), x is greater than z. According to statement (1), x^2 is greater than z^2. This implies that $|x|$ is greater than $|z|$.

There are only two situations in which x is greater than z and the absolute value of x is greater than the absolute value of z. One possibility is that x is positive and z is a lesser positive number. Another possibility is that x is positive and z is a negative number with an absolute value that is less than x. These scenarios are illustrated below.

There are no valid cases in which x is negative because in order to fit statement (2), z would have to be even more negative than x, in which case $|z|$ would be greater than, not less than, $|x|$. Therefore, x is definitely positive.

Statement (1) says that $x^2 > y^2$, which implies that $|x| > |y|$. Since x is positive, $|x| = x$, so $x > |y|$. If x is greater than the absolute value of y, x must also be greater than y itself, so the answer to the question is definitely Yes.

The correct answer is **(C)**.

19. **(E):** In order for the a students to be distributed evenly among the b teachers, a must be divisible by b. This is a factor question in disguise: "Is a divisible by b?"

(1) INSUFFICIENT: The given numbers represent factors of a. If the a students can be divided evenly into a group of 2, then 2 is a factor of a. Likewise, 3 and 5 must be factors of a.

If 2 and 3 are already factors of a, then 6 must also be a factor (since $2 \times 3 = 6$); you can ignore it. Likewise, you've already counted one factor of 3, so you need only one more factor of 3 to make 9. You already have the necessary factors to make both 10 and 15, so ignore those numbers as well. The final list of factors is: 2, 3, 5, and 3.

As a result, a must equal $(2)(3)(5)(3) = 90$ or a multiple of 90. Since the question stem indicated that $a < 150$, a must actually be 90. This statement provides no information about the teachers, however, so it is insufficient.

(2) INSUFFICIENT: If the greatest common factor (GCF) of a and b is 10, then a and b must both be multiples of 10. Since the question stem indicated that $b < 25$, b must be 10 or 20. The value of a is any multiple of 10 up to 140, inclusive. This is not enough to determine whether a is divisible by b. For example, if $a = 50$ and $b = 10$, then a is divisible by b. If $a = 50$ and $b = 20$, then a is not divisible by b.

(1) AND (2) INSUFFICIENT: From statement (1), $a = 90$. From statement (2), $b = 10$ or 20. If $b = 10$, then the 90 students can be divided up evenly into classes of 9 students each. If $b = 20$, then the 90 students cannot be divided up evenly.

The correct answer is **(E)**.

20.   **(D):** All five of the integers in the set are positive, and all of the integers are distinct, or different from each other. Jot down blanks to represent the values in the set.

$$— \quad — \quad — \quad — \quad —$$

The median of the set is 3.

$$— \quad — \quad 3 \quad — \quad —$$

The least two integers in the set must be less than the median, different from each other, and positive: the first two numbers must be 1 and 2.

$$1 \quad 2 \quad 3 \quad — \quad —$$

Finally, the range of the set, or the difference between the greatest and least integers, is 12. Therefore, the greatest integer in the set is 13.

$$1 \quad 2 \quad 3 \quad — \quad 13$$

The only unknown value in the set is the second-greatest integer, which must be between 3 and 13, exclusive. Finding this integer will give you enough information to find the mean of the set.

(1) SUFFICIENT: For a number to be a multiple of 14, it must be a multiple of both 2 and 7. The product of the four known values is already a multiple of 2, since the set already contains the number 2. However, there are no multiples of 7 among the known values. Therefore, the missing fourth value must be a multiple of 7. The only multiple of 7 between 3 and 13 is 7 itself, so this is the missing integer and the mean can now be calculated.

(2) SUFFICIENT: The four known integers sum to 19. Since the unknown integer must be positive, the sum of the entire set must be greater than 19. The next multiples of 13 are $13(2) = 26$ and $13(3) = 39$, which would imply that the missing integer is $26 - 19 = 7$ or $39 - 19 = 20$, respectively. (For greater multiples of 13, the missing integer would have to be even greater than 20.) However, the missing integer must be between 3 and 13, so 20 is too great. The missing integer must be 7, and the mean can be calculated.

The correct answer is **(D)**.

Workout Set 3

21. Let $f(x)$ equal the sum of all of the integers from 1 to x, inclusive, where $x \geq 1$.

    If $g = \dfrac{f(1)}{1^2} + \dfrac{f(2)}{2^2} + \dfrac{f(3)}{3^2} + \cdots + \dfrac{f(10)}{10^2}$, which of the following is true of g ?

    (A) $0 \leq g < 5$

    (B) $5 \leq g < 10$

    (C) $10 \leq g < 15$

    (D) $15 \leq g < 20$

    (E) $20 \leq g < 25$

    [handwritten: $\dfrac{1}{1} + \dfrac{3}{4} + \dfrac{6}{9} + \dfrac{10}{16} + \dfrac{15}{25} + \dfrac{21}{36} , \dfrac{28}{49} + \dfrac{35}{64} + \dfrac{45}{81} , \dfrac{55}{100}$ 1.75 2.45 3.1 3.7   9x.]

22. If x and y are positive integers, what is the remainder when x^y is divided by 10 ?

    (1) $x = 26$

    (2) $y^x = 1$

    [handwritten: $\dfrac{x^y}{10}$?   26   6:0   AD   A   y=1]

23. For all positive integers n, the sequence A_n is defined by the following relationship:

    $$A_n = \frac{n-1}{n!}$$

    What is the sum of all the terms in the sequence from A_1 through A_{10}, inclusive?

    (A) $\dfrac{9! + 1}{10!}$

    (B) $\dfrac{9(9!)}{10}$

    (C) $\dfrac{10! - 1}{10!}$

    (D) $\dfrac{10!}{10! + 1}$

    (E) $\dfrac{10(10!)}{11!}$

    [handwritten: $\dfrac{1-1}{1} \to 0$ $\dfrac{1}{1}$ $\dfrac{10-1}{10!} + \dfrac{9-1}{9!}$ $\dfrac{1}{10(8!)} + \dfrac{1}{10(9)(7!)} \cdots \dfrac{9}{10!}$]

24. If x and y are positive integers and $n = 5^x + 7^{y+3}$, what is the units digit of n ?

    (1) $y = 2x - 16$

    (2) y is divisible by 4. ✓

    [handwritten: $5^x + 7^{y+3}$ units digit   M   B   BD   xxx5 +www3   7 9 3 1]

25. At a certain store, all notebooks have the same price and all pencils have the same price. The price of four notebooks and three pencils is more than $12 and less than $13. The price of two notebooks and five pencils is more than $8 and less than $9. If a notebook costs x more than a pencil, which of the following could be the value of x?

   (A) $0.60

   (B) $1.05

   (C) $1.30

   (D) $2.20

   (E) $2.70

26. A certain sequence is defined by the following rule: $S_n = k(S_{n-1})$, where k is a constant. If $S_1 = 2$ and $S_{13} = 72$, what is the value of S_7?

   (A) 6

   (B) 12

   (C) 24

   (D) 36

   (E) 37

27. If $y = 9^0 + 9^1 + 9^2 + \ldots + 9^n$ and integer n is greater than 2, what is the remainder when y is divided by 5?

   (1) n is divisible by 3.

   (2) n is odd.

28. In a certain sequence, each term after the first is twice the previous term. If the first term of the sequence is 3, what is the sum of the 14th, 15th, and 16th terms in the sequence?

   (A) $3(2^{16})$

   (B) $9(2^{15})$

   (C) $21(2^{14})$

   (D) $9(2^{14})$

   (E) $21(2^{13})$

29. n is an integer such that $n \geq 0$. For $n > 0$, the sequence t_n is defined as $t_n = t_{n-1} + n$. If $t_0 = 3$, is t_n even?

   (1) $n + 1$ is divisible by 3.

   (2) $n - 1$ is divisible by 4.

30. To complete a 120-mile trip, a train first travels at a constant rate of *x* miles per hour (mph) for 80 miles. Then it travels the remaining 40 miles at a constant rate of *y* mph. If the train had instead completed the entire trip at a constant rate of *z* mph, the trip would have taken 1 hour longer. Which of the following is the value of *z* in terms of *x* and *y* ?

(A) $\dfrac{120}{40x + 80y + 1}$

(B) $\dfrac{40x + 80y + xy}{xy}$

(C) $\dfrac{120xy}{40x + 80y + xy}$

(D) $120xy + 40x + 80y$

(E) $\dfrac{121}{xy}$

Handwritten annotations:

80 60

80 + 40 = 120 → 2hrs

2:40 → 3hrs

Workout Set 3 Answer Key

21. **B** √
22. **A** √
23. **C** ✗
24. **B** √
25. **D** √
26. **B** ✗
27. **B** √
28. **E** √
29. **B** √
30. **C** ✗

Workout Set 3 Solutions

21. **(B)** $5 \le g < 10$: $f(x)$ is the sum of all integers from 1 to x, inclusive. Therefore, $f(x)$ equals the average of the integers from 1 to x, which is $\frac{1+x}{2}$, multiplied by the number of integers from 1 to x, which is x. Therefore, $f(x) = \frac{(1+x)(x)}{2}$.

The question asks for the sum of the values of $\frac{f(1)}{1^2}$, $\frac{f(2)}{2^2}$, and so on up to $\frac{f(10)}{10^2}$. Instead of summing these values by hand, look for a pattern, since the problem only asks for a range and not a specific answer.

One possibility is to use algebra. $\frac{f(x)}{x^2}$ can be simplified as follows:

$$\frac{f(x)}{x^2} = \frac{(1+x)(x)}{2x^2}$$
$$= \frac{1+x}{2x}$$

Using this formula, the first few terms of the sum are $\frac{1+1}{2} = 1$, $\frac{1+2}{4} = \frac{3}{4}$, $\frac{1+3}{6} = \frac{2}{3}$, $\frac{1+4}{8} = \frac{5}{8}$, and so on, until the tenth term, which is $\frac{11}{20}$. All of these terms are greater than $\frac{1}{2}$ and no greater than 1. If all of the terms were 0.5, then the sum would be $10(0.5) = 5$. However, if all of the terms were 1, then the sum would be 10. Therefore, the sum must be between 5 and 10.

This problem can also be solved without using a formula for $f(x)$. Manually calculate the first few values of $f(x)$, and look for a pattern.

x	$f(x)$	$\dfrac{f(x)}{x^2}$
1	1	$\dfrac{1}{1} = 1$
2	3	$\dfrac{3}{4}$
3	6	$\dfrac{6}{9} = \dfrac{2}{3}$
4	10	$\dfrac{10}{16} = \dfrac{5}{8}$
5	15	$\dfrac{15}{25} = \dfrac{3}{5}$
6	21	$\dfrac{21}{36} = \dfrac{7}{12}$
7	28	$\dfrac{28}{49} = \dfrac{4}{7}$
etc.	etc.	etc.

The values appear to be decreasing and approaching $\frac{1}{2}$. If each term in the sum is greater than $\frac{1}{2}$ but no greater than 1, their sum will be greater than 5 but no greater than 10.

The correct answer is **(B)**.

22. **(A):** The question asks for the remainder when x^y is divided by 10. The remainder of any number when divided by 10 is equal to the units digit of that number, so the question is really asking for the units digit of x^y.

(1) SUFFICIENT: The tendency is to deem statement (1) insufficient because no information is given about the value of y. But 26 has a units digit of 6, and remember that $6^{\text{any positive integer}}$ has a units digit of 6 (the pattern is a single-term repeat).

$$6^1 = \mathbf{6}$$
$$6^2 = 3\mathbf{6}$$
$$6^3 = 21\mathbf{6}$$

etc.

Thus, 26 raised to ANY positive integer power will also have a units digit of 6 and therefore a remainder of 6 when divided by 10.

(2) INSUFFICIENT: Given that $y^x = 1$, there are a few possible scenarios:

x	y	$y^x = 1$
0	anything nonzero	$(\text{anything nonzero})^0 = 1\ \checkmark$
anything	1	$1^{\text{anything}} = 1\ \checkmark$
even	−1	$-1^{\text{even}} = 1\ \checkmark$

However, the question stem indicates that x and y are POSITIVE integers, so eliminate the first and third scenarios.

The remaining scenario indicates that $y = 1$ and $x =$ any positive integer. Without more information about x, you cannot determine the remainder when x^y is divided by 10.

Since statement (1) indicates the value of x and statement (2) indicates the value of y ($y = 1$), the temptation might be to combine the information to arrive at an answer of (C). This is a common trap on difficult Data Sufficiency problems; in this case, you don't need both statements because statement (1) is sufficient by itself.

The correct answer is **(A)**.

23. **(C)** $\dfrac{10! - 1}{10!}$: Set up a table to list the first few terms of the sequence and also the cumulative sum.

n	$A_n = \dfrac{n-1}{n!}$	Cumulative Sum
1	$A_1 = \dfrac{1-1}{1!} = 0$	0
2	$A_2 = \dfrac{2-1}{2!} = \dfrac{1}{2}$	$\dfrac{1}{2}$
3	$A_3 = \dfrac{3-1}{3!} = \dfrac{2}{6} = \dfrac{1}{3}$	$\dfrac{5}{6}$
4	$A_4 = \dfrac{4-1}{4!} = \dfrac{3}{24} = \dfrac{1}{8}$	$\dfrac{23}{24}$

As you build the table, compare the input column values (n) with the output column values (cumulative sum), looking for a pattern. The denominator of the cumulative sum is $n!$ and the numerator is one less than $n!$. Therefore:

Sum of terms through $A_n = \dfrac{n! - 1}{n!}$

Substitute to find the sum through A_{10}.

Sum of terms through $A_{10} = \dfrac{10! - 1}{10!}$

The correct answer is (C).

24. **(B):** The units digit of n is determined solely by the units digit of the expressions 5^x and 7^{y+3} because when two numbers are added together, the units digit of the sum is determined solely by the units digits of the added numbers.

Since x is a positive integer, and $5^{\text{any positive integer}}$ always has a units digit of 5, 5^x always ends in a 5. However, the units digit of 7^{y+3} is not certain, as the units digit pattern for the powers of 7 is a four-term repeat: [7, 9, 3, 1].

The question can be rephrased as, "What is the units digit of 7^{y+3}?"

Note: Determining y would be one way of answering the question above, but don't rephrase to, "What is y?" Because the units digits of the powers of 7 have a repeating pattern, you might get a single answer for the units digit of 7^{y+3} *despite* having multiple values for y.

(1) INSUFFICIENT: This statement indicates neither the value of y nor the units digit of 7^{y+3}, as y depends on the value of x, which could be any positive integer. For example, if $x = 9$, then $y = 2$, and 7^{y+3} has a units digit of 7. By contrast, if $x = 10$, then $y = 4$, and 7^{y+3} has a units digit of 3. (Note: The statement does indicate that y is an even number, so the exponent $y + 3$ must be odd. As a result, there are only two possible values for the units digit of the desired term: 7 or 3. That could be useful to know if you later need to combine the two statements.)

(2) SUFFICIENT: Regardless of what multiple of 4 you pick, 7^{y+3} will have the same units digit.

y	$y + 3$	Units Digit of 7^{y+3}
4	7	3
8	11	3
12	15	3

Ultimately, this means that n has a units digit of $5 + 3 = 8$.

The correct answer is (B).

25. **(D) \$2.20:** The answer choices in this problem are relatively simple numbers, but they represent the difference between two prices, rather than a single price. Therefore, working backwards may not be possible. Instead, start by translating the information in the problem into math.

Let n be the price of one notebook, and p be the price of one pen. The first piece of information in the problem translates to the following inequality:

$12 < 4n + 3p < 13$

The second piece of information translates to this inequality:

$$8 < 2n + 5p < 9$$

The question asks for the difference between the cost of a notebook and the cost of a pencil. In other words, what is the value of $n - p$?

One option is to use the previous two inequalities to create a third inequality, which includes the combo $n - p$. One way to accomplish this is to multiply the second inequality by -1, taking care to flip the signs. Then, reorder the result so that the inequality signs point in the expected direction:

$$-8 > -2n - 5p > -9$$
$$-9 < -2n - 5p < -8$$

Now, sum the two inequalities. You can add inequalities as long as the inequality signs are facing the same direction:

$$\begin{array}{r}(12 < 4n + 3p < 13)\\ +(-9 < -2n - 5p < -8)\\ \hline = 3 < 2n - 2p < 5\end{array}$$

This simplifies to $1.5 < n - p < 2.5$. The difference between the cost of a notebook and the cost of a pencil must be between \$1.50 and \$2.50, so the only answer choice that is in the correct range is answer (D).

It is also possible to "solve" the two inequalities for n and for p, separately, then to use the resulting ranges to find the possible differences between n and p.

The correct answer is **(D)**.

26. **(B) 12:** To form each new term of the sequence, multiply the previous term by k. If $S_1 = 2$, then $S_2 = 2k$, and $S_3 = 2k^2$, and $S_n = 2k^{n-1}$. Thus, $S_{13} = 2k^{12}$. Since the problem indicates that $S_{13} = 72$, set up an equation to solve for k.

$$2k^{12} = 72$$
$$k^{12} = 36$$
$$k = 36^{\frac{1}{12}}$$

S_7 is equal to $2k^6$. Plug the value of k into that expression to calculate S_7.

$$S_7 = 2\left(36^{\frac{1}{12}}\right)^6$$
$$= 2\left(36^{\frac{1}{2}}\right)$$
$$= 2\sqrt{36}$$
$$= 12$$

The correct answer is **(B)**.

27. **(B):** Remember the units digit pattern for 9^x, where x is an integer. The units digit of 9^x is 9 if x is odd, but the units digit is 1 if x is even: a repeating pattern of [9, 1].

Now, consider the sums of the powers of 9 up to 9^n:

n	$y = 9^0 + 9^1 + 9^2 + \ldots + 9^n$	Units Digit of y
1	$1 + 9 = \mathbf{10}$	0
2	$1 + 9 + 81 = \mathbf{91}$	1
3	$[1 + 9 + 81] + 729 = [\text{units digit of } 1] + \text{units digit of } 9$	0
4	Units digit of 0 + units digit of 1	1
Odd	Units digit: pairs of $(1 + 9)$	0
Even	Units digit: pairs of $(1 + 9) + 1$	1

The alternating 1's and 9's in the units digits pair to a sum of 10, or a units digit of 0. Thus, the units digit of the sum displays another two-term repeating pattern. The units digit of y is 0 if n is odd, but 1 if n is even.

The remainder when y is divided by 5 depends only on the units digit and will be either 0 or 1 as well. The rephrased question is, "Is n odd or even?"

(1) INSUFFICIENT: If n is a multiple of 3, it may be either odd or even.

(2) SUFFICIENT: If n is odd, the units digit of y is 0, and the remainder is 0 when y is divided by 5.

The correct answer is **(B)**.

28. **(E) $21(2^{13})$:** The sequence is 3, 6, 12, 24, 48, and so on. You could write out the first 16 terms and add the 14th, 15th, and 16th together, but such an approach would be prone to error and time-consuming. Additionally, you don't need to calculate the sum explicitly: the answer choices all have some power of 2 as a factor, providing a hint at the best solution method.

Write the sequence in terms of the powers of 2:

3, 6, 12, 24, 48, and so on

$3(2^0), 3(2^1), 3(2^2), 3(2^3), 3(2^4)$, and so on

So S_n, the nth term of the sequence, equals $3(2^{n-1})$.

Thus, the sum of the 14th, 15th, and 16th terms equals $3(2^{13}) + 3(2^{14}) + 3(2^{15})$.

All of the terms share the common factors 3 and 2^{13}, so factor those terms out:

$$3(2^{13})(1 + 2^1 + 2^2)$$
$$3(2^{13})(1 + 2 + 4)$$
$$3(2^{13})(7)$$
$$21(2^{13})$$

The correct answer is **(E)**.

29. **(B):** Sequence problems are often best approached by charting out the first several terms of the given sequence. In this case, keep track of n, t_n, and whether t_n is even or odd.

n	t_n	Is t_n even or odd?
0	3	Odd
1	$3 + 1 = 4$	Even
2	$4 + 2 = 6$	Even
3	$6 + 3 = 9$	Odd
4	$9 + 4 = 13$	Odd
5	$13 + 5 = 18$	Even
6	$18 + 6 = 24$	Even
7	$24 + 7 = 31$	Odd
8	$31 + 8 = 39$	Odd

Notice that beginning with $n = 1$, a four-term repeating cycle of [even, even, odd, odd] emerges for t_n. Thus, a statement will be sufficient only if it indicates how n relates to a multiple of 4 (i.e., $n = a$ multiple of $4 \pm$ known constant).

(1) INSUFFICIENT: This statement does not indicate how n relates to a multiple of 4. If $n + 1$ is a multiple of 3, then $n + 1$ could be 3, 6, 9, 12, 15, etc. This means that n could be 2, 5, 8, 11, 14, etc. From the chart, if $n = 2$ or $n = 5$, then t_n is even. However, if $n = 8$ or $n = 11$, then t_n is odd.

(2) SUFFICIENT: This statement indicates exactly how n relates to a multiple of 4. If $n - 1$ is a multiple of 4, then $n - 1$ could be 4, 8, 12, 16, 20, etc., and n could be 5, 9, 13, 17, 21, etc. From the chart (and the continuation of the four-term pattern), t_n must be even.

The correct answer is **(B)**.

30. **(C)** $\dfrac{120xy}{40x + 80y + xy}$: The answer choices are complex and include two different variables. If you choose to use smart numbers, select your numbers cautiously to simplify the arithmetic.

For instance, if x is equal to y, the problem may be much simpler to solve, although some of the answer choices may then yield the same result. Choose $x = y = 40$, so that the train completes the entire trip at 40 mph, taking $\dfrac{120 \text{ miles}}{40 \text{ mph}} = 3$ hours.

If the train had instead traveled at z mph, it would have taken one more hour, or 4 hours in total. Therefore, $z = \dfrac{120 \text{ miles}}{4 \text{ hours}} = 30$ mph.

The correct answer will yield a value of $z = 30$ mph when $x = 40$ and $y = 40$ are plugged in.

(A) $\dfrac{120}{40(40) + 80(40) + 1}$ is a fraction that is significantly less than 1. Eliminate.

(B) $\dfrac{40(40) + 80(40) + 40(40)}{40(40)} = 1 + 2 + 1 = 4$, which is too low. Eliminate.

(C) $\dfrac{120(40)(40)}{40(40) + 80(40) + 40(40)} = \dfrac{120(40)}{40 + 80 + 40} = \dfrac{120}{1 + 2 + 1} = 30$ Correct!

9

(D) $120(40)(40) + 40(40) + 80(40)$ is much greater than 30. Eliminate.

(E) $\dfrac{121}{40(40)}$ is not an integer, so it cannot equal 30. Eliminate.

Alternatively, solve algebraically by creating an RTD chart.

Rate	Time	Distance
x mph	$\dfrac{80}{x}$ hours	80 miles
y mph	$\dfrac{40}{y}$ hours	40 miles
(Original speed)	$\dfrac{80}{x} + \dfrac{40}{y}$ hours	120 miles
z mph	$\dfrac{80}{x} + \dfrac{40}{y} + 1$ hours	120 miles

Use the last row of the chart to create an equation, which can then be solved for z.

$$z\left(\frac{80}{x} + \frac{40}{y} + 1\right) = 120$$

$$\frac{z(80y + 40x + xy)}{xy} = 120$$

$$z = \frac{120xy}{80y + 40x + xy}$$

The correct answer is (**C**).

Workout Set 4

31. If $x^x y^y = \dfrac{24^3}{2}$, and x and y are integers such that $x < y$, what is the value of $y - x$?

    (A) −1
    (B) 1
    (C) 3
    (D) 5
    (E) 7

32. If $S_n = 5n + 94$ and $K = (S_{80} + S_{82} + S_{84}) - (S_{81} + S_{83} + S_{85})$, what is the value of K?

    (A) −282
    (B) −84
    (C) −30
    (D) −15
    (E) −3

33. Is $xy + xy < xy$?

    (1) $\dfrac{x^2}{y} < 0$

    (2) $x^3 y^3 < (xy)^2$

34. If $y \neq x$, then $\dfrac{x^3 + (x^2 + x)(1 - y) - y}{x - y}$ is the equivalent of which of the following?

    (A) $(x - 1)^2 y$
    (B) $(x + 1)^2$
    (C) $x^2 + x + 1$
    (D) $(x^2 + x + 1)y$
    (E) $(x^2 + x + 1)(x - y)$

35. In the sequence g_n defined for all positive integer values of n, $g_1 = g_2 = 1$ and, for $n \geq 3$, $g_n = g_{n-1} + 2^{n-3}$. If the function $\psi(g_i)$ equals the sum of the terms $g_1, g_2 \ldots g_i$, what is $\dfrac{\psi(g_{16})}{\psi(g_{15})}$?

    (A) g_3

    (B) g_8

    (C) $\psi(g_8)$

    (D) $\psi(g_{16}) - \psi(g_{15})$

    (E) $\dfrac{g_{16}}{2}$

36. If $3^k + 3^k = \left(3^9\right)^{3^9} - 3^k$, then what is the value of k?

    (A) $\dfrac{11}{3}$

    (B) $\dfrac{11}{2}$

    (C) 242

    (D) 3^{10}

    (E) $3^{11} - 1$

37. If x and y are positive integers, what is the value of xy?

    (1) $x! = 6y!$

    (2) $\dfrac{\frac{x!}{y}}{(x-2)!} = \dfrac{30}{y}$

38. If k is an integer and $\dfrac{33!}{22!}$ is divisible by 6^k, what is the maximum possible value of k?

    (A) 3

    (B) 4

    (C) 5

    (D) 6

    (E) 7

39. In a certain sequence, the term S_n is given by the formula $S_n = (n + 1)!$ for all integers $n \geq 1$. Which of the following is equivalent to the difference between S_{100} and S_{99}?

    (A) 101!

    (B) 100!

    (C) $99^2(98!)$

    (D) $100^2(99!)$

    (E) $(100!)^2$

40. If $p = \dfrac{9^7 - 9^5}{7^5 + 7^3}$ and $q = \dfrac{9^5}{7^3}$, what is the value of $\dfrac{q}{p}$?

    (A) $\dfrac{2}{5}$

    (B) $\dfrac{1}{2}$

    (C) $\dfrac{5}{8}$

    (D) $\dfrac{8}{5}$

    (E) $\dfrac{5}{2}$

Answers and explanations follow on the next page. ▶ ▶ ▶

Workout Set 4 Answer Key

31. **B**
32. **D**
33. **E**
34. **C**
35. **A**
36. **E**
37. **C**
38. **D**
39. **D**
40. **C**

Workout Set 4 Solutions

31. **(B) 1:** Simplify the right side of the equation.

$$\frac{(24)(24)(24)}{2}$$
$$(24)(24)(12)$$
$$(3)(8)(3)(8)(3)(4)$$
$$\left(3^3\right)\left(2^8\right)$$

This still needs to be manipulated in order to match the left side of the equation, since the bases need to match their exponents. The number 3^3 is okay, but 2^8 is not. Try turning it into a base of 4 instead.

$$2^8 = 2^{(2)(4)} = 4^4$$

That's it: $x = 3$ and $y = 4$, since the problem states that $y > x$. So $y - x = 4 - 3 = 1$.

The correct answer is **(B)**.

32. **(D) -15:** Note that the expression can be rewritten as follows by pairing up consecutive terms in the sequence.

$$K = \left(S_{80} - S_{81}\right) + \left(S_{82} - S_{83}\right) + \left(S_{84} - S_{85}\right)$$

In each of these pairs, the 94 term cancels out.

$$S_{80} - S_{81} = 5(80) + 94 - \left[5(81) + 94\right] = 5(80) - 5(81)$$
$$S_{82} - S_{83} = 5(82) + 94 - \left[5(83) + 94\right] = 5(82) - 5(83)$$
$$S_{84} - S_{85} = 5(84) + 94 - \left[5(85) + 94\right] = 5(84) - 5(85)$$

Therefore, the value of K is as follows.

$$\begin{aligned}
K &= 5(80) - 5(81) + 5(82) - 5(83) + 5(84) - 5(85) \\
&= 5(80 - 81 + 82 - 83 + 84 - 85) \\
&= 5(-1 - 1 - 1) \\
&= -15
\end{aligned}$$

The correct answer is **(D)**.

33. **(E):** First, rephrase the question stem by subtracting xy from both sides: "Is $xy < 0$?" The question is whether xy is negative, or "Do x and y have opposite signs?"

Be careful! Do *not* rephrase as follows:

Is $xy + xy < xy$?

Is $2xy < xy$?

Is $\dfrac{2xy}{xy} < \dfrac{xy}{xy}$? Incorrect! Dividing by variables is the mistake: What if $xy = 0$? What if $xy < 0$?

Is $2 < 1$? Incorrect as a result of the mistake in the previous step.

Not only does this rephrase make the statements moot (2 is definitely not less than 1, no matter what the statements say), but it also ignores some special cases. If $xy = 0$, then dividing by xy yields an undefined value. If $xy < 0$, you should have flipped the sign of the inequality.

Instead, use the correct rephrasing: "Do x and y have opposite signs?"

(1) INSUFFICIENT: If $\dfrac{x^2}{y} < 0$, then x^2 and y must have opposite signs. Since x^2 must be positive, y must be negative. However, x could be either positive or negative.

(2) INSUFFICIENT: If $x^3y^3 < (xy)^2$, then you can divide both sides by $(xy)^2$ (since that quantity is positive). The simplified inequality is $xy < 1$, which is not sufficient to answer the question.

(1) AND (2) INSUFFICIENT: Each statement indicates that xy could be either positive or negative. The statements are equally insufficient and neither provides any additional information to the other.

The correct answer is **(E)**.

34. **(C)** $x^2 + x + 1$**:** First, distribute the numerator.

$$\frac{x^3 + \left(x^2 + x\right)(1 - y) - y}{x - y} = \frac{x^3 + x^2 + x - x^2y - xy - y}{x - y}$$

None of the answer choices are fractions, so the $x - y$ in the denominator must be canceled by a $x - y$ in the numerator. Group the numerator terms with x and $-y$ in mind.

$$\frac{\left(x^3 + x^2 + x\right) - \left(x^2y + xy + y\right)}{x - y} = \frac{x\left(x^2 + x + 1\right) - y\left(x^2 + x + 1\right)}{x - y}$$

$$= \frac{\left(x^2 + x + 1\right)(x - y)}{x - y}$$

$$= x^2 + x + 1$$

Alternatively, you could *choose smart numbers*. If $x = 2$ and $y = 3$, then.

$$\frac{x^3 + \left(x^2 + x\right)(1 - y) - y}{x - y} = \frac{8 + (4 + 2)(1 - 3) - 3}{2 - 3}$$

$$= \frac{8 + (6)(-2) - 3}{-1}$$

$$= \frac{8 - 12 - 3}{-1}$$

Plug the selected values into the choices. The choice that equals 7 is the correct answer.

(A) $(x - 1)^2 y = (2 - 1)^2(3) = 3$ Eliminate.

(B) $(x + 1)^2 = (2 + 1)^2 = 9$ Eliminate.

(C) $x^2 + x + 1 = 4 + 2 + 1 = 7$ Correct!

(D) $(x^2 + x + 1)y = (4 + 2 + 1)(3) =$ Too great. Eliminate.

(E) $(x^2 + x + 1)(x - y) = (4 + 2 + 1)(2 - 3) =$ Negative. Eliminate.

The correct answer is **(C)**.

35. **(A)** g_3: Begin by listing some values of g_n to get a sense for how g_n progresses.

$$g_1 = 1$$
$$g_2 = 1$$
$$g_3 = g_2 + 2^0 = 1 + 1 = 2 = 2^1$$
$$g_4 = g_3 + 2^1 = 2 + 2 = 4 = 2^2$$
$$g_5 = g_4 + 2^2 = 4 + 4 = 8 = 2^3$$
$$g_6 = g_5 + 2^3 = 8 + 8 = 16 = 2^4$$

For $n \geq 3$, $g_n = 2^{n-2}$.

Now, look for a pattern in the sums defined by $\psi(g_n)$.

$$\psi(g_3) = g_1 + g_2 + g_3 = 1 + 1 + 2 = 4 = 2^2$$
$$\psi(g_4) = (g_1 + g_2 + g_3) + g_4 = \psi(g_3) + g_4 = 4 + 4 + 8 = 2^3$$
$$\psi(g_5) = (g_1 + g_2 + g_3 + g_4) + g_5 = \psi(g_4) + g_5 = 8 + 8 = 16 = 2^4$$

Each value is double the previous value: $\psi(g_n) = 2 \times \psi(g_{n-1})$. Therefore:

$$\frac{\psi(g_{16})}{\psi(g_{15})} = \frac{2 \times \psi(g_{15})}{\psi(g_{15})} = 2$$

Now, all you need to do is scan the answer choices to find an expression that equals 2. You have already discovered that $g_3 = 2$, so you can select g_3 as the answer.

The correct answer is **(A)**.

36. **(E) $3^{11} - 1$:** The common term in this problem is the recurring base of 3. Group like terms (i.e., all the terms with k on the left side, all the other powers of 3 on the right side), then simplify each power of 3 using exponent rules.

$$3^k + 3^k = \left(3^9\right)^{3^9} - 3^k$$

$$3^k + 3^k + 3^k = \left(3^9\right)^{3^9}$$

$$3\left(3^k\right) = \left(3^9\right)^{3^9}$$

$$3^{k+1} = 3^{9 \times 3^9}$$

$$k + 1 = 9 \times 3^9$$

$$k + 1 = 3^2 \times 3^9$$

$$k = 3^{11} - 1$$

The correct answer is **(E)**.

37. **(C):** Note the constraints that x and y are positive integers.

(1) INSUFFICIENT: If $y = 5$ and $x = 6$, then this statement is true: $6! = 6 \times 5!$. Are these the only possible positive integer values for x and y?

The constant 6 is equal to 3!, so there's one more: when $y = 1$ and $x = 3$, the statement is also true: $3! = 6 \times 1!$.

(2) INSUFFICIENT: You can multiply both sides by y to eliminate that variable entirely; in other words, this statement doesn't indicate anything about y.

$$\frac{\frac{x!}{y}}{(x-2)!} = \frac{30}{y}$$

$$\frac{x!}{(x-2)!} = 30$$

(1) AND (2) SUFFICIENT: Continue to simplify the equation from statement (2).

$$\frac{x!}{(x-2)!} = 30$$

$$\frac{x(x-1)(x-2)!}{(x-2)!} = 30$$

$$x(x-1) = 30$$

$$x^2 - x - 30 = 0$$

$$(x+5)(x-6) = 0$$

The quadratic produces two solutions, but only $x = 6$ is valid, since x must be a positive integer. From statement (1), if $x = 6$, then $y = 5$. This is sufficient to calculate a value for xy.

The correct answer is **(C)**.

38. **(D) 6:** The question asks for the greatest value of k such that $\frac{33!}{22!}$ is divisible by 6^k. Since $6 = 3 \times 2$, the greatest value of k will equal the number of 3×2 pairs among the prime factors of $\frac{33!}{22!}$.

To count the number of times 3 appears as a factor of $\frac{33!}{22!}$, rewrite the expression, pulling out any factor(s) of 3 from each term.

$$(33)(32)(31)(30)(29)(28)(27)(26)(25)(24)(23)$$
$$= (\mathbf{3} \times 11)(32)(31)(\mathbf{3} \times 10)(29)(28)(\mathbf{3^3})(26)(25)(\mathbf{3} \times 8)(23)$$

There are six factors of 3 in $\frac{33!}{22!}$.

To count the number of times 2 appears as a factor of $\frac{33!}{22!}$, rewrite the expression, pulling out any factor(s) of 2 from each term.

$$(33)(32)(31)(30)(29)(28)(27)(26)(25)(24)(23)$$
$$= (33)(\mathbf{2^5})(31)(\mathbf{2} \times 15)(29)(\mathbf{2^2} \times 7)(27)(\mathbf{2} \times 13)(25)(\mathbf{2^3} \times 3)(23)$$

There are twelve factors of 2 in $\frac{33!}{22!}$.

Since there are twelve 2's but only six 3's, there are only six 3×2 pairs among the prime factors of $\frac{33!}{22!}$. In general, focus on the greatest prime in the divisor (in this case, the six maximum possible factors of 3 in 6^k), as it will be the limiting factor.

The correct answer is **(D)**.

39. **(D) $(100^2)(99!)$:** $S_{100} = 101!$ and $S_{99} = 100!$.

Factor the difference.

$$
\begin{aligned}
S_{100} - S_{99} &= (101!) - (100!) \\
&= (101)(100!) - 100! \\
&= (100!)(101 - 1) \\
&= (100!)(100) \\
&= (100)(99!)(100) \\
&= \left(100^2\right)(99!)
\end{aligned}
$$

The correct answer is **(D)**.

40. **(C)** $\frac{5}{8}$: Not only does $q = \frac{9^5}{7^3}$, but you can also factor $\frac{9^5}{7^3}$ out of p.

$$p = \frac{9^7 - 9^5}{7^5 + 7^3}$$

$$= \left(\frac{9^5}{7^3}\right)\left(\frac{9^2 - 9^0}{7^2 + 7^0}\right)$$

$$= \left(\frac{9^5}{7^3}\right)\left(\frac{81 - 1}{49 + 1}\right)$$

$$= \left(\frac{9^5}{7^3}\right)\left(\frac{80}{50}\right)$$

$$= \left(\frac{9^5}{7^3}\right)\left(\frac{8}{5}\right)$$

Thus, $p = q\left(\frac{8}{5}\right)$, and $\frac{p}{q} = \frac{8}{5}$. Watch out! This is one of the incorrect answers.

The question asks for $\frac{q}{p}$, which is $\left(\frac{p}{q}\right)^{-1} = \left(\frac{8}{5}\right)^{-1} = \frac{5}{8}$.

The correct answer is **(C)**.

Workout Set 5

41. If x and y are positive integers, what is the value of $\frac{x}{y}$?

    (1) $x^2 = 2xy - y^2$

    (2) $2xy = 8$

42. What is the remainder when $(47)(49)$ is divided by 8 ?

    (A) 1

    (B) 3

    (C) 4

    (D) 5

    (E) 7

43. If $a = 4x^2 + 4xy$ and $b = 4y^2 + 4xy$, which of the following is equivalent to $x + y$?

    (A) $\sqrt{a+b}$

    (B) $2\sqrt{ab}$

    (C) $\frac{a+b}{\sqrt{2}}$

    (D) $2\sqrt{a} - 2\sqrt{b}$

    (E) $\frac{\sqrt{a+b}}{2}$

44. What is the value of $\dfrac{3^{(a+b)^2}}{3^{(a-b)^2}}$?

    (1) $a + b = 7$

    (2) $ab = 12$

45. What is the value of $\left(\sqrt{24 + 5\sqrt{23}}\right)\left(\sqrt{24 - 5\sqrt{23}}\right)$?

    (A) 48

    (B) $\sqrt{24}$

    (C) $5\sqrt{2}$

    (D) 1

    (E) $24 - 5\sqrt{23}$

46. If x is the square of an integer, is y the square of an integer?

    (1) xy is the square of an integer.

    (2) $\dfrac{y}{x}$ is the square of an integer.

47. If x and y are positive integers such that $x > y$ and $2\sqrt{x} - 2\sqrt{y} = \dfrac{(x-y)}{b}$, which of the following is equivalent to $2b$?

(A) $\sqrt{x} - \sqrt{y}$

(B) $\sqrt{x} + \sqrt{y}$

(C) $\dfrac{\sqrt{x}}{\sqrt{y}}$

(D) $2\sqrt{xy}$

(E) $2\sqrt{x-y}$

Handwritten work: $x=9$ $y=4$

$b(2\sqrt{x} - 2\sqrt{y}) = (x-y)$

$\dfrac{x-y}{\sqrt{x}-\sqrt{y}} = 2b$

$b(2\sqrt{x}-2\sqrt{y}) = \dfrac{(x-y)}{(2\sqrt{x}-2\sqrt{y})}$

$\dfrac{2(x-y)}{2\sqrt{x}-2\sqrt{y}}$ $\dfrac{(x-y)^2}{(\sqrt{x}-\sqrt{y})^2}$ $(x-y)(x-y)$ $x-y-\sqrt{2xy}$

$b=2$

48. If $(x+y)^2 = 16$ and $x^2 - y^2 = 16$, what is the value of $2x^2$?

(A) 8

(B) 16

(C) 18

(D) 32

(E) 50

Handwritten work:

$x^2 + 2xy + y^2 = 16$

$+\quad x^2 - y^2 = 16$

$2x^2 + 2xy = 32$

$2x(x+y) = 32$

$2x(4) = 32$

$2x = 8$

$x = 4$

49. Which of the following is equal to $5{,}995^2 - 4{,}796^2$?

(A) $1{,}199^2$

(B) $2{,}687^2$

(C) $3{,}425^2$

(D) $3{,}597^2$

(E) $4{,}820^2$

Handwritten work: $60^2 - 48^2$ ... 3600 ... 2304 ... 48 48 384 1920 2304 ... 1300000

50. If $8xy^3 + 8x^3y = \dfrac{2x^2y^2}{2^{-3}}$, what is the value of xy?

(1) $y > x$

(2) $x < 0$

Handwritten work: (E)

$16x^2y^2 = 8xy^3 + 8x^3y$

$2x^2y^2 = xy^3 + x^3y$

$2x^2y^2 = xy(y^2 + x^2)$

$2xy = y^2 + x^2 \qquad x = y$

$0 = x^2 - 2xy + y^2$

$0 = (x-y)(x-y)$

$0 = (x-y)^2$

Answers and explanations follow on the next page. ▶ ▶ ▶

Workout Set 5 Answer Key

41. **A** ✗
42. **E** ✗
43. **E** ✓
44. **B** ✓
45. **D** ✓
46. **B** ✗
47. **B** ✓
48. **D** ✓
49. **D** ✓
50. **A** ✗

9

Workout Set 5 Solutions

41. **(A):**

    (1) SUFFICIENT: Move all terms to one side.

    $$x^2 = 2xy - y^2$$
    $$x^2 - 2xy + y^2 = 0$$

    Factor this "square of a difference" special product and simplify.

    $$x^2 - 2xy + y^2 = 0$$
    $$(x - y)^2 = 0$$
    $$x - y = 0$$

    Since $x = y$, the value of $\frac{x}{y}$ is 1.

    (2) INSUFFICIENT: If $2xy = 8$, then $xy = 4$. Test different values for x and y.

x (positive)	y (positive)	xy = 4	$\frac{x}{y} = ?$
2	2	$2 \times 2 = 4$ ✓	1
1	4	$1 \times 4 = 4$ ✓	$\frac{1}{4}$

    Alternatively, manipulate the equation $xy = 4$ to get $\frac{x}{y}$ on one side.

    $$xy = 4$$
    $$\frac{xy}{y^2} = \frac{4}{y^2}$$
    $$\frac{x}{y} = \frac{4}{y^2}$$

    The expression $\frac{x}{y}$ does not equal a constant, so $\frac{x}{y}$ could take on many different values.

    The correct answer is **(A)**.

42. **(E) 7:** One way to solve would be to multiply $(47)(49)$, then either divide the result by 8 or repeatedly subtract known multiples of 8 from the result until you are left with a remainder less than 8.

    An alternative is to rewrite the given product as an equivalent yet easier-to-manipulate product. Note that 47 and 49 are equidistant from 48, a multiple of 8. Write each of the original factors as terms in the form $(a + b)$ or $(a - b)$.

    $$(47)(49) = (48 + 1)(48 - 1)$$

    This form is the *difference of two squares* special product, $(a + b)(a - b) = a^2 - b^2$; continue to simplify.

    $$(48 + 1)(48 - 1) = (48^2 - 1^2)$$

    Forty-eight is a multiple of 8, and therefore so is 48^2. Thus, $(48^2 - 1^2)$ is 1 less than a multiple of 8. All such numbers (e.g., 7, 15, 23, 31) have a remainder of 7 when divided by 8.

    The correct answer is **(E)**.

9

43. **(E)** $\dfrac{\sqrt{a+b}}{2}$: Add a and b to get $a + b = 4x^2 + 8xy + 4y^2 = 4(x^2 + 2xy + y^2)$.

The right side is the *square of a sum*, so factor and solve.

$$a + b = 4\left(x^2 + 2xy + y^2\right)$$

$$a + b = 4(x + y)^2$$

$$\frac{a + b}{4} = (x + y)^2$$

$$\sqrt{\frac{a + b}{4}} = (x + y)$$

$$\frac{\sqrt{a + b}}{2} = (x + y)$$

Note that you could safely take the square root of both sides because any square is non-negative.

Alternatively, *choose smart numbers*. For example, if $x = 2$ and $y = 3$, then the final answer $x + y = 5$. For values to plug into the choices, first compute a and b.

$$a = 4x^2 + 4xy = 4\left(2^2\right) + 4(2)(3) = 16 + 24 = 40$$

$$b = 4y^2 + 4xy = 4\left(3^2\right) + 4(2)(3) = 36 + 24 = 60$$

Next, test each answer choice; the one that equals 5 is the correct answer.

(A) $\sqrt{a + b} = \sqrt{40 + 60} = 10$ Eliminate.

(B) $2\sqrt{ab} = 2\sqrt{(40)(60)} = 2\sqrt{(400)(6)} =$ Not an integer. Eliminate.

(C) $\dfrac{a + b}{\sqrt{2}} = \dfrac{40 + 60}{\sqrt{2}} =$ Not an integer. Eliminate.

(D) $2\sqrt{a} - 2\sqrt{b} = 2\sqrt{40} - 2\sqrt{60} =$ Not an integer. Eliminate.

(E) $\dfrac{\sqrt{a + b}}{2} = \dfrac{\sqrt{40 + 60}}{2} = \dfrac{10}{2} = 5$ Correct!

The correct answer is **(E)**.

44. **(B):** Manipulate the question expression, noting the special products in the exponents.

$$\frac{3^{(a + b)^2}}{3^{(a - b)^2}} = \frac{3^{\left(a^2 + 2ab + b^2\right)}}{3^{\left(a^2 - 2ab + b^2\right)}}$$

$$= 3^{\left(a^2 + 2ab + b^2\right) - \left(a^2 - 2ab + b^2\right)}$$

$$= 3^{4ab}$$

The rephrased question is, "What is the value of ab?" Knowing the values of a and b individually would be sufficient, of course, but the individual values are not required as long as you can determine ab.

9

(1) INSUFFICIENT: It is impossible to manipulate $a + b = 7$ to get ab, nor can you solve for a and b individually.

(2) SUFFICIENT: This statement answers the rephrased question directly.

The correct answer is **(B)**.

45. **(D) 1:**

Notice the special product of the form $(a + b)(a - b) = a^2 - b^2$ under the square root symbol.

$$\sqrt{\left(24 + 5\sqrt{23}\right)\left(24 - 5\sqrt{23}\right)} = \sqrt{24^2 - \left(5\sqrt{23}\right)^2}$$
$$= \sqrt{24^2 - (25)(23)}$$
$$= \sqrt{576 - 575}$$
$$= 1$$

The correct answer is **(D)**.

46. **(B):** Jot down the information provided in the question stem. If x is the square of an integer, then $x = i^2$, where i is an unknown integer. Is y a perfect square?

(1) INSUFFICIENT: x is a perfect square, and when multiplied by the unknown value y, it turns into a (possibly different) perfect square.

Case 1: This situation can occur if y is also a perfect square. For example, if $x = 2^2 = 4$, and $y = 3^2 = 9$, then $xy = 36 = 6^2$. Since y is the square of an integer, the answer is Yes.

Case 2: If you only consider integer values for y, it seems as though y must be a square. For instance, if $x = 2^2$, y cannot equal 2, 3, 5, 6, or any non-square, since $2(2^2)$, $3(2^2)$, $5(2^2)$, etc., are not squares.

However, the question does not restrict y to integer values. To find a non-integer value of y that fits the known information, start by choosing square values for both x and xy. Suppose that $x = 2^2 = 4$ and $xy = 3^2 = 9$. In this case, $y = \frac{9}{4}$, which is not a perfect square. Therefore, the answer is No.

(2) SUFFICIENT: $\frac{y}{x}$ is the square of an integer, so $\frac{y}{x} = j^2$, for some unknown integer j. From the question stem, $x = i^2$, for some unknown integer i. Simplify.

$$\frac{y}{x} = j^2$$
$$\frac{y}{i^2} = j^2$$
$$y = i^2 j^2$$
$$y = (ij)^2$$

Therefore, y must be the square of an integer. The answer is definitely Yes, and this statement is sufficient.

The correct answer is **(B)**.

47. **(B)** $\sqrt{x} + \sqrt{y}$: To solve this problem, isolate b in the equation.

$$2\left(\sqrt{x} - \sqrt{y}\right) = \frac{(x - y)}{b}$$

$$2b\left(\sqrt{x} - \sqrt{y}\right) = x - y$$

$$2b = \frac{(x - y)}{\left(\sqrt{x} - \sqrt{y}\right)}$$

Note that it is okay to divide by $\sqrt{x} - \sqrt{y}$, since $x > y$, which implies that $\sqrt{x} - \sqrt{y} \neq 0$.

The question asks for $2b$, but the result does not match any of the answer choices. Most of the choices are not fractions, so try to cancel the denominator. Since $x - y$ is a well-disguised difference of two squares, factor the numerator and denominator.

$$2b = \frac{\left(\sqrt{x} - \sqrt{y}\right)\left(\sqrt{x} + \sqrt{y}\right)}{\left(\sqrt{x} - \sqrt{y}\right)}$$

Cancel $\left(\sqrt{x} - \sqrt{y}\right)$ in the numerator and denominator to get $2b = \sqrt{x} + \sqrt{y}$.

The correct answer is **(B)**.

48. **(D) 32:** Each of the expressions given is equal to 16, so set them equal to each other. Note that you have the square of a sum and the difference of two squares special products. Put them both in distributed form, then simplify.

$$(x + y)^2 = x^2 - y^2$$

$$x^2 + 2xy + y^2 = x^2 - y^2$$

$$2xy + y^2 = -y^2$$

$$2xy + 2y^2 = 0$$

Since $2y(x + y) = 0$, it must be true that either $2y$ or $(x + y)$ is equal to 0. However, $(x + y)$ cannot equal 0, since the problem indicates that $(x + y)^2 = 16$. So it must be that $2y = 0$, and therefore $y = 0$.

Plug in 0 for y in $x^2 - y^2 = 16$ to get $x^2 = 16$. Thus, $2x^2 = 2(16) = 32$.

Alternatively, you can solve this problem by working backwards from the answer choices. Try (B) or (D) first.

(D) If $32 = 2x^2$, then $x = \pm 4$. Use this to solve for y in the second equation.

$$16 - y^2 = 16$$

$$y = 0$$

Do $x = \pm 4$ and $y = 0$ also work in the first equation? Yes!

The correct answer is **(D)**.

9

49.   **(D) $3,597^2$:** There are several ways to approach this problem without extensive calculation.

Units Digit

One option is to note that four of the five answer choices have different units digits. The units digit of $5,995^2$ must equal the units digit of 5^2, which is 5. Similarly, the units digit of $4,796^2$ must equal the units digit of 6^2, which is 6.

Subtracting a number with a units digit of 6 from a number with a units digit of 5 results in a units digit of 9.

However, this does not mean that answer (A) is correct! Since the answer choices are squared, the correct answer must have a units digit of 9 *after* being squared. Therefore, the correct answer is either (B) or (D), since 7^2 has a units digit of 9. See the estimation approach below for one way to differentiate between choices (B) and (D).

Estimation

It is also possible to estimate the answer: 5,995 is approximately equal to 6,000, and 4,796 is approximately equal to 5,000.

$$6,000^2 - 5,000^2$$
$$= 36,000,000 - 25,000,000$$
$$= 11,000,000$$

Since $3,000^2 = 9,000,000$, and $4,000^2 = 16,000,000$, the correct answer must be between $3,000^2$ and $4,000^2$. Eliminate any answer other than answers (C) and (D). Combined with the units digit approach above, this yields the correct answer, choice (D).

Factoring

The number 5,995 is a multiple of 5 just under 6,000, which equals 5(1,200). The number 4,796 is a multiple of 4 just under 4,800, which equals 4(1,200). This "coincidence" suggests factoring.

$$5,995 = 6,000 - 5 = 5(1,200 - 1) = 5(1,199)$$
$$4,796 = 4,800 - 4 = 4(1,200 - 1) = 4(1,199)$$

The shared factor of 1,199 means that simplification is possible.

$$5,995^2 - 4,796^2 = (5 \times 1,199)^2 - (4 \times 1,199)^2$$
$$= \left(1,199^2\right)\left(5^2 - 4^2\right)$$
$$= \left(1,199^2\right)\left(3^2\right)$$
$$= (1,199 \times 3)^2$$
$$= 3,597^2$$

The correct answer is **(D)**.

9

50.   **(A):** Begin by simplifying the equation given in the question.

$$8xy^3 + 8x^3y = \frac{2x^2y^2}{2^{-3}}$$

$$2^{-3}\left(8xy^3 + 8x^3y\right) = 2x^2y^2$$

$$\frac{1}{8}\left(8xy^3 + 8x^3y\right) = 2x^2y^2$$

$$xy^3 + x^3y = 2x^2y^2$$

At this stage, you might be tempted to divide both sides of the equation by xy, in order to arrive at the simpler equation $y^2 + x^2 = 2xy$. However, that would be a mistake—never divide both sides of an equation by an unknown (in this case, xy), unless you are certain that the unknown cannot equal zero. (Division by zero is undefined, and can lead to nonsensical results.) So rather than divide by xy, subtract $2x^2y^2$ from both sides to group all terms on one side of the equals sign.

$$xy^3 + x^3y - 2x^2y^2 = 0$$

$$(xy)\left(y^2 + x^2 - 2xy\right) = 0$$

$$(xy)(y - x)^2 = 0$$

This last line implies that either $xy = 0$ or $y - x = 0$. In other words, either $xy = 0$ or $y = x$.

(1) SUFFICIENT: If $y > x$, then it is impossible that $y = x$. Therefore, $xy = 0$.

(2) INSUFFICIENT: If $x < 0$, then it is possible that $xy = 0$ (i.e., if $y = 0$) or that $y = x$ (i.e., y is negative, too). If $y = x =$ any negative number, then there are infinitely many solutions for xy.

The correct answer is **(A)**.

Workout Set 6

51. Is it possible for a wooden block in the shape of a rectangular solid measuring L by w by h centimeter to pass through a square hole with sides of length 4 centimeter?

    (1) The volume of the wooden block is 16 cm³.

    (2) $L > w > h > 1$

52. Three of the four vertices of a rectangle in the *xy*-coordinate plane are $(-5, 1)$, $(-4, 4)$, and $(8, 0)$. What is the fourth vertex?

    (A) $(-4.5, 2.5)$

    (B) $(-4, 5)$

    (C) $(6, -2)$

    (D) $(7, -3)$

    (E) $(10, 1)$

53. In the coordinate plane, circle C has radius r and its center is at point (x, y). Is at least 50% of the area of circle C contained in a single quadrant of the coordinate plane?

    (1) $x > y > 0$

    (2) $x > r$

54. A group of men and women gathered to compete in a marathon. Each competitor was weighed before the competition; the average weight of the women was 120 pounds, and the average weight of the men was greater than 120 pounds. If the average weight of the entire group was w pounds, what percent of the competitors were women?

    (1) The average weight of the men was 150 pounds.

    (2) The difference between w and the average weight of the women was twice the difference between w and the average weight of the men.

55. What is the average (arithmetic mean) of these numbers: 12; 13; 14; 510; 520; 530; 1,115; 1,120; and 1,125 ?

    (A) 419

    (B) 551

    (C) 601

    (D) 620

    (E) 721

9

56. A set of 5 numbers has an average (arithmetic mean) of 50. The greatest element in the set is 5 greater than 3 times the least element in the set. If the median of the set equals the mean, what is the greatest possible value in the set?

(A) 85

(B) 87

(C) 88

((D)) 92

(E) 93

57.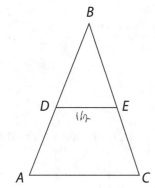

In the triangle above, *DE* is parallel to *AC*. What is the length of *DE* ?

(1) *AC* = 14

(2) *BE* = *EC*

 C

58.   5, 2, 4, *m*, 9, 5   2, 4, 5, 5, 9

For the list of numbers above, what is the median?

(1) The median is an integer.

(2) *m* = 8

 D

59. Set *M* contains seven consecutive integers, and set *N* contains three values chosen from set *M*. Is the standard deviation of set *N* greater than the standard deviation of set *M* ?

(1) Set *N* contains the median of set *M*.

(2) The range of set *M* and set *N* are equal.   B

60. Four different children have jelly beans: Aaron has 5, Bianca has 7, Callie has 8, and Dante has 11. How many jelly beans must Dante give to Aaron to ensure that each child has within 1 jelly bean of all the other children?

((A)) 2

(B) 3

(C) 4

(D) 5

(E) 6

Answers and explanations follow on the next page. ▶ ▶ ▶

$$\frac{(12+2\sqrt{11})^{1/2} - (12-2\sqrt{11})^{1/2}}{\sqrt{12-2\sqrt{11}}}$$

6.5

18.5   12 − 6.5

4.2 −   5.5

②

$$2\sqrt{2} \rightarrow 2(2^{1/2})$$

$$\sqrt{18.63} \sim \sqrt{5.36}$$

4.3

$$\frac{6.15}{\sqrt{18.5}} - \sqrt{5.5}$$

$$\frac{2.5}{9} \quad 4.25 \quad 2\text{-}3 \quad \frac{1.5}{5}$$

②

Workout Set 6 Answer Key

51. **C**
52. **D**
53. **B**
54. **B**
55. **B**
56. **D**
57. **C**
58. **D**
59. **B**
60. **B**

Workout Set 6 Solutions

51. **(C):** Start by considering the different types of blocks that could or could not fit through the hole.

    If all dimensions of the block are less than 4 centimeters (cm), the block can definitely fit through the hole.

    If exactly one of the three dimensions is greater than 4 cm, the block can still definitely fit through the hole. To do so, rotate the block so that the two shorter dimensions are aligned with the sides of the hole.

    However, if at least two of the dimensions of the block are greater than 4 cm, further investigation is required. It may be possible to fit the block through the hole by rotating it to take advantage of the longest dimension of the hole, which is the diagonal of $4\sqrt{2} \approx 5.6$ cm, but if the dimensions of the block are too great, this may be impossible.

    (1) INSUFFICIENT: The block can have any dimensions such that $Lwh = 16$. A block with dimensions 1, 1, and 16 can fit through the hole as shown in the second diagram above. However, a block with dimensions 8, 8, and 0.25 cannot fit through the hole. Since the answer can be Yes or No, this statement is insufficient.

    (2) INSUFFICIENT: A block with dimensions 2, 3, and 4 can fit through the hole, but a block with dimensions 100, 101, and 102 cannot.

    (1) and (2) SUFFICIENT: $Lwh = 16$ and h is greater than 1, so Lw is less than 16. Therefore, L and w cannot both be greater than 4. Since h is the least dimension, it must also be less than 4. Therefore, the block has at least two dimensions that are less than 4, and it can fit through the hole as shown in the second diagram.

    The correct answer is **(C)**.

52. **(D) (7, −3):** Your GMAT scratch pad has a grid; use it to plot the diagram to scale.

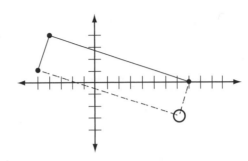

"Eyeball" solution: Complete the rectangle with the dashed lines shown. The fourth point must be located approximately where the bigger dot is drawn. Answers (A), (B), and (E) must be incorrect. The closest answer choice is the point (7, −3). Alternatively, you could plot the remaining two answer choice points to see which one "works" with the three given points.

Alternatively, compute the location of the fourth point, using the fact that the short sides have the same slope. The known short side connects the points (−5, 1) and (−4, 4). In other words, the bottom left corner is 1 to the left and 3 down from the top left corner. The unknown bottom right corner should therefore be 1 to the left and 3 down from the top right corner, or $x = 8 − 1 = 7$ and $y = 0 − 3 = −3$, corresponding to the point (7, −3).

The correct answer is **(D)**.

53. **(B):** The question asks whether at least half of the circle is contained in one quadrant. However, it does not specify a specific quadrant. If at least half of the circle is contained in any one of the four quadrants, the answer to the question will be Yes.

Note that if circle C lies in exactly one or two quadrants, then the answer to the question must be Yes, because at least half of the circle must be in one of those quadrants.

(1) INSUFFICIENT: If $x = 2$, $y = 1$, and $r = 0.5$, then the answer to the question is Yes, since the entire circle is contained in the first quadrant.

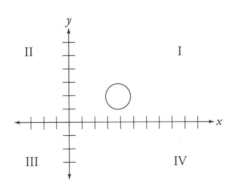

However, if $x = 2$, $y = 1$, and r is much greater than 2, then approximately a quarter of the circle is contained in each quadrant and the answer to the question is No.

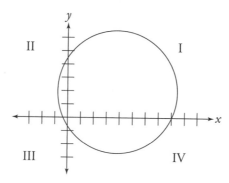

(2) SUFFICIENT: Since the x coordinate is greater than the radius of the circle, no part of the circle can be in the second or third quadrants.

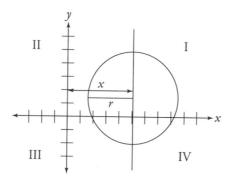

Therefore, at least half of the circle must be in the first quadrant or at least half of the circle must be in the fourth quadrant. The answer to the question is definitely Yes, and this statement is sufficient.

The correct answer is **(B)**.

54. **(B):** The question stem indicates that the average weight of the women was 120 and the average weight of the men was greater than 120. In order to determine what percent of the competitors were women, you would need to know more about the weight of the men and you'd also need to know something about the relative number of women vs. men. If there were not an equal number of each, then this is a weighted average question.

(1) INSUFFICIENT: Statement (1) provides the average weight of the men but does not indicate whether there was an equal number of men and women.

(2) SUFFICIENT: This does not provide the weight of the men or even the value of w, but it does indicate where the weighted average falls between the two values.

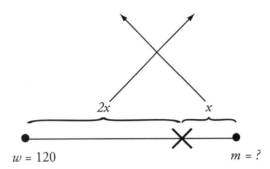

	Women	Men	Difference
Weight	120	m	$m - 120$
# of people	?	?	
Fraction of people	$\dfrac{x}{3x} = \dfrac{1}{3}$	$\dfrac{2x}{3x} = \dfrac{2}{3}$	

If the weighted average is twice as far from the women's end of the line, then the men are responsible for $\frac{2}{3}$ of the total weight and the women are responsible for $\frac{1}{3}$ of the total weight. Therefore, $\frac{1}{3}$, or approximately $33\frac{1}{3}\%$ of the competitors were women. (Note: You do not need to calculate this figure. You can stop whenever you understand that this figure can be calculated.)

The correct answer is **(B)**.

55. **(B) 551:** The simple average formula $\left(\text{Average} = \dfrac{\text{Sum}}{\text{Number of terms}}\right)$ applies to this problem. However, the chance of computational error is high on a problem with this many terms of such great value.

Try grouping the similar terms.

> Group A: 12, 13, 14 (equidistant terms with an average of 13, the middle term)
> Group B: 510, 520, 530 (equidistant terms with an average of 520, the middle term)
> Group C: 1,115; 1,120; 1,125 (equidistant terms with an average of 1,120, the middle term)

Since each group of terms consists of three values (and are therefore equally weighted in the set of nine terms), the average of all nine original terms is the average of the respective averages of Groups A, B, and C.

$$\begin{array}{r} 13 \\ 520 \\ +1,120 \\ \hline 1,653 \end{array}$$

$$\text{Average} = \frac{1,653}{3} = 551$$

You can make that division easier by breaking 1,653 into lesser numbers that are divisible by 3: $1,653 = 1,500 + 150 + 3$. Divide each separately by 3 to get $500 + 50 + 1 = 551$.

The correct answer is **(B)**.

9

56. **(D) 92:** Two techniques will help you efficiently interpret the information given in the question. First, draw a number line with five dots representing the five numbers in the set. Second, label these numbers A, B, C, D, and E, with the understanding that $A \leq B \leq C \leq D \leq E$.

The problem indicates that:

$A + B + C + D + E = 250$ (The set of five numbers has an average of 50.)

$E = 5 + 3A$ (The greatest element is five greater than three times the least element in the set.)

$C = 50$ (The median of the set equals the mean.)

You're asked to maximize E. Arrange the dots on the number line such that you obey the constraints, yet also note where you have some flexibility.

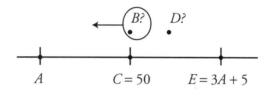

Point D can be anywhere on the line from point C to point E. Given the information from the question stem, you can maximize E by minimizing D. Therefore, make $D = C = 50$.

Similarly, point B can be anywhere on the line from point A to point C. Maximize E by minimizing B, so make $B = A$.

$$A = B \qquad C = D = 50 \qquad E = 3A + 5$$

$$\begin{aligned} A + B + C + D + E &= 250 \\ A + (A) + 50 + 50 + (5 + 3A) &= 250 \\ 105 + 5A &= 250 \\ 5A &= 145 \\ A &= 29 \end{aligned}$$

Therefore, $E = 5 + 3A = 5 + 3(29) = 5 + 87 = 92$.

$$A = B = 29 \qquad C = D = 50 \qquad E = 92$$

The correct answer is **(D)**.

57. **(C):**

(1) INSUFFICIENT: Many elements in this triangle could vary; you don't even know the placement of *B* relative to *AC*, so the triangle itself might stretch. Even for a fixed triangle, *DE* could slide up or down, so various lengths are possible for *DE*, as shown here:

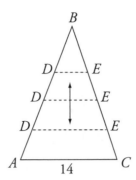

(2) INSUFFICIENT: You don't know the lengths of any sides of the triangle. The side that most affects the length of *DE* is *AC*, so stretch that side. Stretching the triangle out to the right stretches *DE*.

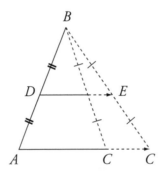

(1) AND (2) SUFFICIENT: *AC* must be 14 and *DE* must be parallel to *AC* and halfway between *AC* and *B*, in order to maintain *BE* = *EC*. Even though vertex *B* is free to move, *DE* will always be the average of the width of the triangle at *AC* (14) and the width at *B* (0). Thus, *DE* must be 7, no matter how the picture shifts.

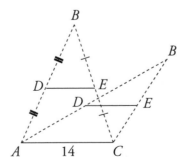

The correct answer is **(C)**.

58.　**(D):** To find the median of a set of numbers, line them up in order of value. The question of interest is, "Where is *m* relative to the other values?" This set has six values, an even number of terms, so the median is the average of the two middle terms.

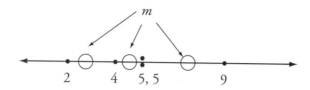

These are the three scenarios shown above.

If $m \leq 4$, then the two middle terms are 4 and 5, and the median is 4.5.

If $4 < m < 5$, then the two middle terms are *m* and 5, and the median is $\frac{m+5}{2}$.

If $m \geq 5$, then the two middle terms are 5 and 5, and the median is 5.

(1) SUFFICIENT: For the case where $4 < m < 5$, the median is $\frac{m+5}{2} = \frac{\text{non-integer} + \text{odd}}{2} = $ non-integer.

Thus, if the median is an integer, it must be 5.

(2) SUFFICIENT: If $m = 8$, then $m \geq 5$, and the median is 5.

The correct answer is **(D)**.

59.　**(B):** Standard deviation is a measure of the "spread" of a group of numbers.

(1) INSUFFICIENT: If set *M* contains the numbers {1, 2, 3, 4, 5, 6, 7}, then 4 is the median. Set *N* could be {3, 4, 5}, which has a lesser standard deviation than set *M* because the two sets have the same average but *N* is not as spread out as *M*.

Alternatively, *N* could be {1, 4, 7}, which has a greater standard deviation than set *M* because the two sets still have the same average, but *N* is now more spread out than M. (It doesn't have additional values that are closer to the average.)

(2) SUFFICIENT: If set *M* contains the numbers {1, 2, 3, 4, 5, 6, 7}, and set *N* has the same range, then *N* must contain 1 and 7. If set *N* contains {1, 4, 7}, then *N* has a greater standard deviation than *M*. If set *N* contains {1, 2, 7}, the standard deviation actually increases even more (because the numbers are no longer evenly distributed}. No matter what combination you try, the standard deviation of *N* has to be greater than the standard deviation of *M*.

The correct answer is **(B)**.

60. **(B) 3:** Conceptually, the transfer of jelly beans from Dante to Aaron reduces the range of the number of jelly beans held by individual children. The constraint is that the final distribution represents a range of just 1 jelly bean, a condition Bianca and Callie already satisfy.

Draw a picture (a number line) to visualize the scenario.

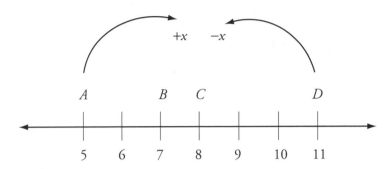

Aaron and Dante must end up with a number of jelly beans that is either 7 or 8. If either Aaron or Dante has a number of jelly beans *other than* 7 or 8, he will differ too much from either Bianca's or Callie's number. You can count out the necessary change on the number line above or you can write out the algebra.

$$A + x = 7 \text{ or } 8$$
$$5 + x = 7 \text{ or } 8$$
$$x = 2 \text{ or } 3$$

$$D - x = 7 \text{ or } 8$$
$$11 - x = 7 \text{ or } 8$$
$$x = 3 \text{ or } 4$$

The solution to both equations is $x = 3$: Add 3 to Aaron to get 8, and subtract 3 from Dante to get 8. The resulting number of jelly beans is $A = 8$, $B = 7$, $C = 8$, and $D = 8$.

The correct answer is **(B)**.

Workout Set 7

61. Is rectangle *R* a square?

    (1) At least one side of rectangle *R* has an integer length.

    (2) The diagonals of rectangle *R* have integer lengths.

62. A group of friends charters a boat for $540 and each person contributes equally to the cost. They determine that if they can get three more of their friends to join them, every person in the group will pay $9 less. If they find three more friends to join them, what is the total number of people renting the boat?

    (A)   6
    (B)   9
    (C)   15
    (D)   18
    (E)   21

63. In Smithtown, the ratio of right-handed people to left-handed people is 3 to 1 and the ratio of men to women is 3 to 2. If the number of right-handed men is maximized, then what percent of all the people in Smithtown are left-handed women?

    (A)   50%
    (B)   40%
    (C)   25%
    (D)   20%
    (E)   10%

64. The sum of the interior angle measures for any *n*-sided polygon equals $180(n - 2)$. If Polygon *A* has interior angle measures that correspond to a set of consecutive integers, and if the median angle measure for Polygon *A* is 140°, what is the least angle measure in the polygon?

    (A)   130°
    (B)   135°
    (C)   136°
    (D)   138°
    (E)   140°

65. When the positive integer *x* is divided by the positive integer *y*, the quotient is 2 and the remainder is *z*. When *x* is divided by the positive integer *a*, the quotient is 3 and the remainder is *b*. Is $z > b$?

    (1) The ratio of *y* to *a* is less than 3 to 2.

    (2) The ratio of *y* to *a* is greater than 2 to 3.

9

66. If a and b are odd integers, $a \triangle b$ represents the product of all odd integers between a and b, inclusive. If y is the least prime factor of $(3 \triangle 47) + 2$, which of the following must be true?

    (A) $y > 50$

    (B) $30 \leq y \leq 50$

    (C) $10 \leq y < 30$

    (D) $3 \leq y < 10$

    (E) $y = 2$

67. Set S is the set of all prime integers between 0 and 20. If three numbers are chosen randomly from set S, and no number is chosen more than once, what is the probability that the sum of all three numbers is odd?

    (A) $\dfrac{15}{56}$

    (B) $\dfrac{3}{8}$

    (C) $\dfrac{15}{28}$

    (D) $\dfrac{5}{8}$

    (E) $\dfrac{3}{4}$

68. Sets A and B each consist of three terms selected from the first five prime integers. No term appears more than once within a set, but any integer may be a term in both sets. If the average of the terms in set A is 4 and the product of the terms in set B is divisible by 22, how many terms are shared by both sets?

    (1) The product of the terms in set B is not divisible by 5.

    (2) The product of the terms in set B is divisible by 14.

69.

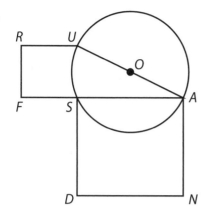

In the figure above, *SAND* and *SURF* are squares, and *O* is the center of the circle. If *Q* is the sum of the areas of squares *SAND* and *SURF* and *C* is the area of the circle, then the fraction $\dfrac{C}{Q}$ is

(A) less than $\dfrac{5}{8}$

(B) between $\dfrac{5}{8}$ and $\dfrac{3}{4}$

(C) between $\dfrac{3}{4}$ and $\dfrac{7}{8}$

(D) between $\dfrac{7}{8}$ and 1

(E) greater than 1

70. Set *S* consists of *n* consecutive positive integers. If $n > 3$, what is the value of *n* ?

(1) The number of multiples of 2 contained in set *S* is equal to the number of multiples of 3 contained in set *S*.

(2) *n* is odd.

Workout Set 7 Answer Key

61. **C**
62. **C**
63. **C**
64. **C**
65. **A**
66. **A**
67. **D**
68. **D**
69. **C**
70. **E**

Workout Set 7 Solutions

61. **(C):** A rectangle is a square if and only if its length equals its width.

(1) INSUFFICIENT: If the length is 1 and the width is 2, the rectangle is not a square. If the length and width are both 2, the rectangle is a square.

(2) INSUFFICIENT: Since R is a rectangle, both of its diagonals have the same length. It is only necessary to examine one of the diagonals. Since the diagonal and two of the sides form a right triangle, the length of the diagonal is always equal to $\sqrt{length^2 + width^2}$.

The diagonal of the rectangle below has an integer length, but the rectangle is not a square:

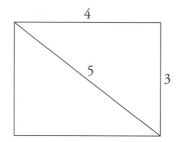

However, in the rectangle below, the diagonal has an integer length and the rectangle is a square. Note that it is not necessary to calculate the exact length of the sides of the square, since this is a Data Sufficiency problem. However, $x = \dfrac{5}{\sqrt{2}}$ in this case.

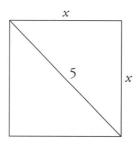

The answer could be Yes or No, so this statement is insufficient.

(1) AND (2) SUFFICIENT: According to the statements, the rectangle has at least one integer side, and it also has integer diagonals.

In a square, the legs and hypotenuse must be in the ratio $x : x : x\sqrt{2}$. To be a square, a rectangle must have a diagonal that is $\sqrt{2}$ times as long as its sides.

However, $\sqrt{2}$ is an irrational number, so if x is an integer, then $x\sqrt{2}$ is not an integer (and vice versa). It is impossible for the rectangle described by these statements to be a square, and the answer to the question is definitely No. The statements together are sufficient.

The correct answer is **(C)**.

62. **(C) 15:** Call the initial number of friends in the group f and the initial cost c. The problem allows you to write two equations.

$$fc = \$540$$
$$(f + 3)(c - 9) = \$540$$

The question asks for $f + 3$. These equations can be solved algebraically, but the math is going to result in having to solve a quadratic. The numbers in the answer choices are fairly small; try plugging them into the problem to find the correct answer. Start with (B) or (D).

	$f + 3$	f	Orig Cost $\frac{540}{f}$	New Cost $\frac{540}{f + 3}$	Are the costs \$9 apart?
(B)	9	6	$\frac{540}{6} = 90$	$\frac{540}{9} = 60$	No

The two costs are much too far apart. More people need to join the group in order to bring the costs closer together. Eliminate (A) and (B). Try (D) next.

	$f + 3$	f	Orig Cost $\frac{540}{f}$	New Cost $\frac{540}{f + 3}$	Are the costs \$9 apart?
(D)	18	15	$\frac{540}{18} = 30$	$\frac{540}{15} = 36$	No

This time, the two costs are only \$6 apart. They're too close. The answer must be between 9 and 18; therefore, the answer must be (C).

Check the math if you're not sure, but do practice this technique enough that you know when you can actually tell what the answer must be (without doing the math).

The correct answer is **(C)**.

63. **(C) 25%:** Use a double-set matrix to solve this problem.

	Right-Handed	Left-Handed	Total
Men			$3x$
Women			$2x$
Total	$3y$	y	$4y = 5x$

There is a *hidden constraint*: the number of people must be an integer. Thus, both x and y are integers. Moreover, the total number of people must be a multiple of 4 and of 5 in order for the given ratios to be possible. From this constraint, there are two ways to solve.

1. *Algebraic Solution*

Since the question specifies that the number of right-handed men be as great as possible, assume that all the men are right-handed; of course, that means that none of the men are left-handed. Because each column in a double-set matrix must total, you can also fill in the number of left-handed women (the group you want).

	Right-Handed	Left-Handed	Total
Men	$3x$	0	$3x$
Women		y	$2x$
Total	$3y$	y	$4y = 5x$

Thus, left-handed women represent $\dfrac{y}{4y} = \dfrac{1}{4} = 25\%$ of the total population.

2. *Smart Number Solution*

Since the total number of people in Smithtown must be a multiple of 20, set the total to 20 and determine the subtotals of men, women, left-handed, and right-handed based on the ratios given in the problem.

	Right-Handed	Left-Handed	Total
Men			12
Women			8
Total	15	5	20

To maximize the number of right-handed men, assign all the men to the "right-handed men" cell, and fill in the remaining cells.

	Right-Handed	Left-Handed	Total
Men	12	0	12
Women	3	5	8
Total	15	5	20

Therefore, left-handed women represent $\dfrac{5}{20} = \dfrac{1}{4} = 25\%$ of the population.

The correct answer is **(C)**.

64. **(C) 136°:** If the median angle measure is 140° and the interior angle measures correspond to a set of consecutive integers, then the average angle measure must equal 140°. Since the sum of the angles must equal $180(n-2)$, the average angle must equal $\dfrac{180(n-2)}{n}$.

$$140 = \frac{180(n-2)}{n}$$
$$140n = 180n - 360$$
$$360 = 40n$$
$$n = 9$$

Therefore, the polygon has nine sides and nine interior angles, and the measures of these angles are equal to a set of consecutive integers *centered at* 140. The set of nine consecutive integers must therefore be:

$$\{136, 137, 138, 139, 140, 141, 142, 143, 144\}$$

The least angle measure is 136°.

The correct answer is **(C)**.

9

65. **(A):** If $\frac{x}{y}$ has a quotient of 2 and a remainder of z, then x is z more than $2y$. Mathematically, $x = 2y + z$. Therefore, $z = x - 2y$.

If $\frac{x}{a}$ has a quotient of 3 and a remainder of b, then x is b more than $3a$. Mathematically, $x = 3a + b$. Therefore, $b = x - 3a$.

The question asks whether $z > b$, and the statements give information about $\frac{y}{a}$. Simplify the question by replacing z and b with their equivalents and solving for the combination $\frac{y}{a}$.

$$z > b\,?$$
$$x - 2y > x - 3a\,?$$
$$-2y > -3a\,?$$
$$\frac{y}{a} < \frac{3}{2}\,?$$

Note that the inequality sign flipped in the last step because of the division by -2. The variable a is a positive integer, so no additional flip is required for that manipulation. Rephrase the question as, "Is $\frac{y}{a} < \frac{3}{2}$?"

(1) SUFFICIENT: This directly answers the rephrased question: "Yes, $\frac{y}{a} < \frac{3}{2}$." Therefore, $z > b$.

(2) INSUFFICIENT: This indicates only that $\frac{y}{a} > \frac{2}{3}$. The answer might be Yes if $\frac{2}{3} < \frac{y}{a} < \frac{3}{2}$. However, the answer might be No if $\frac{y}{a}$ is greater than $\frac{3}{2}$.

The correct answer is **(A)**.

66. **(A) $y > 50$:** The function $(3\,\triangle\,47)$ equals the product $(3)(5)(7)\ldots(43)(45)(47)$. This product is a very large odd number, as it is the product of only odd numbers and thus does not have 2 as a factor. Therefore, $(3\,\triangle\,47) + 2 = $ Odd + Even = Odd, and $(3\,\triangle\,47) + 2$ does not have 2 as a factor either.

Every odd prime number between 3 and 47 inclusive is a factor of $(3\,\triangle\,47)$, since each of these primes is a component of the product. For example, $(3\,\triangle\,47)$ is divisible by 3, since dividing by 3 yields an integer minus the product $(5)(7)(9)\ldots(43)(45)(47)$.

Now consider the sum $(3\,\triangle\,47) + k$, where k is an integer. The sum will only be divisible by 3 if k is also divisible by 3. In other words, when you divide $(3\,\triangle\,47) + k$ by 3, you are evaluating $\frac{3\triangle 47}{3} + \frac{k}{3}$. Because $\frac{3\triangle 47}{3}$ is an integer, $\frac{k}{3}$ must also be an integer to yield an integer sum.

In this problem, $k = 2$, which is not divisible by any of the odd primes between 3 and 47. Since $(3\,\triangle\,47)$ IS divisible, but 2 is NOT divisible, the sum $(3\,\triangle\,47) + 2$ is NOT divisible by any of the odd primes between 3 and 47.

So $(3\,\triangle\,47) + 2$ is not divisible by any prime number less than or equal to 47. The least prime factor of $(3\,\triangle\,47) + 2$ must be greater than 47. Thus, the minimum possible prime factor is 53, since that is the least prime greater than 47.

The correct answer is **(A)**.

67. **(D):** If set S is the set of all prime integers between 0 and 20, then $S = \{2, 3, 5, 7, 11, 13, 17, 19\}$.

    There are seven odd terms and one even term in set S. If the even term is among those selected, the sum will be even $(E + O + O = E)$. The sum will be odd if all three terms selected are odd $(O + O + O = O)$.

    The probability of selecting three odd terms is $\frac{7}{8} \times \frac{6}{7} \times \frac{5}{6} = \frac{5}{8}$.

    The correct answer is **(D)**.

68. **(D):** The first five prime integers are 2, 3, 5, 7, and 11. These are the only terms that can appear in sets A and B. There are some other restrictions on the sets:

    > Set A: The average of the terms in set A is 4, so the sum of the terms is $(4)(3) = 12$. There is only one way for three of the first five primes to sum to 12: $2 + 3 + 7$. Set A is $\{2, 3, 7\}$.

    > Set B: The product of the terms in set B is divisible by 22, so 2 and 11 are terms in set B. Set B is $\{2, 11, x\}$, where x can be 3, 5, or 7, but *not* 2 or 11 (no duplicates).

    > Sets A and B share at least one term: the 2. If x is either 3 or 7, the sets will share two terms. If x is 5, the sets will only share one term.

    The rephrased question is, "Is $x = 5$?" A definite Yes or No answer leads to a definite value answer for the number of shared terms (i.e., Yes = one shared term, No = two shared terms).

    (1) SUFFICIENT: If the product of the terms in set B is not divisible by 5, $x \neq 5$ and the answer to the rephrased question is a definite No.

    (2) SUFFICIENT: If the product of the terms in set B is divisible by 14, then 2 and 7 are terms in B. Therefore, $x = 7$ and the answer to the rephrased question is a definite No.

    The correct answer is **(D)**.

69. **(C) between $\frac{3}{4}$ and $\frac{7}{8}$:** The area of a square is equal to the length of one side squared. The area of a circle is equal to πr^2. The question asks for the fraction $\frac{C}{Q}$.

    $$\frac{C}{Q} = \frac{\text{area of circle}}{\text{sum of areas of squares}}$$

    Inscribed angle USA cuts off a diameter (UA) of the circle, so angle USA must be a right angle. Therefore, the triangle is a right triangle with hypotenuse UA.

    The Pythagorean theorem indicates that $US^2 + SA^2 = UA^2$.

    US^2 also represents the area of the smaller square. SA^2 also represents the area of the larger square. The sum of the two equals the quantity Q mentioned in the question stem, so $Q = UA^2$.

9

UA is a diameter of the circle, so the quantity $Q = (2r)^2 = 4r^2$. The fraction is:

$$\frac{C}{Q} = \frac{\pi r^2}{4r^2} = \frac{\pi}{4}$$

The value of π is approximately 3.14, which falls between 3 and 3.5. Therefore:

$$\frac{3}{4} < \frac{\pi}{4} < \frac{3.5}{4}$$
$$\frac{3}{4} < \frac{\pi}{4} < \frac{7}{8}$$

The correct answer is (**C**).

70.   (**E**): The value of *n* must be 4 or greater. Start with statement (2), as it is much easier than statement (1).

(2) INSUFFICIENT: If *n* is odd, it could equal 3, 5, 7, or so on.

(1) INSUFFICIENT: *Test cases* to figure out what is possible.

n	Set *S*	# Multiples 2 = # Multiples 3?
4	3, 4, 5, 6	Yes: 2 multiples of each
5	3, 4, 5, 6, 7	Yes: 2 multiples of each

(1) AND (2) INSUFFICIENT: The case of *n* = 5 was already proven in the last step. Is there a way to have *n* = another odd number? Keep testing.

n	Set *S*	# Multiples 2 = # Multiples 3?
5	3, 4, 5, 6, 7	Yes: 2 multiples of each
7	3, 4, 5, 6, 7, 8, 9	Yes: 3 multiples of each

Since there are still at least two possible values for *n*, none of the information is sufficient to answer the question.

The correct answer is (**E**).

Workout Set 8

71.

Energy usage (units)	11	10	8	7
Number of days	4	5	n	3

The table above shows daily energy usage for an office building and the number of days that amount of energy was used. If the average (arithmetic mean) daily energy usage was greater than the median daily energy usage, what is the least possible value for n ?

(A) 2

(B) 3

(C) 4

(D) 5

(E) 6

72. A painting crew painted 80 houses. They painted the first y houses at a rate of x houses per week. Then, more painters arrived and everyone worked together to paint the remaining houses at a rate of $1.25x$ houses per week. How many weeks did it take to paint all 80 houses, in terms of x and y ?

(A) $\dfrac{320 - y}{5x}$

(B) $\dfrac{y + 320}{5x}$

(C) $\dfrac{5(80 - y)}{4x}$

(D) $\dfrac{y + 400}{4x}$

(E) $\dfrac{4y + 320}{5x}$

73. $a = x + y$ and $b = x - y$. If $a^2 = b^2$, what is the value of y ?

(1) $\sqrt{x} + \sqrt{y} > 0$

(2) $\sqrt{x} - \sqrt{y} > 0$

74. A herd of 33 sheep is sheltered in a barn with 7 stalls, each of which is labeled with a unique letter from A to G, inclusive. Is there at least one sheep in every stall?

(1) The ratio of the number of sheep in stall C to the number of sheep in stall E is 2 to 3.

(2) The ratio of the number of sheep in stall E to the number of sheep in stall F is 5 to 2.

9

75. If $(s \times 10^q) - (t \times 10^r) = 10^r$, where q, r, s, and t are positive integers and $q > r$, then what is the units digit of t ?

    (A) 0
    (B) 1
    (C) 5
    (D) 7
    (E) 9

76. Is $\sqrt{(y-4)^2} = 4 - y$?

    (1) $|y - 3| \leq 1$
    (2) $y \times |y| > 0$

77. What is the greatest prime factor of $2^{10}5^4 - 2^{13}5^2 + 2^{14}$?

    (A)   2
    (B)   3
    (C)   7
    (D)   11
    (E)   13

78. A decimal is called a "shrinking number" if its value is between 0 and 1 and each digit to the right of the decimal is not less than the digit to its immediate right. For instance, 0.86553221 is a shrinking number. If x is a shrinking number, which of the following must be true?

    I. $\dfrac{9x}{10}$ is a shrinking number.

    II. $\dfrac{x+9}{10}$ is a shrinking number.

    III. $\dfrac{x}{10}$ is a shrinking number.

    (A) I only
    (B) II only
    (C) I and II only
    (D) III only
    (E) I, II, and III

79. Each of the seven paintings in an art gallery has a different price. Is it possible to purchase at least three paintings for no more than $1,800 in total?

    (1) The median price of the seven paintings is $550.

    (2) It is possible to purchase four paintings at the gallery for a total of $2,300.

80. An (x, y) coordinate pair is to be chosen at random from the xy-plane. What is the probability that $y \geq |x|$?

    (A) $\dfrac{1}{10}$

    (B) $\dfrac{1}{8}$

    (C) $\dfrac{1}{6}$

    (D) $\dfrac{1}{5}$

    (E) $\dfrac{1}{4}$

Workout Set 8 Answer Key

71. **E**
72. **B**
73. **B**
74. **C**
75. **E**
76. **A**
77. **C**
78. **B**
79. **D**
80. **E**

9

Workout Set 8 Solutions

71.   **(E) 6:** Here's what you know about the arithmetic mean:

$$\text{Mean} = \frac{4(11) + 5(10) + n(8) + 3(7)}{4 + 5 + n + 3}$$

$$\text{Mean} = \frac{44 + 50 + 8n + 21}{12 + n}$$

$$\text{Mean} = \frac{115 + 8n}{12 + n}$$

In contrast, the median depends on n, but not in a linear way. To find the median, you order the terms and pick the middle one, so try various n values (i.e., vary the number of 8's in the list). This implies the eventual need to plug n values into the mean formula above, so draw a picture to help eliminate some answers first.

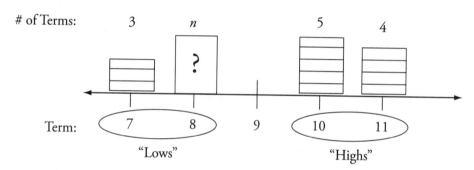

The "low" and "high" grouping is a fast way to find the relationship between median and mean for this set.

If the number of "lows" and "highs" are equal, the median is the average of the middle terms. That is, if $n = 6$, then the median $= 9$.

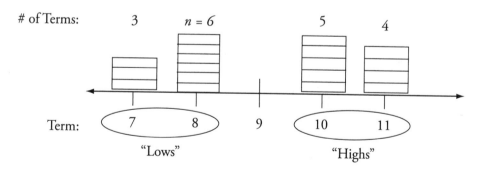

When $n = 6$, the mean must be greater than 9. Why? Pairs of 8 and 10 terms average to 9, but there is one "extra" 8. Pairs of 7 and 11 terms average to 9, but there is one "extra" 11. These "extra" terms differ from 9 by -1 and $+2$ respectively, for a total difference of $+1$. That positive difference implies that (mean > 9), or (mean $>$ median).

To prove that $n = 5$ is too low, you could take a more conventional approach. If $n = 5$, the number of terms is $3 + 5 + 5 + 4 = 17$. The median is the ninth term in this ordered set: 7, 7, 7, 8, 8, 8, 8, 8, **10**, 10, 10, 10, 10, 11, 11, 11, 11. Thus, the median is 10, while the mean is closer to 9.

$$\text{Mean} = \frac{115 + 8n}{12 + n} = \frac{115 + 8(5)}{12 + 5} = \frac{155}{17} \approx 9$$

That is, if $n = 5$, then median > mean.

If $n = 6$, then mean > median.

The correct answer is (**E**).

72. (**B**) $\dfrac{y + 320}{5x}$: This is a combined work problem, so use the work formula: rate × time = work. The work and rates are given, but you need to calculate time, so manipulate the formula: $\text{Time} = \dfrac{\text{work}}{\text{rate}}$. This problem also has variables in the answer choices, so it is efficient to *choose smart numbers*.

There are 80 houses, y houses are painted at a rate of x houses per week, and the rate increases to $1.25x$ houses per week for the remaining $80 - y$ houses. To make the math easier, choose values such that x and $1.25x$ are integers (i.e., x is a multiple of 4) and y and $80 - y$ are divisible by x and $1.25x$, respectively.

	Variable	Value	Units
Total Houses	80	80	Houses
Houses Painted at Slower Rate	y	20	Houses
Houses Painted at Faster Rate	$80 - y$	60	Houses
Initial Rate	x	4	Houses/Week
Increased Rate	$1.25x$	5	Houses/Week

The total painting time is:

20 houses painted at a rate of 4 houses/week = 5 weeks

60 houses painted at a rate of 5 houses/week = 12 weeks

Total time for 80 houses = 5 + 12 = 17 weeks

(A) $\dfrac{320 - y}{5x} = \dfrac{320 - 20}{5(4)} = \dfrac{300}{20} = 15$ Eliminate.

(B) $\dfrac{y + 320}{5x} = \dfrac{20 + 320}{5(4)} = \dfrac{340}{20} = 17$ Correct!

(C) $\dfrac{5(80) - y}{4x} = \dfrac{5(80 - 20)}{4(4)} = \dfrac{300}{16} =$ Not an integer. Eliminate.

(D) $\dfrac{y + 400}{4x} = \dfrac{20 + 400}{4(4)} = \dfrac{420}{16} = \dfrac{105}{4} =$ Not an integer. Eliminate.

(E) $\dfrac{4y + 320}{5x} = \dfrac{4(20) + 320}{5(4)} = \dfrac{20 + 80}{5} = 20$ Eliminate.

The correct answer is (**B**).

73. **(B):** If $a^2 = b^2$, then $(x + y)^2 = (x - y)^2$. Distribute both sides using the *square of a sum* and *square of a difference* special products, then simplify.

$$x^2 + 2xy + y^2 = x^2 - 2xy + y^2$$
$$2xy = -2xy$$
$$4xy = 0$$
$$xy = 0$$

There are three basic scenarios.

x	y	$xy = 0$
0	Any nonzero	✓
Any nonzero	0	✓
0	0	✓

(1) INSUFFICIENT: This statement indicates that x and y must be non-negative for their square roots to be real values. The statement also eliminates the last scenario, in which $x = y = 0$. But y could still be 0 or any positive value.

x	y	$xy = 0$	$\sqrt{x} + \sqrt{y} > 0$
0	Any positive	✓	✓
Any positive	0	✓	✓
0	0	✓	✗

(2) SUFFICIENT: This statement indicates that x and y must be non-negative for their square roots to be real values. This statement eliminates the last scenario. If x and y were both 0, $\sqrt{x} - \sqrt{y}$ would equal 0. It also eliminates the first scenario. If $\sqrt{x} - \sqrt{y} > 0$, then $\sqrt{x} > \sqrt{y}$. Therefore, $x > y$. Thus, you can conclude that $y = 0$.

x	y	$xy = 0$	$\sqrt{x} - \sqrt{y} > 0$
0	Any positive	✓	✗
Any positive	0	✓	✓
0	0	✓	✗

The correct answer is **(B)**.

74. **(C):**

(1) INSUFFICIENT: Set up a table and assign sheep to stalls.

Stall	A	B	C	D	E	F	G
# of Sheep			2x		3x		

Since a fractional sheep is not possible in this problem, x must be a positive integer. Suppose $x = 2$, so there are 4 sheep in C and 6 sheep in E. With 23 sheep remaining, it is possible for each of the other stalls to hold at least 1 sheep (a Yes answer). However, the 23 other sheep might all be in stall B, leaving stalls A, D, F, and G empty (a No answer).

(2) INSUFFICIENT: Set up a table and assign sheep to stalls.

Stall	A	B	C	D	E	F	G
# of Sheep					5y	2y	

If $y = 1$, there are 5 sheep in E and 2 sheep in F. With 26 sheep remaining, it is possible for each of the other stalls to hold at least 1 sheep (a Yes answer). However, 13 sheep might be in both stalls A and B, leaving stalls C, D, and G empty (a No answer).

(1) AND (2) SUFFICIENT: Set up a table and assign sheep to stalls.

Stall	A	B	C	D	E	F	G
# of Sheep			2x		3x = 5y	2y	

Since a fractional sheep is not possible in this problem, x and y must both be positive integers that satisfy the equation $3x = 5y$. The only possibility is $x = 5$ and $y = 3$, since higher multiples would require more than 33 sheep total. Thus, 31 sheep are allocated among these stalls as follows:

Stall	A	B	C	D	E	F	G
# of Sheep			10		15	6	

Thirty-one of the 33 sheep are in three of the 7 pens. With only 2 sheep unaccounted for, there is no way to place at least 1 sheep in each of the remaining four pens (a definite No answer).

The correct answer is **(C)**.

75.   **(E) 9:** Group the 10^r terms together.

$$\left(s \times 10^q\right) - \left(t \times 10^r\right) = 10^r$$

$$s \times 10^q = \left(t \times 10^r\right) + \left(1 \times 10^r\right)$$

$$s \times 10^q = (t + 1) \times 10^r$$

Now, solve for y.

$$s \times 10^q = (t + 1) \times 10^r$$

$$s \times \frac{10^q}{10^r} = t + 1$$

$$s \times 10^{q-r} = t + 1$$

$$s \times 10^{q-r} - 1 = t$$

Since $q > r$, the exponent on 10^{q-r} is positive. Since s is a positive integer, $s \times 10^{q-r}$ is a multiple of 10 and therefore ends in 0. Any multiple of 10 minus 1 yields an integer with a units digit of 9.

The correct answer is **(E)**.

76.   **(A):** The complicated expression in the question stem leads to a disguised Positive/Negative problem. In general, $\sqrt{x^2} = |x|$. Think about this relationship with a real example.

$$\sqrt{3^2} = \sqrt{9} = 3 \qquad\qquad \sqrt{(-3)^2} = \sqrt{9} = 3$$

In both cases (positive or negative 3), the end result is 3. Thus, in general, $\sqrt{x^2}$ will always result in a positive value, or $|x|$. Rephrase the original question using the absolute value symbol in place of the "square root of the square" symbols; then try to make the right-hand side look more like the left.

Is $|y - 4| = 4 - y$?   becomes   Is $|y - 4| = -(y - 4)$?

Since the absolute value of $y - 4$ must be positive or zero, you can rephrase the question further.

Is $-(y - 4) \geq 0$?   becomes   Is $(y - 4) \leq 0$?   and then   Is $y \leq 4$?

(1) SUFFICIENT: The absolute value $|y - 3|$ can be interpreted as the distance between y and 3 on a number line. Thus, y is no more than 1 unit away from 3 on the number line, so $2 \leq y \leq 4$. Thus, $y \leq 4$.

(2) INSUFFICIENT: If $y \times |y| > 0$, then $y \times |y|$ is positive. This means y and $|y|$ must have the same sign. The term $|y|$ is non-negative, so y must be positive. However, knowing that y is positive is not enough to indicate whether $y \leq 4$.

The correct answer is **(A)**.

77. **(C) 7:** A base of 2 is common to each term, and 10 is the smallest exponent appearing with that base. Factor 2^{10} out from all of the terms in the expression.

$$2^{10}5^4 - 2^{13}5^2 + 2^{14} = 2^{10}\left(5^4 - 2^3 5^2 + 2^4\right)$$

Clearly, 2 is a prime factor, but is it the greatest? Examine $(5^4 - 2^3 5^2 + 2^4)$ to determine whether it has a larger prime factor. The expression is of the form $x^2 - 2xy + y^2$, where:

$$x^2 = 5^4, \text{ so } x = 5^2$$
$$y^2 = 2^4, \text{ so } x = 2^2$$

Write the expression in factored form.

$$\left(5^2\right)^2 - 2\left(2^2\right)\left(5^2\right) + \left(2^2\right)^2 = \left(5^2 - 2^2\right)^2$$
$$= (25 - 4)^2$$
$$= 21^2$$

The prime factors of 21 are 3 and 7, so the largest prime factor of the original expression is 7.

Alternatively, if you did not see the quadratic template in $(5^4 - 2^3 5^2 + 2^4)$, you could also perform the computation and factor the result.

$$\left(5^4 - 2^3 5^2 + 2^4\right) = \left(625 - (8)(25) + 16\right)$$
$$= (625 - 200 + 16)$$
$$= (441)$$
$$= (3)(147)$$
$$= (3)(3)(49)$$
$$= (3)(3)(7)(7)$$

The correct answer is **(C)**.

78. **(B) II only:** According to the text, a "shrinking number" is a decimal between 0 and 1 in which each digit to the right of the decimal is no smaller than the digit to its immediate right.

That is, in a shrinking number, each digit is either larger than the one to its right, or the same as the one to its right. As you go through the digits from left to right, the digits will either stay the same or get smaller. For instance, 0.5331 is a shrinking number, but 0.37654 is not a shrinking number.

This Roman Numeral problem asks which of three options must be true. Test cases and eliminate any options that are not necessarily true.

One shrinking number is $x = 0.1000\ldots$ This is a shrinking number because the digits do not get larger after the decimal point. Since this number is relatively easy to do math with, start by using $x = 0.1$ to test cases.

I. As a fraction, $x = \frac{1}{10}$, so $\frac{9x}{10} = \left(\frac{9}{10}\right)\left(\frac{1}{10}\right) = \frac{9}{100} = 0.09$. However, this is not a shrinking number, since 9 is greater than 0. So statement I is not necessarily true. Eliminate choices (A), (C), and (E).

II. $\frac{x+9}{10} = \frac{9.100}{10} = 0.9100$, which is a shrinking number. Statement II could be true.

In fact, statement II must always be true. Adding 9 and then dividing by 10 is equivalent to inserting the digit 9 to the immediate right of the decimal. Since 9 is the largest possible digit, it will never be lower than the digit to its immediate right, so the decimal will still be a shrinking number.

III. $\frac{x}{10} = 0.0100$, which is not a shrinking number, since the digit two places to the right of the decimal is greater than the digit immediately to the right of the decimal. Statement III is not necessarily true. Eliminate choice (D).

The correct answer is **(B)**.

79. **(D):** A gallery has seven paintings with different prices. Is it possible to purchase at least three of the paintings for no more than $1,800? This is possible only if the three least expensive paintings at the gallery have a total price of $1,800 or less. The question can be rephrased as, "Is the total price of the three least expensive paintings $1,800 or less?"

(1) SUFFICIENT: The median price of the seven paintings is $550; since all of the paintings have different prices, the three least expensive paintings have prices below the median. Therefore, the total price of the three least expensive paintings is less than $550 + $550 + $550 = $1,650. The answer is definitely Yes, so this statement is sufficient.

(2) SUFFICIENT: This statement implies that the four least expensive paintings have a total price of $2,300 or less. Jot down some possible cases.

Case 1: $1, $2, $3, and $2,000. The three least expensive paintings can be purchased for $1,800, and the answer to the question is Yes.

Case 2: To find a No answer, try to maximize the lowest three prices out of the four. To do so, make the highest price as low as possible, or only slightly more than one-fourth of the total. Since one-fourth of $2,300 is $575, a good case to test is $573, $574, $576, and $577. However, the sum of the lowest three prices is $1,723, which is still well below $1,800, and the answer is still Yes.

Even when maximizing the lowest of the three prices, the three least expensive paintings can still be purchased for no more than $1,800, and the answer to the question is definitely Yes, so this statement is sufficient.

The correct answer is **(D)**.

80. **(E)** $\frac{1}{4}$: Graph the equation $y = |x|$.

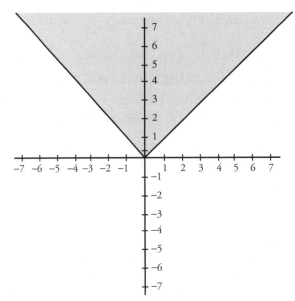

The inequality $y > |x|$ represents everything *above* the line (on either side of the y-axis)—that is, the shaded region. Since the equation $y = |x|$ forms a 45-degree angle from the x-axis, there are 90 degrees above the line (on both sides of the y-axis). This represents one-fourth of the xy-plane. Therefore, if a random pair of (x, y) coordinates is chosen from the plane, the probability is $\frac{1}{4}$ that the point will fit the criterion $y \geq |x|$.

The correct answer is **(E)**.

 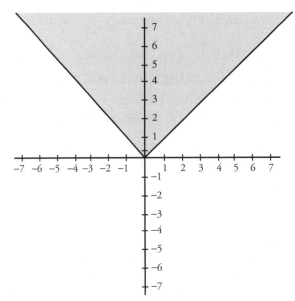

Workout Set 9

81.

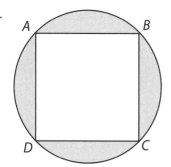

As shown in the figure, square $ABCD$ is inscribed in a circle with circumference $2\pi\sqrt{x}$. What is the area of the shaded region in the diagram above?

(A) $2x$

(B) $\pi x - 2x$

(C) $\pi x - x\sqrt{2}$

(D) $1 - \dfrac{2}{\pi}$

(E) $1 - \dfrac{2}{x}$

82. If $3^a + 3^{a-2} = (90)(3^b)$, what is b in terms of a ?

(A) $a - 4$

(B) $a - 2$

(C) $a + 4$

(D) $3a + 2$

(E) $3a + 4$

83. If $xy \neq 0$, what is the value of $\dfrac{x}{y}$?

(1) $y = 4 - x$

(2) $x(x - 6y) = -9y^2$

84. When one new integer is added to an existing list of six integers, does the median of the list change?

(1) The mean of the original six numbers is 50.

(2) At least two of the numbers in the original list were 50.

85. Let abc and dcb represent three-digit positive integers. If $abc + dcb = 598$, then which of the following must be equivalent to a ?

    (A) $d - 1$

    (B) d

    (C) $3 - d$

    (D) $4 - d$

    (E) $5 - d$

86. For nonzero integers a, b, c and d, is $\dfrac{ab}{cd}$ negative?

    (1) $ad + bc = 0$

    (2) $abcd = -4$

87. Set A consists of 8 distinct prime numbers. If x is equal to the range of set A and y is equal to the median of set A, is the product xy even?

    (1) The smallest integer in the set is 5.

    (2) The largest integer in the set is 101.

88. If $x^3 < 16x$, which of the following CANNOT be true?

    (A) $|x| > 4$

    (B) $x > -4$

    (C) $x < -4$

    (D) $x > 4$

    (E) $x < 4$

89. Is the two-digit positive integer n divisible by 3 ?

    (1) If the digits of n are reversed to produce the two-digit integer m, then m is divisible by 3.

    (2) If the digits of n are reversed to produce the two-digit integer m, then $m + n$ is divisible by 3.

90. Of all the sheets of paper in the tray of Printer A, 20% are removed and transferred to the tray of Printer B. After the transfer, are there more sheets of paper in the tray of Printer B than in the tray of Printer A?

    (1) The transfer increases the number of sheets of paper in the tray of Printer B by more than 25%.

    (2) The transfer increases the number of sheets of paper in the tray of Printer B by less than 30%.

9

Answers and explanations follow on the next page. ▶ ▶ ▶

Workout Set 9 Answer Key

81. **B**
82. **A**
83. **B**
84. **E**
85. **D**
86. **D**
87. **A**
88. **D**
89. **D**
90. **B**

Workout Set 9 Solutions

81. **(B)** $\pi x - 2x$: The circumference of the circle is equal to $2\pi r = 2\pi\sqrt{x}$, so $r = \sqrt{x}$.

    The area of the circle is equal to $\pi r^2 = \pi\left(\sqrt{x}\right)^2 = \pi x$.

    The area of a square is side^2. The diagonal of this square is the diameter of the circle, which is equal to $2r = 2\sqrt{x}$. The diagonal of a square is always $\sqrt{2}$(side), so the side of the square is equal to $\dfrac{\text{diagonal}}{\sqrt{2}}$. Therefore, side $= \dfrac{2\sqrt{x}}{\sqrt{2}} = \sqrt{2x}$ and the area of square $ABCD$ is:

    $$\text{side}^2 = \left(2\sqrt{x}\right)^2 = \frac{4x}{2} = 2x$$

    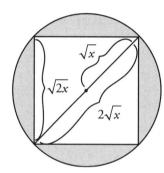

    $\pi x =$ circle's area

    The shaded area is the area of the circle minus the area of the square $= \pi x - 2x$.

    The correct answer is **(B)**.

82. **(A)** $a - 4$: Because the problem never provides real values for a or b, you can choose smart numbers to solve. Choose something for a that will make both exponents on the left side positive. If $a = 3$, then:

    $$3^a + 3^{a-2} = (90)\left(3^b\right)$$
    $$3^3 + 3^{3-2} = (90)\left(3^b\right)$$
    $$27 + 3 = (90)\left(3^b\right)$$
    $$\frac{1}{3} = 3^b$$
    $$3^{-1} = 3^b$$

    Therefore, $b = -1$. Plug $a = 3$ into the answers and look for -1.

    (A) $3 - 4 = -1$ Correct.

    (B) $3 - 1 = 1$ Eliminate.

    (C) $3 + 4 =$ Too big. Eliminate.

    (D) $3(3) + 2 =$ Too big. Eliminate.

    (E) $3(3) + 4 =$ Too big. Eliminate.

Alternatively, you can solve algebraically. Some manipulation is required to determine b in terms of a, but spend a minute thinking strategically about what manipulations to do. It would help to isolate terms with an a by factoring 3^a out on the left side. This will let you compare 3^a to 3^b, and thus compare a to b, once you clean up the constant terms that are left over. Also, 90 is a multiple of 9, which is a power of 3. Ninety is also the sum of 81 and 9, both powers of 3 themselves. It is likely that some constant terms will cancel, as shown below.

$$3^a + 3^{a-2} = (90)(3^b)$$

$$3^a(1 + 3^{-2}) = (90)(3^b) \qquad \text{Factor out } 3^a \text{ on the left side.}$$

$$3^a(3^2 + 1) = (90)(3^b)(3^2) \qquad \text{Multiply both sides by } 3^2 \text{ to cancel the negative exponent.}$$

$$3^a(10) = (90)(3^b)(3^2) \qquad \text{Compute: } 3^2 + 1 = 9 + 1 = 10.$$

$$3^a = (9)(3^b)(3^2) \qquad \text{Divide both sides by 10.}$$

$$3^a = (3^2)(3^b)(3^2) \qquad \text{Express 9 in terms of the common base: } 3^2.$$

$$3^a = 3^{b+4} \qquad \text{Combine terms on the right side.}$$

$$a = b + 4 \qquad \text{Set the exponents on each side equal.}$$

Therefore, $b = a - 4$.

The correct answer is **(A)**.

83. **(B):** The constraint in the question stem indicates that neither x nor y equals zero.

(1) INSUFFICIENT: You can prove insufficiency by testing cases. If $y = 1$, then $x = 3$, in which case $\frac{x}{y}$ is 3. If $y = 2$, then $x = 2$, in which case $\frac{x}{y}$ is 1.

(2) SUFFICIENT: Testing cases might not be such a great idea for this statement because there are multiple instances of each variable. Begin by distributing the left-hand side of the equation.

$$x^2 - 6xy = -9y^2$$

Now, you've got a quadratic, so solve that way.

$$x^2 - 6xy + 9y^2 = 0$$

$$(x - 3y)^2 = 0$$

$$x - 3y = 0$$

$$x = 3y$$

$$\frac{x}{y} = 3$$

The correct answer is **(B)**.

9

84. **(E):** You can test cases to try to prove or disprove the statements.

(1) INSUFFICIENT: If the original set is 50, 50, 50, 50, 50, 50, the mean and median were 50 originally. The new term may be any value and the median will not change.

If, on the other hand, the original set is 0, 0, 0, 100, 100, 100, the mean and median were 50 originally. If the new term is 75, the median increases to 75. More generally for this set, if the new term is not equal to the original median of 50, the median will change.

(2) INSUFFICIENT: If the original set is 50, 50, 50, 50, 50, 50, the median was 50 originally. The new term may be any value and the median will not change.

If, on the other hand, the original set is 0, 0, 0, 50, 50, 50, the median was 25 originally. If the new term is 40, the median increases to 40. More generally for this set, if the new term is not equal to the original median of 25, the median will change.

(1) AND (2) INSUFFICIENT: The mean must be 50 and at least two terms in the original set must be 50.

If the original set is 50, 50, 50, 50, 50, 50, the mean and median were 50 originally. The new term may be any value and the median will not change.

If the original set is 0, 0, 0, 50, 50, 200, the mean was 50 and the median was 25 originally. If the new term is greater than 25, the median increases. If the new term is less than 25, the median decreases.

The correct answer is **(E)**.

85. **(D) $4 - d$:** Set up the addition and extract several equations by summing each digit place individually.

$$\begin{array}{r} abc \\ +\,dcb \\ \hline 598 \end{array}$$

Note that both the ones digit and tens digit come from the sum $c + b$. Since the result is different in the ones digit (8) and the tens digit (9), a 1 must be carried from the ones to the tens digit. Thus, $c + b \neq 8$; instead, $c + b = 18$.

If $c + b = 18$, then both c and b must be 9 (the largest digit). Place an 8 in the ones digit of the sum and carry a 1 to the tens place. The sum in the tens digit is thus $1 + b + c = 1 + 18 = 19$. Next, place a 9 in the tens digit of the sum and carry a 1 to the hundreds place.

In the hundreds place, the sum is $1 + a + d = 5$.

Now, solve for a.

$$\begin{aligned} 1 + a + d &= 5 \\ a + d &= 4 \\ a &= 4 - d \end{aligned}$$

The correct answer is **(D)**.

9

86. **(D):** If an even number (0, 2, or 4) of the integers a, b, c, and d is negative, each pair of negatives will cancel, because $(-1)(-1) = +1$ and $\frac{(-1)}{(-1)} = +1$. This would yield a positive result for $\frac{ab}{cd}$.

Thus, a way to rephrase the question is, "Among the integers a, b, c, and d, are an odd number (*one or three*) of them negative?"

(1) SUFFICIENT: This statement can be rephrased as $ad = -bc$.

a	d	b	c	$ad = -bc$	Odd number of negatives?
+	+	−	+	✓	Yes
+	−	+	+	✓	Yes
−	−	−	+	✓	Yes
+	−	−	−	✓	Yes

Though the table doesn't list all possibilities, it lists enough to realize that, in order for the signs of ad and bc to be opposite one another, either one or three of the four integers must be negative.

(2) SUFFICIENT: You might recognize that the $(-1)(-1) = +1$ property implies that $abcd$ is only negative when there are non-paired negatives among the integers. That is, an odd number (one or three) of the integers a, b, c, and d must be negative. If not, you could list a few cases to see the pattern.

a	b	c	d	$abcd$ = negative	Odd number of negatives?
+	+	−	+	✓	Yes
+	−	+	+	✓	Yes
−	+	−	−	✓	Yes
−	−	+	−	✓	Yes

The correct answer is **(D)**.

87. **(A):** The product xy will be even if x is even, y is even, or both are even.

The prime numbers include 2, 3, 5, 7, 11, 13, 17, 19, etc. The smallest possible term in set A is 2, which is the only even prime.

x = the range of set A = largest term − smallest term in set A. If the smallest term in set A is 2, then x = odd − even = odd. If the smallest term in set A is odd (i.e., not 2), then x = odd − odd = even.

The median of set A is the average of the two middle terms, since the number of terms in the set is even. Thus, $y = \frac{\text{odd} + \text{odd}}{2} = \frac{\text{even}}{2}$ = integer. However, y could be either even (e.g., when the middle terms are 11 and 13) or odd (e.g., when the middle terms are 7 and 11).

A useful rephrase of this question is, "Is either x or y even?"

(1) SUFFICIENT: If the smallest prime in the set is 5, x = even, and therefore xy is even.

(2) INSUFFICIENT: If the largest integer in the set is 101, the range of the set can be odd or even (e.g., $101 - 3 = 98$ or $101 - 2 = 99$). The median of the set can also be odd or even, as discussed. Therefore, xy can be either odd or even.

The correct answer is **(A)**.

88. **(D)** $x > 4$: It may be tempting to simplify this way:

$$x^3 < 16x$$
$$x^2 < 16$$
$$-4 < x < 4$$

The first step of this solution is wrong because you can't divide by x without knowing its sign. If x is negative, you would have to flip the sign.

Check both cases.

x	$x^3 < 16x$ becomes:	Take square root:	Solve for x:
Positive	$x^2 < 16$ (don't flip)	$\lvert x \rvert < 4$	$0 < x < 4$
Negative	$x^2 > 16$ (flip)	$\lvert x \rvert > 4$	$x < -4$

There are two ranges of solutions for x. The question asks for something that is definitely NOT true. Check the answer choices for an answer that does NOT include any values in these two ranges. All of the answer choices include some of the values above, except for (D): if x must be either between 0 and 4, or less than -4, it cannot be the case that $x > 4$. However, it is possible, for certain values of x, for each of the other answer choices to be true.

Alternatively, there is a way to do algebra with inequalities containing variables. Instead of dividing by the variable, subtract it from both sides, then factor.

$$x^3 - 16x < 0$$
$$x\left(x^2 - 16\right) < 0$$
$$x(x - 4)(x + 4) < 0$$

In order for the product of three numbers to be negative, either all three need to be negative, or exactly one of the three needs to be negative. This cannot occur if x is greater than 4, since all three values would be positive. Therefore, (D) cannot be true.

The correct answer is **(D)**.

89. **(D):** Before diving into the statements, remind yourself of the divisibility rules. One way to check for divisibility by 3 is to add the digits. If their sum is divisible by 3, then the number itself is divisible by 3.

(1) SUFFICIENT: If m is divisible by 3, then the sum of the digits of m must be divisible by 3 as well. Since m has the same digits as n, the sum of the digits of n must also be a multiple of 3. Therefore, n itself is divisible by 3.

9

(2) SUFFICIENT: This statement requires a bit more work because it's not immediately clear what would happen when you add m and n. Because the question asks you to move digits around to different places (the tens place, the units place), rewrite the information using place-value notation, where $a =$ the tens digit of n and $b =$ the units digit of n.

$n = 10a + 1b$

Therefore, $m = 10b + 1a$.

The sum $m + n = 11a + 11b = 11(a + b)$.

The statement indicates that the sum $m + n$ is divisible by 3, so $11(a + b)$ must also be divisible by 3. Eleven itself is not divisible by 3, so the sum $a + b$ must be divisible by 3. This sum represents the sum of the two digits of the number m as well as the sum of the two digits of the number n; if the sum of n's two digits is divisible by 3, then n is also divisible by 3.

The correct answer is (**D**).

90.   (**B**): You can solve this problem algebraically or by testing cases. Both methods are shown.

(1) INSUFFICIENT: If Printer A starts out with 100 sheets, then 20 sheets are moved to Printer B, and Printer A ends up with 80 sheets. If B started out with 75 sheets, then an increase of 20 sheets would be more than 25% of the starting number, and B would end up with 95 sheets. In this case, B has more sheets than A after the transfer.

If, instead, B started out with 40 sheets, then an increase of 20 sheets would be more than 25% of the starting number, and B would end up with 60 sheets. In this case, B has fewer sheets than A after the transfer.

(2) SUFFICIENT: If Printer A starts out with 100 sheets and 20 are moved to Printer B, then A ends up with 80 sheets. If B started out with 2,000 sheets, then an increase of 20 sheets would be less than 30% of the starting number, and B would end up with many more sheets than A.

If B started out with 80 sheets, then a 20-sheet increase would still be less than 30% of the starting number, and again B would end up with more sheets than A.

How low can B go? If the 20 sheets represent a less-than-30% increase, then use 30% as the limiting figure. If 20 represented exactly 30% of B's sheets, then B would have to start with $66\frac{2}{3}$ sheets (ignore the fact that this isn't an integer). In this case, B would end up with $88\frac{2}{3}$ sheets, which is still greater than A's 80 sheets. After the transfer, B can't drop below A.

Algebraically, use a for the original number of sheets in Printer A and use b for the original number of sheets in Printer B.

After the transfer, A has $a - 0.2a = 0.8a$ sheets. B has $b + 0.2a$ sheets. Rephrase the question: "Is $b + 0.2a > 0.8a$?" Or, "Is $b > 0.6a$?"

(1) INSUFFICIENT: Translate the statement into algebra.

$$b + 0.2a > 1.25b$$
$$0.2a > 0.25b$$
$$0.8a > b$$

Flip the statement around to compare it more easily to the rephrased question: $b < 0.8a$. Is it true that $b > 0.6a$? Maybe.

(2) SUFFICIENT: Translate the statement into algebra.

$$b + 0.2a < 1.3b$$
$$0.2a < 0.3b$$
$$2a < 3b$$

Therefore, $\frac{2a}{3} < b$ or $b > \frac{2a}{3}$.

The decimal equivalent of $\frac{2}{3}$ is $0.\overline{6}$, so b is indeed always greater than $0.6a$.

The correct answer is **(B)**.

Workout Set 10

91. If $|x| \neq |y|$, $xy \neq 0$, $\dfrac{x}{x+y} = n$, and $\dfrac{x}{x-y} = m$, then $\dfrac{x}{y}$ is equal to which of the following?

    (A) $\dfrac{3mn}{2}$

    (B) $\dfrac{3m}{2n}$

    (C) $\dfrac{n(m+2)}{2}$

    (D) $\dfrac{2nm}{(m-n)}$

    (E) $\dfrac{n^2 - m^2}{nm}$

92. If a certain culture of bacteria increases by a constant factor of x every y minutes, how long will it take for the culture to increase to 10,000 times its original size?

    (1) $\sqrt[y]{x} = 10$

    (2) In two minutes, the culture will increase to 100 times its original size.

93. A cylinder of height h is $\dfrac{3}{4}$ full of water. When all of the water is poured into an empty cylinder whose radius is 25% larger than that of the original cylinder, the new cylinder is $\dfrac{3}{5}$ full. The height of the new cylinder is what percent of h ?

    (A) 25%

    (B) 50%

    (C) 60%

    (D) 80%

    (E) 100%

94. If a and b are distinct positive integers, what is the units digit of $2^a 8^b 4^{a+b}$?

    (1) $b = 24$ and $a < 24$

    (2) The greatest common factor of a and b is 12.

95. Employees of a certain company are each to receive a unique seven-digit identification code consisting of the digits 0, 1, 2, 3, 4, 5, and 6 such that no digit is used more than once in any given code. In valid codes, the second digit in the code is exactly twice the first digit. How many valid codes are there?

    (A)   42

    (B)   120

    (C)   210

    (D)   360

    (E)   840

96. An *n*-sided die has sides labeled with the numbers 1 through *n*, inclusive, and has an equal probability of landing on any side when rolled. If the die is rolled twice, what is the probability of rolling 1 both times?

    (1) If the die is rolled twice, the probability that the two rolls are different is 80%.

    (2) If the die is rolled twice, the probability that the two rolls are equal is $\dfrac{1}{n}$.

97. If *w*, *x*, *y*, and *z* are positive integers and $\dfrac{w}{x} < \dfrac{y}{z} < 1$, what is the proper order, increasing from left to

    right, of the following quantities: $\dfrac{x}{w}, \dfrac{z}{y}, \dfrac{x^2}{w^2}, \dfrac{xz}{wy}, \dfrac{x+z}{w+y}, 1$?

    (A) $1, \dfrac{z}{y}, \dfrac{x}{w}, \dfrac{x+z}{w+y}, \dfrac{x^2}{w^2}, \dfrac{xz}{wy}$

    (B) $1, \dfrac{z}{y}, \dfrac{x+z}{w+y}, \dfrac{x}{w}, \dfrac{xz}{wy}, \dfrac{x^2}{w^2}$

    (C) $1, \dfrac{z}{y}, \dfrac{x}{w}, \dfrac{x+z}{w+y}, \dfrac{xz}{wy}, \dfrac{x^2}{w^2}$

    (D) $1, \dfrac{z}{y}, \dfrac{x}{w}, \dfrac{xz}{wy}, \dfrac{x+z}{w+y}, \dfrac{x^2}{w^2}$

    (E) $1, \dfrac{z}{y}, \dfrac{x+z}{w+y}, \dfrac{xz}{wy}, \dfrac{x^2}{w^2}, \dfrac{x}{w}$

98. What is the value of $|a + b|$?

    (1) $(a + b + c + d)(a + b - c - d) = 16$

    (2) $c + d = 3$

99. Set *A* consists of all the integers between 10 and 21, inclusive. Set *B* consists of all the integers between 10 and 50, inclusive. If *x* is a number chosen randomly from set *A*, *y* is a number chosen randomly from set *B*, and *y* has no factor *z* such that $1 < z < y$, what is the probability that the product *xy* is divisible by 3 ?

    (A) $\dfrac{1}{4}$

    (B) $\dfrac{1}{3}$

    (C) $\dfrac{1}{2}$

    (D) $\dfrac{2}{3}$

    (E) $\dfrac{3}{4}$

9

100. At a birthday party, x children will be seated at two different tables. At the table with the birthday cake on it, exactly y children will be seated, including the birthday girl, Sally. How many different groups of children may be seated at the birthday cake table?

(A) $\dfrac{(x-1)!}{(y-1)!(y-1)!}$

(B) $\dfrac{x!}{y!(x-y)!}$

(C) $\dfrac{y!}{x!(x-y)!}$

(D) $\dfrac{(y-1)!}{(x-y)!(y-1)!}$

(E) $\dfrac{(x-1)!}{(x-y)!(y-1)!}$

Answers and explanations follow on the next page. ▶ ▶ ▶

Workout Set 10 Answer Key

91. **D**
92. **D**
93. **D**
94. **B**
95. **D**
96. **A**
97. **B**
98. **C**
99. **B**
100. **E**

Workout Set 10 Solutions

91. **(D)** $\dfrac{2nm}{m-n}$: If $x = 2$ and $y = 3$, then $n = \dfrac{2}{5}$ and $m = \dfrac{2}{-1} = -2$. The target number for testing the answer choices is $\dfrac{x}{y} = \dfrac{2}{3}$.

(A) $\dfrac{3mn}{2} = $ Negative. Eliminate.

(B) $\dfrac{3m}{2n} = $ Negative. Eliminate.

(C) $\dfrac{n(m+2)}{2} = 0$ Eliminate.

(D) $\dfrac{2nm}{(m-n)} = \dfrac{2\left(\frac{2}{5}\right)(-2)}{-2 - \frac{2}{5}} = \dfrac{\frac{-8}{5}}{\frac{-10}{5} - \frac{2}{5}} = \dfrac{\frac{-8}{5}}{\frac{-12}{5}} = \dfrac{8}{12} = \dfrac{2}{3}$ Correct.

(E) $\dfrac{n^2 - m^2}{nm} = \dfrac{\frac{4}{25} - 4}{\frac{-4}{5}} = \dfrac{\frac{4}{25} - \frac{100}{25}}{\frac{-20}{25}} = \dfrac{-96}{-20} = $ Greater than 1. Eliminate.

This problem can be solved algebraically, but this path is not recommended.

$$\dfrac{x}{x+y} = n \qquad\qquad \dfrac{x}{x-y} = m$$

$$\left(\dfrac{x}{x+y}\right)^{-1} = n^{-1} \quad \text{and} \quad \left(\dfrac{x}{x-y}\right)^{-1} = m^{-1}$$

$$\dfrac{x+y}{x} = \dfrac{1}{n} \qquad\qquad \dfrac{x-y}{x} = \dfrac{1}{m}$$

Now that the fractions have a common denominator of x, subtract one from the other.

$$\left(\dfrac{x+y}{x}\right) - \left(\dfrac{x-y}{x}\right) = \dfrac{1}{n} - \dfrac{1}{m}$$

$$\dfrac{x+y-x-(-y)}{x} = \dfrac{m}{nm} - \dfrac{n}{nm}$$

$$\dfrac{2y}{x} = \dfrac{m-n}{mn}$$

$$\dfrac{y}{x} = \dfrac{m-n}{2mn}$$

$$\dfrac{x}{y} = \dfrac{2mn}{m-n}$$

You are not alone if the algebraic solution was not obvious to you! Algebraic "false starts" are common in this type of problem. In addition, there are other, equally valid algebraic paths whose final forms would not match any of the answers.

When you encounter a tough "pure algebra" problem that has variables in the answer choices, picking numbers and testing the answer choices is often the best approach; it's fast, easy, and correct.

The correct answer is **(D)**.

92. **(D):** To understand the question stem, pick some numbers: the bacteria culture begins with an initial quantity of $I = 100$ and increases by a factor of $x = 2$ every $y = 3$ minutes. Construct a table to track the growth of the bacteria.

Time (min.)	Bacteria
3	$100(2) = 100(2)^1$
6	$100(2)(2) = 100(2)^2$
9	$100(2)(2)(2) = 100(2)^3$
12	$100(2)(2)(2)(2) = 100(2)^4$
...	...
$3n = t$	$100(2)^n$

n represents the number of growth periods, and $n = \dfrac{t}{y}$ where t is time in minutes. For example, the fourth growth period in the table above ended at 12 minutes, and $4 = \dfrac{12 \text{ minutes}}{3 \text{ minutes}}$.

From this example, construct a general formula for the quantity of bacteria, F.

$$F = I(x)^{\frac{t}{y}}$$

This question asks how long it will take for the bacteria to grow to 10,000 times their original amount. In other words, "What is t when $F = 10,000I$?"

$$F = 10,000I = I(x)^{\frac{t}{y}}$$
$$10,000 = (x)^{\frac{t}{y}}$$

The rephrased question is, "What is t when $10,000 = (x)^{\frac{t}{y}}$?"

(1) SUFFICIENT: Note that the yth root of x is equivalent to x to the $\dfrac{1}{y}$ power. This statement indicates that $x^{\frac{1}{y}} = 10$. If you plug this value into the equation, you can solve for t (though stop the calculation at the point that you can tell that you can solve for t).

$$10,000 = (x)^{\frac{t}{y}}$$
$$10,000 = \left[(x)^{\frac{1}{y}}\right]^t$$
$$10,000 = 10^t$$
$$10^4 = 10^t$$
$$t = 4$$

(2) SUFFICIENT: The culture grows one-hundredfold in 2 minutes. In other words, the sample grows by a factor of 10^2. Since exponential growth is characterized by a constant factor of growth (i.e., by a factor of x every y minutes), in another 2 minutes, the culture will grow by another factor of 10^2. Therefore, after a total of 4 minutes, the culture will have grown by a factor of $10^2 \times 10^2 = 10^4$, or 10,000.

The correct answer is **(D)**.

93. **(D) 80%:** The answer choices contain percentages, and the problem never offers a real value for h. Choose a smart number.

Also note that the problem mentions the volume of the cylinder ($V = \pi r^2 h$), so you're going to need a radius. That radius needs to be increased by 25% later in the problem, so pick a small integer that is easy to increase by 25%, such as 4.

$$r = 4$$

The problem also contains two fractions, $\frac{3}{4}$ and $\frac{4}{5}$. Since one number is already a multiple of 4, make the other number a multiple of 5.

$$h = 5$$

Now, solve the problem using these numbers. Remember that the original cylinder is only $\frac{3}{4}$ full.

$$\text{Three-quarters of original cylinder volume} = \frac{3}{4}\left[\pi\left(4^2\right)(5)\right]$$
$$= 60\pi$$

$$\text{New radius} = 4 + (0.25)4 = 5$$

The amount of water in the new cylinder has to be the same 60π. Remember that it is only $\frac{3}{5}$ full.

$$60\pi = \pi\left(5^2\right)(h)\left(\frac{3}{5}\right)$$
$$60 = 15h$$
$$4 = h$$

The new height is 4. The original height was 5, so the new height is $\frac{4}{5}$, or 80%, of the original height.

The correct answer is **(D)**.

94. **(B):** This problem contains a common trap seen in many difficult DS questions. Answer choice (C) is a tempting short-cut answer as the combined statements would provide the values of both a and b, which could be plugged into the expression to answer the question.

Rephrase the question:

$$2^a 8^b 4^{a\,+\,b} = 2^a \left(2^3\right)^b \left(2^2\right)^{a\,+\,b}$$
$$= 2^a \left(2^{3b}\right)\left(2^{2a\,+\,2b}\right)$$
$$= 2^{3a\,+\,5b}$$

Remembering the units digit patterns for powers of 2 will help on this problem:

$$2^1 = 2$$
$$2^2 = 4$$
$$2^3 = 8$$
$$2^4 = 16$$
$$2^5 = 32$$
$$\ldots \quad \text{etc.}$$

The units digits for powers of 2 is a repeating pattern of [2, 4, 8, 6].

If you can determine the relationship of $3a + 5b$ to a multiple of 4 (i.e., where $2^{3a + 5b}$ is in the predictable four-term repeating pattern of units digits), you will be able to answer the question. This question can be rephrased as, "What is the remainder when $3a + 5b$ is divided by 4?"

(1) INSUFFICIENT: If $b = 24$, then $5b$ is a multiple of 4. However, a could be any integer less than 24. Possible remainders when $3a$ is divided by 4 are 0, 1, 2, or 3.

(2) SUFFICIENT: If the greatest common factor of a and b is 12, then 12 must be a factor of both variables. That is, both a and b are multiples of 12 and thus also multiples of 4. As a result, $3a$ and $5b$ will be multiples of 4 as well, so the remainder will be 0 when $3a + 5b$ is divided by 4.

The correct answer is **(B)**.

95. **(D) 360:** Valid codes must have a second digit that is exactly twice the first digit. There are three ways to do this with the available digits.

> Scenario A: 12*XXXXX*
>
> Scenario B: 24*XXXXX*
>
> Scenario C: 36*XXXXX*

For each of these basic scenarios, there are 5! ways to shuffle the remaining five numbers (represented by *X*'s above).

Thus, the total number of valid codes is $3 \times 5! = 3 \times 120 = 360$.

The correct answer is **(D)**.

96. **(A):** When an n-sided die is rolled once, the probability of rolling any particular number (such as 1) is equal to $\frac{1}{n}$. Therefore, the probability of rolling 1 both times is equal to $\left(\frac{1}{n}\right)\left(\frac{1}{n}\right) = \frac{1}{n^2}$. Rephrase the question as, "What is the value of n?"

(1) SUFFICIENT: The probability that the two rolls are different is 80%, or $\frac{4}{5}$.

When rolling an n-sided die twice, the first roll can have any value from 1 to n, inclusive. Regardless of the value of the first roll, the probability is $\frac{1}{n}$ that the second roll will have that same value. Therefore, the overall probability of rolling the same value twice is $\frac{1}{n}$, and the probability of rolling two different values is $1 - \frac{1}{n}$.

Therefore, according to this statement, $1 - \frac{1}{n} = \frac{4}{5}$. The value of n is 5, and this statement is sufficient.

(2) INSUFFICIENT: The probability that two rolls of an n-sided die will have the same value is $\frac{1}{n}$, regardless of the value of n. This statement would be true for any value of n, so the value of n cannot be determined and this statement is insufficient.

The correct answer is **(A)**.

97.   **(B)** $1, \frac{z}{y}, \frac{x+z}{w+y}, \frac{x}{w}, \frac{xz}{wy}, \frac{x^2}{w^2}$: It would require a lot of tricky work to solve this algebraically, so

test cases instead. Make sure to pick values for the unknowns such that $\frac{w}{x} < \frac{y}{z} < 1$ holds true. For

example, if $w = 1$, $x = 2$, $y = 3$, and $z = 4$, then $\frac{1}{2} < \frac{3}{4} < 1$ is true.

Before plugging those values in for the quantities, check the answers. All of them begin with 1 and $\frac{z}{y}$, so don't bother to test $\frac{z}{y}$. In addition, check the answer choices after each term that you evaluate.

$$\frac{x}{w} = \frac{2}{1} = 2$$

$$\frac{x^2}{w^2} = \frac{2^2}{1^2} = 4$$

$$\frac{xz}{wy} = \frac{(2)(4)}{(1)(3)} = \frac{8}{3}$$

$$\frac{x+z}{w+y} = \frac{2+4}{1+3} = \frac{6}{4} = \frac{3}{2}$$

Now, place in ascending order: $1 < \frac{z}{y} < \frac{3}{2} < 2 < \frac{8}{3} < 4$.

The third term is $\frac{x+z}{w+y}$, so cross off answers (A), (C), and (D). The fourth term is $\frac{x}{w}$, so cross off answer (E).

The correct answer is **(B)**.

98.   **(C):** The question asks for the absolute value of $a + b$, so try to manipulate the statements to isolate that combination of variables, $a + b$. Statement (2) looks much easier, so start there.

(2) INSUFFICIENT: This provides information about c and d, and the relationship between them, but no information about a or b.

(1) INSUFFICIENT: Manipulate the equation to group $(a + b)$ and $(c + d)$ terms.

$$(a + b + c + d)(a + b - c - d) = 16$$
$$[(a + b) + (c + d)][(a + b) - (c + d)] = 16$$

Note that this is of the form $(x + y)(x - y)$, where $x = (a + b)$ and $y = (c + d)$. This is the *difference of squares* special product, $(x + y)(x - y) = x^2 - y^2$. Use this to transform this expression.

$$[(a + b) + (c + d)][(a + b) - (c + d)] = 16$$
$$(a + b)^2 - (c + d)^2 = 16$$
$$(a + b)^2 = 16 + (c + d)^2$$

This is not enough to determine the value of $(a + b)^2$.

(1) AND (2) SUFFICIENT: From statement (2), $(a + b)^2 = 16 + (c + d)^2$. From statement (1), $c + d = 3$. You can substitute for $c + d$ and solve. The solution is shown below, but note that you don't have to do that math: The question asked for the absolute value of $a + b$, so the fact that the equation has $(a + b)^2$ doesn't matter.

$$(a + b)^2 = 16 + (c + d)^2$$
$$(a + b)^2 = 16 + 3^2$$
$$(a + b)^2 = 16 + 9$$
$$(a + b)^2 = 25$$
$$(a + b) = 5 \text{ or } -5$$
$$|a + b| = 5$$

The correct answer is **(C)**.

99.　**(B)** $\frac{1}{3}$: If y has no factor z such that $1 < z < y$, then y must be prime. Examine a few examples to see why this is true.

> 6 has a factor 2 such that $1 < 2 < 6$: 6 is NOT prime.
> 15 has a factor 5 such that $1 < 5 < 15$: 15 is NOT prime.
> 3 has NO factor between 1 and 3: 3 IS prime.
> 7 has NO factor between 1 and 7: 7 IS prime.

Because y is selected from set B, it is a prime number between 10 and 50, inclusive. The only prime number that is divisible by 3 is 3, so y is definitely not divisible by 3.

Thus, xy is only divisible by 3 if x itself is divisible by 3. Rephrase the question: "What is the probability that a multiple of 3 will be chosen randomly from set A?"

There are $21 - 10 + 1 = 12$ terms in set A. Of these, 4 terms (12, 15, 18, and 21) are divisible by 3. Thus, the probability that x is divisible by 3 is $\frac{4}{12} = \frac{1}{3}$.

The correct answer is **(B)**.

100.　**(E)** $\dfrac{(x - 1)!}{(y - 1)!(x - y)!}$: This problem contains variables in the answer choices, so choose smart numbers.

$$x = 8$$
$$y = 5$$

There are 8 children at the party, and 5 will sit at the table with the cake. Sally must sit at the birthday cake table, so pick $5 - 1 = 4$ of the other $8 - 1 = 7$ children to sit at that table with her. How many different ways can you choose 4 from a group of 7? Set up an anagram grid, where Y means "at the cake table" and N means "at the other table."

A	B	C	D	E	F	G
Y	Y	Y	Y	N	N	N

Now, you can calculate the number of possible groups:

$$\frac{7!}{4!3!} = \frac{(7)(6)(5)}{(3)(2)(1)} = 35$$

Note that the answer choices are in factorial form; it may be the case that you will find the unsimplified factorial form, rather than 35. Test each answer choice by plugging in $x = 8$ and $y = 5$.

(A) $\dfrac{(x-1)!}{(y-1)!(y-1)!} = \dfrac{(8-1)!}{(5-1)!(5-1)!} = \dfrac{7!}{4!4!} =$ Not a match. Eliminate.

(B) $\dfrac{x!}{y!(x-y)!} = \dfrac{8!}{5!(8-5)!} = \dfrac{8!}{5!3!} =$ Not a match. Eliminate.

(C) $\dfrac{y!}{x!(x-y)!} = \dfrac{5!}{8!(8-5)!} = \dfrac{5!}{8!3!} =$ Not a match. Eliminate.

(D) $\dfrac{(y-1)!}{(x-y)!(y-1)!} = \dfrac{1}{(8-5)!} =$ Not a match. Eliminate.

(E) $\dfrac{(x-1)!}{(x-y)!(y-1)!} = \dfrac{(8-1)!}{(8-5)!(5-1)!} = \dfrac{7!}{3!4!} =$ Correct.

As an alternative to testing all five choices, you could use a hybrid approach to determine the formula using variables.

The number of possible groups was $\dfrac{7!}{4!3!}$, but remember that this formula took Sally into account.

> The 7 came from $8 - 1 = x - 1$.
> The 4 came from $5 - 1 = y - 1$.

The 3 came from the difference between these numbers: $7 - 4 = (x - 1) - (y - 1) = (x - y)$.

Substitute these variable expressions in place of the numbers.

$$\frac{7!}{4!3!} = \frac{(x-1)!}{(y-1)!(x-y)!}$$

The correct answer is **(E)**.

Workout Set 11

101. A casino pays players with chips that are either turquoise or violet colored. If each turquoise-colored chip is worth t dollars and each violet-colored chip is worth v dollars, where t and v are integers, what is the combined value of four turquoise-colored chips and two violet-colored chips?

    (1) The combined value of six turquoise-colored chips and three violet-colored chips is $42.

    (2) The combined value of five turquoise-colored chips and seven violet-colored chips is $53.

102. Jonas and Amanda stand at opposite ends of a straight road and start running toward each other at the same moment. Their rates are randomly selected in advance so that Jonas runs at a constant rate of 3, 4, 5, or 6 miles per hour and Amanda runs at a constant rate of 4, 5, 6, or 7 miles per hour. What is the probability that Jonas has traveled farther than Amanda by the time they meet?

    (A) $\dfrac{3}{16}$

    (B) $\dfrac{5}{16}$

    (C) $\dfrac{3}{8}$

    (D) $\dfrac{1}{2}$

    (E) $\dfrac{13}{16}$

103. If p is a positive integer, is p^2 divisible by 96 ?

    (1) p is a multiple of 8.

    (2) p^2 is a multiple of 12.

9

104.

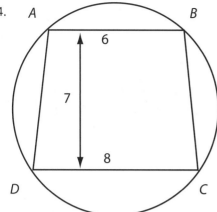

In the figure above, the trapezoid *ABCD* is inscribed in a circle. Parallel sides *AB* and *CD* are 7 inches apart and 6 and 8 inches long, respectively. What is the radius of the circle in inches?

(A) 4

(B) 5

(C) 7

(D) $4\sqrt{2}$

(E) $5\sqrt{2}$

105. If $9^y + 3^b = 10(3^b)$, then $2y$ is equal to which of the following?

(A) $b - 2$

(B) $b - 1$

(C) b

(D) $b + 1$

(E) $b + 2$

106. The radius of a circle is *r* yards. Is the area of the circle at least *r* square yards? (1 yard = 3 feet)

(1)   The diameter of the circle is more than 2 feet.

(2)   If the radius of the same circle is *f* feet, the area of the circle is more than $2f$ square feet.

107. For how many values of *x* from 1 to 300, inclusive, is the sum of the integers from 1 to *x*, inclusive, divisible by 3 ?

(A)   30

(B)   99

(C)   100

(D)   199

(E)   200

108. If x and y are integers and $|xy| = 8$, what is the value of $|x + y|$?

    (1) x and y are both divisible by 2.

    (2) $xy > 0$

109. Set X consists of exactly four distinct integers that are greater than 1. For each integer in the set, all of that integer's unique prime factors are also in the set. For example, if 20 is in set X, then 2 and 5 must also be in set X. How many of the distinct integers in set X are prime?

    (1)   The product of the integers in set X is divisible by 36.

    (2)   The product of the integers in set X is divisible by 60.

110. If $p = (2^2)(3x)$ and $r = (2^2)(3y)$, where x and y are prime numbers and $x \neq y$, which of the following represents the least common multiple of p and r ?

    (A) $12xy$

    (B) $6xy$

    (C) xy

    (D)   12

    (E)   6

Answers and explanations follow on the next page. ▶ ▶ ▶

9

Workout Set 11 Answer Key

101. **D**
102. **A**
103. **C**
104. **B**
105. **E**
106. **A**
107. **E**
108. **C**
109. **B**
110. **A**

Workout Set 11 Solutions

101. **(D):** The question asks for the value of $4t + 2v$, where t and v represent the values of the turquoise and violet chips, respectively. Note that the question asks for a combination of variables, or a *combo*; it may not be necessary to be able to solve for the individual values of t and v.

    (1) SUFFICIENT: Translate and simplify the statement.

$$6t + 3v = 42$$
$$3(2t + v) = 42$$
$$2t + v = 14$$

    You can't solve for t and v, so this statement might look sufficient—but remember what the question is asking! You need to find the value of $4t + 2v$. Multiply the equation by 2: $4t + 2v = 28$.

    (2) SUFFICIENT: Translate the statement.

$$5t + 7v = 53$$

    There isn't a way to simplify this one, but notice all those prime numbers. Primes tend to minimize the number of allowable scenarios, especially when the question also specifies that the variables have to be integers. See what combinations of integers would actually work here.

    The $5t$ term could be 5, 10, 15, 20, and so on. This term can contribute only numbers that end in 5 or 0. If that's the case, the $7v$ term must have a units digit of either 3 or 8. List out the possibilities for $7v$, and try only the ones that end in 3 or 8.

    $7v$: 7, 14, 21, 28, 35, 42, 49

    Only one ends in 3 or 8. If $7v = 28$, then $v = 4$ and the $5t$ term must equal 25, so $t = 5$. This one scenario works and it is the only possible scenario for this equation, given that v and t must be integers.

    The correct answer is **(D)**.

102. **(A)** $\frac{3}{16}$: If Jonas and Amanda run at the same rate, they will meet each other exactly in the middle. Jonas will only run farther than Amanda if Jonas' rate is greater than Amanda's. In math terms, Distance = rate × time, and since Jonas and Amanda run for the same time, their relative distances depend solely on their relative rates. Rephrase the question as, "What is the probability that Jonas ran faster than Amanda?"

    There are four possible rates for Jonas (3, 4, 5, and 6) and four for Amanda (4, 5, 6, and 7). In total, there are $(4)(4) = 16$ possible rate scenarios.

    Of Jonas' four possible rates, only two (5 and 6) are greater than some of Amanda's possible rates (4 and 5). List the three rate scenarios that result in a faster speed (greater distance) for Jonas.

    Jonas ran 5 miles per hour (mph), and Amanda ran 4 mph.

    Jonas ran 6 mph, and Amanda ran 4 mph.

    Jonas ran 6 mph, and Amanda ran 5 mph.

    Since there are 16 possible combinations of rates, the probability that Jonas ran farther than Amanda is $\frac{3}{16}$.

    The correct answer is **(A)**.

103. **(C):** The prime factorization of 96 is $(2)(2)(2)(2)(2)(3) = (2^5)(3^1)$. In order for p^2 to be divisible by 96, p^2 would have to have the prime factors $2^5 3^1$ in its prime box. The rephrased question is therefore, "Does p^2 have *at least* five 2's and one 3 in its prime box?"

(1) INSUFFICIENT: If p is a multiple of $8 = (2)(2)(2)$, p has 2^3 in its prime box. Therefore, p^2 has $(2^3)^2 = 2^6$ in its prime box, and thus has the required five 2's. However, it is uncertain whether p^2 has at least one 3 in its prime box.

(2) INSUFFICIENT: If p^2 is a multiple of $12 = (2)(2)(3)$, p^2 has two 2's and one 3 in its prime box. It is uncertain whether p^2 has at least five 2's total as there may or may not be three more 2's in the prime box.

(1) AND (2) SUFFICIENT: Statement (1) indicates that p^2 has 2^6 in its prime box and statement (2) indicates that p^2 has a 3 in its prime box. Therefore, it is certain that p^2 has *at least* five 2's and one 3 in its prime box.

The correct answer is **(C)**.

104. **(B) 5:** Redraw the figure as closely to scale as possible (remember that the official scrap paper is graph paper!), labeling the known dimensions and the radius in question.

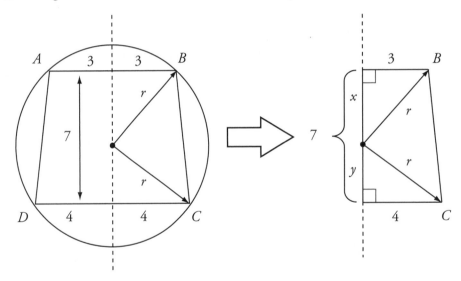

In order for the trapezoid vertices to lie on the circle, the trapezoid must be symmetrical about the dotted line, which passes through the center of the circle. Draw this vertical and the radii to points B and C to create two right triangles, allowing you to use the Pythagorean theorem.

In fact, you might play an educated hunch that the triangles are $3-4-5$ common right triangles. This checks out: If hypotenuse r is 5, then each triangle has a 3 and 4 side. The unknown vertical sides are thus 4 and 3, which sum to 7 as they must.

Algebraically, set up the following equations from the picture.

$$x^2 + 3^2 = r^2$$
$$y^2 + 4^2 = r^2$$
$$x + y = 7$$

Setting the two equations for r^2 equal.

$$x^2 + 3^2 = y^2 + 4^2$$
$$x^2 - y^2 = 4^2 - 3^2$$
$$(x + y)(x - y) = 7$$

Since $(x + y)(x - y) = 7$, $(x - y) = 1$.

Solve for x and y.

$$(x + y) = 7$$
$$+(x - y) = 1$$
$$2x = 8$$
$$x = 4$$
$$y = 7 - x = 3$$

The radius of the circle is 5, because $r^2 = 3^2 + 4^2 = 25$.

The correct answer is (**B**).

105. (**E**) $b + 2$: First, simplify the given equation.

$$9^y + 3^b = 10\left(3^b\right)$$
$$\left(3^2\right)^y + 3^b = 10\left(3^b\right)$$
$$\left(3^2\right)^y = 10\left(3^b\right) - 3^b$$
$$3^{2y} = 3^b(10 - 1)$$
$$3^{2y} = 3^b\left(3^2\right)$$
$$3^{2y} = 3^{b+2}$$
$$2y = b + 2$$

The correct answer is (**E**).

9

106. **(A):** First, translate the question stem: Is $\pi r^2 \geq r$? Simplify.

$$\text{Is } \pi r \geq 1?$$

$$\text{Is } r \geq \frac{1}{\pi}?$$

Note that the question is stated in yards, but the statements use feet, so convert the question stem to feet.

$$\text{Is } r \geq \frac{1}{\pi} \text{ yards?}$$

$$\text{Is } r \geq \frac{3}{\pi} \text{ feet?}$$

(1) SUFFICIENT: $D > 2$ feet. Therefore, $r > 1$ foot. The value of $\frac{3}{\pi}$ is approximately $\frac{3}{3.14}$, or a little bit less than 1. Yes, $r \geq \frac{3}{\pi}$ feet.

(2) INSUFFICIENT: According to this statement, $\pi f^2 > 2f$. Simplify.

$$\pi f^2 > 2f$$
$$\pi f > 2$$
$$f > \frac{2}{\pi}$$

In other words, $f > \frac{2}{3.14}$ or approximately $\frac{2}{3}$. Therefore, f could be smaller than $\frac{3}{\pi}$ feet (just a bit smaller than 1) but it could also be larger.

The correct answer is **(A)**.

107. **(E) 200:** Start at $x = 1$, then $x = 2$, and so on, looking for a pattern.

x	Sum of the integers from 1 to x, inclusive	Is the sum divisible by 3?
1	1	No
2	3	Yes
3	6	Yes
4	10	No
5	15	Yes
6	21	Yes
7	28	No

It appears that the pattern is No, Yes, Yes, No, Yes, Yes, etc., repeating every three terms. Therefore, 2 out of every 3 values of x yield a sum that is divisible by 3. So 200 of the 300 values of x will yield a sum that is divisible by 3. The answer is 200.

The correct answer is **(E)**.

108. **(C):** If the two variables must be integers and the absolute value of their product is 8, then x and y have to represent either the factor pair $(1, 8)$ or the factor pair $(2, 4)$, in either order and with either sign (positive or negative). This narrows the possible number of cases considerably.

(1) INSUFFICIENT: List out the possible cases allowed by this statement. If x and y are both divisible by 2, then you're dealing with the factor pair $(2, 4)$. After you try your first case, ask yourself what different case would be most likely to return a *different* answer to the question.

x	y	$|xy| = 8$	$|x + y| = ?$
2	4	✓	6
−2	4	✓	2

In this case, just reversing the numbers $(4, 2)$ won't make a difference to the final question, so don't list that case second. Try one of the cases that allows a negative value. Now that you have two different values, you know the statement is not sufficient.

(2) INSUFFICIENT: Follow the same process. This statement indicates that the two values have the same sign: both positive or both negative.

x	y	$|xy| = 8$	$|x + y| = ?$
1	8	✓	9
2	4	✓	6

Again, list cases until you have two contradictory results (or until you've tried all cases and realized that there is only one possible answer).

(1) AND (2) SUFFICIENT:

x	y	Both divisible by 2? Same signs?	$|xy| = 8$	$|x + y| = ?$
2	4	✓	✓	6
		✓		
−2	−4	✓	✓	6
		✓		

Only four possible cases are allowed: the variables must match the $(2, 4)$ factor pair and the signs have to be the same. The chart above shows two of the four possible cases, but you could also reverse the order: $(4, 2)$ and $(−4, −2)$. Since you're just adding at the end, though, the order of the two variables doesn't matter. In all four cases, $|x + y| = 6$.

The correct answer is **(C)**.

109. **(B):** Set X contains exactly four distinct integers; *distinct* means the four integers must be different. Also, if a number is contained in the set, all of its unique prime factors must also be in the set. If a prime number, such as 3, is in the set, no additional numbers are required in the set: the only prime factor of 3 is 3 itself, which is already included. However, if the composite number 8 is in the set, its one unique prime factor, 2, must also be included.

To better understand the question, jot down some four-integer sets that fit the description. Specifically, look for sets that have different numbers of primes.

$\{2, 3, 5, 7\}$ is a valid set that contains four primes.

$\{2, 4, 8, 16\}$ is a valid set that contains only one prime, since all of the terms are powers of 2.

(1) INSUFFICIENT: The question deals with primes and divisibility; start by factoring 36.

The prime factorization of 36 is $36 = 2 \times 2 \times 3 \times 3$. For the product of the four integers in the set to be divisible by 36, the four integers must include 2, 2, 3, and 3 as prime factors, in some combination. Therefore, based on the definition of the set, 2 and 3 must both be included in the set. The remaining two numbers must include at least one 2 and at least one 3 as prime factors between them. However, there are several different valid sets that fit this criterion.

Case 1: $\{2, 3, 6, 9\}$ has a product divisible by 36, since it includes at least two 2's and at least two 3's in its prime factors. Also, it is a valid set since it includes all of the unique prime factors of 6 (2 and 3) and all of the unique prime factors of 9 (only 3). This set has two primes.

Case 2: The primes 2 and 3 must be included in the set; include a third prime as well, such as 5. The final number in the set must include 2 and 3 as prime factors in order for the product of the whole set to be divisible by 36. $\{2, 3, 5, 6\}$ is one example of a valid set that contains three primes and has a product divisible by 36. This set has three primes.

Because the set might have either two primes or three primes, the statement is insufficient.

(2) SUFFICIENT: Based on similar reasoning to that from statement (1), note that 2, 3, and 5 must be included in the set. The product of 2, 3, and 5 is 30, so the product of the set will definitely be divisible by 30.

In order for the product to be divisible by 60, there must be at least one additional multiple of 2 in the set. Because this number is a multiple of 2, and because 2 itself is already included in the set, it is not a prime. Therefore, the only primes in the set are 2, 3, and 5, and the answer to the question is 3.

The correct answer is **(B)**.

110. **(A) 12xy:** p and r share three prime factors: 2, 2, and 3. Each also has an additional prime factor that is not shared by the other. Draw overlapping circles in which to place the shared and non-shared prime factors of p and r. To find the least common multiple (LCM), multiply from left to right and include all the common factors in the product.

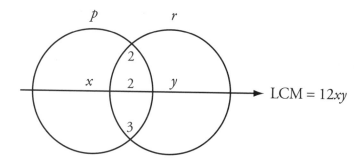

The correct answer is **(A)**.

9

Workout Set 12

111.

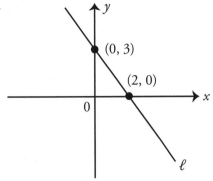

Which of the following equations represents a line parallel to line ℓ in the figure above?

(A) $2y - 3x = 0$

(B) $2y + 3x = 0$

(C) $2y - 3x = 6$

(D) $3y + 2x = 6$

(E) $3y - 2x = 9$

112. If $y = |x - 1|$ and $y = 3x + 3$, then x must be between which of the following values?

(A) 2 and 3

(B) 1 and 2

(C) 0 and 1

(D) −1 and 0

(E) −2 and −1

113. If a is a positive integer, is a^2 a multiple of 8 ?

(1) a^3 is a multiple of 16.

(2) $(a + 4)^2$ is a multiple of 8.

9

114.

1 mile stretch of highway

black line   black line

A road crew painted two black lines across a road, as shown in the figure above, to mark the start and end of a one-mile stretch. Between the two black lines, they will paint across the road a red line at each third of a mile, a white line at each fifth of a mile, and a blue line at each eighth of a mile. What is the smallest distance (in miles) between any of the painted lines on this stretch of highway?

(A) 0

(B) $\dfrac{1}{120}$

(C) $\dfrac{1}{60}$

(D) $\dfrac{1}{40}$

(E) $\dfrac{1}{30}$

115. Set S consists of n consecutive integers, where $n > 1$. What is the value of n ?

(1) The sum of the integers in set S is divisible by 7.

(2) The sum of the integers in set S is 14.

116. A trapezoid is symmetrical about a vertical center line. If a circle is drawn such that it is tangent to exactly three points on the trapezoid and is enclosed entirely within the trapezoid, what is the diameter of the circle?

(1) The parallel sides of the trapezoid are 10 inches apart.

(2) Of the parallel sides of the trapezoid, the shorter side is 15 inches long.

117. Three boys are ages 4, 6, and 7, respectively. Three girls are ages 5, 8, and 9, respectively. If two of the boys and two of the girls are randomly selected and the sum of the selected children's ages is z, what is the difference between the probability that z is even and the probability that z is odd?

(A) $\dfrac{1}{9}$

(B) $\dfrac{1}{6}$

(C) $\dfrac{2}{9}$

(D) $\dfrac{1}{4}$

(E) $\dfrac{1}{2}$

118. If two distinct integers x and y are randomly selected from the integers between 1 and 10, inclusive, what is the probability that $\dfrac{x^2 - y^2}{4}$ is a positive odd integer?

    (A) $\dfrac{1}{15}$

    (B) $\dfrac{1}{9}$

    (C) $\dfrac{2}{15}$

    (D) $\dfrac{2}{9}$

    (E) $\dfrac{3}{10}$

119. Positive integers a and b are less than or equal to 9. If a and b are assembled into the six-digit number $ababab$, which of the following must be a factor of $ababab$?

    (A) 3

    (B) 4

    (C) 5

    (D) 6

    (E) None of the above

120. The two-digit positive integer s is the sum of the two-digit positive integers m and n. Is the units digit of s less than the units digit of m ?

    (1) The units digit of s is less than the units digit of n.

    (2) The tens digit of s is not equal to the sum of the tens digits of m and n.

9

Answers and explanations follow on the next page. ▶ ▶ ▶

Workout Set 12 Answer Key

111. **B**
112. **D**
113. **D**
114. **D**
115. **E**
116. **C**
117. **A**
118. **A**
119. **A**
120. **D**

Workout Set 12 Solutions

111. **(B) $2y + 3x = 0$:** Parallel lines have the same slope. The slope of line ℓ is $\dfrac{\text{rise}}{\text{run}} = \dfrac{\text{change in } y}{\text{change in } x} = \dfrac{0-3}{2-0} = -\dfrac{3}{2}$. Work backwards from the answers by rearranging into slope-intercept form:

$y = mx + b$ form, where the slope is m. Since only one answer can be correct, only one answer will have a slope of $-\dfrac{3}{2}$; stop when you find the one with the matching slope.

(A) $2y = 3x$	$y = \dfrac{3}{2}x$	Slope $= \dfrac{3}{2}$ Incorrect
(B) $2y = -3x$	$y = \dfrac{-3}{2}x$	Slope $= -\dfrac{3}{2}$ Correct

Alternatively, use the slope to write the equation, manipulate, and look for a match.

$$y = \left(-\frac{3}{2}\right)x + b$$
$$2y = -3x + b$$

Only answer (B) is a match for the x and y portions.

The correct answer is **(B)**.

112. **(D) -1 and 0:** Set the two equations for y equal and algebraically solve $|x - 1| = 3x + 3$ for x. This requires two solutions: one for the case that $x - 1$ is positive, the other for the case that $x - 1$ is negative.

$x - 1$ is positive:
$$(x - 1) = 3x + 3$$
$$-4 = 2x$$
$$-2 = x$$

$x - 1$ is negative:
$$-(x - 1) = 3x + 3$$
$$-x + 1 = 3x + 3$$
$$-2 = x$$
$$-\frac{2}{4} = -\frac{1}{2} = x$$

In the $x - 1$ is positive case, the answer is $x = -2$. In this case, $x - 1$ is not actually positive, so this is a false case. Discard it. As a result, there is only *one* solution: $x = -\dfrac{1}{2}$.

The correct answer is **(D)**.

113. **(D):** In order for a^2 to be a multiple of 8, the prime factorization of a^2 must include all of the prime factors of 8. That is, to be a multiple of 8, a^2 would have to include 2, 2, and 2 among its prime factors.

When an integer is squared, all of its prime factors are duplicated. Therefore, if a only includes a single 2 among its prime factors, a^2 might only include two 2's. In order to guarantee that a^2 includes at least three 2's, a must include at least two 2's in its prime factors.

The question translates to: "Does the prime factorization of a include at least two 2's?" Or, "Is a divisible by 4?"

9

(1) SUFFICIENT: The positive integer a, when cubed, is a multiple of 16. Odd integers, when cubed, will always yield an odd result, so a cannot be odd. What positive even values could a have?

If $a = 2$, then $a^3 = 8$, which is not a multiple of 16. Neither is 6^3 or 10^3. However, if $a = 4$, then $a^3 = 64$, which is a multiple of 16, as are $8^3 = (4^3)(2^3)$ and $12^3 = (4^3)(3^3)$. Therefore, this statement indicates that a is a multiple of 4. When a multiple of 4 is squared, the result is always a multiple of 8, so the answer is definitely Yes.

(2) SUFFICIENT: Start by multiplying out the expression in the statement.

$(a + 4)^2$ is a multiple of 8.

$a^2 + 8a + 16$ is a multiple of 8.

$a^2 + 8(a + 2)$ is a multiple of 8.

The second part of the expression, $8(a + 2)$, is a multiple of 8 for any value of integer a. In order for the entire expression to be a multiple of 8, the first part of the expression must be a multiple of 8 as well. So according to this statement, a^2 is a multiple of 8. The answer is a definite Yes, so this statement is sufficient.

The correct answer is **(D)**.

114. **(D)** $\frac{1}{40}$: When comparing fractional pieces of a whole, find a common denominator. In this case, the one-mile stretch is divided into thirds, fifths, and eighths. The smallest common denominator of 3, 5, and 8 is 120. If the one-mile highway is divided into 120 equal increments, where will the red, white, and blue marks fall?

> Red (thirds): 40, 80 (out of 120 increments)
>
> White (fifths): 24, 48, 72, 96 (out of 120 increments)
>
> Blue (eighths): 15, 30, 45, 60, 75, 90, 105 (out of 120 increments)

The smallest distance between two marks is $75 - 72 = 3$ or $48 - 45 = 3$. This equates to $\frac{3}{120}$, or $\frac{1}{40}$ miles.

The correct answer is **(D)**.

115. **(E):** Both statements provide information about the sum of the set, so rephrase with this in mind.

> Sum of consecutive set = (Median)(Number of terms)
>
> Sum of consecutive set = (Median)(n)

For $n =$ odd, the median is the middle term, an integer. For $n =$ even, the median is the average of the two middle terms, a non-integer of the form "integer + 0.5." You can determine n if you can determine both the median of set S and the sum of the integers in set S.

Next, glance at the statements. Statement (2) is actually a subset of statement (1): if the sum is exactly 14, then the sum is divisible by 7. As a result, the answer can't be (A), because if statement (1) is sufficient, then statement (2) would also have to be sufficient. The answer also can't be (C), because statement (2) doesn't add new information to statement (1). Cross off answers (A) and (C) and start with statement (2).

(2) INSUFFICIENT: Since *n* must be an integer, use divisibility rules to narrow down possible median values.

$$\text{Sum of consecutive set} = (\text{Median})(n)$$
$$14 = (\text{Median})(n)$$
$$(2)(7) = (\text{Median})(n)$$

Check some possible median and *n* values (remember that $n > 1$).

n = 2 and median = 7: Set *S* can't have an integer median if there are only two terms. Ignore.

n = 7 and median = 2: Set *S* is {−1, 0, 1, 2, 3, 4, 5}, which has a sum of 14. Okay.

n = 4 and median = 3.5: Set *S* is {2, 3, 4, 5}, which has a sum of 14. Okay.

There are at least two possible values for *n*.

(1) INSUFFICIENT: The two possible cases for statement (2) also apply to statement (1), since the numbers chosen for statement (2) must also work in statement (1).

(1) AND (2) INSUFFICIENT: As noted, the final two cases tested for statement (2) are also allowed by statement (1), so there are still at least two possible values for *n*.

The correct answer is **(E)**.

116. **(C):** There are four basic ways this picture could look as there are four sides of the trapezoid that could serve as the non-tangent side.

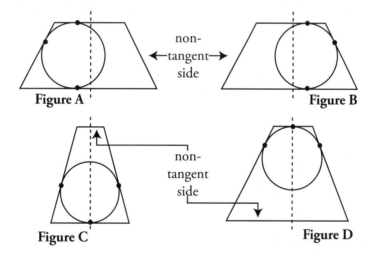

(1) INSUFFICIENT: If the circle is tangent to both of the parallel sides (Figure A or B), then the diameter must be 10. If the circle is tangent to only one of the parallel sides (Figure C or D), then the diameter is less than 10. Since there are multiple possibilities for the diameter of the circle, statement (1) does not contain enough information to answer the original question.

(2) INSUFFICIENT: Just knowing the length of the shorter parallel side is not enough to determine which of the basic figures above describes the correct situation. If Figure A or B represents the correct situation, the diameter of the circle is determined solely by the distance between the parallel sides; the diameter is independent of the length of the shorter parallel side. If Figure C or D describes the correct situation, then the diameter would depend on not only the 15-inch side but also the longer parallel side, which has an unknown length.

(1) AND (2) SUFFICIENT: In Figures C and D, the diameter must be less than 10 but also greater than the length of the smaller parallel side. If the length of the smaller parallel side is 15, then the diameter would have to be greater than 15 for Figures C and D, but this is impossible (since the diameter has to be less than 10). Therefore, Figure A or B represents the correct situation, and the diameter of the circle must equal 10.

Alternatively, notice that Figure D could not represent the situation since the circle would have to have a diameter larger than 15 inches in order to be tangent to the short parallel side and the non-parallel sides of the trapezoid. The parallel sides of the trapezoid are only 10 inches apart, so the circle would be too large to be drawn entirely within the trapezoid as required. Similar logic explains why Figure C is also impossible when considering (1) and (2) together.

The correct answer is (**C**).

117. (**A**) $\frac{1}{9}$: List the possible cases. Wherever possible, avoid computing; use Odd & Even principles to reduce your computation.

Boys	Girls	Sum z
4, 6 = Even	5, 8 = Odd	E + O = O
4, 6 = Even	5, 9 = Even	E + E = E
4, 6 = Even	8, 9 = Odd	E + O = O
4, 7 = Odd	5, 8 = Odd	O + O = E
4, 7 = Odd	5, 9 = Even	O + E = O
4, 7 = Odd	8, 9 = Odd	O + O = E
6, 7 = Odd	5, 8 = Odd	O + O = E
6, 7 = Odd	5, 9 = Even	O + E = O
6, 7 = Odd	8, 9 = Odd	O + O = E

Of the nine scenarios listed, five yield an even z and four yield an odd z.

The difference between the probability that z is even and the probability that z is odd is therefore $\frac{5}{9} - \frac{4}{9} = \frac{1}{9}$.

The correct answer is (**A**).

118. **(A)** $\frac{1}{15}$: This problem involves both probability and special quadratics. In order to find the probability that $\frac{x^2 - y^2}{4}$ is a positive odd integer, you must find the number of values of x and y for which this is the case. The problem is really asking you to count the values of x and y for which $\frac{x^2 - y^2}{4}$ is a positive odd integer.

Because $x^2 - y^2$ is a special quadratic, the expression can be simplified to $\frac{(x-y)(x+y)}{4}$.

This expression is an integer when $(x-y)(x+y)$ is divisible by 4. Note that $x - y$ and $x + y$ are always either both even or both odd. Whenever $x - y$ and $x + y$ are both even, their product will be divisible by 4. In other words, when x and y are either both even or both odd, $\frac{(x-y)(x+y)}{4}$ is an integer. But when x and y are different in parity (one even and the other odd), $\frac{(x-y)(x+y)}{4}$ is not an integer.

The expression also needs to be positive. This will occur whenever x is greater than y. Otherwise, $x - y$ would not be positive and the entire expression would be negative or zero.

Finally, when is $\frac{(x-y)(x+y)}{4}$ an ODD integer? Test a few cases to determine when this occurs. Based on the reasoning above, you only need to test cases in which x is greater than y and in which x and y are either both even or both odd.

x	y	$\dfrac{(x-y)(x+y)}{4}$	Odd or even?
5	3	$\dfrac{2 \times 8}{4} = \dfrac{16}{4} = 4$	Even
7	3	$\dfrac{4 \times 10}{4} = \dfrac{40}{4} = 10$	Even
9	3	$\dfrac{6 \times 12}{4} = \dfrac{72}{4} = 18$	Even
3	1	$\dfrac{2 \times 4}{4} = \dfrac{8}{4} = 2$	Even
7	1	$\dfrac{6 \times 8}{4} = \dfrac{48}{4} = 12$	Even

It appears that whenever x and y are both odd, $\dfrac{(x-y)(x+y)}{4}$ will be even. Therefore, x and y cannot both be odd. Test some cases in which x and y are both even:

x	y	$\dfrac{(x-y)(x+y)}{4}$	Odd or even?
4	2	$\dfrac{2\times6}{4} = \dfrac{12}{4} = 3$	Odd
6	2	$\dfrac{4\times8}{4} = \dfrac{32}{4} = 8$	Even
8	2	$\dfrac{6\times10}{4} = \dfrac{60}{4} = 15$	Odd
10	2	$\dfrac{8\times12}{4} = \dfrac{96}{4} = 24$	Even
6	4	$\dfrac{2\times10}{4} = \dfrac{20}{4} = 5$	Odd
8	4	$\dfrac{4\times12}{4} = \dfrac{48}{4} = 12$	Even

If x and y are both even, then whether the case is valid depends on whether x and y differ by a multiple of 4. Whenever $x - y$ is a multiple of 4 in the table above, so is $x + y$, and vice versa.

Therefore, whenever $x - y$ is a multiple of 4, $\dfrac{(x-y)(x+y)}{4}$ is an even integer.

In summary:

- x and y must both be even.
- x must be greater than y.
- $x - y$ must NOT be a multiple of 4.

That leaves only a few cases to count:

x	y
10	8
10	4
8	6
8	2
6	4
4	2

There are six valid cases. In total, there are $(10)(9) = 90$ ways to choose two distinct values for x and y from the integers between 1 and 10, inclusive. So the probability is $\dfrac{6}{90} = \dfrac{1}{15}$.

The correct answer is **(A)**.

119. **(A) 3:** This problem is most efficiently solved by working backwards from the answers.

    (A) 3: The sum of the digits of *ababab* is $3(a + b)$. This must be a multiple of 3. On the test, stop here and select answer (A). Below, you'll find explanations for the other answers.

    (B) 4: An integer is divisible by 4 if its last two digits represent a two-digit number that is itself divisible by 4. It is uncertain whether the two-digit integer *ab* is divisible by 4.

    (C) 5: An integer is divisible by 5 if the last digit is 0 or 5. It is uncertain whether the positive integer *b* is 5.

    (D) 6: An integer is divisible by 6 if it is even and divisible by 3. Answer (A) established that *ababab* is divisible by 3, but it is uncertain whether the last digit *b* is even, a requirement for *ababab* to be even. Note that you can also use logic to eliminate this answer. If *ababab* were divisible by 6, it would also have to be divisible by 3, but that would lead to two correct answers!

    The correct answer is **(A)**.

120. **(D):** Try out a few randomly chosen numbers to help you understand the question.

    If $m = 10$ and $n = 10$, then $s = 20$ and the units digits of m and s are equal.
    If $m = 11$ and $n = 12$, then $s = 23$ and the units digit of s is greater than the units digit of m.
    If $m = 19$ and $n = 11$, then $s = 30$ and the units digit of s is less than the units digit of m.

What's going on with all of these cases? Basically, if the units digits of m and n are small enough, then the units digit of s will be equal to or greater than the units digit of m (and of n).

On the other hand, if the units digits of m and n are large enough to cause you to carry over a 1 to the tens digit, then the units digit of s will end up being smaller than the units digit of m (and of n).

(1) SUFFICIENT: If the units digit of s is definitely less than the units digits of one of the smaller numbers, then the carryover situation must apply, in which case the units digits of both m and n must be larger than the units digit of s.

(2) SUFFICIENT: There are only two ways in which the tens digit will not equal the tens digits of the two smaller numbers:

Case 1: The tens digits of the two smaller numbers result in a number that needs to carry over into the hundreds digit. This is impossible for this problem because s is also a two-digit number.

Case 2: The units digits of the two smaller numbers result in a number that carries over into the tens digit. This must be what is happening in this case. If so, then the units digit of the larger number, s, must be smaller than the units digits of the two smaller numbers, m and n.

The correct answer is **(D)**.

Workout Set 13

121. If x and y are positive integers such that $x^2 - y^2 = 48$, how many different values of y are possible?

    (A) Two

    (B) Three

    (C) Four

    (D) Five

    (E) Six

122. If the number 200! is written in the form $p \times 10^q$, where p and q are integers, what is the maximum possible value of q ?

    (A) 40

    (B) 48

    (C) 49

    (D) 55

    (E) 64

123. If x and y are integers, and $x \neq 0$, what is the value of x^y ?

    (1) $|x| = 2$

    (2) $64^x 6^{2x+y} = 48^{2x}$

124. The three sides of a triangle have lengths p, q, and r, each an integer. Is this triangle a right triangle?

    (1)   The perimeter of the triangle is an odd integer.

    (2)   If the triangle's area is doubled, the result is not an integer.

125. If x is positive, what is the least possible value of $\dfrac{x}{2} + \dfrac{2}{x}$?

    (A) $\dfrac{1}{2}$

    (B) 1

    (C) 2

    (D) 3

    (E) 4

126. The average (arithmetic mean) cost of three computer models is $900. If no two computers cost the same amount, does the most expensive model cost more than $1,000 ?

    (1)   The most expensive model costs 25% more than the model with the median cost.

    (2)   The most expensive model costs $210 more than the model with the median cost.

127.

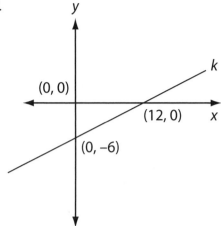

Which of the following equations represents a line perpendicular to line k in the figure above?

(A) $3y + 2x = -12$

(B) $2y + x = 0$

(C) $2y - x = 0$

(D) $y + 2x = 12$

(E) $y - 2x = 12$

128. Is $x > 0$?

    (1) $|2x - 12| < 10$

    (2) $x^2 - 10x \geq -21$

129. *K*-numbers are positive integers with only 2's as their digits. For example, 2, 22, and 222 are *K*-numbers. The *K*-weight of a number n is the minimum number of *K*-numbers that must be added together to equal n. For example, the *K*-weight of 50 is 5, because $50 = 22 + 22 + 2 + 2 + 2$. What is the *K*-weight of 600 ?

(A) 10

(B) 11

(C) 12

(D) 13

(E) 14

130. If the reciprocals of two consecutive positive integers are added together, what is the sum in terms of the greater integer x ?

(A) $\dfrac{3}{x}$

(B) $x^2 - x$

(C) $2x - 1$

(D) $\dfrac{2x - 1}{x^2 + x}$

(E) $\dfrac{2x - 1}{x^2 - x}$

9

Workout Set 13 Answer Key

121. **B**
122. **C**
123. **B**
124. **D**
125. **C**
126. **D**
127. **D**
128. **A**
129. **A**
130. **E**

Workout Set 13 Solutions

121. **(B) Three:** The choices themselves, as well as *how many* in the question text, suggest that y could have more than one value. To begin, simplify the given information using algebra and logical reasoning.

$$x^2 - y^2 = 48$$
$$(x - y)(x + y) = 48$$

Since x and y are integers, both $x - y$ and $x + y$ are integers. The product of two integers is 48. One of those integers is equal to $x + y$ and the other is equal to $x - y$. Since $x^2 - y^2$ is positive and x and y are both positive, x must be greater than y. Therefore, $x + y$ and $x - y$ are a pair of positive factors of 48, with $x + y$ being the greater of the two factors. List the pairs of factors of 48 and solve for the values of x and y.

Note one thing first. Since the factors are y above and y below x, the value of x equals the average. Therefore, if for a particular case the average of $(x - y)$ and $(x + y)$ is not an integer, that case is not valid. In order for the average of the two terms to be an integer, the sum has to be even, so if the sum is odd, eliminate that possibility immediately.

$x - y$	$x + y$	x	y
1	48	n/a (sum not even)	
2	24	13	11
3	16	n/a (sum not even)	
4	12	8	4
6	8	7	1

Of the five factor pairs, three yield integer values for x and y. Double-check that they fit the equation.

$$13^2 - 11^2 = 169 - 121 = 48$$
$$8^2 - 4^2 = 64 - 16 = 48$$
$$7^2 - 1^2 = 49 - 1 = 48$$

The correct answer is **(B)**.

122. **(C) 49:** To maximize the value of q, you would need to constrain p to NOT be a multiple of 10. In other words, q should count *every* factor of 10 in 200!, and p would be the product of the remaining factors of 200!.

To count factors of 10 in 200!, you could start by counting the multiples of 10 between 1 and 200, inclusive. But this method would undercount the number of 10's that are factors of 200! because it would miss other pairs that can create 10, such as:

200! has 2 and 5 as factors, which multiply to 10, creating another factor of 10.

200! has 6 and 15 as factors, which multiply to 90, creating another factor of 10.

Therefore, this problem is really about counting the number of 2×5 factor pairs that can be made from the factors of 200.

Of 2 and 5, there will be fewer 5's overall, so count the number of 5's found among the factors of 200!.

	Number of Multiples between 1 and 200, Inclusive
Multiples of 5 ($= 5^1$)	$\dfrac{200}{5} = 40$
Multiples of 25 ($= 5^2$)	$\dfrac{200}{25} = 8$
Multiples of 125 ($= 5^3$)	125 is the only one: 1

The higher multiples contribute *more than one* factor of 5 to the total.

There are eight multiples of 25 in the range (namely, 25, 50, 75, 100, 125, 150, 175, and 200). Each of these is also a multiple of 5, so each has already been counted once, and thus each of the eight multiples of 25 contributes one *additional* factor of 5. Finally, 125 contributes a total of three 5's to the count—but two have already been counted, leaving only one *additional* factor of 5 to include.

Therefore, the prime factorization for 200! includes $40 + 8 + 1 = 49$ factors of 5.

The correct answer is **(C)**.

123. **(B):** Since $x \neq 0$, x^y does not equal 0^y or 0.

(1) INSUFFICIENT: This statement indicates that x is equal to 2 or -2. The statement indicates nothing about y.

(2) SUFFICIENT: Simplify using exponent rules, noting the common factors of 6 and 8 on each side of the equation.

$$64^x 6^{2x+y} = 48^{2x}$$
$$\left(8^2\right)^x 6^{2x+y} = (6 \times 8)^{2x}$$
$$8^{2x} 6^{2x} 6^y = 6^{2x} 8^{2x}$$
$$6^y = 1$$
$$y = 0$$

Since $y = 0$ and $x \neq 0$ (as stated in the question stem), this information is sufficient to conclude that $x^y = x^0 = 1$.

The correct answer is **(B)**.

124. **(D):** The question stem specifies that the triangle's sides all have integer lengths.

(1) SUFFICIENT: Perimeter is calculated by summing the three side lengths. In order for that sum to be odd, either all three numbers have to be odd or one of the three numbers has to be odd.

$$O + O + O = \text{odd}$$
$$O + E + E = \text{odd}$$

If the triangle is a right triangle, then the Pythagorean theorem ($a^2 + b^2 = c^2$) holds. If all three side lengths are odd, this would mean $\text{odd}^2 + \text{odd}^2 = \text{odd}^2$. This is impossible, however; odd + odd = even.

If one side length is odd and the other two are even, then there are two possibilities:

$$\text{odd}^2 + \text{even}^2 = \text{even}^2 \text{ (impossible: odd + even = odd)}$$
$$\text{even}^2 + \text{even}^2 = \text{odd}^2 \text{ (also impossible: even + even = even)}$$

Every right triangle possibility is impossible, so the triangle cannot be a right triangle.

(2) SUFFICIENT: $A = \frac{1}{2}bh$, or $2A = bh$. If, as this statement indicates, $2A$ is not an integer, then A itself is not an integer. As a result, at least one of b and h is also not an integer.

For right triangles, b and h are the two shorter sides of the triangle. The question stem specifies that all three sides are integers, so if the triangle were a right triangle, then b and h would both have to be integers. This is impossible, so the triangle cannot be a right triangle.

The correct answer is **(D)**.

125. **(C) 2:** The problem specifies that x has to be positive, so try some small positive integers to see how the expression $\frac{x}{2} + \frac{2}{x}$ works.

If $x = 1$, then the expression becomes $\frac{1}{2} + 2 = 2.5$. If $x = 2$, then the expression becomes $1 + 1 = 2$. Since x can equal 2, eliminate answers (D) and (E).

What if x is a fraction, such as $\frac{1}{2}$? In that case, the expression becomes $\frac{\frac{1}{2}}{2} + \frac{2}{\frac{1}{2}}$ or $\frac{1}{4} + 4 \ldots$ interesting. It's even bigger than the integer options above. How come?

The expressions $\frac{x}{2}$ and $\frac{2}{x}$ are reciprocals of each other. As long as x is positive, there are two broad scenarios possible:

1. If one expression is less than 1, then the other has to be greater than 1.
2. If one expression equals 1, then the other also equals 1.

Answers (A) and (B), then, are impossible.

The correct answer is **(C)**.

126. **(D):** If the average of the cost of the three models is $900, then the sum is $2,700. Call the three models a, b, and c, in order from least expensive to most.

(1) SUFFICIENT: The statement indicates that $c = 1.25b$, so $a + b + 1.25b = 2,700$. This isn't enough to solve for specific values, but it might be enough to tell whether $c > \$1,000$. Keep working.

$$a + b + 1.25b = \$2,700$$
$$a + 2.25b = \$2,700$$

By definition, $a < b$, so plug LTb (less than b) into the equation for a.

$$\text{LT}b + 2.25b = 2,700$$
$$\text{LT}3.25b = 2,700$$
$$\text{LT}b = \frac{2,700}{3.25}$$
$$\text{LT}b = \frac{2,700}{\frac{13}{4}}$$
$$\text{LT}b = 2,700\left(\frac{4}{13}\right)$$

From here, estimate: 13 goes into 2,600 a total of 200 times and it goes into 100 approximately 7 times. Therefore, LT$b = (207)(4) = 828$.

If b is approximately 830, then 125% of b is definitely larger than 1,000. Therefore, the most expensive model does cost more than $1,000.

(2) SUFFICIENT: Follow a similar path: $c = b + 210$. Therefore:

$$\text{LT}b + b + (b + 210) = 2,700$$
$$\text{LT}b + 2b = 2,490$$
$$\text{LT}3b = 2,490$$
$$\text{LT}b = 830$$

If b is a bit more than 830, then $b + 210$ is definitely over 1,000. Therefore, the most expensive model does cost more than $1,000.

The correct answer is **(D)**.

127. **(D)** $y + 2x = 12$: The product of the slopes of two perpendicular lines is -1. The slope of line k is:

$$\frac{\text{rise}}{\text{run}} = \frac{\text{change in } y}{\text{change in } x} = \frac{0 - (-6)}{12 - 0} = \frac{6}{12} = \frac{1}{2}$$

Thus, the slope of a line perpendicular to k is -2.

Use the desired slope to create a slope-intercept equation and look for a match among the answers.

$$y = -2x + b$$
$$y + 2x = b$$

Only answer **(D)** offers a match for the left side of the equation.

Alternatively, put each choice in slope-intercept form: $y = mx + b$, where the slope is m. Stop when you find the correct answer.

(A) $3y + 2x = -12$	$y = -\dfrac{2}{3}x - 4$	Slope $= -\dfrac{2}{3}$ Not a match. Eliminate.
(B) $2y + x = 0$	$y = -\dfrac{1}{2}x$	Slope $= -\dfrac{1}{2}$ Not a match. Eliminate.
(C) $2y - x = 0$	$y = \dfrac{1}{2}x$	Slope $= \dfrac{1}{2}$ Not a match. Eliminate.
(D) $y + 2x = 12$	$y = -2x + 12$	Slope $= -2$ Correct.

The correct answer is **(D)**.

128. **(A):** The question stem asks a Yes/No question: Is x positive?

(1) SUFFICIENT: Manipulate the absolute value expression to represent this inequality on a number line.

$$|2x - 12| < 10$$
$$|2(x - 6)| < 10$$
$$2|x - 6| < 10$$
$$|x - 6| < 5$$

This can be interpreted as, "The distance between x and 6 is less than 5." On a number line, this is the region between 1 and 11.

All possible values for x are positive, so the answer to the question is a definite Yes.

(2) INSUFFICIENT: Manipulate the inequality to get 0 on one side, then factor the resulting quadratic.

$$x^2 - 10x \geq -21$$
$$x^2 - 10x + 21 \geq 0$$
$$(x - 7)(x - 3) \geq 0$$

The factored quadratic on the left side will equal 0 when $x = 3$ and 7. These are the boundary points. On a number line, check the regions on either side of these boundary points to determine the valid region(s) for x.

Note that when $3 < x < 7$, $(x - 7)(x - 3) = (\text{neg})(\text{pos}) = \text{neg}$.

Since both positive and negative values are possible for x, the answer is Maybe.

The correct answer is **(A)**.

129. **(A):** Since you are looking for the *minimum* number of *K*-numbers that sum to 600, a practical place to start is with the *largest K*-number less than 600, or 222. There are between two and three multiples of 222 in 600, so subtract out the two whole multiples.

$$\begin{array}{r} 600 \\ -444 \, (= 2 \times 222) \\ \hline 156 \end{array}$$

Now, the next largest *K*-number is 22. Again, subtract as many whole multiples as possible.

$$\begin{array}{r} 156 \\ -154 \, (= 7 \times 22) \\ \hline 2 \end{array}$$

The next largest *K*-number is 2.

$$\begin{array}{r} 2 \\ -2 \, (= 1 \times 2) \\ \hline 0 \end{array}$$

Thus, $600 = 222(2) + 22(7) + 2(1)$, and the *K*-weight of 600 is $2 + 7 + 1 = 10$.

The correct answer is **(A)**.

9

130. **(E):** If the greater of the two integers is x, then the two integers can be expressed as $x - 1$ and x. The sum of the reciprocals would therefore be:

$$\frac{1}{x-1} + \frac{1}{x} = \frac{x + (x-1)}{(x-1)x}$$
$$= \frac{2x-1}{x^2 - x}$$

Alternatively, choose smart numbers. For example, let the larger number $x = 3$. The smaller number would therefore be $3 - 1 = 2$. The sum of the reciprocals would be:

$$\frac{1}{3} + \frac{1}{2} = \frac{2}{6} + \frac{3}{6} = \frac{5}{6}$$

Plug $x = 3$ into the answers, and find the one that equals $\frac{5}{6}$.

(A) $\dfrac{3}{x} = \dfrac{3}{3} = 1$ Eliminate.

(B) $x^2 - x =$ An integer. Eliminate.

(C) $2x - 1 =$ An integer. Eliminate.

(D) $\dfrac{2x-1}{x^2 + x} = \dfrac{5}{9+3} = \dfrac{5}{12}$ Eliminate.

(E) $\dfrac{2x-1}{x^2 - x} = \dfrac{6-1}{9-3} = \dfrac{5}{6}$ Correct.

The correct answer is **(E)**.

Workout Set 14

131. The sequence A is defined as follows: $A_1 = 1$, and $A_n = A_{n-1} + (-1)^{n+1}(n^2)$ for all integer values $n > 1$. What is the value of $A_{15} - A_{13}$?

    (A)   14
    (B)   29
    (C)   169
    (D)   196
    (E)   421

132. If d represents the hundredths digit and e represents the thousandths digit in the decimal $0.4de$, what is the value of this decimal rounded to the nearest tenth?

    (1) $d - e$ is a positive perfect square.
    (2) $\sqrt{d} > e^2$

133. If x is a positive integer greater than 1, and y is the smallest positive integer that is evenly divisible by every integer between 1 and x, inclusive, what is the value of x ?

    (1) $y = 10x$
    (2) $y = 60$

134. A chain is comprised of 10 identical links, each of which independently has a 1% chance of breaking under a certain load. If the failure of any individual link means the failure of the entire chain, what is the probability that the chain will fail under the load?

    (A) $(0.01)^{10}$
    (B) $10(0.01)^{10}$
    (C) $1 - (0.10)(0.99)^{10}$
    (D) $1 - (0.99)^{10}$
    (E) $1 - (0.99)^{(10 \times 9)}$

135.

	City A to City B	City B to City C	City C to City A
First Bus Departs	5:00	5:00	5:00
Length of Trip	25 minutes	35 minutes	60 minutes
Subsequent Departures	Every 20 minutes	Every 30 minutes	Every 20 minutes

The table above shows the schedule for the bus routes between three pairs of cities. If Ash plans to travel by bus from City A, to City B, to City C, and back to City A, what is the shortest possible duration, in minutes, of his entire trip?

(A) 120

(B) 130

(C) 140

(D) 150

(E) 160

136. Are the positive integers x and y consecutive?

(1) $x^2 - y^2 = 2y + 1$

(2) $x^2 - xy - x = 0$

137. What is the value of $y - x^2 - x$?

(1) $y = -3x$

(2) $y = -4(x + 1)$

138. If $f(x) = (x + 6)^2$ and $g(x) = 9x$, which of the following specifies all the possible values of x for which $f(g(x)) < g(f(x))$?

(A) $-2 < x < 2$

(B) $x > 2$

(C) $0 < x < 3$

(D) $-4 < x < 2$

(E) $6 < x < 9$

9

139.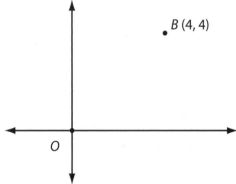

In the figure above, *ABCD* is a rectangle, and each of *AP* and *CQ* is perpendicular to *BD*. If $DP = PQ = QB = 1$, what is the length of *AB* ?

(A) $\sqrt{2}$

(B) $\sqrt{3}$

(C) $\sqrt{6}$

(D) $2\sqrt{2}$

(E) $2\sqrt{3}$

140.

In the rectangular coordinate system above, point *A* is not shown. If the area of triangle *OAB* is at least 16, which of the following could NOT be the coordinates of point *A* ?

(A) $(1, 8)$

(B) $(4, 14)$

(C) $(5, -4)$

(D) $(8, -1)$

(E) $(14, 4)$

Answers and explanations follow on the next page. ▶ ▶ ▶

Workout Set 14 Answer Key

131. **B**
132. **E**
133. **A**
134. **D**
135. **C**
136. **D**
137. **C**
138. **A**
139. **C**
140. **A**

9

Workout Set 14 Solutions

131. **(B) 29:** Generate the first several values of the sequence, using the given relationship. Notice that a component such as $(-1)^{n+1}$ switches the sign of the additive term back and forth. Use a table to keep your work organized.

n	$A_n = A_{n-1} + (-1)^{n+1}(n^2)$
1	1
2	$1 + (-1)^{2+1}(2^2) = 1 - 4 = -3$
3	$-3 + (-1)^{3+1}(3^2) = -3 + 9 = 6$
4	$6 + (-1)^{4+1}(4^2) = 6 - 16 = -10$
5	$-10 + (-1)^{5+1}(5^2) = -10 + 25 = 15$
6	$15 + (-1)^{6+1}(6^2) = -15 - 36 = -21$

What is the pattern? The sign alternates between positive and negative. Ignoring the sign of the terms (taking absolute values) might help to determine the full pattern.

n	$A_n = A_{n-1} + (-1)^{n+1}(n^2)$	$|A_n|$	Change from Previous Term
1	1	1	
2	-3	3	$+2$
3	6	6	$+3$
4	-10	10	$+4$
5	15	15	$+5$
6	-21	21	$+6$

That is, the absolute value of each term equals the absolute value of the previous term plus n. Following this pattern, $|A_{15}|$ is 15 greater than $|A_{14}|$, and $|A_{14}|$ is 14 greater than $|A_{13}|$. Thus, $|A_{15}| - |A_{13}| = +15 + 14 = 29$.

Since the odd-numbered terms in the original sequence are positive, the absolute value of any odd-numbered term equals the term itself, so $|A_{15}| - |A_{13}| = A_{15} - A_{13} = 29$.

The correct answer is **(B)**.

132. **(E):** When rounding to the nearest tenth, use the hundredths digit, or d in this case. If $d \geq 5$, the decimal $0.4de$ is rounded up to 0.5. If $d \leq 4$, the decimal $0.4de$ is rounded down to 0.4. Thus, a rephrase of this question is, "Is $d < 5$ (or, equivalently, is $d \geq 5$)?"

(1) INSUFFICIENT: Since $d - e$ is positive, $d > e$. Since d and e are digits (i.e., 0, 1, 2 ... 7, 8, 9), there is a maximum value for the difference: $d - e \leq 9$. There are only three perfect squares less than or equal to 9: $d - e = 1$, 4, or 9.

d	e	$d - e =$ Perfect Square	Is $d < 5$?
9	0	$9 - 0 = 9$ ✓	No
1	0	$1 - 0 = 1$ ✓	Yes

It is possible for d to round up or down, so this statement isn't sufficient.

(2) INSUFFICIENT: Since d and e are positive, you can square each side of the inequality without worrying about flipping the sign: $d > e^4$. Since d and e are digits (i.e., 0, 1, 2 … 7, 8, 9), $9 \geq d > e^4$, which means that e can only be 0 or 1. (Note that $2^4 = 16$, which is too large.) Test cases again; whenever possible, reuse numbers that you tried in the last statement, assuming those numbers are allowed by the new statement.

d	e	$\sqrt{d} > e^2$	Is $d < 5$?
9	0	$3 > 0$ ✓	No
1	0	$\sqrt{1} > 0$ ✓	Yes

It is again possible for d to round up or down, so this statement isn't sufficient.

(1) AND (2) INSUFFICIENT: Taking both statements together, e must be 0 or 1 and $d - e$ must equal 9, 4, or 1.

You've already tested the $d = 9$ and $d = 1$ scenarios for both of the statements individually, so you don't need to retest them here. Even together, the two statements allow d to round up or down.

The correct answer is (**E**).

133. (**A**): List a few values of x and y to gain understanding; doing so also prepares you to most easily interpret the statements.

x	y
2	2
3	6
4	12
5	60
6	60
7	420

(1) SUFFICIENT: Look in the table above for cases in which $y = 10x$. There is only one: $x = 6$ and $y = 60$.

To be completely confident that this is the only valid case, approach the problem theoretically. In order for y to equal $10x$, $10x$ would have to be divisible by 1, 2, 3 … $(x - 1)$, and x. However, x itself cannot have any common factors with $x - 1$, so 10 must be divisible by $x - 1$. So $x - 1$ equals 1, 2, 5, or 10, so x must be 2, 3, 6, or 11.

Therefore, $x = 2$ and $x = 3$ have already been eliminated as possibilities and $x = 6$ has already been confirmed to work. The only remaining case that needs to be checked is $x = 11$. Since 110 is not divisible by every number smaller than 11 (e.g., 110 is not divisible by 3 or 4), $x = 11$ is not a valid case. The only possible answer is $x = 6$, so this statement is sufficient.

9

(2) INSUFFICIENT: Based on the table above, $y = 60$ when $x = 5$ or 6. There are two possible answers, so the statement is insufficient.

The correct answer is **(A)**.

134. **(D)** $1 - (0.99)^{10}$: Qualitatively, many failure scenarios could occur.

- None of the links will fail.
- Exactly one of the links will fail.
- Exactly two of the links will fail.
- And so on.

Given the complexity of the failure scenarios, it is easier to look at the opposite scenario.

Probability that at least one link will fail $= 1 -$ probability that No links will fail

For each of the links, the probability that it will not fail is $1 - 0.01 = 0.99$. The probability that all 10 will not fail is thus $(0.99)^{10}$, since the probability that all 10 will not fail equals the product of the probabilities of the individual links not failing.

Therefore, the probability that at least one link will fail equals $1 - (0.99)^{10}$.

The correct answer is **(D)**.

135. **(C) 140:** Ash's round trip consists of two parts: the time spent on the bus and the time spent waiting for the next bus. No matter which buses he takes, the time spent on the bus will always be equal: $25 + 35 + 60$ minutes $= 120$ minutes. This question is really about minimizing the time that Ash spends waiting. Note the mismatch between the departure frequencies and the trip durations; it is unlikely that the waiting time is 0, so eliminate (A).

Because buses leave each city every 20 or 30 minutes, and both of these time periods divide evenly into one hour, the pattern of departures will always repeat every hour. Therefore, it is only necessary to check three different scenarios: Ash will leave City A either on the hour, 20 minutes after the hour, or 40 minutes after the hour.

Then, to minimize waiting, Ash should take the first available buses in City B and City C. For each of the three possible times that Ash could leave City A, note the next available buses for each leg of his trip.

Leave A	Arrive in B	Leave B	Arrive in C	Leave C	Arrive in A	Total Time
5:00	5:25	5:30	6:05	6:20	7:20	2 hr 20 min
5:20	5:45	6:00	6:30	6:40	7:40	2 hr 20 min
5:40	6:05	6:30	7:05	7:20	8:20	2 hr 40 min

Therefore, the shortest possible duration of the entire trip is $2(60) + 20 = 120 + 20 = 140$ minutes.

The correct answer is **(C)**.

136. **(D):** Consecutive integers differ by exactly 1. For x and y to be consecutive, either $x = y + 1$ or $x = y - 1$. Rephrase the question as, "Does x equal either $(y + 1)$ or $(y - 1)$?"

(1) SUFFICIENT: There's only one term with x but a couple with y, so it is easiest to solve for x.

$$x^2 - y^2 = 2y + 1$$
$$x^2 = y^2 + 2y + 1$$
$$x^2 = (y + 1)^2$$
$$\sqrt{x^2} = \sqrt{(y + 1)^2}$$
$$|x| = y + 1$$

Since x and y are both positive, you can drop the absolute value signs and conclude that $x = y + 1$.

(2) SUFFICIENT: Factor out a common term.

$$x^2 - xy - x = 0$$
$$x(x - y - 1) = 0$$

Therefore, $x = 0$ or $x - y - 1 = 0$. The question stem indicates that x is positive, so x cannot equal 0. As a result, it must be the case that $x - y - 1 = 0$, or $x = y + 1$. The two integers are consecutive.

The correct answer is **(D)**.

137. **(C):**

(1) INSUFFICIENT: Solve for the expression in question by adding $(-x^2 - x)$ to both sides.

$$y = -3x$$
$$y + \left(-x^2 - x\right) = -3x + \left(-x^2 - x\right)$$
$$y - x^2 - x = -x^2 - 4x$$

The answer depends on the value of x, which is not given.

(2) INSUFFICIENT: Solve for the expression in question by adding $(-x^2 - x)$ to both sides.

$$y = -4(x + 1)$$
$$y + \left(-x^2 - x\right) = -4(x + 1) + \left(-x^2 - x\right)$$
$$y - x^2 - x = -4x - 4 - x^2 - x$$
$$y - x^2 - x = -x^2 - 5x - 4$$

The answer depends on the value of x, which is not given.

(1) and (2) SUFFICIENT: Each statement provides a different expression equal to $y - x^2 - x$. Set these two equal to each other and solve.

$$-x^2 - 5x - 4 = -x^2 - 4x$$
$$-5x - 4 = -4x$$
$$5x + 4 = 4x$$
$$x = -4$$

Once the squared terms drop out, the equation is solvable. Stop when you know you can solve!

The correct answer is **(C)**.

138. **(A)** $-2 < x < 2$: This problem asks you to compare two "nested" functions: $f(g(x))$ and $g(f(x))$. To simplify a nested function, replace the variable term in the outer function with the entire inner function.

$$f(g(x)) = (g(x) + 6)^2 = (9x + 6)^2$$
$$g(f(x)) = 9f(x) = 9(x + 6)^2$$

To find the values of x for which $f(g(x)) < g(f(x))$, simplify the following inequality.

$$(9x + 6)^2 < 9(x + 6)^2$$

One possibility is to multiply out both quadratics and then simplify as much as possible.

$$81x^2 + 108x + 36 < 9(x^2 + 12x + 36)$$
$$81x^2 + 108x + 36 < 9x^2 + 108x + 324$$
$$72x^2 < 288$$
$$x^2 < 4$$

In turn, this simplifies to $-2 < x < 2$.

Another approach involves using the multiples of 9 in the initial inequality. Factor out a 9 on the left side of the inequality.

$$(9x + 6)^2 < 9(x + 6)^2$$
$$(3(3x + 2))^2 < 9(x + 6)^2$$
$$(3^2)(3x + 2)^2 < 9(x + 6)^2$$
$$(3x + 2)^2 < (x + 6)^2$$

Then, simplify:

$$(3x + 2)^2 < (x + 6)^2$$
$$9x^2 + 12x + 4 < x^2 + 12x + 36$$
$$8x^2 < 32$$
$$x^2 < 4$$
$$-2 < x < 2$$

The correct answer is **(A)**.

139. **(C)** $\sqrt{6}$: Start by labeling the three line segments with length 1. Label the unknown length as x.

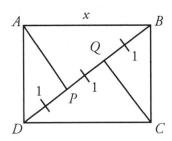

From here, there are two ways to approach the problem. One approach is to use the Pythagorean theorem to label the lengths of the missing sides. Triangle ABP is a right triangle, so the following is true:

$$AP^2 + BP^2 = AB^2$$
$$AP^2 + 2^2 = x^2$$
$$AP = \sqrt{x^2 - 4}$$

Similarly, APD is a right triangle, and the following is true:

$$AP^2 + DP^2 = AD^2$$
$$\left(\sqrt{x^2 - 4}\right)^2 + 1^2 = AD^2$$
$$x^2 - 3 = AD^2$$
$$AD = \sqrt{x^2 - 3}$$

Finally, since BAD is a right triangle, the Pythagorean theorem can be used to solve for the value of x.

$$AB^2 + AD^2 = BD^2$$
$$x^2 + \left(\sqrt{x^2 - 3}\right)^2 = 3^2$$
$$x^2 + x^2 - 3 = 3^2$$
$$2x^2 = 12$$
$$x^2 = 6$$
$$x = \sqrt{6}$$

The other solution uses the fact that triangles *APD* and *BPA* are similar. To prove this, note that *APD* is a right angle. Therefore, angles *PAD* and *ADP* sum to 90 degrees. According to the diagram, angles *PAD* and *BAP* also sum to 90 degrees. Therefore, *ADP* and *BAP* have the same degree measure. Since triangles *APD* and *BPA* have two pairs of matching angles, the third pair of angles must match as well, and the two triangles are similar. The sides line up as follows:

	Triangle *PAD*	Triangle *PBA*
Shortest Side	side *PD*	side *AP*
Middle Side	side *AP*	side *BP*
Longest Side	side *AD*	side *AB*

Since $PD = 1$, $BP = 2$, and $AP = AP$, you can set up a proportion to find the length of side *AP*.

$$\frac{1}{AP} = \frac{AP}{2}$$
$$2 = (AP)^2$$
$$AP = \sqrt{2}$$

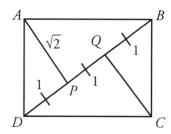

Finally, use the Pythagorean theorem to determine the length of *AB*.

$$BP^2 + AP^2 = AB^2$$
$$2^2 + \left(\sqrt{2}\right)^2 = AB^2$$
$$6 = AB^2$$
$$AB = \sqrt{6}$$

Alternatively, since the diagram is drawn to scale, you can try to estimate. Side *AB* appears to be longer than *BP*, but shorter than *BD*. Its length should be between 2 and 3. Estimate the values of the answer choices.

(A) $\sqrt{2}$ = Less than 2. Eliminate.

(B) $\sqrt{3}$ = Less than 2. Eliminate.

(C) $\sqrt{6}$ = between 2 and 3.

(D) $2\sqrt{2}$ = between 2 and 3.

(E) $2\sqrt{3}$ = More than 3. Eliminate.

Only answers (C) and (D) are close to the correct number.

The correct answer is (**C**).

140. **(A) (1, 8):** First, identify any answer choices that will be easy to eliminate before you begin calculating the areas of triangles. Answers (B) and (E) are symmetrical; the triangles they yield will have the same area. Therefore, neither can be the correct answer. Eliminate answers (B) and (E).

The question is asking for triangles with area less than 16 square units, so first try drawing a triangle with an area of exactly 16 square units. If the base of the triangle is OB, it has a length $4\sqrt{2}$. Use the area formula to find the height.

$$A = \frac{bh}{2}$$

$$16 = \frac{b(4\sqrt{2})}{2}$$

$$32 = b(4\sqrt{2})$$

$$\frac{32}{4\sqrt{2}} = b$$

$$\frac{8}{\sqrt{2}} = b$$

$$\frac{8\sqrt{2}}{2} = b$$

$$4\sqrt{2} = b$$

The height is also $4\sqrt{2}$. Draw the height of the triangle perpendicular to OB through the origin in either quadrant II or quadrant IV. The vertex of the height is at either $(-4, 4)$ or $(4, -4)$.

Any triangle with the same height will have the same area. Therefore, if A lies on the line $y = x + 8$ or on the line $y = x - 8$, the triangle will have an area of 16. If A lies anywhere between those two lines, then the triangle will have an area less than 16. Of the answers, only $(1, 8)$ lies between the two lines.

Alternatively, plot the triangles formed by the remaining answer choices on your paper.

(A)

(C)

(D)
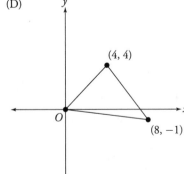

Rather than calculating the exact area of each triangle, notice that each one is fairly close to a triangle whose area is easier to calculate.

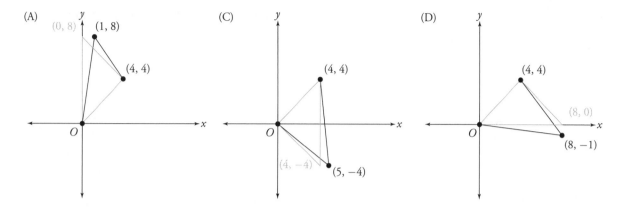

In choice (A), the triangle has a slightly smaller area than the triangle with vertices at $(0, 8)$, $(4, 4)$, and $(0, 0)$. The latter triangle has an area of exactly 16 square units. Therefore, triangle (A) has an area smaller than 16 square units, so answer (A) is correct.

In choice (C), the triangle has a slightly greater area than the triangle with vertices at $(4, 4)$, $(4, -4)$, and $(0, 0)$. The latter triangle has an area of exactly 16 square units. Therefore, the area of triangle (C) is slightly greater than 16.

In choice (D), the triangle has a slightly greater area than the triangle with vertices at $(4, 4)$, $(8, 0)$, and $(0, 0)$. The latter triangle has an area of exactly 16 square units. Therefore, the area of triangle (D) is slightly greater than 16.

The correct answer is **(A)**.

Workout Set 15

141. If $\dfrac{(ab)^2 + 3ab - 18}{(a-1)(a+2)} = 0$, where a and b are integers and a does not equal 1 or −2, which of the following could be the value of b ?

    I.   1

    II. 2

    III. 3

(A) I only

(B) II only

(C) I and II only

(D) I and III only

(E) I, II, and III

142. The currencies of three countries are called credits, units, and bells. If 12 credits can be exchanged for a total of exactly 8 units and 5 bells, what is the smallest integer number of units that can be exchanged for an integer number of bells, with no change left over?

(1)   15 credits can be exchanged for 4 units and 25 bells, with no change left over.

(2)   25 bells can be exchanged for 8 units, with no change left over.

143. What is the area of the quadrilateral bounded by the lines $y = \dfrac{3}{4}x + 6$, $y = \dfrac{3}{4}x - 6$, $y = -\dfrac{3}{4}x + 6$, and $y = -\dfrac{3}{4}x - 6$?

(A)   48

(B)   64

(C)   96

(D) 100

(E) 140

144. Each digit 1 through 5 is used exactly once to create a five-digit integer. If the 3 and the 4 cannot be adjacent digits in the integer, how many five-digit integers are possible?

(A)   48

(B)   66

(C)   72

(D)   78

(E)   90

9

145. For positive integers a, b, and c, b is 120% greater than a, and c is 25% less than the sum of a and b. Which of the following could be the value of $|a - c|$?

    (A)   6
    (B)   7
    (C)   8
    (D)   9
    (E)   10

146. A soccer competition consisted of two rounds. In each round, the 20 teams competing were divided randomly into 10 pairs, and each pair played a single game. None of the games resulted in a tie, and of the teams that lost in the first round, 7 also lost in the second round. How many teams won both of their games?

    (A) 3
    (B) 4
    (C) 5
    (D) 6
    (E) 7

147. What is the units digit of the positive integer x ?

    (1) $\dfrac{x}{5} = y + 0.2$, where y is a positive integer.

    (2) $\dfrac{x}{2} = z + 0.5$, where z is a positive integer.

148. If x and y are positive integers, what is the value of $x + y$?

    (1) $(x + y - 1)! < 100$
    (2) $y = x^2 - x + 1$

9

149.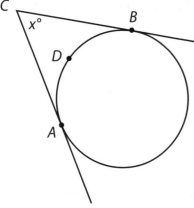

In the figure above, two lines are tangent to a circle at points *A* and *B*. What is *x*?

(1) The area of the circle is 81π.

(2) The length of arc *ADB* is 7π.

150. For all *n* such that *n* is a positive integer, the terms of a certain sequence *B* are given by the following rules:

$B_n = B_{n-1} + 5$ if *n* is odd and greater than 1

$B_n = -B_{n-1}$ if *n* is even

$B_1 = 3$

What is the sum of the first 65 terms in the sequence?

(A) −5

(B) 0

(C) 3

(D) 5

(E) 8

Answers and explanations follow on the next page. ▶ ▶ ▶

Workout Set 15 Answer Key

141. **C**
142. **D**
143. **C**
144. **C**
145. **B**
146. **E**
147. **C**
148. **E**
149. **C**
150. **C**

Workout Set 15 Solutions

141. **(C) I and II only:** Factor the numerator:

$$\frac{(ab)^2 + 3ab - 18}{(a-1)(a+2)} = \frac{(ab+6)(ab-3)}{(a-1)(a+2)} = 0$$

Since the fraction equals 0, either $ab + 6 = 0$ or $ab - 3 = 0$. Thus, $ab = -6$ or 3. Since a and b are integers, and $ab = -6$ or $ab = 3$, it must be the case that b is a factor of either -6 or 3. Note that $a \neq 1$ and $a \neq -2$.

I.   POSSIBLE: If $b = 1$, then $a = -6$ or $a = 3$, which are both allowed.

II. POSSIBLE: If $b = 2$, then $a = -3$ or $a = \frac{3}{2}$. One of those $(a = -3)$ is allowed.

III. IMPOSSIBLE: If $b = 3$, then $a = -2$ or $a = 1$, neither of which is allowed.

The correct answer is **(C)**.

142. **(D):** Use three variables to represent the unknown values in this problem. Let c represent the value of one credit, u represent the value of one unit, and b represent the value of one bell. The given information translates to the following equation:

$$12c = 8u + 5b$$

The question asks about exchanging an integer number of units for an integer number of bells. Therefore, your goal is to find the relationship between the value of a unit and the value of a bell.

(1) SUFFICIENT: This statement can be rewritten as the following equation, using the same variables as above.

$$15c = 4u + 25b$$

Combine this with the equation from the question stem. Because the goal is to find the relationship between b and u, focus on eliminating the other variable, c. First, multiply the equations by 5 and 4, respectively, so that the coefficient of c is 60 in both.

$$5(12c = 8u + 5b)$$
$$4(15c = 4u + 25b)$$

$$60c = 40u + 25b$$
$$60c = 16u + 100b$$

Next, subtract one equation from the other and simplify.

$$0 = 24u - 75b$$
$$75b = 24u$$
$$25b = 8u$$

Therefore, 8 units are worth the same amount as 25 bells. Because the ratio 8 : 25 cannot be reduced further, 8 is the smallest number of units that can be exchanged for an integer number of bells. For instance, 4 units could only be exchanged for 12.5 bells, which is not an integer. The answer to the question is 8.

9

(2) SUFFICIENT: If 8 units can be exchanged for 25 bells, then because 8 and 25 have no common factors, no smaller integer number of units can be exchanged for bells, as described above. The answer to the question is 8, and this statement is sufficient.

The correct answer is **(D)**.

143. **(C) 96:** All of these line equations are of the form $y = mx + b$, where m is the slope and b is the y-intercept. Two of these lines have a slope of $\frac{3}{4}$ and are thus parallel to each other. The other two lines are parallel to one another with a slope of $-\frac{3}{4}$. Two of the lines have a y-intercept of 6 while the other two lines have a y-intercept of -6.

Sketch the lines.

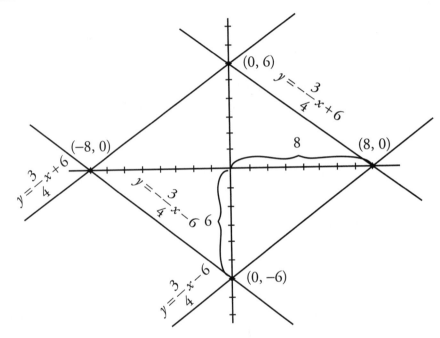

In *each* quadrant, there is a triangle with the dimensions 6—8—10, a multiple of the common 3—4—5 right triangle.

$$Area = 4\left(\frac{1}{2}bh\right)$$
$$= 2bh$$
$$= 2(6)(6)$$
$$= 96$$

9

Alternatively, recognize that the quadrilateral is a rhombus (four equal sides of length 10) and use the formula for the area of a rhombus: $\dfrac{D_1 \times D_2}{2}$, where D indicates the length of the diagonals.

$$\text{Area} = \frac{12 \times 16}{2} = 96$$

The correct answer is **(C)**.

144. **(C) 72:** In a constrained combinatorics question such as this one, it is often easier to consider the "violating" cases instead of the "okay" cases.

> \# of permutations that obey the constraint = \# of permutations total − \# of permutations that violate the constraint

At first glance, ignore the constraint that 3 and 4 cannot be adjacent to determine the total number of five-digit integers possible:

> \# of permutations total = 5! = (5)(4)(3)(2)(1) = 120

Now, consider the basic ways that 3 and 4 might be adjacent to each other in a five-digit number:

3	4	x	x	x

x	3	4	x	x

x	x	3	4	x

x	x	x	3	4

For each of these four base cases, there are two ways to order the 3 and 4 (3, 4 and 4, 3), as well as 3! ways the other digits (1, 2, and 5) can be arranged in the x positions. Thus:

> \# of permutations that violate the constraint = $4 \times 2 \times 3! = (4)(2)(3)(2)(1) = 48$

Therefore, the number of permutations that do not violate the constraint equals $120 - 48 = 72$.

The correct answer is **(C)**.

145. **(B) 7:** Start by translating the text into math. Note that b is 120% greater than a, not 120% of a.

$$b = 2.2a$$
$$c = 0.75(a + b)$$

There are three variables and only two equations, so you won't be able to solve in the traditional sense, but you may be able to determine something about these integers. Substitute for b in the second equation.

$$c = 0.75(a + 2.2a)$$
$$c = 0.75(3.2a)$$
$$c = 2.4a$$
$$10c = 24a$$
$$5c = 12a$$

Both a and c are integers, and 5 and 12 share no prime factors. So a must be divisible by 5 and c must be divisible by 12. Try $a = 5$ and $c = 12$ to see whether b is a positive integer in this case.

$$a = 5$$
$$b = 2.2a = 2.2(5) = 11$$
$$c = 0.75(a + b) = 0.75(16) = 12$$

This is a valid case because b is a positive integer. In this case, the value of $|a - c| = |5 - 12| = |-7| = 7$, which is one of the answer choices.

The correct answer is **(B)**.

146. **(E) 7:** Each team either won or lost the first game and either won or lost the second game. Therefore, this problem can be approached using *overlapping sets*. Create a Double-Set Matrix.

	Won first game	Lost first game	Total
Won second game			
Lost second game		7	
Total			20

Initially, it appears that there is not enough information to determine how many teams won both games. However, note that there were no ties and each round consisted of exactly 10 games.

Since each of the 10 games yielded one winner and one loser, there were exactly 10 teams that won in the first round and 10 teams that lost in the first round. Similarly, there were 10 teams that won in the second round and 10 teams that lost in the second round.

9

Based on this information, fill in the remainder of the matrix.

	Won first game	Lost first game	Total
Won second game	7	3	10
Lost second game	3	7	10
Total	10	10	20

Seven teams won both of their games.

The correct answer is **(E)**.

147. **(C):**

(1) INSUFFICIENT: Manipulate the statement.

$$\frac{x}{5} = y + 0.2$$
$$x = 5(y + 0.2)$$
$$x = 5y + 1$$

Thus, x is 1 greater than a multiple of 5. Since all multiples of 5 end in either 0 or 5, x must end in either 1 or 6.

Alternatively, you could list numbers. Since y is a positive integer, $5y$ could be 5, 10, 15, 20, etc. Thus, x could be 6, 11, 16, 21, etc. The units digit of x could be 1 or 6.

(2) INSUFFICIENT: Manipulate the statement.

$$\frac{x}{2} = z + 0.5$$
$$x = 2(z + 0.5)$$
$$x = 2z + 1$$

This indicates that x is odd, because $2z$ is an even number. Any odd single-digit integer is a possible units digit for x: 1, 3, 5, 7, or 9.

(1) AND (2) SUFFICIENT: Statement (1) indicates that x must end in either 1 or 6. Because statement (2) indicates that x is odd, x must end in 1 and cannot end in 6.

The correct answer is **(C)**.

148. **(E):** The question stem asks for the value of the combo $x + y$.

(1) INSUFFICIENT: $(x + y - 1)! < 100$. To see the possible values of $(x + y - 1)$, list the factorials of the first few integers.

$$1! = 1$$
$$2! = 2$$
$$3! = 6$$
$$4! = 24$$
$$5! = 120 \text{ (too large)}$$

Therefore, $(x + y - 1) \leq 4$, and $(x + y) \leq 5$.

(2) INSUFFICIENT: Add x to both sides of $y = x^2 - x + 1$ to create $(x + y)$ on one side of the equation.

$$y = x^2 - x + 1$$
$$x + y = x + x^2 - x + 1$$
$$x + y = x^2 + 1$$

The exact value of $(x + y)$ is unknown, as it depends on the value of x^2, which could be any positive integer.

(1) AND (2) INSUFFICIENT: $(x + y) \leq 5$ and $x + y = x^2 + 1$ combine to indicate that $x^2 + 1 \leq 5$. There are two integer solutions: $x = 1$ or $x = 2$. Therefore:

If $x = 1$, then $y = 1^2 - 1 + 1 = 1$ and $x + y = 1 + 1 = 2$.
If $x = 2$, then $y = 2^2 - 2 + 1 = 3$ and $x + y = 2 + 3 = 5$.

The correct answer is **(E)**.

149. **(C):** The size of the angle depends on two things.

<u>The size of the circle</u>

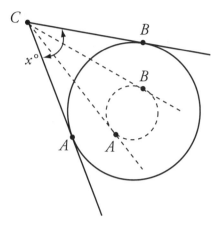

<u>The distance of C from the circle</u>
(inversely related to arc length ADB)

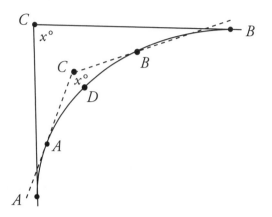

Larger circle → Larger x

Farther C → smaller x

Larger arc ADB → smaller x

(1) INSUFFICIENT: The rubber band picture on the right indicates that for a circle of fixed size, x can still vary with the length of arc ADB (i.e., x varies with the placement of C).

(2) INSUFFICIENT: Draw some cases to prove that x can vary for a given arc ADB.

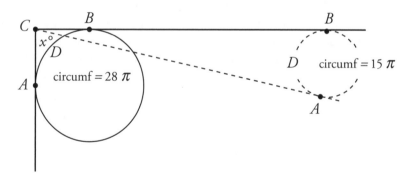

For a circle with circumference 28π, the arc ADB is $\frac{7\pi}{28\pi} = \frac{1}{4}$ of the circle, so x is $90°$. For a circle with circumference 15π, the arc ADB is $\frac{7\pi}{15\pi} = \frac{7}{15}$, or nearly half of the circle, and the lines tangent to the circle at A and B will join at a smaller angle x.

(1) AND (2) SUFFICIENT: If the area of the circle is $\pi r^2 = 81\pi$, then $r = 9$. The circumference of the circle is $2\pi r = 18$. Thus, arc ADB is $\frac{7\pi}{18\pi} = \frac{7}{18}$ of the circumference of the circle. There is only one way to draw the lines tangent to the circle at A and B, so x must be one specific value.

9

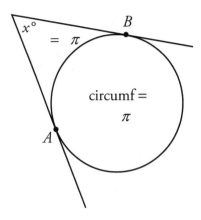

The correct answer is **(C)**.

150. **(C) 3:** List the first few terms of the sequence according to the given rules.

$$B_1 = 3$$
$$B_2 = -B_1 = -3$$
$$B_3 = B_2 + 5 = -3 + 5 = 2$$
$$B_4 = -B_3 = -2$$
$$B_5 = B_4 + 5 = -2 + 5 = 3$$
$$\cdots \text{ etc.}$$

Note that the pattern is a four-term repeat: 3, −3, 2, −2. Also note that the sum of this repeating group is $(3) + (-3) + (2) + (-2) = 0$. This repeating group will occur 16 times through term number 64. (Note: Because the sum of the four terms is 0, you don't actually have to figure out how many times the pattern repeats.) Thus, the sum of the first 64 terms will be 0. This leaves the 65th term, which will have the same value as B_1: 3. Therefore, the sum of the first 65 terms is 3.

The correct answer is **(C)**.

Workout Set 16

151.

Model	Profit as a Percent of Model's Total Sales
Model A	12%
Model B	16%
Model C	20%

A bicycle store earned a different percent profit on each of the three models of bicycles it sells, as shown in the table above. If the store made a total profit of 16% on sales of these three models of bicycles last month, and these three models represented the entirety of the store's profits, what percent of its total profits last month came from sales of Model A bicycles?

(1) The store earned 20% of its profits last month from sales of Model B bicycles.

(2) The store earned 50% of its profits last month from sales of Model C bicycles.

152. A beaker contains 100 milligrams of a solution of salt and water that is x% salt by weight such that $x < 90$. If the water evaporates at a rate of y milligrams per hour, how many hours will it take for the concentration of salt to reach $(x + 10)$%, in terms of x and y ?

(A) $\dfrac{100 - 100x}{xy + 10y}$

(B) $\dfrac{1{,}000 + 99x}{xy + 10y}$

(C) $\dfrac{100y + 100xy}{x + 10}$

(D) $\dfrac{1{,}000}{xy + 10y}$

(E) $\dfrac{1{,}000}{xy + 10}$

153. Set A consists of five consecutive positive integers. Set B consists of every integer that is in set A as well as the sum of every pair of two distinct integers from set A, discarding any numbers that already appear in set B. What is the greatest integer in set B ?

(1) The range of set B is 13.

(2) There are exactly 12 integers in set B.

154. A survey included two questions, each of which could be answered with either Yes or No. A total of 100 respondents took the survey, and every respondent answered both questions. How many respondents answered both questions with a Yes?

(1) Of the respondents who answered Yes to the first question, 40% answered Yes to the second question.

(2) Of the respondents who answered Yes to at least one question, 30% answered Yes to both questions.

9

155. If x is a positive two-digit integer, is x divisible by 17 ?

    (1) x is divisible by 7.

    (2) x has exactly 3 unique prime factors.

156. Green paint is made by mixing blue paint with yellow paint in a ratio of 2 to x. Turquoise paint is made by mixing green paint with blue paint in a ratio of y to 2. In terms of x and y, how many gallons of yellow paint are required to make 10 gallons of turquoise paint?

    (A) $\dfrac{10xy}{(x+2)(y+2)}$

    (B) $\dfrac{20x}{(x+2)(y+2)}$

    (C) $\dfrac{20x}{y+2}$

    (D) $\dfrac{10(x+2)}{y+2}$

    (E) $\dfrac{10}{xy+4}$

157. Erin writes a list of every sixth integer in increasing order, starting with the positive integer x. Harry writes a list of every ninth integer in increasing order, starting with the positive integer y. Will any integer appear on both Erin's list and Harry's list?

    (1) x is a multiple of y.

    (2) $x - y$ is a multiple of 3.

158. The students in a certain college class took a midterm exam and a final exam, both of which were scored out of a total of 100 points. What percent of the students earned a higher score on the final than on the midterm?

    (1) Of the students in the class, 28% scored at least 6 points higher on the final than on the midterm.

    (2) Of the students who scored higher on the final than on the midterm, 40% scored at least 6 points higher on the final.

9

159. A triathlon consists of three legs: a swim, a bike ride, and a run. A race organizer analyzes the results of a certain triathlon and observes that the ratio of swim distance to bike distance to run distance was 1 to 50 to 12, and that the ratio of average swim time to average bike time to average run time for all participants was 3 to 10 to 6. If the average speed of racers in each leg of the race does not change, but the race organizer changes the distance of each leg of the race so that the average swim time, average bike time, and average run time are now equal to each other, what fraction of the total distance of the race will be represented by the swim leg of the triathlon?

    (A) $\dfrac{1}{63}$

    (B) $\dfrac{1}{22}$

    (C) $\dfrac{2}{23}$

    (D) $\dfrac{3}{21}$

    (E) $\dfrac{1}{3}$

160. An unpainted wall with a total area of 100 square feet needed to be painted with three coats of paint. Nelson began the job by painting an area of 60 square feet. Then, Jamaica painted a total area of 70 square feet. Finally, Bryan painted a total area of 80 square feet. After Bryan finished painting, an area of q square feet of the wall was covered in three coats of paint. If the entire surface area of the wall had received at least one coat of paint, which of the following specifies all the possible values of q ?

    (A) $0 \leq q \leq 50$

    (B) $0 \leq q \leq 60$

    (C) $10 \leq q \leq 50$

    (D) $10 \leq q \leq 55$

    (E) $10 \leq q \leq 60$

Workout Set 16 Answer Key

151. **D**
152. **D**
153. **A**
154. **E**
155. **D**
156. **A**
157. **B**
158. **C**
159. **B**
160. **D**

9

Workout Set 16 Solutions

151. **(D):** A store sold three different models of bicycles last month. For each of these models, the profit earned by the store represents a different percentage of the sales of that model. The question stem also states that the total profit was 16% of the total sales.

One way to handle the question stem is to use variables A, B, and C to represent the total sales of Model A, B, and C bicycles, respectively. Then, the profit from Model A bicycles is $0.12A$, the profit from Model B bicycles is $0.16B$, and the profit from Model C bicycles is $0.20C$. Also, the total dollar amount of sales is $A + B + C$, so the following is true and can be simplified:

$$\text{Total profit} = 0.16(\text{total sales})$$
$$0.12A + 0.16B + 0.20C = 0.16(A + B + C)$$
$$0.12A + 0.20C = 0.16A + 0.16C$$
$$0.04C = 0.04A$$
$$C = A$$

You might also notice that 16% is exactly in the middle of the three percentages provided in the question stem. The problem is effectively a weighted average problem: if more dollars worth of Model A bicycles were sold, then the average profit would be pulled downwards, closer to 12%. If more dollars worth of Model C bicycles were sold, then the average profit would be pulled upwards, closer to 20%. Since the actual profit was in the middle, at 16%, the dollar value of the Model A bicycles sold and the dollar value of the Model C bicycles sold must be equal.

The question asks about the share of profits that came from Model A bicycles. This question can be rephrased as, "What is $\dfrac{0.12A}{0.16(A + B + C)}$?" which can then be simplified as follows:

What is $\dfrac{0.12A}{0.16(A + B + A)}$?

What is $\dfrac{3A}{4(2A + B)}$?

What is $\dfrac{3A}{8A + 4B}$?

The variables would cancel entirely if you could determine a known ratio of A to B.

(1) SUFFICIENT: 20% of the store's profits came from Model B bicycles, which can be translated and simplified as follows, remembering that $A = C$ and the total profit equals $0.16(A + B + C)$:

$$(0.2)(0.16)(A + B + C) = 0.16B$$
$$(0.2)(0.16)(A + B + A) = 0.16B$$
$$(0.2)(A + B + A) = B$$
$$(0.2)(2A + B) = B$$
$$0.4A + 0.2B = B$$
$$0.4A = 0.8B$$
$$A = 2B$$

Substituting $A = 2B$ into the question causes all unknowns to cancel out, yielding an answer of $\frac{6}{20}$, or 30%.

(2) SUFFICIENT: The store earned 50% of its profits from sales of Model C bicycles, which can be translated and simplified as follows, remembering that $A = C$ and the total profit equals $0.16(A + B + C)$.

$$(0.50)(0.16)(A + B + C) = 0.20C$$
$$(0.50)(0.16)(A + B + A) = 0.20A$$
$$(0.08)(2A + B) = 0.20A$$
$$0.16A + 0.08B = 0.20A$$
$$0.08B = 0.04A$$
$$2B = A$$

This is the same result that statement (1) produced. The answer is again 30%, as shown above, so this statement is sufficient.

The correct answer is **(D)**.

152. **(D)** $\frac{1,000}{xy + 10y}$: The answer choices in this mixture problem include variables. Therefore, it is possible to use smart numbers.

Suppose that $x = 10$ (initial concentration) and $y = 2$ (water evaporation rate in milligrams [mg] per hour). Therefore, the beaker initially contains 10% of 100 mg = 10 mg of salt. The question asks how many hours it will take for the concentration of salt to reach $(x + 10)\%$, or 20%.

The beaker will always contain 10 mg of salt, since the salt does not evaporate. The 10 mg of salt will represent 20%, or $\frac{1}{5}$, of the total weight when the total solution weight has been reduced to 50 mg. To get to this point, 50 mg of water must evaporate. This will take a total of $\frac{50 \text{ mg}}{2 \text{ mg/hr}} = 25$ hours.

Plug in $x = 10$ and $y = 2$ to see which answer choice equals 25 hours.

(A) $\frac{100 - 100(10)}{20 + 20}$ Negative. Eliminate.

(B) $\frac{1,990}{20 + 20} = $ A non-integer close to 50. Eliminate.

(C) $\frac{2,200}{10 + 10} = 110$. Eliminate.

(D) $\frac{1,000}{20 + 20} = 25$. Correct.

(E) $\frac{1,000}{20 + 10} = \frac{100}{3}$. Eliminate.

Alternatively, approach the problem with algebra. Initially, the beaker contains x mg of salt in a total solution of 100 mg. After h hours, hy mg of the solution will have evaporated, so the solution will have a total weight of $(100 - hy)$ mg, and the amount of salt will still be x mg. So the new concentration, as a percentage, will be $100\% \left(\dfrac{x}{100 - hy} \right)$. This percent should equal $(x + 10)\%$. Set up an equation and solve for h, the number of hours.

$$\frac{100x}{100 - hy} = x + 10$$

$$100x = (100 - hy)(x + 10)$$

$$\frac{100x}{x + 10} = 100 - hy$$

$$hy = 100 - \frac{100x}{x + 10}$$

$$hy = \frac{100x + 1{,}000 - 100x}{x + 10}$$

$$hy = \frac{1{,}000}{x + 10}$$

$$h = \frac{1{,}000}{xy + 10y}$$

The correct answer is **(D)**.

153. **(A):** To better understand how the sets are constructed, write out an example. Suppose that set A consists of the integers 1, 2, 3, 4, and 5. Then, set B will initially include 1, 2, 3, 4, and 5, and more numbers will be added to it as follows, discarding any numbers that already appear in set B.

- $1 + 2 = 3$ discard
- $1 + 3 = 4$ discard
- $1 + 4 = 5$ discard
- $1 + 5 = 6$ will be added to set B
- $2 + 3 = 5$ discard
- $2 + 4 = 6$ discard
- $2 + 5 = 7$ will be added to set B
- $3 + 4 = 7$ discard
- $3 + 5 = 8$ will be added to set B
- $4 + 5 = 9$ will be added to set B

Thus, if set A contains the integers from 1 to 5, set B consists of 1, 2, 3, 4, 5, 6, 7, 8, and 9. The question asks for the greatest integer in set B.

(1) SUFFICIENT: The range of a set is the difference between the greatest and the smallest numbers in that set. The smallest number in set B is the smallest number from set A, since all of the additional numbers in set B are constructed by summing numbers together and will therefore be greater. Call this number x.

The greatest number in set B is created by summing the two greatest numbers from set A. Those numbers are $x + 3$ and $x + 4$, and their sum is $2x + 7$.

Therefore, the range of set B is $(2x + 7) - x$. Set this equal to the given range of 13, and solve for x:

$$(2x + 7) - x = 13$$
$$x + 7 = 13$$
$$x = 6$$

The smallest number in set A is 6, and both sets can be listed with certainty. There is only one answer to the question, so this statement is sufficient.

(2) INSUFFICIENT: There are exactly 12 integers in set B, and you will likely have to test cases to determine how this could happen. Above, it was determined that if set A contains the integers 1, 2, 3, 4, and 5, then set B contains 9 integers in total: the integers from 1 to 9, inclusive. This is not enough integers: Find a case with fewer duplicates to discard. Try larger numbers.

Case 1: If set A contains the integers 5, 6, 7, 8, and 9, then set B contains 5, 6, 7, 8, 9, 11, 12, 13, 14, 15, 16, and 17. This set B contains 12 integers, and the greatest integer is 17.

Case 2: If set A contains the integers 100, 101, 102, 103, and 104, then set B contains 100, 101, 102, 103, 104, 201, 202, 203, 204, 205, 206, and 207. This set B again contains 12 integers, but its greatest integer is 207.

The correct answer is **(A)**.

154. **(E):** This is an Overlapping Sets problem. Create a Double-Set Matrix and fill out the known information.

	Yes to Question 1	No to Question 1	Total
Yes to Question 2			
No to Question 2			
Total			100

The question asks for the number of respondents who gave two Yes answers. Try to determine the number that belongs in the top left of the matrix.

(1) INSUFFICIENT: Let x represent the number of people who answered Yes to the first question. The matrix can be filled out as follows:

	Yes to Question 1	No to Question 1	Total
Yes to Question 2	0.4x		
No to Question 2	0.6x		
Total	x	$100 - x$	100

If $x = 5$, then the answer is $0.4(5) = 2$. If $x = 90$, then the answer is $0.4(90) = 36$. More than one value is possible for the answer, so this statement is not sufficient.

(2) INSUFFICIENT: Let y represent the number of people who answered No to both questions. Then, the number of people who answered Yes to at least one question is $100 - y$. Since 30% of these people answered Yes to both questions, the matrix can be filled out as shown.

	Yes to Question 1	No to Question 1	Total
Yes to Question 2	$0.3(100 - y)$		
No to Question 2		y	
Total			100

If $y = 10$, the answer is $0.3(90) = 27$. If $y = 80$, the answer is $0.3(20) = 6$. Since more than one value is possible for the answer, this statement is insufficient.

(1) AND (2) INSUFFICIENT: Using the information in both statements, you can conclude that $0.3(100 - y) = 0.4x$. This simplifies to $0.4x + 0.3y = 30$, but both x and y can still have multiple values.

Accordingly, the matrix can be filled out with numbers in several different ways.

	Yes to Question 1	No to Question 1	Total
Yes to Question 2	24	20	44
No to Question 2	36	20	56
Total	60	40	100

	Yes to Question 1	No to Question 1	Total
Yes to Question 2	12	10	22
No to Question 2	18	60	78
Total	30	70	100

The correct answer is **(E)**.

155. **(D):** The question stem includes a constraint that x is positive and has two digits. Without this constraint, the answer would be (E), since knowing whether x is divisible by 7 or has other prime factors does not help you determine whether x is divisible by 17.

Use the constraint as you solve the problem. Since x is a positive two-digit integer, x is between 10 and 99, inclusive. The question asks whether x is divisible by 17. Since there are only a few integers in this range that are divisible by 17, jot them down for later reference: 17, 34, 51, 68, and 85. The question can be rephrased as, "Is x equal to 17, 34, 51, 68, or 85?"

(1) SUFFICIENT: Positive two-digit integer x is a multiple of 7. Since none of the numbers listed earlier (17, 34, 51, 68, 85) are multiples of 7, x is definitely not one of these numbers. Therefore, x is not a multiple of 17, and the answer is definitely No.

Alternatively, use logical reasoning to prove that the statement is sufficient without doing too much arithmetic. Seven and 17 are both prime numbers, so the smallest number that is divisible by both of them is their product, $(7)(17) = 119$. However, you already know that x is smaller than 119, since x only has two digits. Therefore, x cannot be a multiple of both 7 and 17, so the answer is definitely No.

(2) SUFFICIENT: None of the numbers listed earlier have exactly three unique prime factors: 17 is prime, while 34, 51, 68, and 85 each have exactly two unique prime factors. Therefore, x is not one of these numbers, so x is not a multiple of 17 and the answer to the question is No.

It is also possible to show that x cannot be a multiple of 17 while doing minimal arithmetic. If x has exactly three unique prime factors, then x will only be divisible by 17 if 17 is among those factors. However, the smallest number that has three unique prime factors that include 17 is $(2)(3)(17) = 102$, which is too large to be the value of two-digit integer x. Therefore, x can not be divisible by 17 and the answer is definitely No.

The correct answer is **(D)**.

156. **(A)** $\dfrac{10xy}{(x+2)(y+2)}$: Since the answer choices include variables, choose smart numbers. It will be simpler to choose y first, since the value of y is more closely related to the 10 gallons of turquoise paint. Choose $y = 8$, so that the sum of y and 2 in the ratio of the paints used to make turquoise can be $8 + 2 = 10$. In this case, it takes 8 gallons of green paint and 2 gallons of blue paint to make 10 gallons of turquoise paint.

Next, choose a value for x. Because the total amount of green paint should be 8 gallons, choose $x = 6$, so that the sum of x and 2 in the ratio to make green paint is $2 + 6 = 8$. In total, it will take 6 gallons of yellow paint to create the turquoise paint, so the answer to the question is 6.

Plug $x = 6$ and $y = 8$ into the answer choices. The correct answer will simplify to 6.

(A) $\dfrac{10(6)(8)}{(6+2)(8+2)} = \dfrac{480}{80} = 6$. Correct.

(B) $\dfrac{20(6)}{(6+2)(8+2)} = \dfrac{120}{80} =$ Not an integer. Eliminate.

(C) $\dfrac{20(6)}{8+2} = \dfrac{120}{10} = 12$ Eliminate.

(D) $\dfrac{10(6+2)}{(8+2)} = \dfrac{80}{10} = 8$ Eliminate.

(E) $\dfrac{10}{(6)(8)+4} = \dfrac{10}{52} =$ Not an integer. Eliminate.

The correct answer is **(A)**.

9

157. **(B):** Erin's list starts with an unknown positive integer and then includes every sixth integer. So Erin's list could be any of the following, depending on the value of x:

x	Erin's List
1	1, 7, 13, 19, 25 …
2	2, 8, 14, 20, 26 …
3	3, 9, 15, 21, 27 …
etc.	etc.

Similarly, Harry's list could be any of the following:

y	Harry's List
1	1, 10, 19, 28, 37 …
2	2, 11, 20, 29, 38 …
3	3, 12, 21, 30, 39 …
etc.	etc.

(1) INSUFFICIENT:

Case 1: If $x = y = 1$, then x is a multiple of y, and the number 1 appears on both lists. Therefore, the answer to the question is Yes.

Case 2: If $x = 3$, all of the numbers on Erin's list are multiples of 3. If $y = 1$, none of the numbers on Harry's list are multiples of 3. Therefore, x is a multiple of y, but no numbers appear on both lists, so the answer to the question is No.

(2) SUFFICIENT: If $x - y$ is a multiple of 3, then $x - y = 3n$, for some integer n. So $x = 3n + y$. The integers on the two lists are as follows:

Erin's list: $3n + y, 3n + y + 6, 3n + y + 12, 3n + y + 18$ …

Harry's list: $y, y + 9, y + 18, y + 27$ …

If n is a multiple of 3, then $3n$ is a multiple of 9, so $3n + y$ appears on both lists. If n is 1 more than a multiple of 3, then $3n + 6 = 3(n + 2) = 3$(multiple of 3) is a multiple of 9, so $y + 3n + 6$ appears on both lists. Finally, if n is 2 more than a multiple of 3, then $3n + 12 = 3(n + 4) = 3$(multiple of 3) is a multiple of 9 so $y + 3n + 12$ appears on both lists. Regardless of the value of n, some number appears on both Erin's and Harry's lists, so the answer to the question is Yes.

The correct answer is **(B)**.

9

158. **(C):** According to the question stem, each student in the class earned a certain score on the midterm and a certain score on the final. A student's final score could have been higher than, equal to, or lower than his or her midterm score. To answer the question, you'll need to determine what percent of the students fell into the first of these three categories.

(1) INSUFFICIENT: It is possible that all of the remaining students scored between 1 and 5 points higher on the final than on the midterm, which would make the answer to the question 100%. It is also possible that all of the remaining students scored higher on the midterm than on the final, which would make the answer to the question 28%.

(2) INSUFFICIENT: This statement relates the percent of students who scored higher on the final to the percent of students who scored at least 6 points higher on the final. However, without any information about either of these percents, the question cannot be answered definitively.

For instance, 50% of the students could have scored higher on the final, and 40% of this 50% could have scored at least 6 points higher. Or, only 10% of the students could have scored higher on the final, and 40% of this 10% could have scored at least 6 points higher.

(1) AND (2) SUFFICIENT: According to statement (1), the following is true:

$$0.28(\text{total students}) = \text{students who scored 6+ points higher on the final}$$

According to statement (2), the following is true:

$$0.4(\text{students who scored higher on the final}) = \text{students who scored 6+ points higher on the final}$$

Combine these two equations.

$$0.28(\text{total students}) = 0.4(\text{students who scored higher on the final})$$

Simplify this equation to calculate the percent of students who scored higher on the final.

$$\frac{\text{Students who scored higher on the final}}{\text{Total students}} = \frac{0.28}{0.4} = 70\%$$

Since an exact answer to the question can be calculated, the statements together are sufficient.

The correct answer is **(C)**.

159. **(B)** $\frac{1}{22}$**:** This problem provides two pieces of information. The first is the ratio of the swim distance to the bike distance to the run distance: 1 to 50 to 12. The second piece of information is the ratio of the average swim time to average bike time to average run time: 3 to 10 to 6.

Use an unknown multiplier for each of these ratios.

	Distance	Time
Swim	d	$3t$
Bike	$50d$	$10t$
Run	$12d$	$6t$

Now, use an RTD (rate/time/distance) chart to calculate the average speed for competitors in each of the three legs, in terms of d and t.

	Rate	Time	Distance
Swim	$\dfrac{d}{3t}$	$3t$	d
Bike	$\dfrac{5d}{t}$	$10t$	$50d$
Run	$\dfrac{2d}{t}$	$6t$	$12d$

The question asks about a scenario in which the average swim time, bike time, and run time are equal, but the rates stay the same. In this scenario, the following will be the case:

	Rate	Time	Distance
Swim	$\dfrac{d}{3t}$	t	?
Bike	$\dfrac{5d}{t}$	t	?
Run	$\dfrac{2d}{t}$	t	?

Use the RTD formula to fill in the missing column of this chart.

	Rate	Time	Distance
Swim	$\dfrac{d}{3t}$	t	$\dfrac{d}{3}$
Bike	$\dfrac{5d}{t}$	t	$5d$
Run	$\dfrac{2d}{t}$	t	$2d$

The distances are in a ratio of $\dfrac{1}{3}$ to 5 to 2, or 1 to 15 to 6. The swim distance represents $\dfrac{1}{1+15+6} = \dfrac{1}{22}$ of the total distance.

The correct answer is (**B**).

160. **(D)** $10 \le q \le 55$: The problem does not specify the extent to which each person paints over the area that was already painted by the previous person. For instance, when Jamaica painted 70 square feet (sq ft) of the wall, she might have painted over the entire 60 sq ft already painted by Nelson, or she might have painted over only some of it.

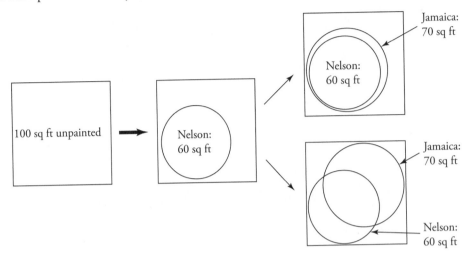

However, by the time Bryan finished painting, the entire wall had been painted with at least one coat of paint, and some of it might have been painted with as many as three coats. The question asks how much of the wall had three coats, and the answer choices represent ranges from minimum to maximum area.

First, make q as large as possible. In order to do so, the amount of paint used on the remainder of the wall must be minimized. The area q will be as large as possible when the remaining $100 - q$ square foot area is covered in only a single coat.

The entire amount of paint applied by all three painters is $60 + 70 + 80 = 210$ sq ft. If q sq ft of the wall has three coats of paint, and the remaining $100 - q$ has only one coat, the following is true:

$$3(\text{area with 3 coats}) + 1(\text{area with 1 coat}) = \text{total paint applied}$$

Turn this into an equation and solve for q.

$$3q + (100 - q) = 210$$
$$100 + 2q = 210$$
$$2q = 110$$
$$q = 55$$

The greatest possible value of q is 55 sq ft. Therefore, answer (D) must be correct.

It is also possible to determine the greatest possible value of q by working backwards from the choices, testing their extreme values using pictures. If the painting is done as shown below, then 55 sq ft of the wall will have three coats of paint and the rest will have only one coat.

Total $= 5 + 15 + 25 + 55 = 100$ sq ft

Jamaica painted 70 sq ft total.

Nelson painted 60 sq ft total.

15   0   5

55

0   0

25

Bryan painted 80 sq ft total.

To find the smallest possible number of square feet with three coats, do the opposite: Assume that the rest of the wall has as much paint as possible. In that case, the remaining $100 - q$ sq ft of wall will have two coats of paint, so the following will be true:

$$3q + 2(100 - q) = 210$$
$$q + 200 = 210$$
$$q = 10$$

The smallest possible value of q is 10. Here is another way to visualize the minimization of the three-coat area.

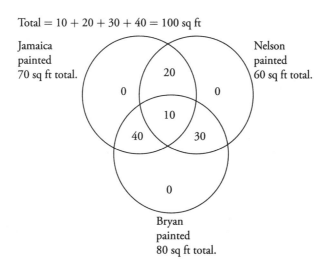

Total $= 10 + 20 + 30 + 40 = 100$ sq ft

Jamaica painted 70 sq ft total.

Nelson painted 60 sq ft total.

0   20   0

10

40   30

0

Bryan painted 80 sq ft total.

The correct answer is **(D)**.

Go beyond books.
Try us for free.

In Person

Find a GMAT course near you and attend the first session free, no strings attached.

**Find your city at
manhattanprep.com/gmat/classes**

Online

Enjoy the flexibility of prepping from home or the office with our online course.

**See the full schedule at
manhattanprep.com/gmat/classes**

On Demand

Prep where you are, when you want with GMAT Interact™— our on-demand course.

**Try 5 full lessons for free at
manhattanprep.com/gmat/interact**

Not sure which is right for you? Try all three! Or, give us a call, and we'll help you figure out which program fits you best.

Toll-Free U.S. Number 800.576.4628 | International 001 212.721.7400 | Email gmat@manhattanprep.com

Prep made personal.

Whether you want quick coaching in a particular GMAT subject area or a comprehensive study plan developed around your goals, we've got you covered. Our expert GMAT instructors can help you hit your top score.

CHECK OUT THESE REVIEWS FROM MANHATTAN PREP STUDENTS.

Highly recommend MPrep for a 700 score
☆☆☆☆☆
Company: Manhattan Prep
Course: Manhattan Prep Private Tutoring
GMAT Scores — Before: 680 **After:** 720

I bought the MPrep books and started studying on my own. Along with using the MPrep materials I also met with a Manhattan Prep private tutor. He was fantastic. He really [listened] to my concerns and tried to understand what was holding me back. He's very down to earth and pragmatic. Not only did he help me understand the test material better, he helped me to have a better mental game while taking it. After meeting with him and studying with the MPrep materials I boosted my score to a 720.

A one hour private tutoring session took me to the next level.
☆☆☆☆☆
Company: Manhattan Prep
Course: Manhattan Prep Private Tutoring
GMAT Scores — Before: N/A **After:** 730

I purchased the MPrep materials second-hand and pursued a self-study strategy. I was stuck between 700 and 720 on all my practice exams, but was hoping to get into the mid-700s. I thought a private tutoring session would really help me go to the next level in my scoring. [My instructor] asked me beforehand (via email) what I was struggling with and what I thought I needed. He was able to quickly talk me through my struggles and give me concise, helpful tips that I used during the remainder of my study time and the actual exam.

Best prep out there!
☆☆☆☆☆
Company: Manhattan Prep
Course: Manhattan Prep Private Tutoring
GMAT Scores — Before: 560 **After:** 750

I just took my GMAT and scored a 750 (Q49, V42). This was a pretty amazing feat for me considering I scored only 560 my first time taking the GMAT. Only by sitting down with the Manhattan Prep books and really learning the content contained in them was I able to get into the 700 range. Then, when I was consistently scoring in the 90+ percentile, Manhattan Prep tutoring got me my 750 and into the 98th percentile. If you want a 700+ on the GMAT, use Manhattan Prep. PERIOD!!

Manhattan Prep is Best in Class
☆☆☆☆☆
Company: Manhattan Prep
Course: Manhattan Prep Private Tutoring
GMAT Scores — Before: N/A **After:** 750

I signed up for the self study so that I could review the materials on my own time. After completing the basic course content and taking a couple practice tests, I signed up for private tutoring. [My instructor] helped me to develop a game plan to address my weaknesses. We discussed the logic behind the problem and practical strategies for eliminating certain answers if time is running short. Originally, I had planned on taking the GMAT two times. But, MPrep and [my instructor] helped me to exceed my goal on the first attempt, allowing me to focus on the rest of my application.

Contact us at 800-576-4628 or gmat@manhattanprep.com for more information about your GMAT study options.